THE

SCHOOL OF RAPHAEL

OR THE

STUDENT'S GUIDE

TO

EXPRESSION IN HISTORICAL PAINTING

ILLUSTRATED BY EXAMPLES ENGRAVED BY DUCHANGE, AND OTHERS, UNDER THE
INSPECTION OF SIR NICHOLAS DORIGNY, FROM
HIS OWN DRAWINGS

AFTER

The most celebrated heads in the Cartoons at the King's Palace.

TO WHICH ARE NOW ADDED

THE OUTLINES OF EACH HEAD,

AND ALSO

SEVERAL PLATES OF THE MOST CELEBRATED ANTIQUE STATUES, SKELETONS, AND
ANATOMICAL FIGURES,

Engraved by an Eminent Artist

WITH INSTRUCTIONS FOR YOUNG STUDENTS IN THE ART OF DESIGNING,

AND

THE PASSIONS

AS CHARACTERISED BY RAPHAEL IN THE CARTOONS.

DESCRIBED AND EXPLAINED

BY BENJAMIN RALPH.

LONDON:

PRINTED FOR JOHN BOYDELL, ENGRAVER.

Published by Tom Richardson
ISBN 978-0-9821678-4-7

THE

SCHOOL OF RAPHAEL;

OR, THE

STUDENT'S GUIDE

TO

EXPRESSION IN HISTORICAL PAINTING.

ILLUSTRATED BY EXAMPLES ENGRAVED BY DUCHANGE, AND OTHERS, UNDER THE
INSPECTION OF SIR NICHOLAS DORIGNY, FROM
HIS OWN DRAWINGS

AFTER

𝕿𝖍𝖊 𝖒𝖔𝖘𝖙 𝖈𝖊𝖑𝖊𝖇𝖗𝖆𝖙𝖊𝖉 𝕳𝖊𝖆𝖉𝖘 𝖎𝖓 𝖙𝖍𝖊 𝕮𝖆𝖗𝖙𝖔𝖔𝖓𝖘 𝖆𝖙 𝖙𝖍𝖊 𝕶𝖎𝖓𝖌'𝖘 𝕻𝖆𝖑𝖆𝖈𝖊.

TO WHICH ARE NOW ADDED,

THE OUTLINES OF EACH HEAD,

AND ALSO

SEVERAL PLATES OF THE MOST CELEBRATED ANTIQUE STATUES, SKELETONS, AND
ANATOMICAL FIGURES,

Engraved by an Eminent Artist.

WITH INSTRUCTIONS FOR YOUNG STUDENTS IN THE ART OF DESIGNING.

AND

THE PASSIONS

AS CHARACTERISED BY RAPHAEL IN THE CARTOONS.

DESCRIBED AND EXPLAINED

BY BENJAMIN RALPH.

LONDON:

PRINTED FOR JOHN BOYDELL, ENGRAVER.

CONTENTS

∽

LIST OF ILLUSTRATIONS

∽

INTRODUCTION TO THIS EDITION

The School of Raphael, or the Student's Guide to Expression in Historical Painting by Nicholas Dorigny with commentary by Benjamin Ralph might be the most beautiful art instruction book ever published. Admiration for the beauty and skill of Raphael's drawing was certainly the reason to make the prints, and though Mr. Ralph acknowledges the beauty of the engravings and the drawings they were based on, that was not his only reason for making the book.

Jennifer Montagu in her book,[1] argues that while the art world was influenced by Charles LeBrun's *Méthode pour Apprendre à Dessiner les Passions*, it increasingly criticized his work as mannered. Styles of art were undergoing a change and the new taste admired neo-classic ideals. The study of expression continued to be regarded as a primary component of art education so a new source of examples was sought.

Benjamin Ralph turned to Raphael Sanzio d'Urbino (1483-1520) as a source and used the prints made from tracings and drawings by Nicholas Dorigny of Raphael's cartoons which were commissioned by Pope Leo X for tapestries for the Sistine Chapel and the Vatican Palace. The tapestries still hang on special occasions beneath Michelangelo's famous ceiling. The cartoons were greatly admired in the 18th century because they were original works from his studio and reproductions of them were available in prints. Raphael completed ten cartoons of an original order for sixteen. Only seven survive. The cartoons were completed in 1516 and sent off to be rendered as tapestries. About 1630 Peter Paul Rubens informed Charles I of the cartoons and they were acquired at considerable espense.[2] The cartoons are now at the Victoria and Albert Museum, London.

The majority of the cartoons were in the Netherlands "but in 1630, through the mediation of Rubens, they were sold to England, where they were regarded as Raphael's most valuable creations.

"After the beheading of Charles I., scarcely any of Raphael's pictures were to be found in England...but the Cartoons for the Tapestries seem to have been regarded even by the Puritans as a precious possession"[3]

Jonathon Richardson published his *Essay on the Theory of Painting* around

---

1 The Expression of the Passions: the Origin and Influence of Charles LeBrun, Yale University Press, 1994., p. 91.
2 Notes on the cartoons of Raphael now in the South Kensington Museum, Charles Ruland, London, 1867., p. 9.
3 The Life of Raphael, Herman Friedrich Grimm, Sarah Halland Adams, Alexander Gardner, 1887., p. 271.

this time also. He called the cartoons "the greatest achievement of the Roman School."[4]

Here is another description by Johann David Passavant:

"Being furnished with a note extraordinary to the house-keeper, we were allowed ample time for the examination of THE SEVEN CARTOONS OF RAPHAEL.

"Among the various objects of attraction in Hampton Court, these seven celebrated cartoons, from the Acts of the Apostles, by Raphael, demanded our undivided attention, and richly answered the high reputation which they enjoy.

"It is well known that Raphael executed ten cartoons[5] in water colours, which were subsequently sent to Arras in the Netherlands, where they served as models for as many pieces of tapestry. These latter were worked with gold thread, and were of such magnificence, that on being brought to Rome Pope Leo X, paid the sum of fifty thousand ducats for them. In the meantime the original cartoons remained at the manufactory and as years passed away, were laid aside, and their very existence forgotten. The honor of discovering them was reserved for Rubens who, aided by the directions of Dorigny, succeeded in rescuing seven of them from their oblivion, and being at that time ambassador to England, he offered them to the amateur King, Charles I., by whom they were eventually purchased...

"What raises these cartoons above all others of Raphael's works is their peculiarly simple and comprehensive style, which is eminently in harmony with the character of the Gospel, and places the subject so clearly before the spectator, that "all who may read." So, high as Raphael as a historical painter, in the limited sense of the word, ranks among his compeers, so among the chef-d'oeuvres which he has bequeathed to the world, may these cartoons be reckoned as belonging to his finest."[6]

The cartoons are painted in glue distemper on multiple sheets of paper which were glued together. According to one reference,[7] they were cut apart and reglued together at a later time at which time they were also affixed to a canvas backing for preservation.

Nicholas Dorigny (1658-1746) was from a famous French artistic family. He was trained by his father Michael and worked mainly as an engraver. He continued his studies in Rome and stayed there 28 years where he made his name making engravings of Italian works of art especially the works of Raphael (whose reputation rivaled Michaelangelo's among art enthusiasts of the time) including a well received portfolio of prints of Raphael's frescoes of the Wedding of Psyche and Cupid in the Villa Farnesina in Rome. In Rome he became know to "several

4   Raphael, Alfred Robert Dryhurst, Methuen & Co. London, 1905., p. 183

5   The missing cartoons are The Stoning of St. Peter, The Conversion of Saul, and St. Paul in Prison at Philippi.

6   Tour of a German Artist in England: With Notices of Private Galleries and Remarks on the State of Art, M. Johann David Passavant, Vol. I., Saunders and Otley, London, 1836., p. 79.

7   ibid., p. 82.

Englishmen of rank, who persuaded him to come to England, and engrave the cartoons. He arrived in June 1711, but did not begin his drawings till the Easter following, the intervening time being spent in raising a fund for his work. At first it was proposed that the plates should be engraved at the Queen's expense and to be given as presents to the nobility, foreign princes and ministers. Lord Treasurer Oxford was much his friend: but Dorigny demanding 4,000£ or 5,000£ put a stop to that plan; yet the queen gave him an apartment, at Hampton Court, with necessary perquisites."[8]

The work proceeded on a subscription basis. Dorigny soon was overwhelmed and sent to Paris for assistants, among them Charles Dupuis. Dorigny presented the engravings to King George I in April of 1719. He was knighted in 1719 shortly after their completion. He retired to France in 1924. His collection of drawings had been sold in 1723. Among the "drawings were a hundred and four heads, hands and feet, traced from the cartoons."[9] "The heads were afterwards engraved by various French artists and published by John Boydell as *The School of Raphael, or the Student's Guide to Expression in Historical Painting*"[10] in 1759. The images reproduced here are from a later 1782 edition which included more illustrations than the original, namely the outline prints of the heads and the 12 plates illustrating the principles of geometry, hands, arms and legs and the plates after Albinus and the Torso of Michelangelo, Apollo, Venus, and Hercules. The additional studies were by John Boydell and the book published under the title *The School of Raphael, or the Student's Guide to Expression in Historical Painting: illustrated by Duchange and others, under the inspection of Sir Nicholas Dorigny, from his own drawings after the most celebrated Heads in the Cartoons at the King's Palace*[11] according to the *Penny Cyclopedia of the Society for the Diffusion of Useful Knowledge.*

This is the listing from the *Catalogue No. 113 Archæology. Books on Ancient Art Beginning from Archaic Times.* Karl W. Hiersemann, Leipzig, 1893:

"**Cartons in Hampton Court** - Dorigny, L., the School of Raphael; or the Student's Guide to expression in historical painting, illustr. by examples engr. after the most celebrated Heads in the Cartons at the Queen's Palace; to which are added the outlines of each head, and 12 plates of statues, skeletons and anatom. figures. With text by B. Ralph. fol. London 1782. ...Tafeln dargestellt u. N. Pigne, G. Duchange, S. Thomassin, L. Desplaces, D. Beauvais, C. Dupuis, N. Tardieu, B. Lepissie gestochen."[12]

The original book is a huge folio sized edition and the imprints of the individual plates are on average 10 ¾ inches wide and 7½ inches tall. The first

---

8 Anecdotes of Painting in England: with some account of the principal artists, Horace Walpole, James Dallaway, Ralph Nicholson Wornum, George Vertue, Vol III, 1876., p. 246.
9 ibid., p. 247.
10 The English Cyclopedia: a new dictionary of universal knowledge, Vol. 2., edited by Charles Knight, 1856.
11 The Supplement to the Penny Cyclopedia of the Society for the Diffusion of Useful Knowledge, Vol. 1. 1851., p.490
12 *Catalogue No. 113 Archæology. Books on Ancient Art Beginning from Archaic Times.* Karl W. Hiersemann, Leipzig, 1893., p. 496

ninety plates consist of images of two heads each. The ninety plates consist of forty-five images, with two heads to an image, the first of each set of images is a fully rendered, shaded version of the heads from the figures of Raphael's cartoons, the second is an outline version in which dotted lines show where the highlights and shadows will appear in the fully rendered version.

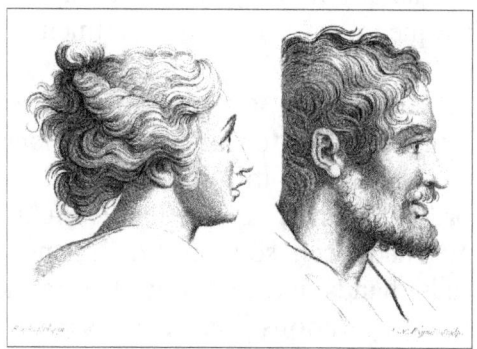

Plate 1.

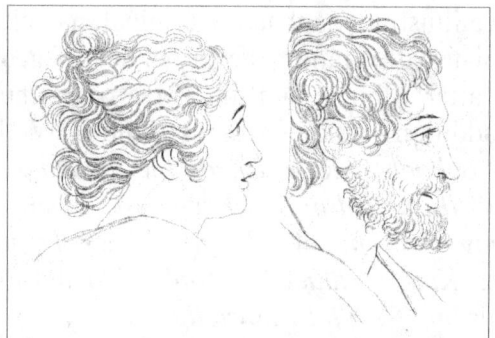

Plate 1. Outline Version

    Because of the size of this book, I divided each of the first ninety plates in half and printed each head on an opposite facing page so that they can be rendered full scale and as close as possible to their original appearance.

    The last twelve plates are the previously mentioned studies of geometry, anatomy and ancient sculptures. These do not lend themselves to dividing, so they are reproduced as large as possible on one page.

    You can easily find color reproductions of Raphael's cartoons but for convenience of referring back to the full versions while reading Benjamin Ralph's introduction I include black and white versions here.

-Tom Richardson, 2010

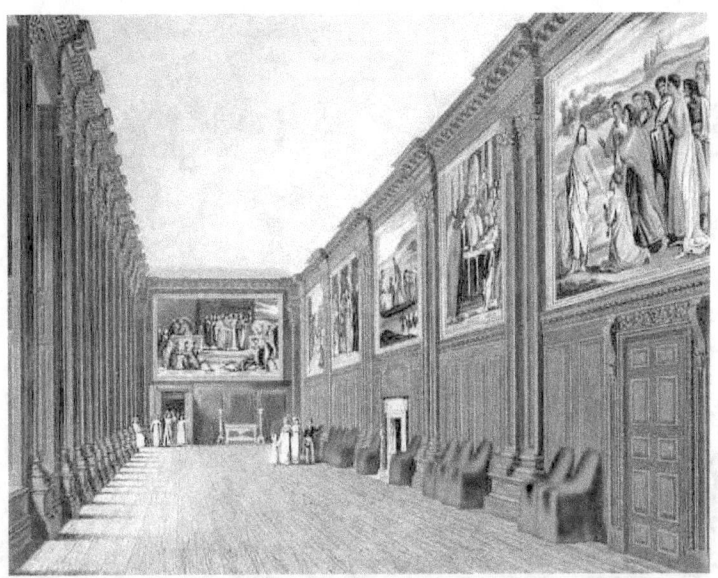

The Cartoon Gallery at Hampton Court, "...William III had them fitted into their original forms, and pasted upon canvas. He further completed the good work by building a gallery, especially for their reception, in Hampton Court...."[13]

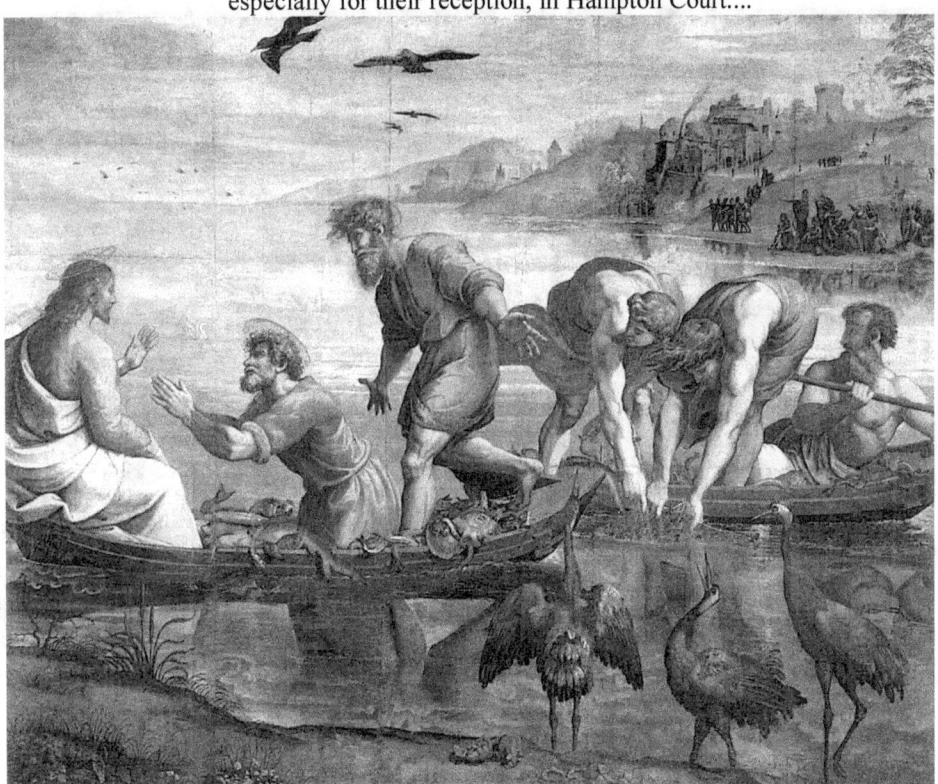

Cartoon 1. The Miraculous Draught of Fishes

13 Tour of a German Artist in England, Johann David Passavant, p. 82.

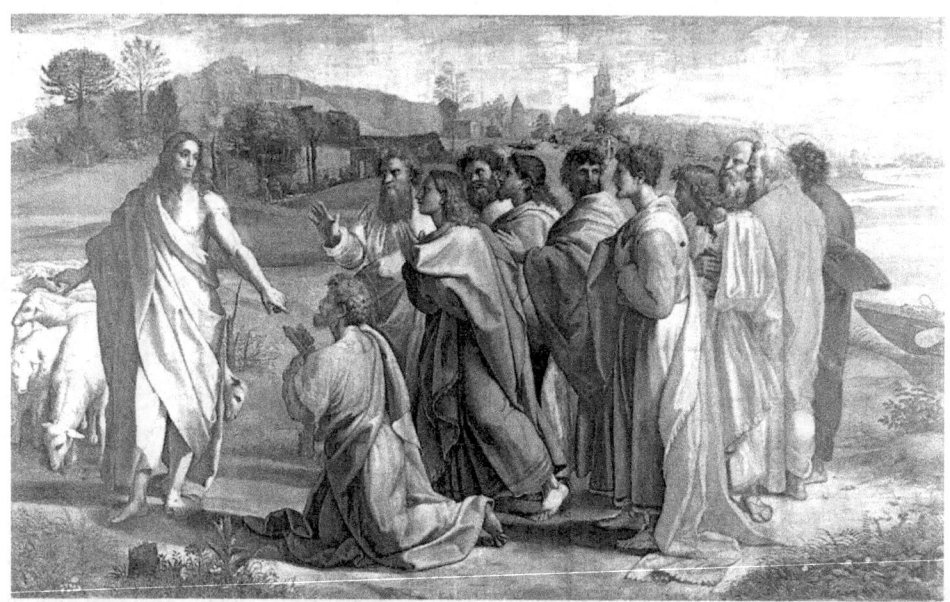

Cartoon 2. Christ's Charge to Peter

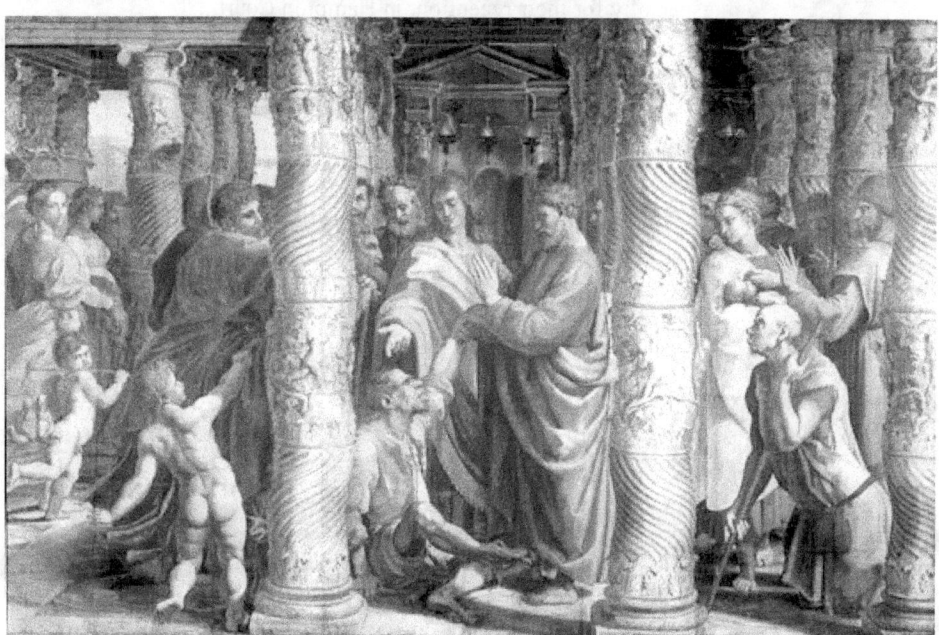

Cartoon 3. The Lame Man Healed

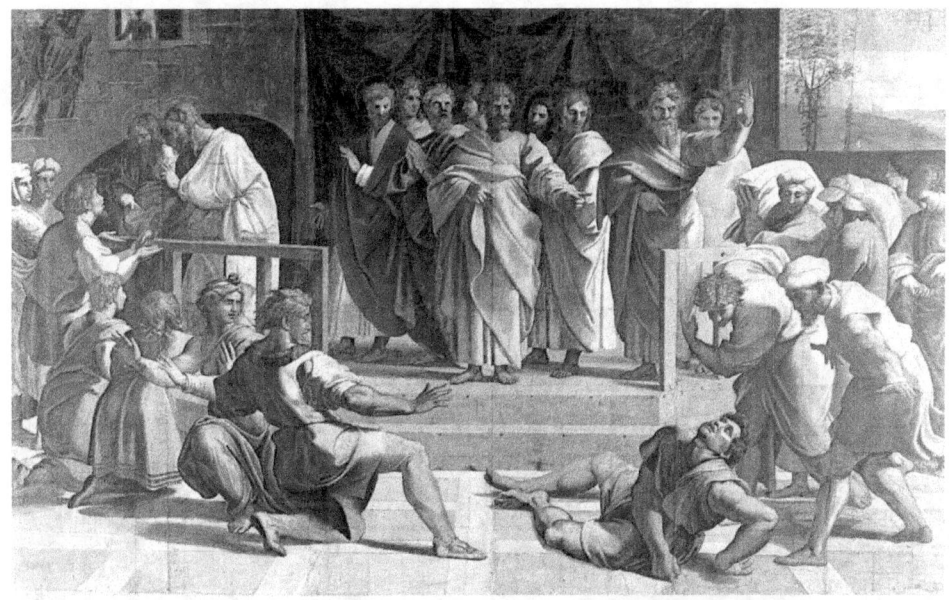

Cartoon 4. The Death of Ananias

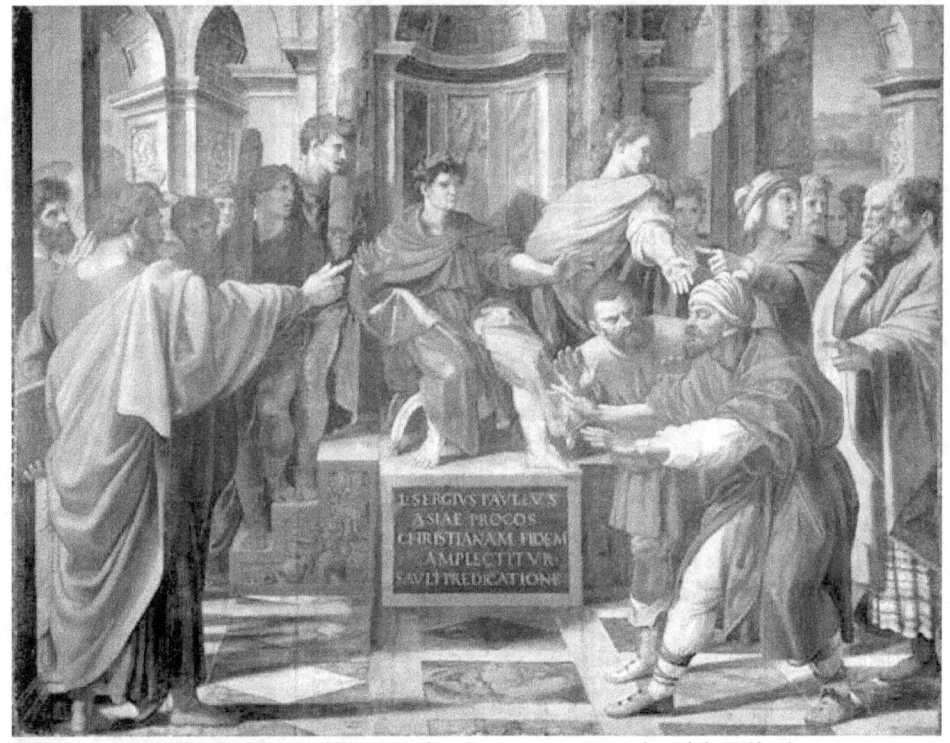

Cartoon 5. Elymas the Sorcerer Struck with Blindness

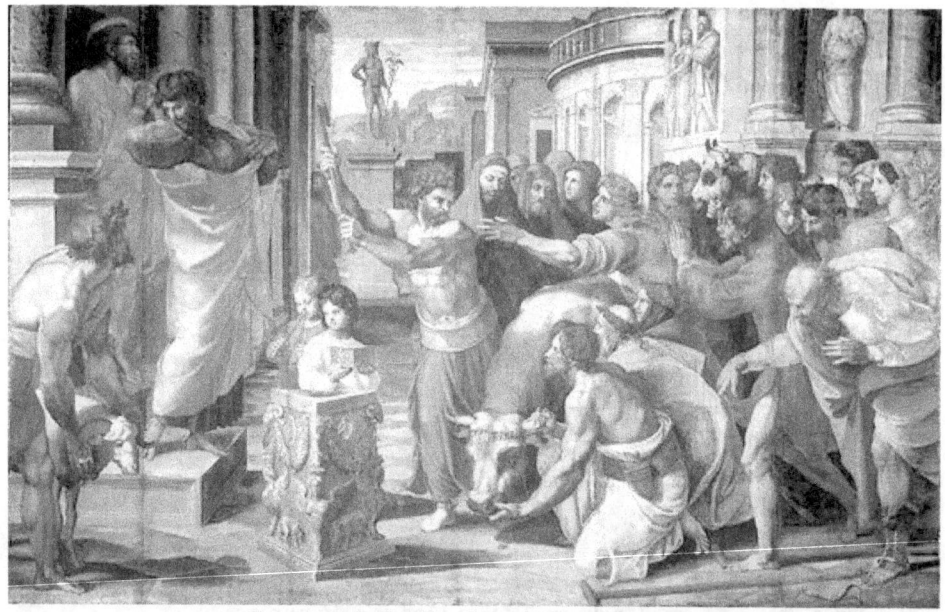

Cartoon 6. St. Paul and Barnabas at Lystra

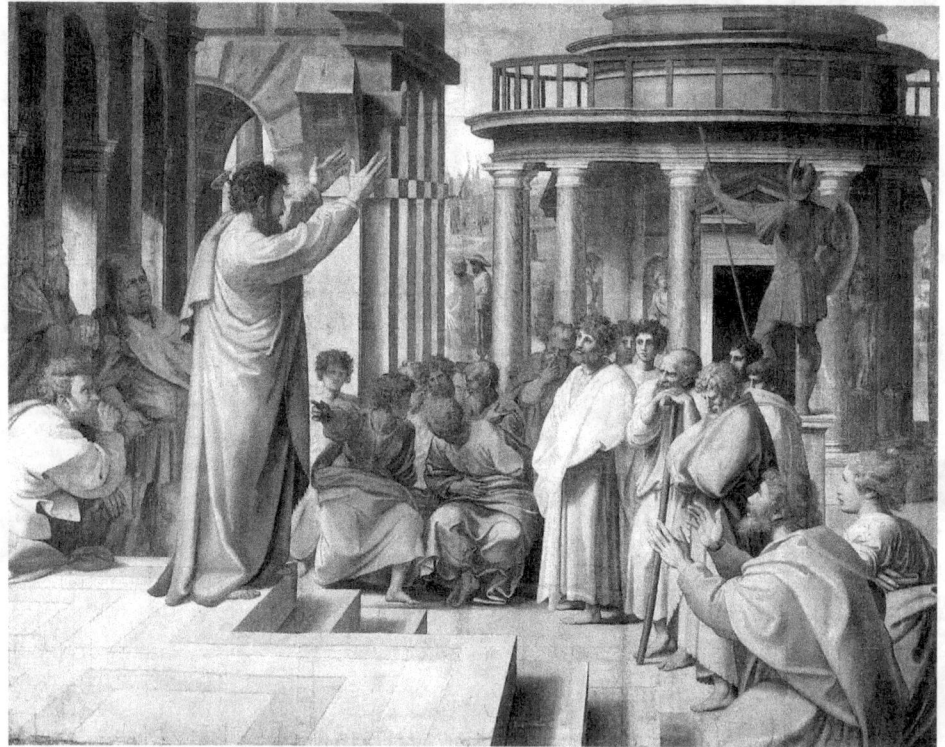

Cartoon 7. St. Paul Preaching at Athens

INTRODUCTION

IT is usual for the compilers of Drawing-books, not only to complain of the ignorance and inaccuracy of all that have preceded them, but to raise new expectation without any sense of the danger of new disappointment. The author of the following sheets, however, intends not, by depreciating the labours of others, to procure that credit for his own, which the same arts of supplantation may as effectually destroy: from a sincere love for the art itself, from a desire of communicating the means of improvement to others, and from a well-established hope, that the *science of painting* (for in historical compositions it is surely more than an art) is reviving in all its splendour in this island, he has been induced to recommend the incomparable examples in this book; and he is persuaded they will contribute to the proficiency of every one, whose happy genius urges him to excel in a study, that not only leads to the knowledge of TRUE BEAUTY, but directs the application of it to innumerable purposes of entertainment and use.

It was indeed, at first, determined to give only the outlines and finished heads, with an explanation of the characters, from a consideration that such a collection was peculiarly adapted to the use of painters, or at least of those who had already attained to a competent degree of excellence in the art. But, as no bounds can be set to the genius of youth, so no limits ought to be put to the means of improvement; and, in order to render this work useful to the learner as well as the proficient, it was afterwards thought necessary to prefix some examples even of the rudiments of design, as well as of those of the most elegant of the human form, and to give with them the best instructions that could be collected: and as it is undoubtedly true, that the Grecian and Italian schools are the only treasuries of design, from which could examples be taken with so much propriety as from the Grecian statues and the works of Raphael? Accordingly, all the examples have been taken from them, except the geometrical figures and the bones and muscles of the human body, which are selected from the works of those authors that are esteemed most correct; to whom, however, no recourse would have been had, if the subjects could have been supplied from the same source.

Though no examples of perspective are given, yet it must not be inferred, that this omission of so useful a part of science is occasioned either by ignorance of the art itself, or inattention to the just improvement of this work, to the design of which the examples of perspective are wholly foreign: it is, indeed, a complete study of itself; and, as such, the practice of that incomparable method laid down by Dr. Brooke Taylor, and with great pains and ingenuity explained by Mr. Kirby, is earnestly recommended.

The principal design of this work is to encourage the study of the most profound part of painting, the *characteristics of the passions*; in order to which, the sacred histories, represented in the inimitable Cartoons of Raphael, have been considered separately, and the principal characters in each described and referred to in the several heads in the work; and an Index is given for finding the passions under their proper denomination, referring to the description of each, and also to the design of the character itself.

Le Brun, the only author who has written on the passions as a painter, and given rules for describing them, has certainly succeeded very well, so far as he goes; but his examples, instead of answering all the purposes of study, appear, upon comparing them with those in the Cartoons, to be extremely defective; nay, it may be affirmed, that a person who has only studied Le Brun, will be at a loss when he views some of the characters in the Cartoons to know what passions are expressed in them, and yet the ideas will be found to be, in the highest degree, exalted, just, and significant; and he will be struck with astonishment and disgust, when he returns to his former study, in which he will find no traces to lead his ideas back to the point from which they first set out.*

The Cartoons are, indeed, a vast fund of variety, from which every man may enrich himself without diminishing the heap, or depriving those who come after him of their share of the inexhaustible treasure bequeathed to the whole world by that incomparable painter.

If, therefore, the explanation of the Cartoons should be found defective, let it be remembered, that the attempt is new: that the characters described are those of the Holy Jesus and his immediate followers, who were the greatest and best of mankind; and that the Cartoons are the labours of the first genius in painting that has appeared in the world since those of ancient Greece, of whose stupendous performances we have nothing left but the names.

---

* This author, however he may be censured or ridiculed for such an assertion, cannot help saying, that a collection of the passions as they are found in nature, might be made from the works of Mr. Hogarth, which would do honour to that master, and prove of great utility to young students.

OBSERVATIONS

ON THE

ART OF DESIGNING OR DRAWING.

∽

THE *theory of design* is the knowledge which is acquired by reading the best authors who have laid down rules for the attainment of the art scientifically, and given their judgment upon the performances of the greatest painters. By a thorough knowledge of the theory of design, those who are themselves unable to draw the most simple objects, may be qualified to pass sentence upon the works of the best masters; and in this case theory being separated from practice, is usually considered in another light, and distinguished by the appellation of *taste*. There is also another way of acquiring *taste* without reading, and that is by frequently examining good pictures in the presence of such as are esteemed judges of the art, who seldom fail of giving their opinion without reserve; and thus, according to the portion of knowledge they possess, and the understanding of those who are attentive to their decisions, theory or taste may be obtained in a greater or lesser degree.

Theory, therefore, in this sense of the word, has hitherto been the great support of painting: had taste been confined to *practical study* only, so many noble and invaluable pieces would not now have been found in the palaces of Princes, and the houses of great men, whose avocations could not perhaps otherwise permit them to acquire any taste at all for this art, and consequently painting would have found no patronage.

The practical part of design is the constant application of the hand, assisted by the understanding, in the imitation of variety of forms.

Those objects, whether persons or places, of which we have but a transient view, are, in the memory, like sketches made with charcoal upon paper, which either the slightest rubbing. or a blast of wind will entirely deface: how then shall the hand, unaccustomed to exercise in this art, perform its function, when the mind itself, after the object has been removed from before it a short time, can retain only a confused idea of its resemblance? Theory and practice, therefore, ought to be inseparable; and the knowledge of either without its associate, can never produce any thing like perfection.

From what has been already said it is obvious, that drawing, considered only as such, is nothing more than a habit, by which the hand, being accustomed to follow the traces of the eye, conveys upon paper or other materials the similitude of objects, and can only be obtained by unwearied application and great attention.

By practice the hand acquires a facility which gives freedom, and this freedom must constantly be corrected by judgment in placing every particular part in the object to be delineated in its proper order: it must be observed, that judgment is not here meant to be that exertion of the understanding which would be requisite to compose an historical picture, or a well-imagined landscape, but relates only to proportion, or an accurate consideration of the distance of one feature, limb, or part from another; it being no unusual thing for such as draw very well practically, to be utterly incapable of composing or inventing, which ought to be with more propriety ascribed to genius.

The *Manual Part of Designing* consists in two Operations,

OUTLINE AND RELIEF.

The first of these, with regard to *human figures*, comprehends *anatomy* and *proportion*.

The second, *light* and *shadow*; and these are produced by *hatching* with chalks, pen and ink, and black lead, or *washing* with Indian ink, bistre, &c.

Proportion and *relief* are also absolutely necessary in other parts of design, as landscape, ornaments, &c.

The necessary materials for designing are charcoal, red, black, and white chalk, Indian ink, bistre, black lead pencils, crow quill pens, and camel-hair pencils.

The charcoal should be chosen with a fine grain, such as will mark freely, and may be discharged easily by brushing it either with a feather or silk handkerchief; it is of great use in sketching or marking out the general idea of the figure or part to be designed; and the strokes being easily effaced, the drawing may, by degrees, be brought to its due proportion, and be afterwards more correctly finished with either of the chalks.

It has been already said of what importance the geometrical figures in Plate I. are to the art of designing: let them therefore be carefully studied and frequently drawn, even while the student thinks himself qualified to proceed further; for as confinement to dry studies often creates disgust, it is rather recommended to the learner to blend the practice of them with the most easy examples in the other plates.

Let not the student be deterred from proceeding by the appearance of difficulties; what is thought insurmountable may be conquered by repeated trials; and the wonder will be, that it should ever have appeared in so discouraging a light.

It will be found extremely advantageous to hold the port crayon, or other instrument, something more than two inches from the bottom; for freedom is the very essence of design.

Begin rather with parts than a whole figure.

An attempt to draw the figure of a man by one who is unable to mark the outline of a head will be unsuccessful, and such an effort instead of applause will certainly meet with contempt.

Proceed, therefore, with designing the different features of the face, and each of them in different positions; and when these can be performed with accuracy, it will be proper to begin with a whole head.

The examples of the oval for drawing the face and head in Plate I. should now be carefully considered, and Fig. XIV. in that plate, is an example of a head according to the most exact proportion. The oval is divided by a perpendicular line from top to bottom, and that line into four equal parts: the upper division describes the space from the top of the head to the lowest hair upon the forehead; the next division passes between the eye-brows and eye-lids, and not through the eyes, as has been erroneously taught; from thence to the bottom of the third division is the length of the nose; and the fourth contains the mouth and chin: this last is again divided into three equal parts; the first of which shews the space from the bottom of the nose to the middle of the mouth, the second contains the under lip and the space between that and the chin, and the chin fills the third part of the lower division of the face: the length of the eye is reckoned one fifth part of the breadth of the face which is also the breadth of the nose from the extremity of each nostril, and the mouth is nearly of the same measure: the ear is of the same length with the nose.

Observe, therefore, to place every feature properly: let the nose be set directly under the centre of the forehead, and the middle of the mouth exactly under that of nose; place the eyes upon a line, that there may appear no distortion, and be careful that the eyes and mouth are parallel to each other.

Of three quarter faces and profiles there are many fine examples in this book, and therefore little more need be said of them. It has been sometimes recommended to provide a piece of box turned in the shape of an egg, to mark off the several divisions upon it, and, by turning it various ways to observe the different appearance of the lines; but it would be much better to try the same experiment with a small plaster head, which may be more easily procured, and will certainly answer the purpose much better.

The student having frequently and carefully designed the head and its parts, may now turn his attention to the other extremities of the human body, which are, the hands and feet; these have ever been esteemed a difficult part of design; and various authors considering them as almost always appearing foreshortened, have given their proportions and laid down rules for drawing them under those appearances. But these, it is apprehended, are so many fetters to the understanding, and stumbling blocks in the way of genius; cautious judgment should be our conductor; the eye hardly ever sees them in any other situation, and it is by the eye the hand should be guided; the hand must mark nothing but what the eye directs, and the eye can discern no part but what the docile hand may delineate in its proper place. In short, a strict attention to nature, or good imitations of her, will always lead to truth and elegance; and if the design of any subject whatever happens not to be perfect when finished, our observations must have been erroneous ; and nothing remains but by repeated efforts to amend those parts which the judgment will discover to be incorrect.

The foregoing study will naturally lead to the *arms*, *trunk*, and *thighs;* of all which several elegant examples may be found in Plates III, IV, and V: in Plate V. are two views of the celebrated Torso of Michael Angelo, of which no greater recommendation can be given, than that it was the chief study of the great painter and sculptor whose name it bears.

It will next be proper to attempt designing a whole figure; and as this depends in a great measure, upon proportion as the foundation of symmetry, it may not be impertinent to give the measures of the human body, according to the rules laid down by M. Du Piles in his Observations on Fresnoy's Art of Painting.

THE MEASURES OF A HUMAN BODY.

"The ancients have commonly allowed eight heads to their figures, though some of them have but seven. But we ordinarily divide the figures into ten[*] faces; that is to say, from the crown of the head to the sole of the foot, in the following manner:

From the crown of the head to the forehead, is the third part of the face.

The face begins at the root of the lowest hairs which are upon the forehead, and ends at the bottom of the chin.

The face is divided into three proportionable parts;[†] the first contains the forehead, the second the nose, and the third the mouth and chin.

From the chin to the pit betwixt the collar bones, are two lengths of a nose.

From the pit betwixt the collar bones to the bottom of the breast, one face.

[‡]From the bottom of the breasts to the navel, one face.

[$]From the navel to the genitories, one face.

From the genitories to the upper part of the knee, two faces.

The knee contains half a face.

From the lower part of the knee to the ancle, two faces.

From the ancle to the sole of the foot, half a face.

---

[*] This depends on the age and quality of the persons. The Apollo and Venue de Medicis have more than ten faces. See the figures, Plates X. and XI.

[†] See plate I. Fig. XIV.

[‡] The Apollo has a nose more.

[$] The Apollo has half a nose more; and the upper half of the Venus de Medicis is to the lower part of the belly, and not to the privy parts.

A man when his arms are stretched out, is, from the longest finger of his right hand to the longest of his left, as broad as he is long.

From one side of the breasts to the other, two faces.

The bone of the arm, called *humerus*, is the length of two faces, from the shoulder to the elbow.

From the end of the elbow to the root of the little finger, the bone called *cubitus*, with part of the hand, contains two faces.

From the box of the shoulder-blade to the pit betwixt the collar bones, one face. If you would be satisfied in the measures of breadth, from the extremity of one finger to the other, so that this breadth should be equal to the length of the body, you must observe, that the boxes of the elbows with the *humerus*, and of the *humerus* with the shoulder-blade, bear the proportion of half a face, when the arms are stretched out.

The sole of the foot is the sixth part of the figure.

The hand is the length of a face.

The thumb contains a nose.

The inside of the arm, from the place where the muscle disappears, which makes the breast (called the pectoral muscle) to the middle of the arm, four noses. From the middle of the arm to the beginning of the hand, five noses.

The longest toe is a nose long.

The two outmost parts of the teats and the pit, betwixt the collar-bones of a woman, make an equilateral triangle.

For the breadth of the limbs, no precise measure can be given; because the measures themselves are changeable, according to the quality of the persons, and according to the movement of the muscles.

The foregoing rules, strongly impressed upon the memory, will prove of infinite advantage, as well in comparing the proportions of the antique statues with one another, as in judging of the different productions of nature in the formation of the human body, when considered in designing from the life; but as variety in composition is absolutely necessary, care must be taken that too strict an observance of the above measures may not destroy it; nor will the subject always allow that the figures should preserve the same proportion; which the ingenious author of the Analysis of Beauty has, in his chapter of *Proportion*, very judiciously remarked in is, Observations upon the celebrated Statue of the *Apollo-Belvedere*,* in the following words:

"May be, I cannot throw a stronger light on what has been hitherto said of proportion, than by animadverting on a remarkable beauty in the Apollo-Belvedere, which hath given it the preference even to the Antinous: I mean a super-addition of *greatness*, to at least as much beauty and grace as is found in the latter.

* See the Figure, Plate X.

These two master-pieces of art are seen together in the same apartment at Rome, where the Antinous fills the spectator with admiration only, whilst the Apollo strikes him with surprise; and, as travellers. express themelves, with appearance of something *more than human*: which they *of course* are always at a loss to describe: and this effect, they say, is the more astonishing, as, upon examination, its disproportion is evident, even to a common eye. One of the best sculptors we have in England, who lately went to see, them, confirmed to me what has been now said, particularly as to the legs an thighs being too long, and too large for the upper parts. And Andrea Sacchi, one of the Italian painters, seems to have been of the same opinion, or he would hardly have given his Apollo, crowning Pasqualini the musician, the exact proportion. of the Antinous (in a famous picture.of his, now in England) as otherwise it seems to be a direct copy from the Apollo.

Although in very great works we often see an inferior part neglected, yet here it cannot be the case; because, in a fine statue, just proportion is one of its essential beauties: therefore it stands to reason, that these limbs must have been, lengthened on purpose, otherwise it might have easily been avoided.

So that if we examine the beauties of this figure thoroughly, we may reasonably conclude, that what has been hitherto thought so unaccountably *excellent* in its general appearance, hath been owing to what hath seemed a *blemish* in a part of it: but let us endeavour to make this. matter as clear as possible, as it may add more force to what has been said.

Statues, by being bigger than life (as this is one, and larger than the Antinous) always gain some nobleness in effect, according to the principle of quantity; but this alone is not sufficient to give what is properly to be called *greatness* in proportion."

Here the author refers to two figures of dwarfs or lilliputians, in the prints given with his 'book, and proceeds with saying, that "were they to be drawn, or carved, by a scale of ten feet high, they would still be but pigmy proportions; as, on the other hand, a figure of but two inches may represent a gigantic height.

Therefore *greatness* of proportion must be considered as depending on the application of *quantity* to those parts of.the body where it can give more scope to its grace in movement; as to the neck for the larger and swan-like turns of the head, and to the legs and thighs for the more ample sway of all the upper parts together."

All Objects are *greater*, or *less*, by Comparison.

There is no other way of conveying the idea of a giant than by comparison; he must be accompanied by one or more figures of the same proportion, but they must be drawn upon a lesser scale; but if to an extraordinary stature it should be requisite to add superior strength, it must be done, as the before-mentioned author ingeniously observes, by a judicious exaggeration of particular parts of the body:

the Farnesian Hercules is a fine example of uncommon bodily strength. See Plate VII.

It is entirely owing to the neglect of comparing objects, that particular views of mountains, rocks, and lakes of water, are almost generally deficient: the trees, buildings, vessels, and figures, which are necessarily introduced with the principal object, are usually drawn in much greater proportions than they ought to be, and this error never fails to destroy the effect desired: that which was intended to represent a stupendous mountain, conveys the idea of a paltry hill; huge rocks appear like inconsiderable heaps of stone, and vast lakes of water are diminished to the size of ordinary fish-ponds.

The Knowledge of ANATOMY is the Basis of Design.

The truth of this assertion is clearly proved by M. Du Piles, who, in his Principles of Painting, says, "As it is in vain to desire to profit by a bare sight of fine things, if we do not well conceive them; so it is impossible thoroughly to understand the beauty of the antique, anymore than truth in, nature, without the help of anatomy. We may, indeed, by seeing and designing the antique, acquire a certain greatness of design: and, in the main, get a practice tending to good taste and delicacy; but these advantages, if void of knowledge and principles, can only dazzle the spectator by a specious show, and by ill-placed remembrances of things. A man may be in raptures on seeing the fine works of antiquity, and yet be far from knowing the genuine source of those beauties which he admires; at least, if he be ignorant of that fundamental part of design, anatomy.

If then anatomy be the basis of design, and enables us to discover the beauties of the antique, I cannot but observe, that the knowledge of so much of it as the painter and sculptor require, is easily retained; and that the neglect of this attainment proceeds only from its being thought to lead towards dryness of design, and pedantry of manner.

ANATOMY is a knowledge of the parts of the human body; but to painters that only which relates to the bones, and the principal muscles which cover them, is needful.

Nature has furnished us with bones for the solidity of the body, and strength of the members: to them she has fixed the muscles, as exterior agents, to draw them whither she pleases: the bones determine the measures of length, and the muscles those of bigness in the parts of nature; at least, it is the office of the-muscles to settle the form and exactness of outlines.

'Tis indispensably necessary to be well acquainted with the forms and joints of the bones, because motion often alters their measures; and likewise to understand the situation and office of the muscles, since the most striking truth in design depends upon them.

The bones themselves are motionless, and stir only by the help of the muscles. The muscles have their origins and insertions: by their origins they are fastened to a bone, which they were never intended to stir; and by their insertions to another bone, which they draw when they please towards their origins.

Every muscle has its opposite muscle; when one acts the other yields, like well-buckets, one of which descends as the other comes up: the acting muscle swells, and contracts next to its origin; the other that obeys, dilates, and relaxes.

The largest bones, which are moved with the greatest difficulty, are covered with the largest muscles; these are often aided by others, which are designed for the same office, and thereby increase the force of motion and make the part more apparent.

We often observe, in the naked parts of antique figures, and even in nature itself, certain swells, the reason of which we cannot discover, without considering the situation and office of the muscle which is the cause of them. But those who are skilful in anatomy, see all in seeing a part, and know how to remove from the eye what the skin and fat seem to conceal, and what is hid to those who are ignorant of this science."

As the knowledge of anatomy is absolutely necessary for the attainment of perfection in design, a very particular attention to the examples of the bones and muscles in Plates VI. VII. VIII. and IX. is recommended.

When the student has acquired a tolerable habit of designing, and also made himself equally conversant with the bones and muscles, it will be found of the utmost advantage, in drawing the human body, to sketch out in the first place the osteology, or skeleton of the figure, in its proper proportion, and in the attitude required; which may be done either from a print, painting, or nature itself: the next operation will be to delineate the proper muscles, marking each distinctly in its place in a bold manner; after which the figure will probably appear over-charged with muscles. And now it will be of the utmost importance to recollect the idea of the waving line, which is described in Plate I. Fig. X. for it will be only by a thorough comprehension of the use of that line that the drawing will appear to be well or ill executed, when finished: the skilful in anatomy know, that where the insertions of the muscles appear too hard and overcharged, and the hollows too deep, which is always the case in a prepared muscular figure, that nature has wisely contrived to remedy the defect and fill up those vacancies, by placing therein certain quantities of fat, which softens the harshness and inequality of the lines, and produces that inexpressible grace which is always found in the outlines of well-proportioned bodies, and which has been so happily imitated by the ancients.

As naked figures cannot be introduced with any propriety, except in some particular subjects, where there is an absolute necessity for them, it becomes a matter of the greatest importance to clothe them gracefully: it will now therefore be proper to give some

RULES FOR DESIGNING OF DRAPERIES.

The gradation before recommended for designing naked figures, by beginning with the osteology, may, with equal propriety, be applied to the designing of Draperies: for as that method will be found of the utmost utility for placing the muscles correctly; so first designing the figure naked, and afterwards proceeding to cast the Drapery, will be found in this point equally beneficial. It will not be necessary to finish with that exactness which is required for such as are intended to remain in that state; but the just proportion being given, and the parts boldly marked, the mistakes that are found in the performances of those who proceed with less caution, will be prevented. The best authors, who have treated upon the manner of designing Draperies, concur in enforcing the utility of this method.

It will also be necessary in designing Draperies to observe the following precepts:

1. Carefully avoid overcharging the figure with an unnecessary quantity.

2. Shew as much of the form of the body under it as possible.

3. Where large draperies are requisite, throw them into few folds, but let those be large and graceful.

4. On the contrary, loosen those from the body which are close and short, by small folds judiciously placed; which will take off that stiffness which would be the consequence of their sitting too strait.

5. When much drapery is necessary, let the greater part of it (if convenient) be thrown into shadow.

6. Observe to give tender shadows to those folds which fall in the lights, that the hollow parts may not appear too deep and cutting.

7. Let the folds be well contrasted, and avoid straight lines as much as possible.

8. Make the folds contrast the body and limbs.

9. A judicious repetition of folds in a circular form, contributes greatly to characterize. a fore-shortened limb.

10. The drapery of figures moving with great activity, should play as if agitated by the wind; but that in proportion only to the velocity with which the figure appears to move: on the contrary, in fixed attitudes keep the drapery still.

11. Numberless examples of fine draperies maybe found in prints after the great masters; but none are fitter to be consulted than those of the Cartoons: let them be designed carefully, and the artist will be better enabled to cast them himself in a true taste, when he afterwards makes designs from real draperies.

When the student has made a considerable progress, and is able to copy a picture, drawing, or print, with freedom and exactness, let him proceed to finish his studies by considering the antique and nature. The collection of casts from the antique statues, at the Royal Academy for Painting and Sculpture, are accessible to the ingenious.

It will be necessary to conclude with one useful caution: let the student be careful how he studies the statues; let him remember, that the best of them are only memorials of the intense application of those great artists, whose lives were spent in endeavours to express their own idea of perfection, which varied according to the different genius or taste of each master, and the different nature of the materials he wrought upon; and that those performances which come nearest to nature are the best. And let it be further remembered, that a design correctly made after the finest statue, will never convey any other idea than that of a statue: there is a stiffness inseparable from marble or plaster, which is conveyed to, and infallibly distinguishes the designs made after them from those made after nature; and that stiffness should be avoided with the utmost care and assiduity.

OF THE

STUDY OF GEOMETRICAL FIGURES

THOUGH this part of the Work will undoubtedly be censured by those who are contented with a superficial knowledge Of the Art of Designing, yet the end proposed will be sufficiently answered, if it met with the approbation of the few; let those who deride admonition, and choose to wanton upon the surface of the stream, float gently down it, and divert themselves with the sticks and weeds with which they will be insensibly and inevitably entangled.

> "Errors, like straws, upon the surface low,
> Those who would search for pearls must dive below."

However, it is not expected, nor is it indeed necessary, that a perfect designer should be a perfect geometrician; but it is certainly expected that he should be acquainted with the form and construction of the most simple geometrical figures, which are, in fact, the basis of the art he would study: to those, therefore, who would attain to a masterly manner of designing, it is recommended to study carefully the figures described in Plate I; to make them familiar, and to endeavour to imitate their forms rather by the hand, guided by judgment, than the rule and compass; for, as Fresnoy judiciously observes, *The compass should rather be in the painter's eyes, than his hands*. But as the true construction of these figures is easily attained, it will probably argue either self-sufficiency or indolence not to be acquainted with it.

EXPLANATION OF THE GEOMETRICAL FIGURES IN THE FIRST PLATE.

FIGURE I.
To bisect (or cut in two equal parts) a given Line.

Set one point of the compasses in A, and, opening them something more than half the length of the line, describe a semicircle, and from the point B do the same, and draw a line through their intersections.

FIGURE II.
To divide a given Circle into four equal Parts.
Draw a line through the centre C, and proceed as in FIG. I.

FIGURE III.
From a given point C, in a right Line, to erect a Perpendicular.
Set one point of the compasses in C, and, opening them at pleasure, set off the distances A B, and proceed as in Fie. I.

FIGURE IV.
Upon a Point, situate at or near the end of a Line, to erect a Perpendicular.
From the point B, on the line A B, extend the compasses, at pleasure, to the centre C, from which describe a circle, and from the intersection in the line A B at D, draw a line through C, which will cut the circumference at E, from which draw a line to the point B.

FIGURE V.
Shews the manner of drawing parallel lines, which needs no explanation, and may be drawn to any distance required.

FIGURE VI.
To form a Square from a given Line.
Erect a perpendicular (by the rule given in FIG. IV.) upon which and the base line, set off with the compasses the line proposed, and keeping the same distance, draw the circular lines C D B, and A D B, from whose intersections at D draw the lines DC and DA.

FIGURE VII.
From two given Lines to form a Parallelogram, or long Square.
Draw the line C B at pleasure, upon which set off the longest given line A, erect a perpendicular at E, upon which set off the given line B, mark off the line from F, and the line B from A, and draw the lines A G and G F.

FIGURE VIII.
From a given Line to form an equilateral Triangle.
Take the length of the given line A B with the compasses, and from the point. A and B draw circular lines, from whose intersection draw A D and C B.

FIGURE IX.
Is an attempt to shew, with certainty, how to draw that curved line which the Author of the Analysis of Beauty has, with as great propriety as *authority*, termed the *line of beauty*; and upon the use and properties of which he has obliged

the world with a very elegant, ingenious, and instructive Treatise: it has however been objected, that he has omitted to give a rule whereby *precise line of beauty* may be found; in consequence of which objection, and in order to enforce the study of that line, this figure is given; not as a mathematical demonstration, nor as an insult upon the author of the Analysis of Beauty (whose meaning is very obvious, though perhaps not so fully explained as to silence the clamours of ignorance and detraction,) but as a line extremely well worth studying, being itself simple, elegant, easily drawn, and the precise line of beauty described by that great artist, whose plain unaffected manner of referring to the most familiar objects or the explanation of his ideas, we shall endeavour to follow, and inform the Reader, that it is to be found in an ornament well known to every school-boy; that of a six-pointed star, of which the contrasted halves of any two opposite give the line required.

The Construction of the Ninth Figure.

Divide a circle into four equal parts by the rule before given. The semi-diameter, or the distance from A to C will, if the figure be drawn exactly, be equal to one sixth part of the circumference, set off therefore half the diameter from D to B, and from E to F, and keeping the same distance from the point F draw E C and from the point B draw C D.

FIGURE X.

This figure is founded upon a precept said to be given by the celebrated MICHAEL ANGELO TO to his scholar Marcus de Scienna, which according to *Lomazzo*, was "that *he should always make a figure pyramidal, serpent like, and multiplied by one, two, and three,*"[*] which precept, as the Author of the Analysis, observes, hath remained a mystery down to this time; and indeed it appears not only to be mysterious but absurd; to talk of *multiplying by the number One* is a gross impropriety; and that MICHAEL ANGELO should advise his scholar *always* to make a figure pyramidal and serpentine, and multiplied by those numbers, must be a mistake, for every figure in a picture cannot possibly admit of such a rule: for instance, it is not to be preserved in a figure sitting or stooping, and consequently MICHAEL ANGELO, who well knew the necessity of such attitudes, would never impose such a stricture. The truth is, this famous precept had suffered the fate of many other excellent traditional rules before it came to *Lomazzo*, who transcribed it as it was delivered to him, contenting himself with the authority of the master, and the ambiguity of the precept itself. It is perhaps more rational to believe, that MICHAEL ANGELO endeavoured to persuade his pupil to accustom himself to draw a figure *or line* which was pyramidal, serpentine, and *increasing in the proportion of*

---

* See Haydocke's Translation printed at Oxford in 1598.

one, two, and three, as a sure means of acquiring a habit of designing the outlines of the human body in a masterly manner, and thereby as the Author of the Analysis terms it, always expressing the lines of beauty and grace; LOMAZZO proceeds to explain the foregoing precept thus: "In which precept (in mine opinion) the whole mysterie of the. arte consisteth. For the greatest grace and life that a picture can have is, that it expresse *motion*, which the painters call the *spirite* of a picture: nowe there is no forme so fitte to expresse this *motion*, as that of the flame of fire; which, according to *Aristotle* and the other philosophers, is an elemente most active of all others; because the form of the flame thereof is most apt for motion, for it hath a *conus* or sharpe pointe, wherewith it seemeth to divide the aire, that so it may ascende to his proper sphere. So that a picture having this forme will be most beautiful.

"Now this is to be understood after two sortes; either that the *conus* of the *pyramis* be placed upwardes, and the base downwardes, as in the fier: or else contrary wise with the *base* upwardes, and the *conus* downwardes. In the first it expresseth the width and largenesse of a picture about the legges and garmentes below: shewing it slender above *pyramidall* wise, by discovering one shoulder and hiding the other, which is shortened by the turning of the body. In the seconde, it sheweth. the arms biggest in the upper partes; by representing either both the shoulders, or both the armes, shewing one legge, and hiding the other, or both of them after one sorte, as the skilful painter shall judge fittest for his purpose. So that his (Michael Angelo's) meaning is,that it should resemble the forme of the letter S placed right, or else turned the wronge way, as; Ƨ ,because then it hath this beauty. Neither ought he only to observe this forme in the whole body; but even in every part; so that in the legge when a muscle is raysed outwardes on the one side, that which answereth directly on the contrary side must be drawn in and hid (as may be seene in the life.)

"The last parte of Michael Angelo his observation was, that a picture ought to be multiplied by one, two, and three. And herein consisteth the chiefest. skill of that proportion whereof I mean to intreate more at large in this booke. For the diameter of the biggest place, betweene the knee and the foote is double to the least, and the largest part of the thigh triple."

In the observations on the Art of Painting of Du Fresnoy,[†] it is said, "That the outlines, give not only a grace to the parts, but also to the whole body, as we see, in the Antinous, Venus de Medicis, and others." And further it is said, "Besides, that the figures and their parts ought almost always to have a serpentine and flaming form naturally; these sorts of outlines have I know not what of life and seeming motion in them, which very much resembles the activity of the flame and of the serpent."

Elsum, in his Art of Painting,[*] after he has quoted the above precept of

---

† See Dryden's Translation of Du Fresnoy's Art of Painting, p. 125.
* See Elsum's Art of Painting after the Italian manner, printed at London, 1703.

Michael Angelo, has this remarkable passage:

"But for as much as there are *two* sorts of pyramids, the one straight as is that near St. Peter's in Rome, called the *pyramid of Julius Cæsar*; the other waived like flame, and is called *Michael Angelo's serpentine*. This latter also a painter must imitate, his contours must *turn and wind like a serpent*."

It is presumed that the tenth figure has all the properties mentioned by the foregoing authors; it actually expresses motion as that of a flame, of a streamer agitated by the wind, is a true representation of the decreasing swell of a wave, and is consequently a proper study for those who are emulous of excelling in designing the outlines of the human body; and though it may not carry with it sufficient proof of it being the very precept of Michael Angelo, it is hoped the time which is bestowed on its consideration will not be thrown away.

The Construction of the Tenth Figure.

Upon the line A B, draw a circle C at pleasure, take the diameter of that circle, and from the circumference of the circle C, upon the line A B draw the circle D, which will be twice the diameter of C, then take the distance from the centres C and D, and from the circumference of the circle D draw the circle E, which will be three timeá the diameter of C the lesser circle, and proceed to draw the curves in the same manner as described in FIG. X.

FIGURE XI.
Shews the manner of dividing a Line into any number of equal Parts.

This figure will be found to be of great use in forming squares for drawings from pictures, whether they are to be enlarged or reduced, and is constructed in the following manner:

Draw A B, the line proposed, and from A draw the line A D at pleasure, then setting the compasses in A, cut the lines A B and A D in E F, and, keeping the same distance in the compasses from B, cut the line A B at G, then take the distance E F; and, setting it off from G to H, draw the line B I, upon which (the line in the example being divided into eight parts) set off at pleasure even equal parts, and do the same upon A D, (observing always to set off one part less than the number requird,) draw lines from the marks in I B to those in A D, and the line A B will be divided into eight equal parts.

DESCRIPTION

OF THE

CARTOONS OF RAPHAEL URBIN.

WHEN a man enters into that awful Gallery at Hampton Court, (says Mr. Richardson, in his Essay on the Theory of Painting,) he finds himself amongst a sort of people superior to what he has ever seen, and very probably to what those really were. Indeed this is (speaking of grace and greatness,) the principal excellence of those wonderful pictures, as it must be allowed to be that part of painting which is preferable to all others. These inimitable pieces are called CARTOONS, from their being executed upon paper; and are nothing more than coloured drawing upon a washed ground previously prepared for that purpose, the shadows of which are made by hatching with the point of a large pencil, and the whole are very highly finished. They were originally intended as patterns for tapestery, and were entirely the work of that great master Raphael Urbin. It is almost impossible to consider these pictures, without supposing that, as the Miraculous Draught of Fishes is the only miracle of our Saviour's to be found among them, it is more than probable, that what this country now happily possesses, is but a part of a most stupendous work of this great man, and that many more glorious Cartoons of the life and miracles a our Saviour have perished in oblivion; for it can hardly be conceived, that this single subject could particularly engage the attention of Raphael, among many others which would undoubtedly have made better pictures, and been more suitable to genius; and the Cartoon of Christ's Charge to Peter, and the regular succession the acts of the Apostle, seem greatly to confirm this opinion. However, as it is a argument that probably will not be contested, and cannot be proved, it can only be lamented, that perhaps some accident, or the premature death of that great master,* has deprived the world of an invaluable treasure.

---

* Anno 1522, Æt. 37.

CARTOON I.

THE MIRACULOUS DRAUGHT OF FISHES.

And Jesus said unto Simon, Fear not, from henceforth thou shalt catch men. **Luke v. 10.**

THIS was an amazing event; but as the principal persons were few, and half of them necessarily engaged in the management of their nets, the historical expression is confined to three figures only, which are those of our Saviour, Peter, and James. The principal figure of this picture is Christ, who is pronouncing the words above quoted, in order to remove the apprehension of Peter, who, in a fine posture of supplication, has just uttered these words, "Depart from me, for I am a sinful 0 Lord." Our Saviour's figure and action are perfectly great and graceful; and in his character, divinity, benignity, arid tenderness, are expressed in the highest degree. In Peter's countenance,[*] fear, wonder, and solicitude are blended in a most extraordinary manner, and compose a character of expression worthy of Raphael;[†] the figure in the same boat, supposed to be that of James, is also finely imagined and drawn; awe and attention are strongly marked in his face, and he seems, by his action, to have acquiesced in the supplication of Peter, as acknowledging himself unworthy of being the companion of Divinity.[‡] The rest of the figures, as has already been said, are chiefly concerned in attending to their employment which, as they were in another vessel, naturally engrossed their attention; only the nearest of them seems to have caught some part of the conversation, and appears to listen: this last figure, and another, who are pulling up. the net, are finely drawn, contrasted, and foreshortened; and the whole figure of the old man in the stern of the boat, who is very attentive to his business, is extremely fine.

The perspective in this Cartoon (in which the point of sight is placed pretty high) occasions the sea to make a fine back ground for the figures, which, from its natural hue, fails not of shewing the colouring of the figures to the utmost advantage. At a great distance, upon the sea-shore, appear several groupes of figures, designed in a manner, the principal of which seems to consist of a number of persons; are employed in the baptism of infants. Nothing need be said to the objection commonly made by small critics to the size of the boats, that having been fully answered by Mr. Richardson; who has also mentioned the effect of the sea-fowl, which artfully and judiciously placed in the fore ground, and indeed could be very ill spared.

---

* Plate 29. No. I.
† Plate 18. No. I.
‡ Plate 13. No. II.

CARTOON II.

CHRIST'S CHARGE TO PETER; COMMONLY CALLED THE DELIVERY OF THE KEYS.

He said unto him the third time, Simon, son of Jonas, lovest thou me? Peter was grieved because he said unto him the third time, Lovest thou me? And he said unto him Lord, thou knowest all things, thou knowest that I love thee. Jesus saith unto him, Feed my sheep. John xxi. 17.

THE principal figure in this picture is that of our Saviour, which Mr. Richardson is of opinion has received some injury, and is not at present what Raphael made it. This supposition,* it is believed, has never been contradicted; and whoever attentively compares the taste of design in this figure with those of the apostles in the same Cartoon, or that of our Saviour in the Miraculous Draught of Fishes, must be convinced that it falls many degrees short of that great painter. Perhaps, by some who may contend for its being Raphael's, it may be urged, that, like Leonardo da Vinci, in a similar case, he was baffled by the greatness of his own idea: but whichever argument holds good, we must be content to take it as it appears. Mr. Richardson also observes, that the time chosen is the moment of our Lord's having just spoken; and that in consequence of our Saviour's interrogating Peter, "Lovest thou me more than these ?" the rest of the apostles were eager to reply to that question, by assuring their Lord, that their love for him was at least equal to Peter's; and this solicitude is finely expressed in every character. The next principal figure is that of Peter, who, according to the history, is represented upon his knees, with the utmost humility attending to and receiving the charge given him by his divine Master. The head is drawn in profile, and the face is entirely in shadow.† It may be here observed, that the shadow cast by Peter's body serves admirably to bring the figure of our Saviour forward, and also to keep the principal groupe together. The third principal figure is St. John, whose expression and attitude Mr. Richardson mentions as an improvement upon the story. He says, our Saviour, by commanding Peter to feed his sheep seemed to indicate a preference in favour of that apostle, as has been observed; anti that St. John, who was the beloved disciple, may, therefore, be supposed to have been under a particular concern on that account. Accordingly he appears to address himself to our Lord with extreme ardour, as if earnestly endeavouring to convince him of the sincerity of his love.‡ The attention of all the apostles is directed to our Saviour, except one,¶ who seems to press forward: and, by turning his head, which is seen between two profiles, hinders the repetition which would have unavoidably happened if he had been looking the same way. The heads of the apostles are amazingly designed,

---

* Plate 35. No. I.
† Plate 29. No. I
‡ Plate 18. No. I.
¶ Plate 13. No. II.

and full of expression; and their attitudes are finely varied and contrasted. The draperies are noble and well-cast; that of our Saviour only appears to be rather heavy, and unsuitable to him at this time, as being after his resurrection. But admitting that this figure has suffered, the injury may, in this particular, be attributed to the alteration of it by some other hand. Mr. Richardson, who had studied the Cartoons observes, that the small piece of drapery in a part of the outermost apostle, is of great consequence to this picture; which, being folded as under his arm, breaks the straight line of an unpleasing mass of light, and gives a more graceful form to the whole: which artifice is also assisted by the boat. Of the same consequence to the principal figure is the flock of sheep placed behind, which helps to break the lines of the drapery, detach the figure from its ground, and illustrate the history.

CARTOON III.

THE LAME MAN HEALED; COMMONLY CALLED THE BEAUTIFUL GATE OF THE TEMPLE.

Then Peter said, Silver and gold have I none, but such as 1 have give I thee: in the name of Jesus Christ of Nazareth, rise up and walk.
And he took him by the right hand, and lifted him up, and immediately his feet. and ancle bones received strength. **Acts iii. 6, 7.**

THIS truly great composition is divided into three distinct groupes, by means of the magnificent columns which appear in the front of the picture, and are a part of the colonade which supports the roof of the portico. The two apostles Peter and John, the cripple, and four figures, whose heads only are seen, compose the groupe in the centre; one side of the picture is filled with people going to the temple, and its opposite with others coming from it; which disposition Raphael has advantageously employed in contrasting these two subordinate groupes, by opposing the backs of some of the figures to others which are seen in front, and further contrasting these by several which are in profile.

There is not, perhaps, in the world, a picture so thoroughly characterised, or so artfully managed, as this Cartoon. The moment of Peter's having pronounced the words, "In the name of Jesus Christ of Nazareth, rise up and walk," is the time chosen by Raphael; and is the instant when the lame man finds himself suddenly enabled to rise; when the muscles of his limbs, released from the contraction which till now withheld and deprived him of their use, are expanding, and an extraordinary impulse urges him to the exertion of their hitherto useless functions; all which is most amazingly conceived and expressed. At this period, those who were apprized. of some thing extraordinary which was then transacting, are endeavouring to thrust forward on the side of the picture where the cripple is placed; and these, with a woman an boy who are hastily passing onto the temple, together with the inimitable boy in the front of the picture, who is eagerly pulling back one of the figures, remarkably characterize the principal subject of the cartoon, which is that of the agent of Divine Power giving strength and agility to the torpid limbs of a man who was born lame. Wonder and amazement are finely expressed in the characters of the spectators; and on the side of the picture next to Peter, who with great dignity has conferred the divine gift, every thing is still, but expressing silent amazement. Thus in the parts where dignity should be preserved, all is quiet; and where strength and activity are given every thing is in motion. The character of the cripple is finely imagined; it is perfectly that of a mean person; and the expression of joy and gratitude which appears in it, is finely balanced by a mixture of doubt and astonishment; and he seems scarcely to believe the reality of the blessing he is receiving. The character of Peter is devout and majestic;* and that of John is full of divinity, and superlatively graceful;† he is represented with the utmost pity and affability, concurring with Peter in this act of true piety and charity. The rest of the heads in the same groupe are finely invented and drawn, particularly that of the old man leaning upon his crutch,‡ and of him who is looking over John's shoulder.§

It is remarkable, that the same airs of the head, which Raphael has given to the two apostles, are nearly the same with those of the man and woman on that side of the picture;‖ and the action of Peter's arm is repeated in the same man with a very little variation. He has also introduced another cripple into this groupe whose character is not altogether unlike that of him who is healed; but the expression is of another kind, and shews a malevolence and disinclination to believe the truth of this miracle; which seems to be one reason why he was placed behind the apostle,¶ as a situation most properly adapted to one of his way of thinking; but this figure is of prodigious use, and is moreover a fine contrast to the other; and the repetition in the rest is so judiciously managed, that it has no ill effect; but of this groupe particular notice will be taken in speaking of the by-works or ornaments of this Cartoon.

There is a wonderful expression of malignity in the character of the man who presses his lips with his finger, in the same groupe. The woman with the child in her arms has a character full of expression, is exquisitely designed, and perfectly great and graceful. The fine boy* in the fore part of the picture, who being unconcerned is eager to be going, and pulls the man's garment, is a fine contrast to the figure of the cripple; and at the same time breaks a mass of shadow, which

---

* Plate 6 No. II.
† Plate 31. No. I.
‡ Plate 31. No. II.
§ Plate 24. No. II.
‖ Plate 5. No. I.
¶ Plate 27. No. II.
* Plate 29. No. II.

would otherwise have had a very disagreeable effect. This boy is also contrasted by another,[†] who is led along hastily by a woman with a basket upon her head;[‡] and these, as has already been observed, give motion to that side of the picture. The drapery upon this woman's arm is artfully swelled and folded towards the elbow, and breaks the straitness which would have appeared from her action, and could not but have offended the eye. It will now be proper to speak of the ornaments, and other accidental decorations, which are usually called bye works.

The principal of these are the columns, which with regard to the picture, are the finest that could possibly be imagined, and in themselves are a proof of the amazing genius of Raphael. The effect of the waving line, as an ornament, is perhaps no where made use of to such advantage, nor better proves its gracefulness. To confirm this assertion, let one any substitute in their stead, or ideally substitute the Ionic or Corinthian, or any other order; and let it be enriched with flutings, and all the decorations that can possibly be given to those orders, and then compare it with Raphael's. What an astonishing alteration must ensue! How cutting, how disagreeably heavy will the innovation appear! and how-very considerably must the picture suffer by the change! Besides, as the columns were arbitrary, and the painter had once deviated from the established rules, he was at liberty to do what he pleased; and therefore Raphael has apparently made use of this licence for the purpose following: It was doubtless necessary that the principal groupe should not only possess the center of the picture, but occupy more space than the others, in order to maintain its character of distinction from the subordinate ones: in consequence of which, Raphael has made the intercolumniation greater between the first and second column, than between the second and third, a part of which is cut off by the side of the picture. This being allowed, it will not be difficult to give what is apprehended will be thought a sufficient reason for the repetitions before mentioned,; and why the same number of figures, nearly in the same attitudes, the cripple excepted, were introduced into this groupe. It is certain, that if this part of the picture had been otherwise managed, than it is, by too great a variation in the attitudes from those of the principal groupe, the inequality of the intercolumniation would have been more apparent; and consequently every common observer would have taken the liberty of condemning it as an oversight in Raphael. The great artifice, therefore, is concealed in the similitude of the figures which compose these groupes. The same number are employed in both. In the principal groupe, the whole figure of the cripple is seen; in the other the body is large, but being upon his knees, his legs are hid by the column, and the space occupied by his hand and arm, which rests upon a staff is by no means equivalent to the room gained by the disappearing of his legs; and yet this staff and limb seem to fill up the space. The distance from the knees of the cripple to the column, is greater than that between the feet of the lame man and

† Plate 15. No. II.
‡ Plate 9. No. II.

the same column; and both being near the ground-line or front of the picture, cause a great deception. The woman with the child in her arms is similar to John; but she is placed much nearer the column. John's arm is moderately extended, and his hand appears directly over the cripple's head; the woman's arm is employed in holding the child, and consequently does not appear; and a light, well-folded piece of drapery supplies the place, and forms a mass which receives the shadowed parts of the cripple's head and body. The man is in an attitude similar to that of Peter; but the column is placed so as to be partly hid by his hand, by which he expresses his astonishment,* falls exactly in the centre between the two columns, as does that of Peter in the principal groupe: but lest this should be too remarkable, the hand of the woman is seen close by it, naturally and gracefully applied to her breast; and this, with the infant's head, makes a sufficient variation, and does not in the least destroy the principal intention. It being absolutely necessary to introduce the whole arm of the figure of the man, and the hand being be placed in the centre, the arm is unavoidably required to be bent rather more than that of Peter; but this was not a sufficient variation, and therefore a kind of short open sleeve, which reaches about half way down to the elbow, was added; and this also produces another variation. To carry on this artifice in every part, Raphael judged it expedient to have the same number of figures in each groupe; but whereas in the principal one there are three heads between that of John and the column, and none between that of his and Peter's, so in this there appears but a part of one between the woman and the column, and the other three are placed in the space between the man and woman. The same artifice is also finely kept up in the distant colonnade; where, in the same space, two rows of the same columns appear in perspective, and by their contrast occasion the distance between the columns on the opposite side to appear larger than it really is. In short, this Cartoon is altogether the most consummate piece of art that probably ever was or ever will be produced.

CARTOON IV.

THE DEATH OF ANANIAS.

But Peter said, Ananias, why hath Satan filled thine heart to lie to the Holy Ghost, and to keep back part of the price of the land? Whilst it remained, was it not thine own? And after it was sold, was it not in thine own power? why hast thou conceived this thing in thine heart? Thou hast not lied unto men, but unto God. And Ananias hearing these words fell down, and gave up the ghost. And great fear came on all that heard these things Acts v. 3 - 5.

OF all the various ways ordained by the Almighty for putting a period to the present existence of human nature, there is none so affecting or alarming as the stroke of sudden death; whenever, therefore this happens, it appears more or less

---

* Plate 11. No. I.

terrible to those who survive, according to the state of the soul at that moment when it is separated from the body. The death of Ananias was, therefore, a subject capable of exciting horror in an extraordinary degree, supposing it to have been only a common accident: but the circumstance of his death was much more terrifying, as it was a manifestation of the divine wrath upon him, "who had not lied unto men, but unto God." This alarming event happened at a time when the minds of the people were filled with the amazing things which they both saw and heard; when universal benevolence possessed the hearts of those who adhered to the doctrine taught by the apostles. Therefore such an event must have struck those who were witnesses to it with horror and reverence; with detestation of the act itself, and with reverential awe for the apostle, whose fore-knowledge of the fraud practised by Ananias, made him openly accuse him in the words above mentioned. Raphael has told this story in a manner worthy of his sublime genius; and the time chosen is so very evident that it needs not be mentioned.

This Cartoon is composed of three distinct groupes, and Ananias is the principal figure; but it required no less than the profound skill of this great master to make him appear so; the figure being prostrate by necessity, must have appeared to some disadvantage, had the spectators been all standing, even though they had inclined as much as the two men who are stooping over him. Raphael, therefore, has most judiciously given all the figures in the forepart of the picture such attitudes, as at once perfectly correspond with the story, and make the figure of Ananias more conspicuous. Accordingly, the subordinate figures are all either kneeling or stooping; and these, at the same time, give an inexpressible dignity to the apostles, who are standing, and form a distinct groupe in the middle of the back part of the picture, in the centre of which Peter is placed, who is described as having just pronounced the accusation. The whole figure of Ananias is inimitably fine; but the expression in his character is amazing. There appears to be strongly marked in the features not only the stroke of death as a corporeal suffering, but the agonies of a wounded conscience;[*] from which immediately proceeds the writhing contortions of the body and limbs the very extremities of which appear contracted and convulsed. The character of Peter is also finely imagined and designed: there is a holy severity in his countenance which is inexpressibly great; his attitude[†] is majestic; and though his situation is something remote, it is impossible to avoid seeing that his is the second principal figure in the picture. The whole groupe of apostles are characters of great dignity; each seems collected within himself, and revolving upon this terrible catastrophe: and one of them, who is next to Peter, appears with reverential awe to address himself to the Almighty, and is a fine character.[‡] Horror, fear, and amazement, are blended in the character of the man

---

* Plate 7. No. I.
† Plate 35. No. II.
‡ Plate 7. No. II.

who is opposed to Ananias;[§] who by his situation attitude appears also to be rendering up his goods to the apostles, and possibly intended for Joses called Barnabas, who is mentioned in the latter part of the preceding chapter and this figure makes the finest contrast imaginable to that of the dying man. The woman next to him discovers her terror in a manner perfectly adapted to her sex, as well as the circumstances of the story.[¶] Her fear compels her to turn round, the natural preparative for flight; and this occasions her figure to contrast that of the man before described in a fine manner. The character of John, who is very properly employed in relieving the necessitous persons who compose a part of one of the subordinate groupes, is extremely graceful; compassion and benevolence are strongly expressed in his countenance,[£] and his action discovers, that he not only relieves them with money, but likewise bestows with it his advice, and appears to exhort the make a proper use of it. The apostle, who seems, to beckon to some who are supposed to be out of the picture, to bear testimony of the punishment inflicted on Ananias, is a character of great dignity, and his attitude is finely varied from that of Peter's.[$]

The draperies in this Cartoon are perfectly fine, and extremely well cast; particularly those of the apostles, which are remarkably graceful, and the folds finely posed and contrasted. That of Ananias requires particular observation: he has less than any other figure in the picture, his arms, legs, and feet being entirely naked. This possibly to some may appear absurd, but it is a fine artifice; the violent agitation of the muscles is thereby made apparent; and the limbs of the figures near being mostly covered, serve to shew his figure more distinctly, and of course help to discover its consequence. In short, the whole composition of this picture is perfectly great and striking, and is a remarkable instance of the genius of Raphael. In the Cartoon of the lame man healed, there is a luxury of fancy displayed in the ornaments with which it is enriched; in this its grandeur, dignity and effect, are totally derived from the invention and disposition of the characters. Ornaments there are none and the bye-works are extremely plain and agreeable to the simplicity of the church of Christ in its in infant state; the chief of them is the curtain, which is behind the apostles; it is indeed simple, but then it is finely folded, and serves admirably to break the straight line, which is made by the heads of the apostles, which without this help, must have appeared somewhat disagreeably. The back ground is also artfully varied, and relieved by an opening on one side, and a flight of steps, with figures ascending them, on the other.

§ Plate 10. No. I
¶ Plate 10. No. I.
£ Plate 2. No. II.
$ Plate 22. No. II.

CARTOON V.

ELYMAS THE SORCERER STRUCK WITH BLINDNESS.

And now behold the hand of the Lord is upon thee; and thou shalt be blind, not seeing the light, of the sun for a season. And immediately there fell on him a mist and a darkness, and he went about seeking some to lead him by the hand.—Acts xiii. 11.

THOUGH terror and astonishment are strongly expressed in this picture, yet it appears of a different kind, and produces a different effect from that in the Cartoon of the Death of Ananias. The punishment of Elymas was to him dreadful and grievous, and to the beholders terrifying and wonderful; but is apparently considered by them no otherwise than as it relates to this, instance of the divine judgment inflicted on him. The death of Ananias inspired horror also, not without a mixture of pity for the sufferer, who, before the discovery of his crime, was probably esteemed as a good and devout man; on the contrary, the sorcerer was a person, of whom it may reasonably be judged the people stood in awe; and that he was rather feared on account of his power than beloved for his virtues. This will evidently appear, when the manner in which Raphael has told this story is considered. Every one of the spectators discovers terror and surprise; but none (except one of the lictors, who stands near the proconsul) discovers the least expression of pity. Elymas, though in the midst of numbers, appears to be alone: and he extends his arms in vain, "seeking some to lead him by the hand;" nor does the admirable figure, who stands between him and the proconsul, and who, with the utmost amazement, looks steadfastly in his face, seem inclinable to offer him the least assistance. Indeed, there are but few of the spectators who appear to give any attention at all to him; the majority of them being employed either in relating, or attending to the relation of the punishment inflicted upon him. Elymas who is the principal figure in this picture, according to the observation of Mr. Richardson, is blind from head to foot, and is altogether a most inimitable character. Perhaps Raphael hardly ever conceived one more expressive; and though this great master thought proper to assist the understanding by making the subordinate figures more fully explain the principal subject, yet this figure was alone sufficient to have done it. Dejected arrogance is amazingly described in his character,[+] together with that shame and confusion, which must naturally have appeared in it when he felt the irresistible force and superiority of the divine power. His attitude is also extremely fine, and can only be thoroughly understood by viewing the picture itself, or a good copy or print after it. The apostle Paul is the next principal figure; he is placed opposite to the sorcerer, and is represented with one arm extended, as having just denounced sentence upon him, to the execution of which with a look of holy satisfaction, he seems to demand the proconsul's attention. He is likewise distinguished by a book, which he holds under the other arm. In his character,

---

+   Plate 26. No. I.

which appears in profile, the expression is awful and majestic; his whole figure is finely imagined and drawn, full of dignity and perfectly graceful.* The next is the proconsul Sergius Paulus, who is more affected than any of the spectators: terror and astonishment are, expressed in his countenance,† and evidently discover that he feels the force, and is sensible of the equity of the divine judgment; but it appears in a manner perfectly becoming his- character, and he sits amazed at the punishment of Elymas, and convinced of the truth of the doctrine preached by the holy apostles. The apostle Barnabas, who stands behind the sorcerer, is employed in explaining his fate to those who, by their situation, must necessarily be ignorant of it, as being placed behind him, which he is represented as doing with great zeal and energy. The man, who stands between Elymas and the proconsul,‡ is prodigiously fine; he is, indeed, all amazement and attention; and in his character there is expressed a mixture of doubt, and an eagerness to discover whether the sorcerer's blindness is real or not. The man, whose head appears between that of Paul and the side of the picture,§ is also full of expression; he is apparently a believer, which is shewn by a fine mixture of fear and devotion in his countenance. There is like-wise great expression in the lictors, who stand upon the steps;£ and also in the rest of the characters which compose this picture.¶ The draperies in general are extremely fine, particularly that of Paul, which is noble, well-cast, and folded: that of the sorcerer is also finely imagined, and suitable to his character. The scenery or background of this Cartoon is magnificent, and well-adapted; it will be sufficient to say that in order to break the stiffness of uniformity, Raphael has taken some liberties in the architecture, which produce an effect that makes ample amends for any seeming irregularity.

CARTOON VI.

PAUL AND BARNABAS AT LYSTRA.

And there sat a certain man at Lystra, impotent in his feet, being a cripple from his mother's womb, who never had walked. The same heard Paul speak, who steadfastly beholding him, and perceiving that he had faith to be healed said with a loud voice, Stand upright on thy-feet; and he leaped and walked. And when the people saw what Paul had done, they lifted up their voices, saying in the speech of Lycaonia, the gods are come down to us in the likeness of men. And they called Barnabas Jupiter, and Paul Mercurius, because he was chief speaker. Then the priest of Jupiter, which was before their city, brought oxen and garlands into the gates, and would have done sacrifice with the peaple. Which when the apostles Barnabas and Paul heard of, they rent their clothes, and ran in among the people, crying out.—Acts xiv. 8—14.

---

* Plate 21. No. II.
† Plate 38. No. I.
‡ Plate 1. No. II.
§ Plate 26. No. II.
£ Plate 12. No. II.
¶ Plate 4. No. II.

IN this Cartoon the simplicity and purity of the Christian religion is finely opposed to the pompous idolatry and superstition of the heathens: the divine behaviour and modesty of the two apostles is infinitely more striking and greater than all the tumult and parade of the sacrifice, which the priests, attended by the people, are about to make to them. The manner in which Raphael has described this ceremony, is perfectly fine, and agreeable to the custom of the Romans; and is entirely taken from the bass-relief of the Trajan column, the priests and boys employed in the intended sacrifice being almost exactly copied from thence, particularly the priest of Jupiter,[*] who is in all respects, except in the drapery, the figure in the column being without any. In the characters of the priests and people there is a general expression of enthusiasm and superstitious fear, which is finely described. Paul is the principal figure in this picture: he is represented as standing upon a kind of step, from whence he is about to descend, in order to stop the mistaken religious fury of the people; and at the same time with the utmost grief and perturbation, which is admirably expressed, in his countenance, is rending his garment, and exposes part of his breast, which produces a fine effect in the imagination.[†] The apostle Barnabas, who stands behind him, is a fine character; he is seen entirely in shadow; but his attitude and expression are incomparable; grief and pity are blended in his countenance, and he clasps his hands together with a fervour not to be described. Mr. Richardson, in speaking of this Cartoon, and the sacrifice represented in it, says, "the occasion of all that is finely told. The man who was healed of his lameness, is one of the forwardest to express his sense of the divine power, which appeared in those apostles; and to shew it to be him, not only a crutch is under his feet on the ground, but an old man takes up the lappet of his garment, and looks upon the limb, which he remembered to have been crippled, and expresses great devotion and admiration;[‡] which sentiments are also seen in the other, with a mixture of joy." Mr. Richardson might have added gratitude also, which is visibly expressed in the character of the cripple.[§] And, indeed, if it be allowable to censure so great a master, the place in which this man is found is liable to some objection. Paul, in looking steadfastly upon him perceived "he had faith to be healed;" and he is here represented among the crowd of idolaters, and appears to be one of the most zealous to assist at a ceremony so utterly disagreeable to his holy benefactors. To this it may be objected, that as he probably had not had time to be fully instructed in the Christian faith, this was the only way in which he could possibly testify his gratitude; but it is submitted whether he might not, with more propriety and equal advantage to the picture, have been introduced in the place of the man, who is on the same side of the picture with the apostles, employed in bringing a ram to the sacrifice;[¶] or at least in some other

---

*   Plate 45. No. II.
†   Plate 20. No. I.
‡   Plate 13. No. I.
§   Plate 23. No. I.
¶   Plate 3. No. I.

situation, in this particular more agreeable to his disposition to receive the religion of Christ. The whole figure of this man is finely designed, and vastly expressive; but the leg, which the old man is looking at, is remarkably elegant, and was undoubtedly painted from nature. The figure of the old man is also finely drawn and imagined and his attitude, which is stooping, brings several subordinate figures into view, which could not otherwise have been seen. The architecture in the back ground of this Cartoon is magnificent; the forms of the buildings are finely varied; and the whole together exhibits a noble composition.

CARTOON VII.

PAUL PREACHING AT ATHENS.

Then Paul stood in the midst of Mars hill, and said, Ye men of Athens, I perceive that in all things ye are too superstitious: For as I passed by and beheld your devotions, I found an altar with this inscription, TO THE UNKNOWN GOD; whom, therefore, ye ignorantly worship, him declare I unto you.—Acts xvii. 22, 23.

IF invention, expression, design, variety, and decorum, are allowed to constitute a fine historical composition, this Cartoon certainly deserves the character it has long maintained, of being one of the greatest performances of Raphael.

This fine picture is divided into three groupes; the first of which is composed of four figures, among whom the apostle is eminently distinguished as indeed he is from every other in the picture; his situation being so extremely remarkable, that he is shewn to the greatest advantage that can possibly be conceived. The man who is about to ascend the steps, the woman behind him, and eight other figures who are represented standing, compose the second groupe; and the third is formed by six persons who are sitting. This last is placed between the first and second, nearly in the centre of the picture.

The character of Paul is universally allowed to be the most sublime performance that ever was produced by the pencil of Raphael; and Mr. Richardson, who passionately admired this figure, with a warmth peculiar to himself (which, perhaps, upon this, and some similar occasions carried him a little too far), says, "But no historian or orator, can possibly give me so great an idea of that eloquent and zealous apostle, as that figure of his does; all the fine things related, as said or wrote by him, cannot; for there I see a person, face, air, and action, which no words can sufficiently describe, but which assure me as much as those can, that that man must speak good sense, and to the purpose." Thus much is beyond contradiction, that nothing hitherto produced can give so great an idea of the person of Paul, or can better help to illustrate the divine zeal and elocution which that apostle so eminently possessed, than the awful, majestic, and expressive character, which the hand of Raphael has given them.*

Raphael has employed every artifice, in order to make the apostle particularly conspicuous; all the figures in the picture are subservient to that purpose; the man and woman at the bottom of the steps are actually nearer to the eye than the apostle, but their situation causes the base line of the picture to cut off part of their height and as they are both stooping, they are effectually prevented from lessening the importance of the apostle. He has managed the figures that appear behind the apostle in the same manner, by placing two of them lower than Paul, and the third sitting upon the upper step; by which means they are sufficiently degraded. The figures in the second groupe, who are seen standing, are situated upon the ground, their heads mostly inclined, and are also at a considerable distance; and those who compose the middle groupe are at a still greater distance and are represented sitting. But the gigantic statue of Mars, which is introduced with great propriety is of infinite service to the picture; it is placed beyond the outermost figures of the second groupe; therefore the distance of this statue being considered, and the height and bulk of it compared with the figure of the apostle, it will be found to reduce the last to a moderate size, and also serves admirably, by its magnitude, to balance that side of the picture.

Among a great variety of fine characters in this picture, next to that of the apostles, is that of the man who is ascending the steps, in whose countenance awe and reverence are finely blended;† nor need the most common observer be told, that this man and the woman behind him are intended to represent Dionysius and Damarius,‡ who we are informed by the history were converted.

The expression of extreme attention in the three figures nearest to Dionysius in the second groupe, is most admirably described;§ nor is that of the man in the same groupe, who presses his lips with his finger, less to be admired.£ The three figures behind the apostle, who are apparently displeased with his discourse, are finely invented,$ particularly that of him who is sitting and rests his chin upon his hand- in his character envy and malignity are finely described.þ

Leonardo da Vinci, in his treatise upon Painting, has given it as a precept, that "In grave and serious compositions, when assemblies are held, and matters of importance debated, let but few young men be present; it being contrary to custom to intrust affairs of this nature in the hands of youth, who are not less able to give counsel, than they are willing to receive it; and who, therefore, have two reasons for absenting themselves from these kinds of meetings."¶ This precept is no where

---

* Plate 27. No. I.
† Plate 37. No. II
‡ Plate 1. No. I.
§ Plate 19. No. I.
£ Plate 36. No. II.
$ Plate 33. No. II.
þ Plate 17. No. I.
¶ See the Translation printed at London, 1721

better illustrated than in this Cartoon, where there is a wonderful expression of attention, decorum, and gravity, in the old men; and, on the contrary, the few young persons who are introduced in the picture appear froward, impatient, and impetuous, and contempt and dislike are strongly expressed in each of their characters; for which reason part of these turbulent persons are judiciously thrown into the most distant groupe, and others are placed behind the older men.[$]

In the distance between the buildings, in the center of the picture, are seen two figures, who appear to be talking together, and seem to be of no consequence to the composition; but their use is great: they not only serve to break the straight line made by the heads of those who are sitting, as also the parallel lines made by the columns of the temple and the adjacent piazza, but connect the principal and two subordinate groupes together; and without them the picture must have suffered considerably.

The attitudes of the figures are extremely fine and expressive; the draperies noble and well cast, particularly that of the apostle, which is admirably designed. The architecture is elegant, not rich, but suitable to the taste of the Athenians, and properly adapted to the picture; as is the distant view of the country, it being customary for them to place the statue of Mars, as the guardian of the city, at the entrance into it.

Upon the whole, it may not be improper to conclude, with comparing the ideas of two such great painters as Raphael and Leonardo da Vinci in similar subjects, by the following extract from the writings of the latter, who, in describing the manner in which a public oration should be represented, says, "To represent a person haranguing a multitude, consider, in the first place, the subject-matter on which he is to entertain them, in order to give him an action suitable to the occasion; for instance, if the business be to persuade, let it appear in his gestures; if it be to argue and deduce reasons, let him hold one of the fingers of his left hand between two of those of the right, keeping the other two shut; let his face be turned to the assembly, and his mouth half open, so that he may appear to speak; if he be sitting, let him seem as about to rise, advancing his head a little forwards; if he be represented standing let him incline a little with his head and breast towards the people; and let the assembly be seen listening with silence and attention; let all their eyes be fastened on the speaker, and let their actions discover somewhat of admiration; let some old man be seen wondering at what he hears, with his mouth shut, his lips drawn close, wrinkles about the corners of his mouth, the bottom of his cheeks, and in the forehead, occasioned by the eyebrows, which must be raised near the setting on of the nose; let others be represented sitting, with their fingers clasped within each other, bearing up their left knee, another old man may be seen with his knees thrown across each other, his elbow leaning on his knee, and with his hand supporting his chin, which may be covered with a venerable beard."

The similarity of the ideas of these two great men will be better discovered

---

[$] Plate 20. No. II, Plate 30. No. I. Plate 41. No. II., Plate 42 No. I. and II.

by comparing the Cartoon with the foregoing quotation, where, though several things are differently expressed, yet upon the whole, the thought is so nearly alike, that it may be almost implied, that either Leonardo's idea had been put in execution by Raphael, or, could there have been a probability of it, that the latter had dictated to the former when he was composing his book.

INDEX.

———

INDEX.

INDEX.

PASSIONS.	CARTOONS.	PLATE	NUMBER.
Surprise - - - - -	The lame Man healed - - - - - - - -	29	2
Surprise and Gratitude	The same - - - - - - - - - - -	6	2
—— with Doubt -	Paul and Barnabas - - - - - - - -	13	1
—— and Attention	The same - - - - - - - - -	19	2
Terror, with Compassion	Death of Ananias - - - - - - - - -	14	2
Thoughtfulness - - -	Paul Preaching - - - - - - - - -	36	2
Wonder - - - - -	The same - - - - - - - - - - -	8	1
Wonder and Astonishment	The lame Man healed - - - - - - - -	4	2
Zeal - - - - - - -	Elymas the Sorcerer - - - - - - - -	1	2
	The same - - - - - - - - - - -	21	2

THE PLATES

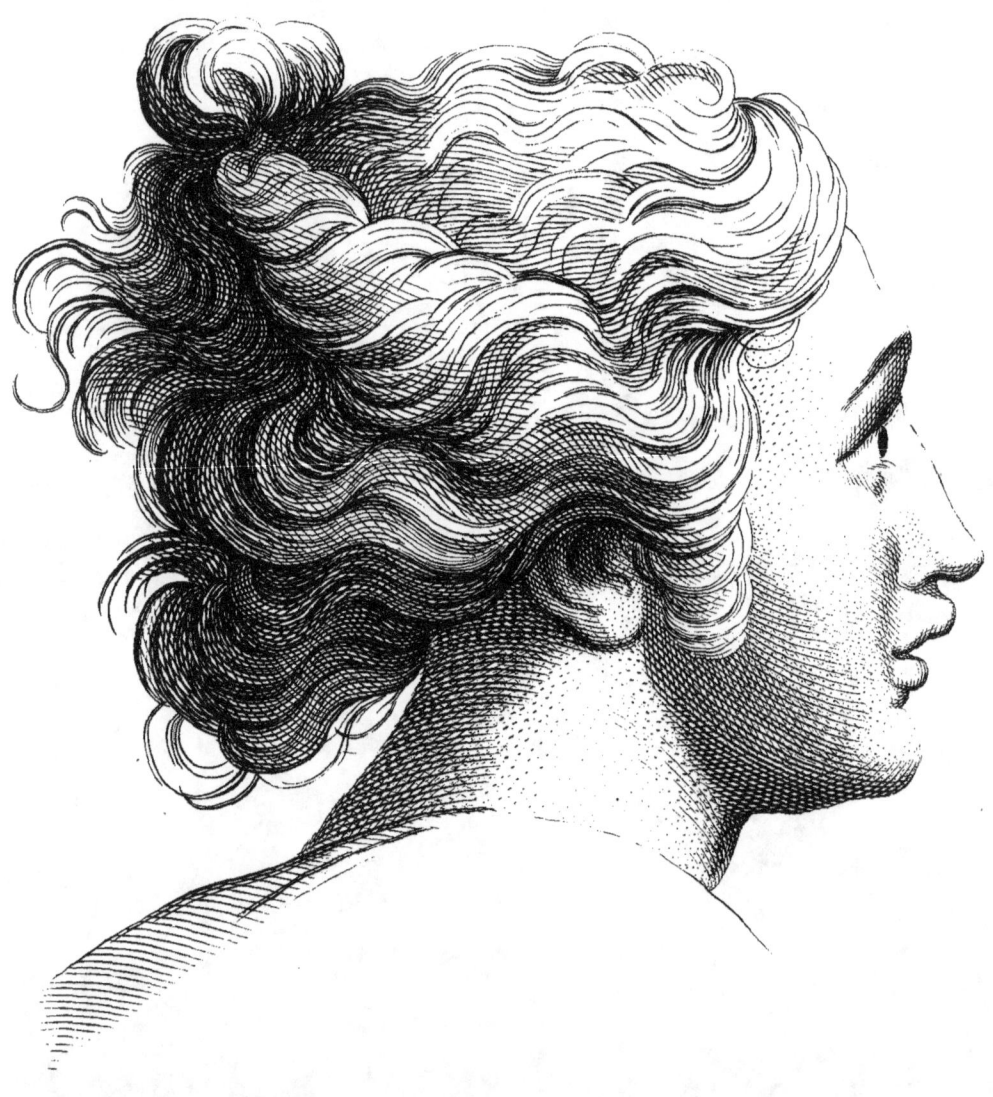

Raph. Urb. pin.

Plate 1. I. - from Paul Preaching at Athens

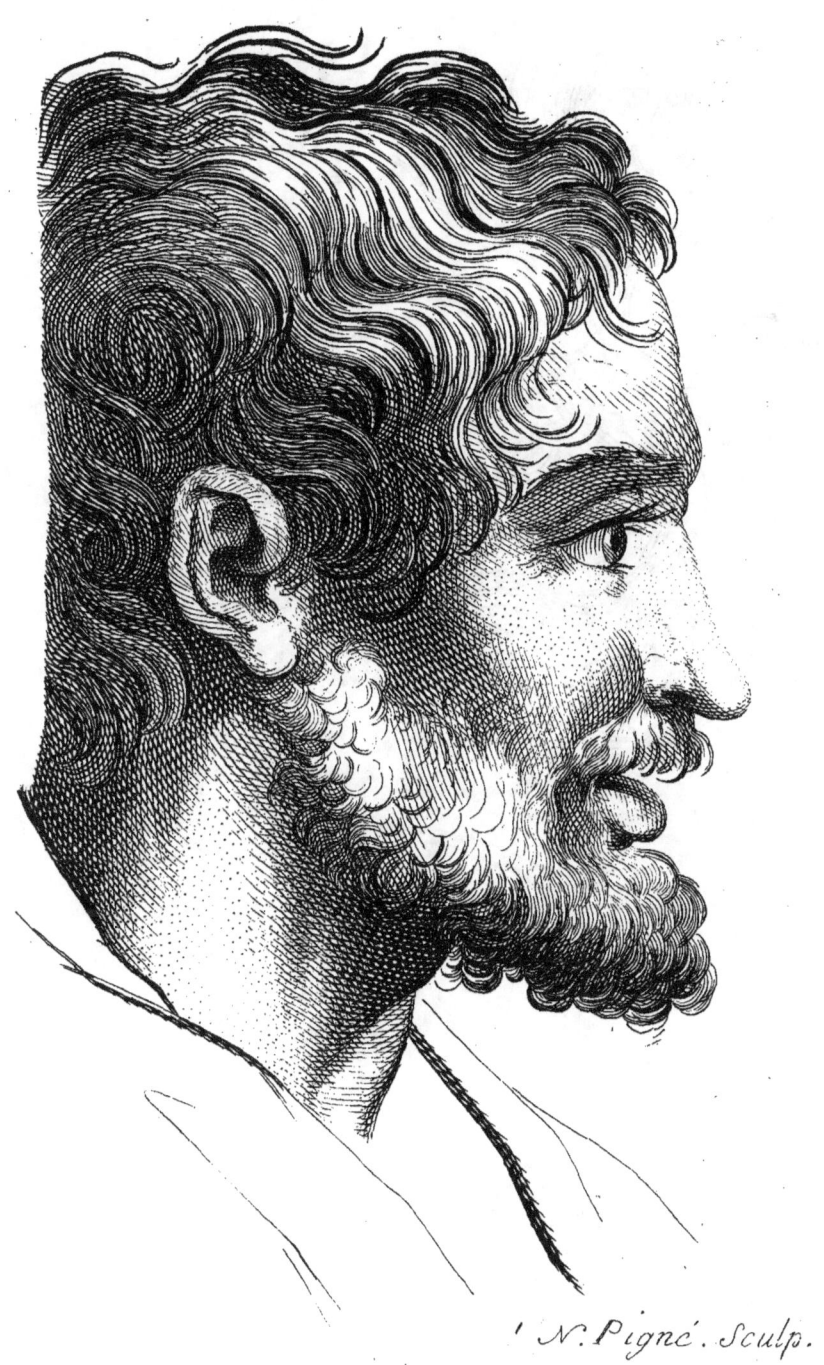

N. Pigné. Sculp.

Plate 1. II. - from Elymas the Sorcerer

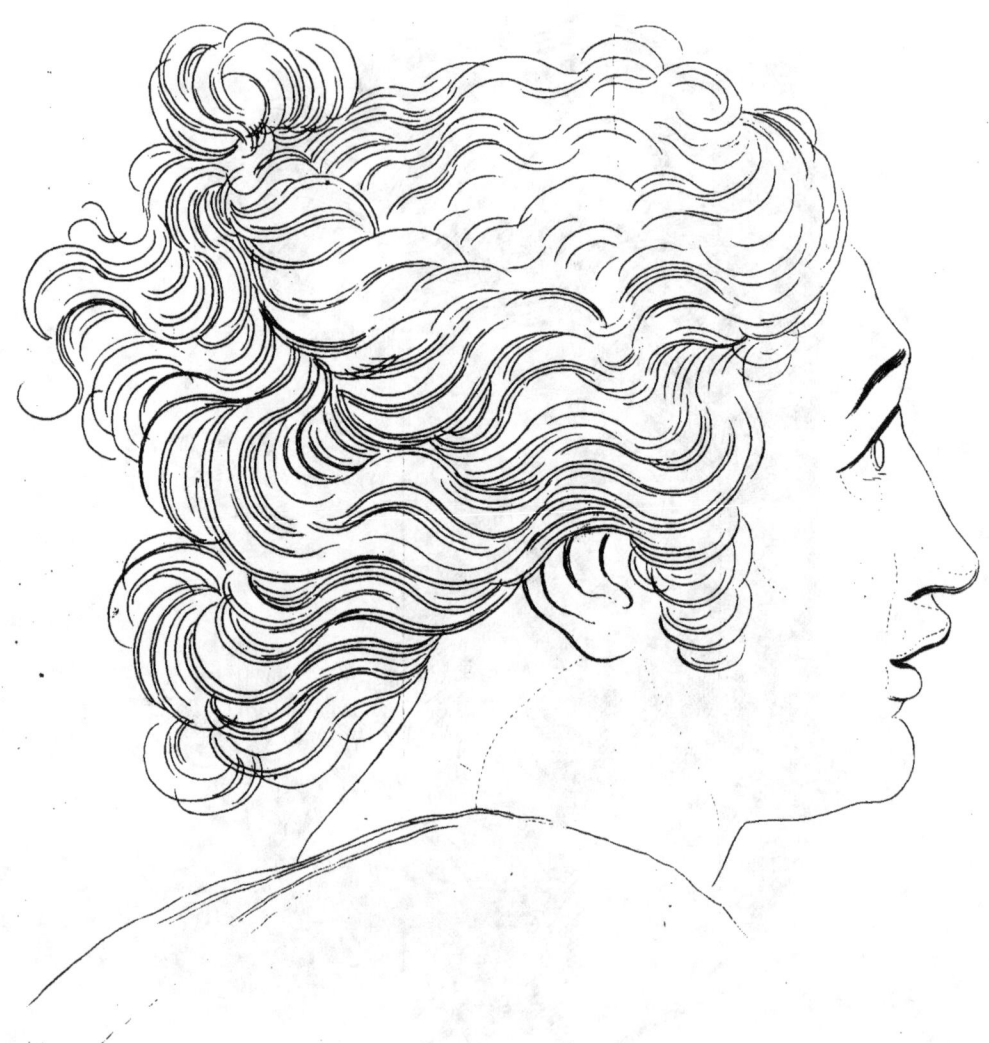

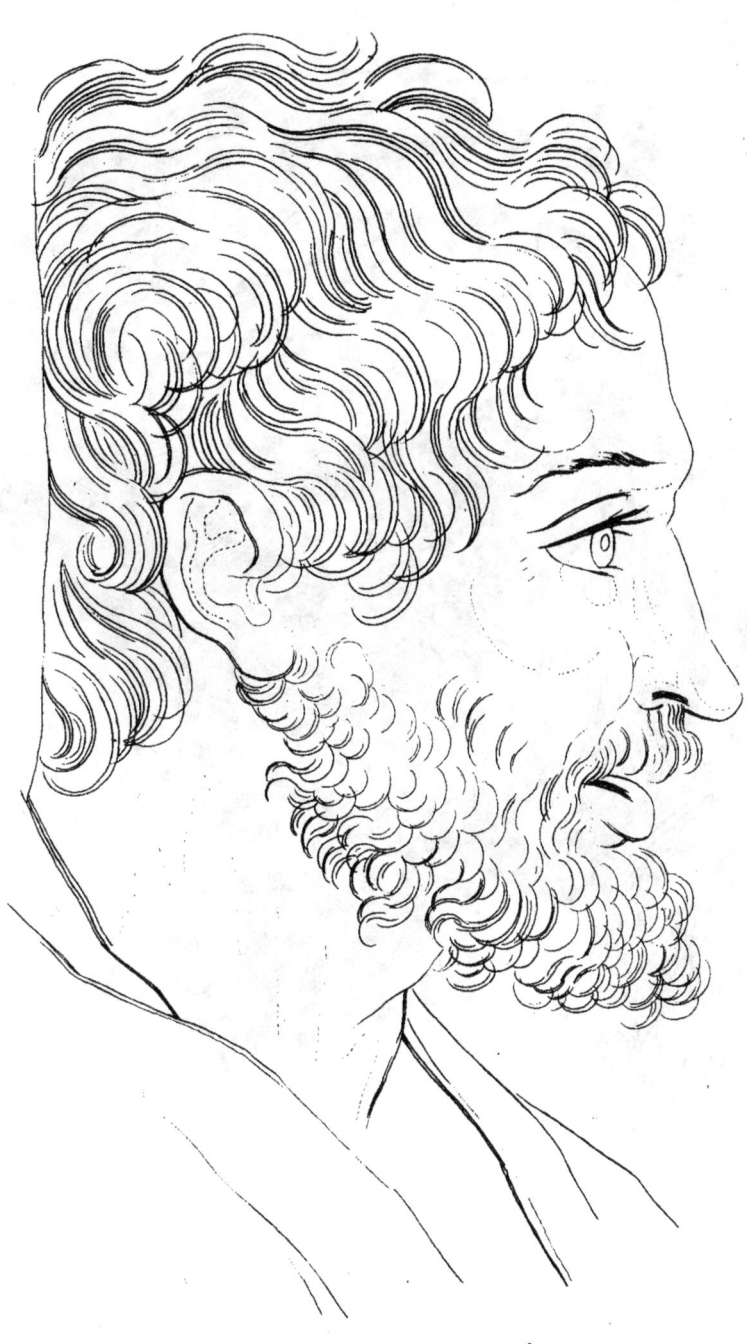

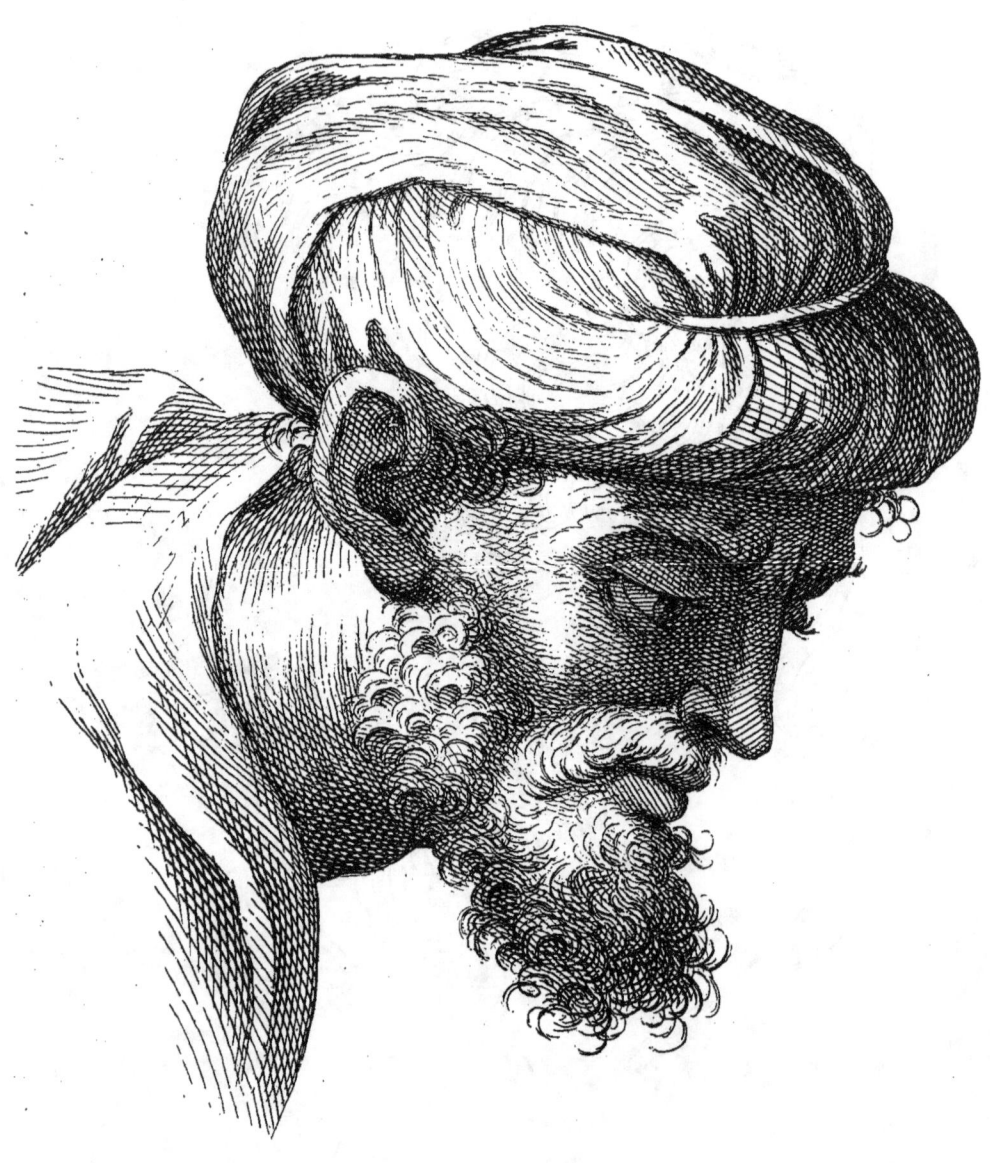

Raph. Vrb pinx.

Plate 2. I. - from The Death of Ananias

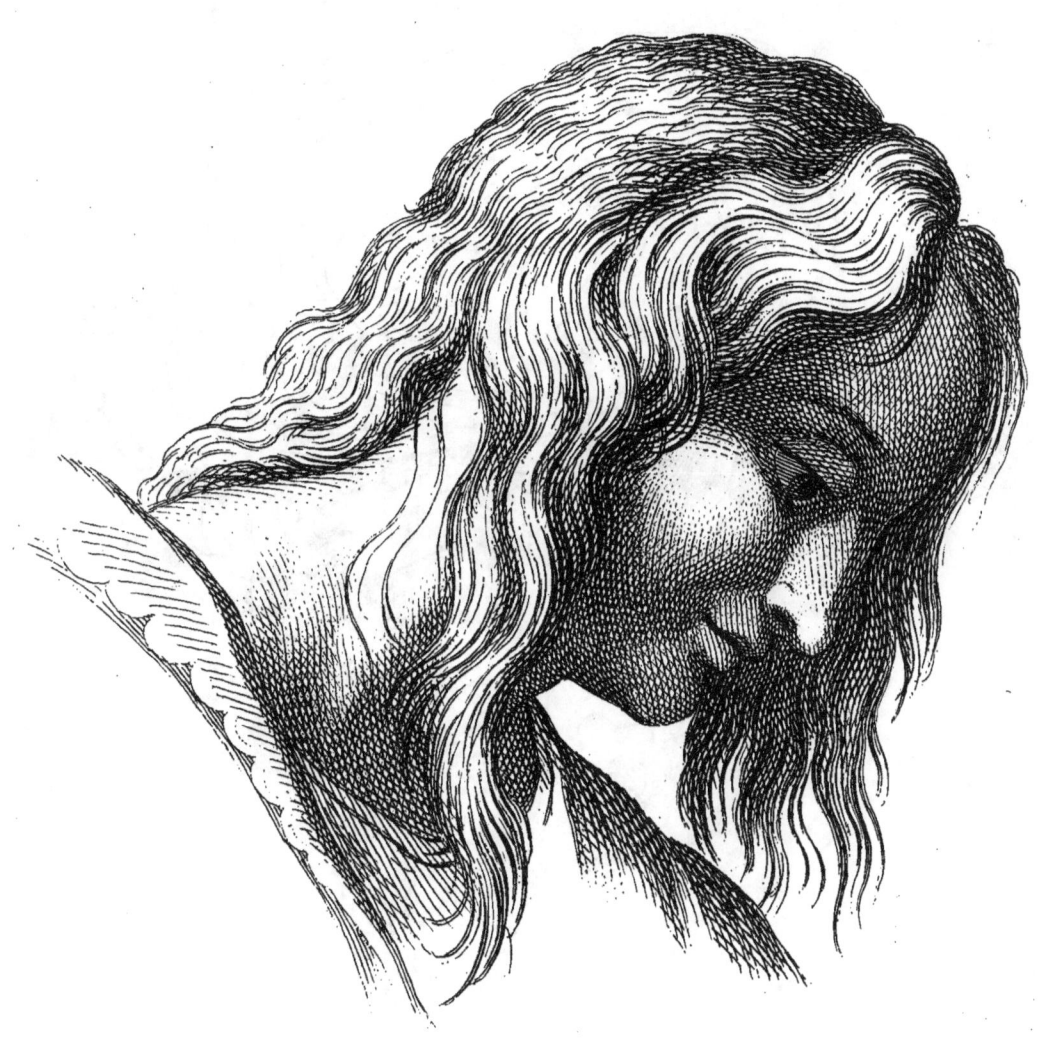

C. Dupuis scu.

Plate 2. II. - from the Death of Ananias

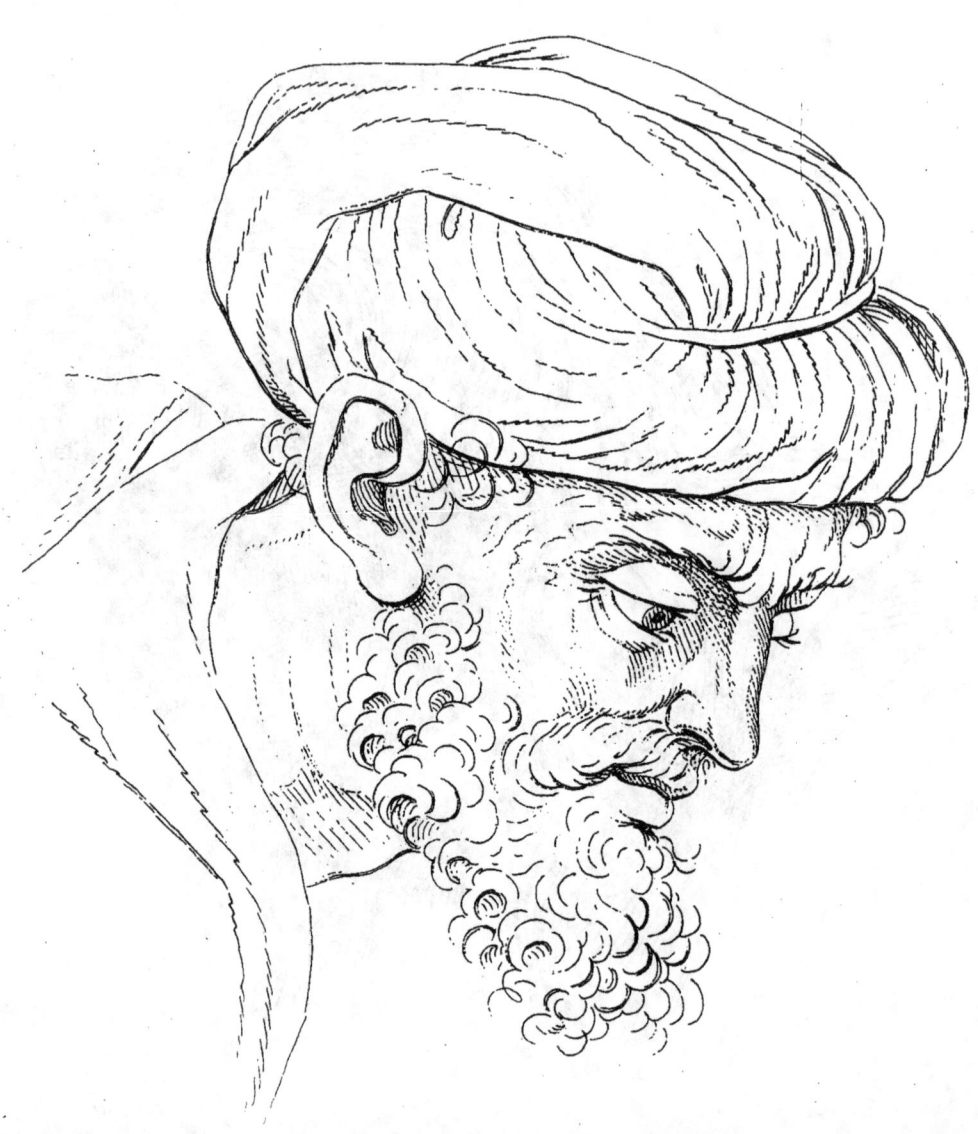

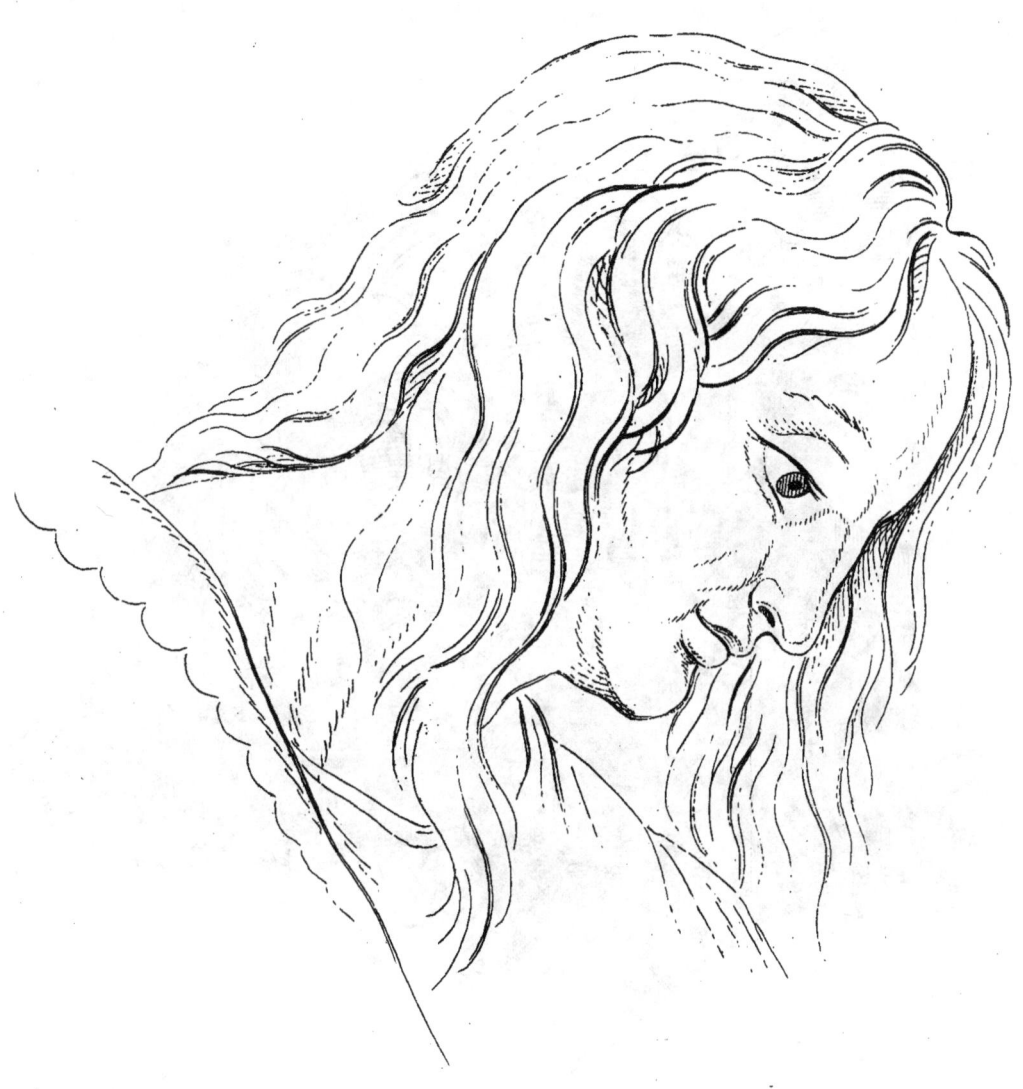

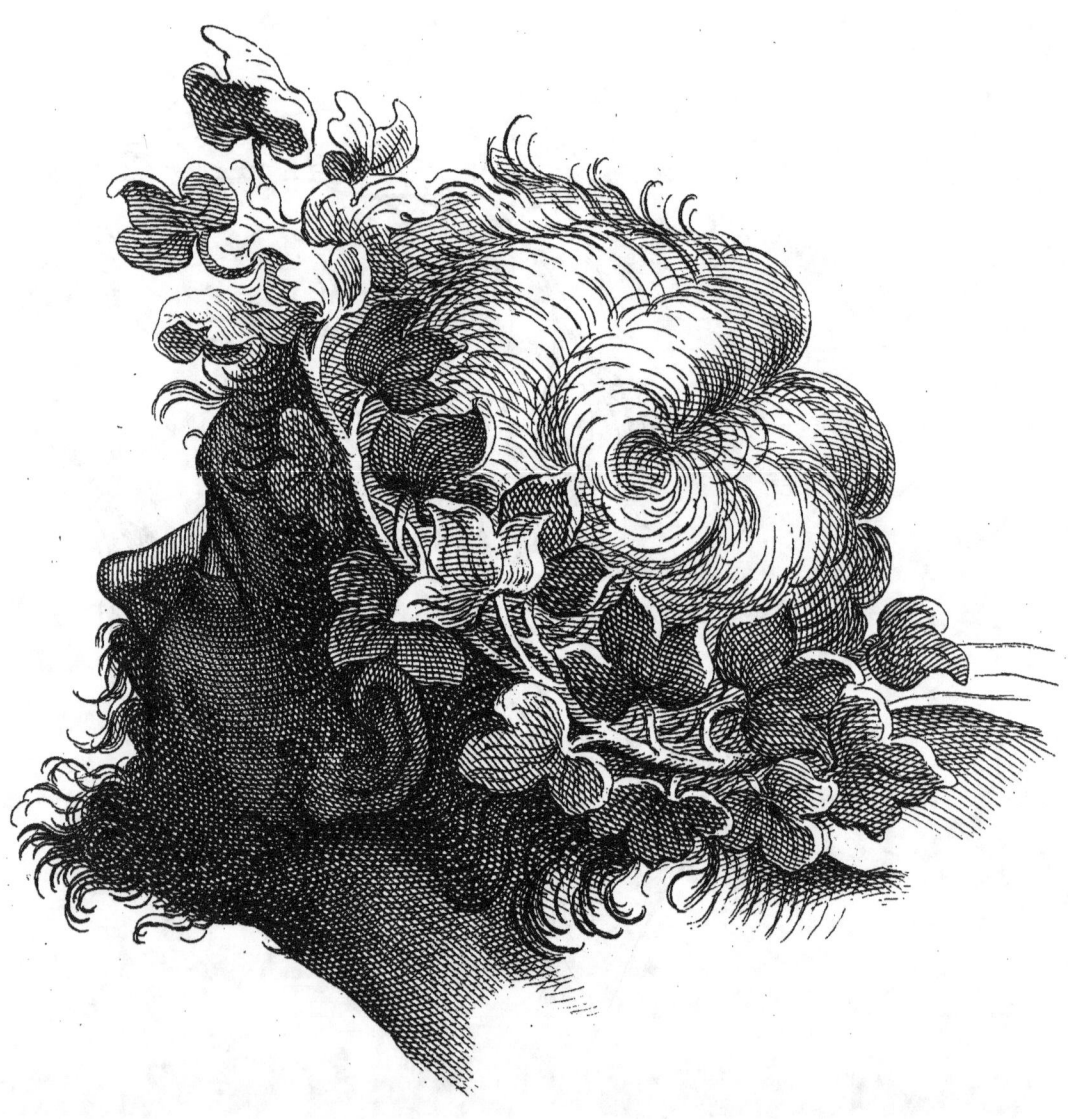

Raph. Vrbin pinx.

Plate 3. I. - from Paul and Barnabas

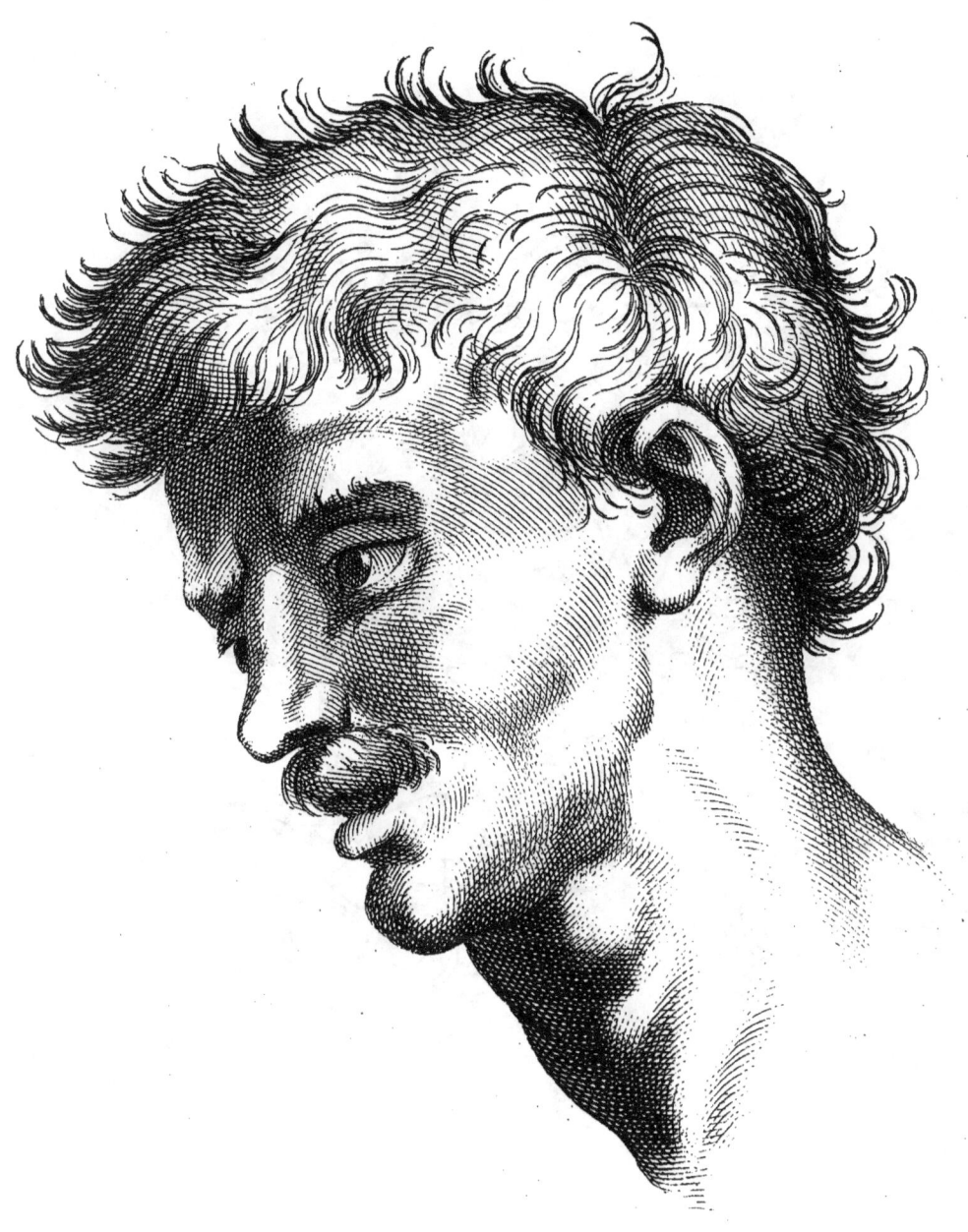

Plate 3. II. - from Elymas the Sorcerer

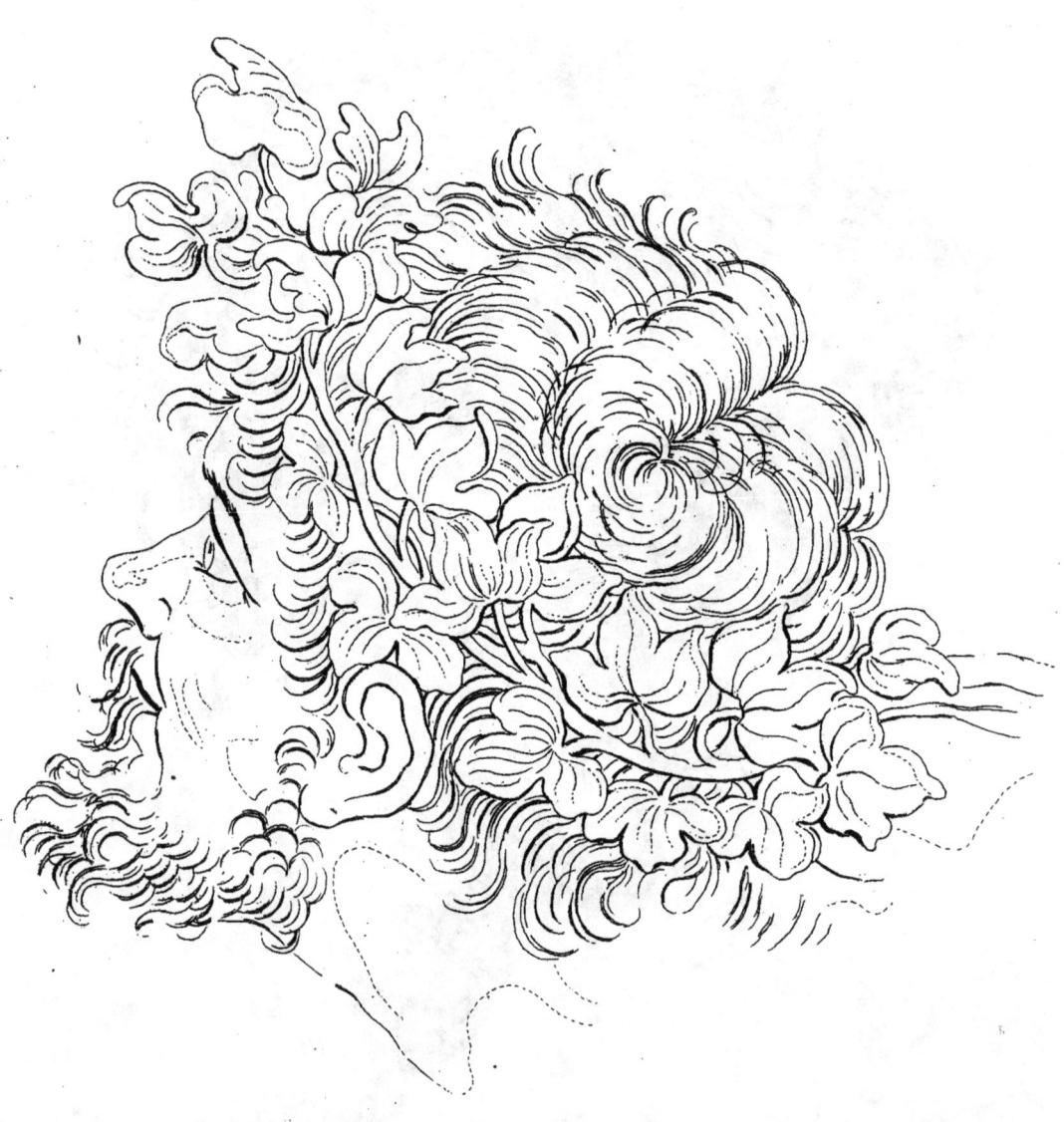

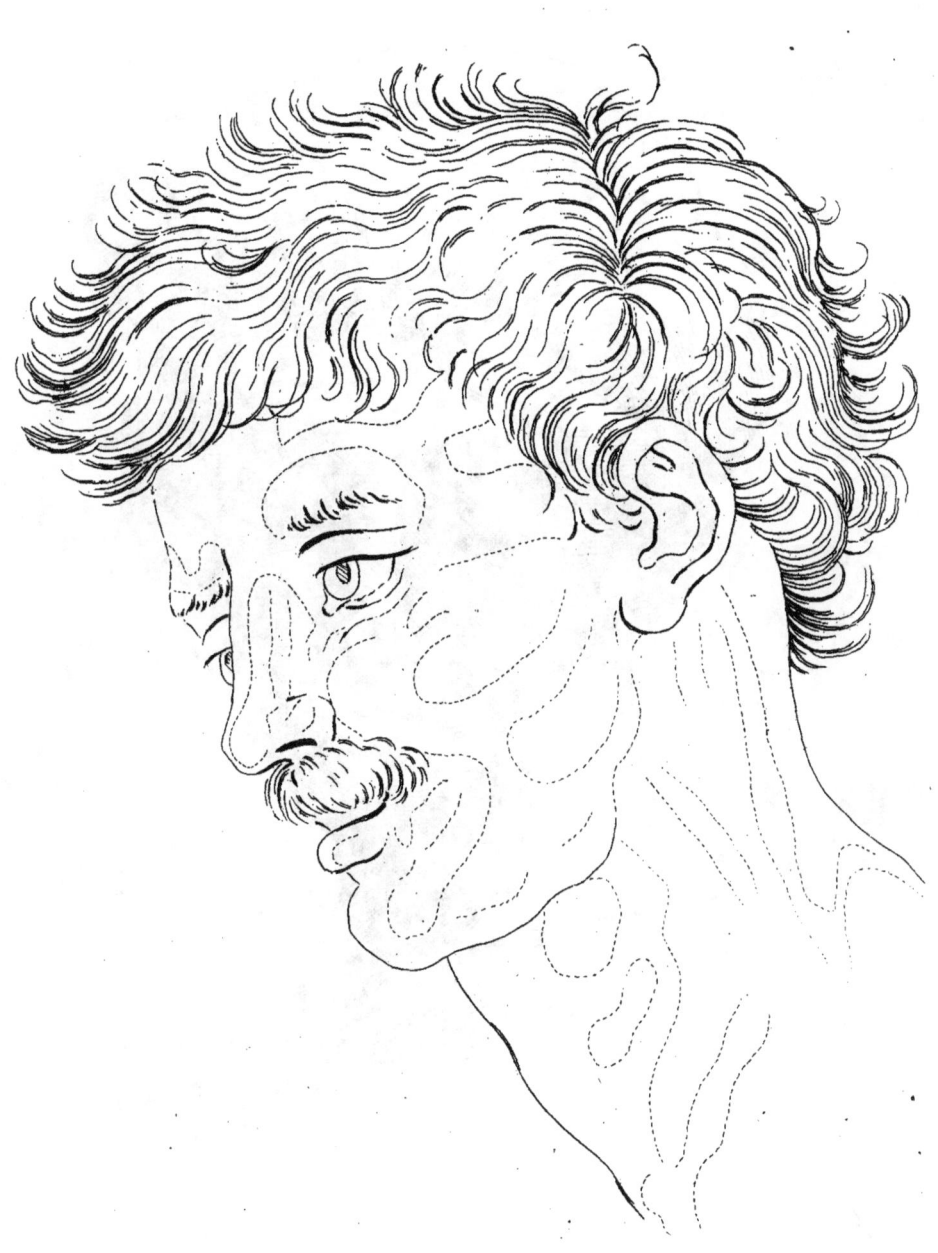

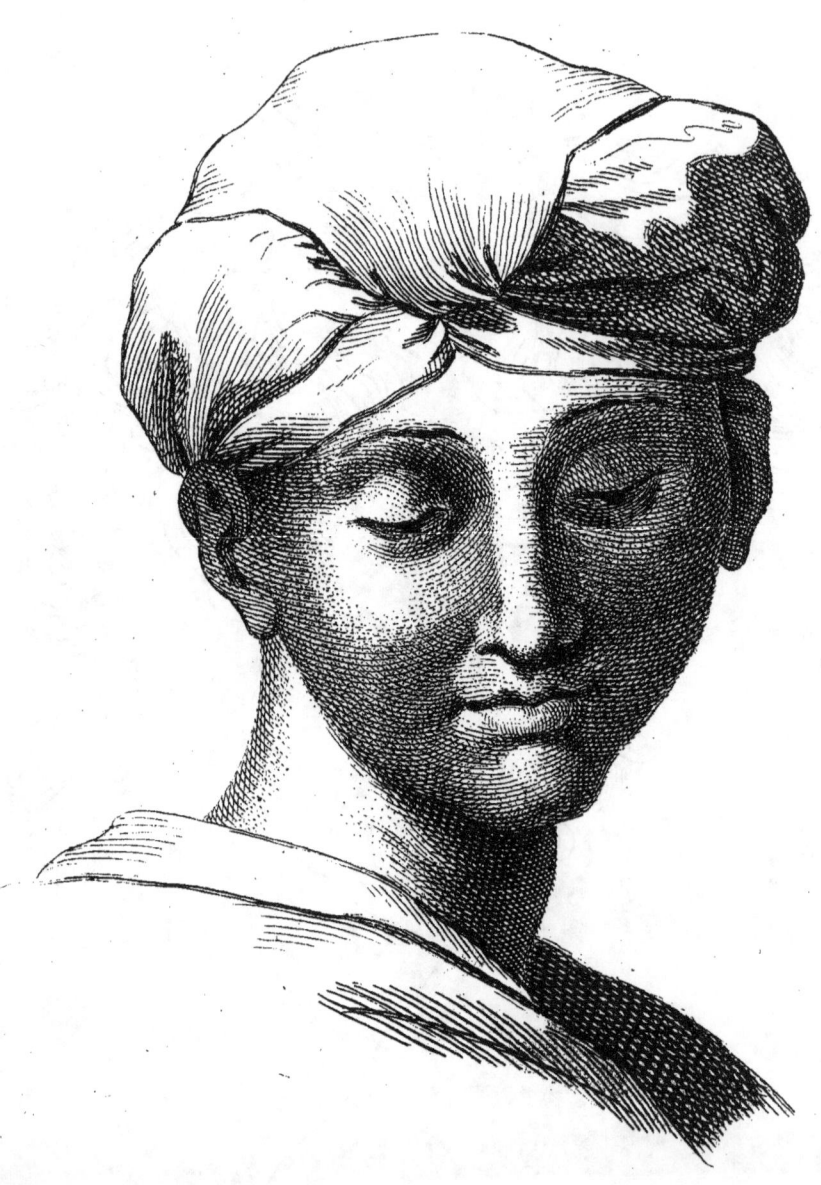

Raph.Vrb.pin.
N. Dorigny 6q. delin.

Plate 4. I. - from The Death of Ananias

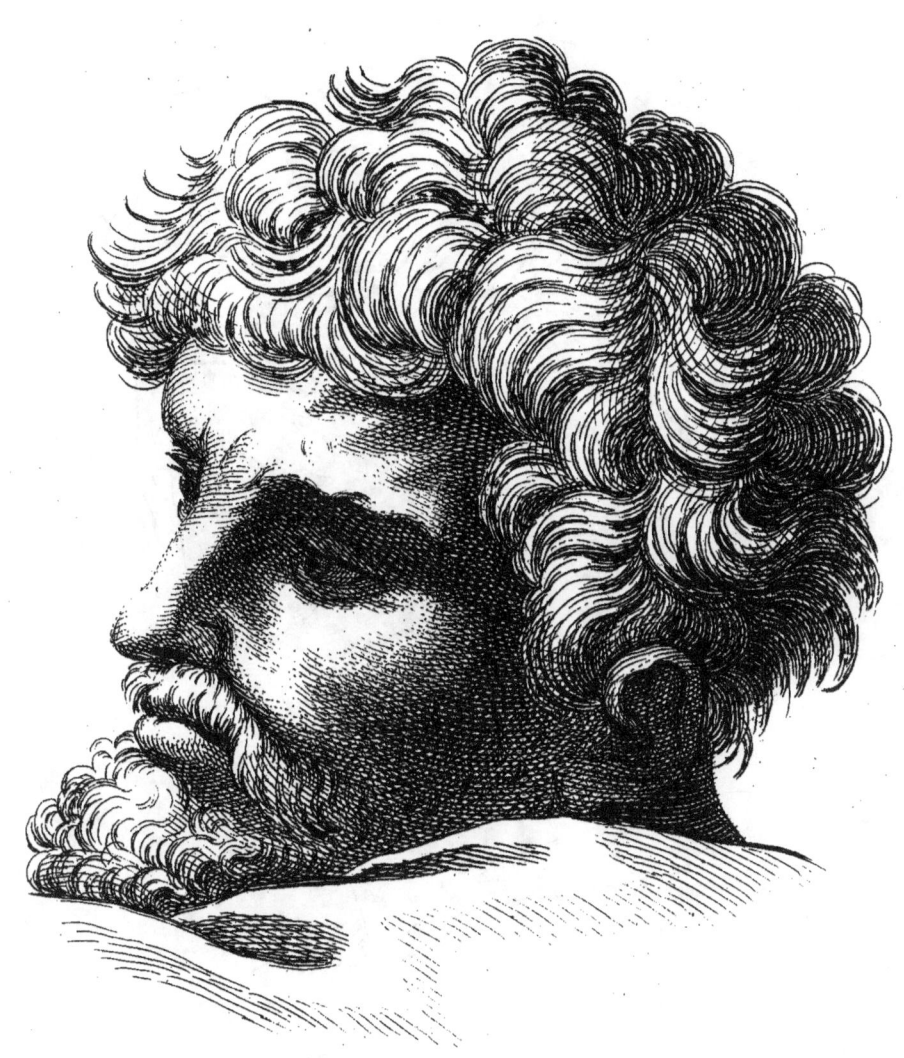

N. Pigné. termi.

Plate 4. II. - from The Lame Man Healed

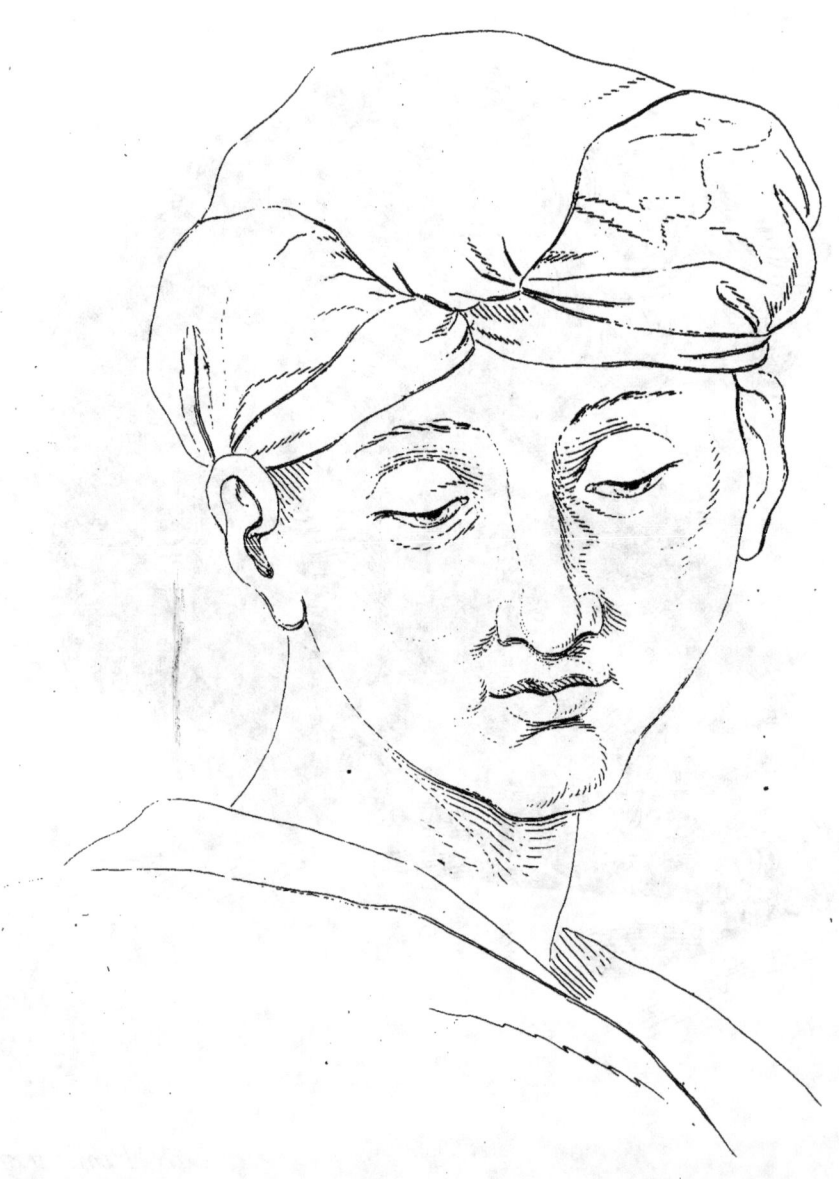

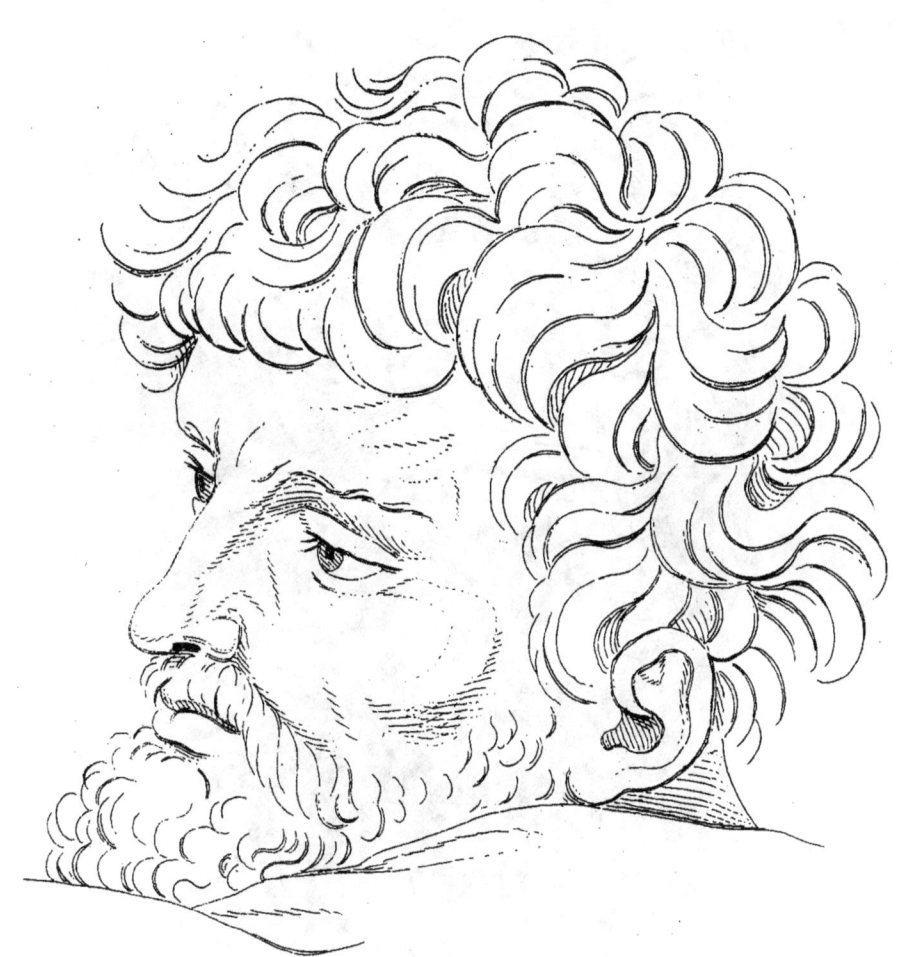

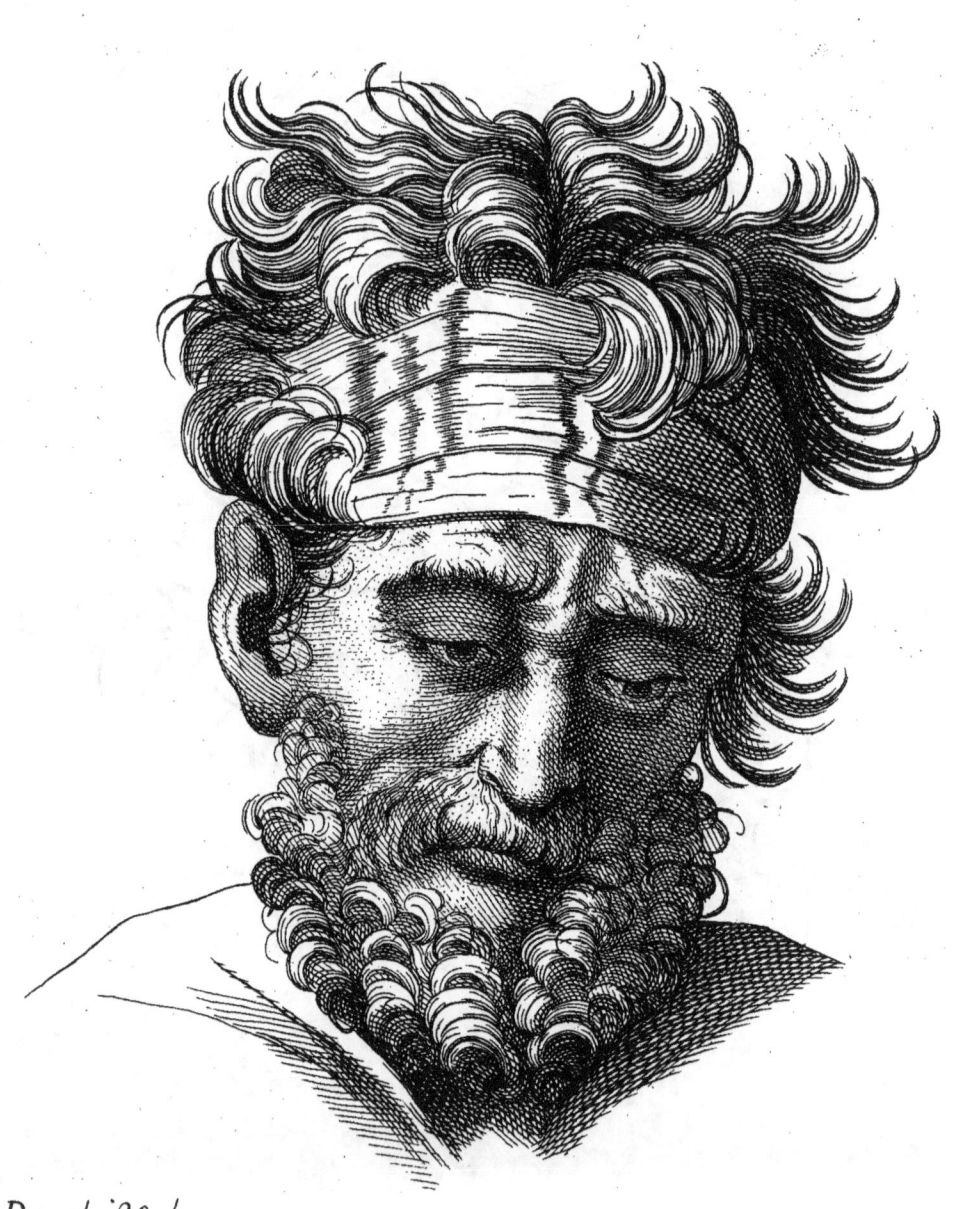

Raph. Vrb. pin.

Plate 5. I. - from The Lame Man Healed

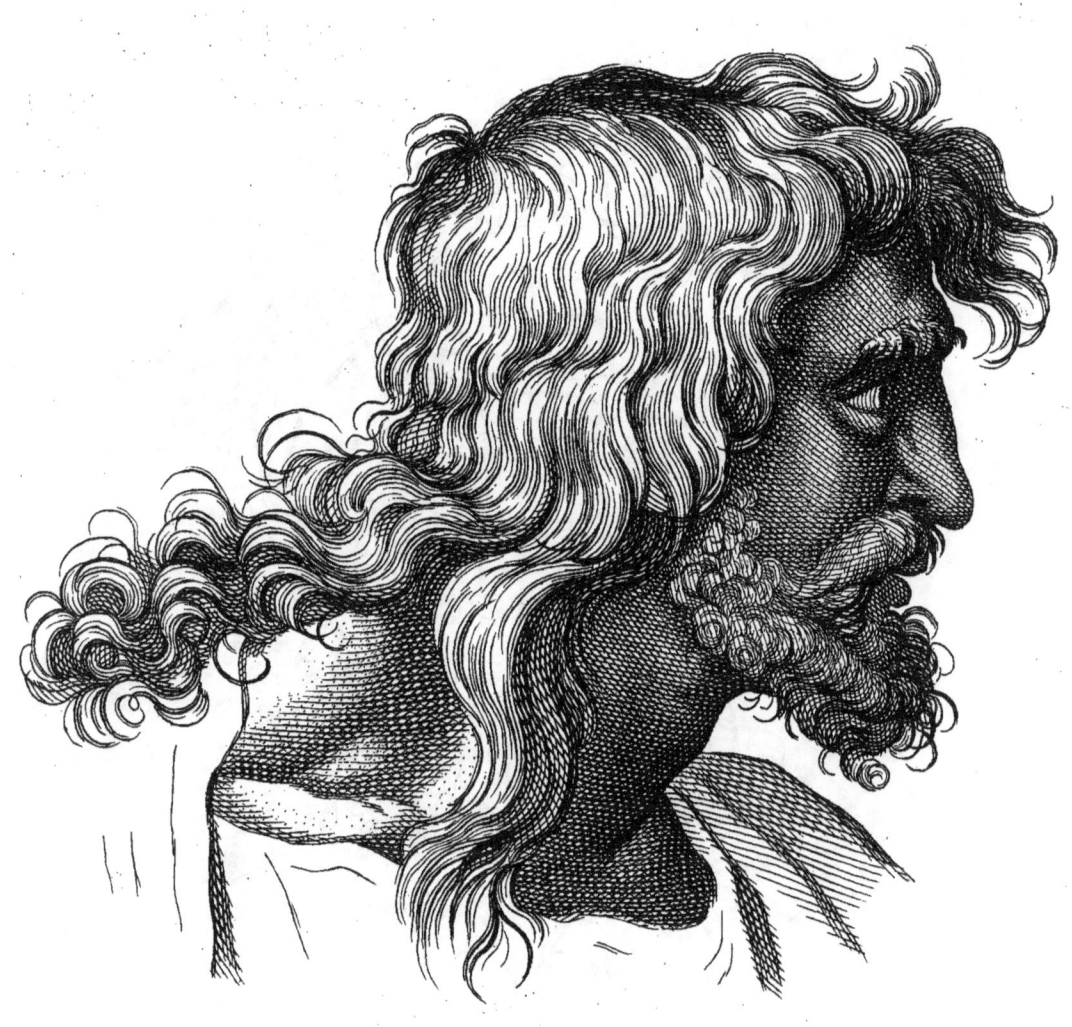

N. Pigné. Sculp.

Plate 5. II. - from Christ's Charge to Peter

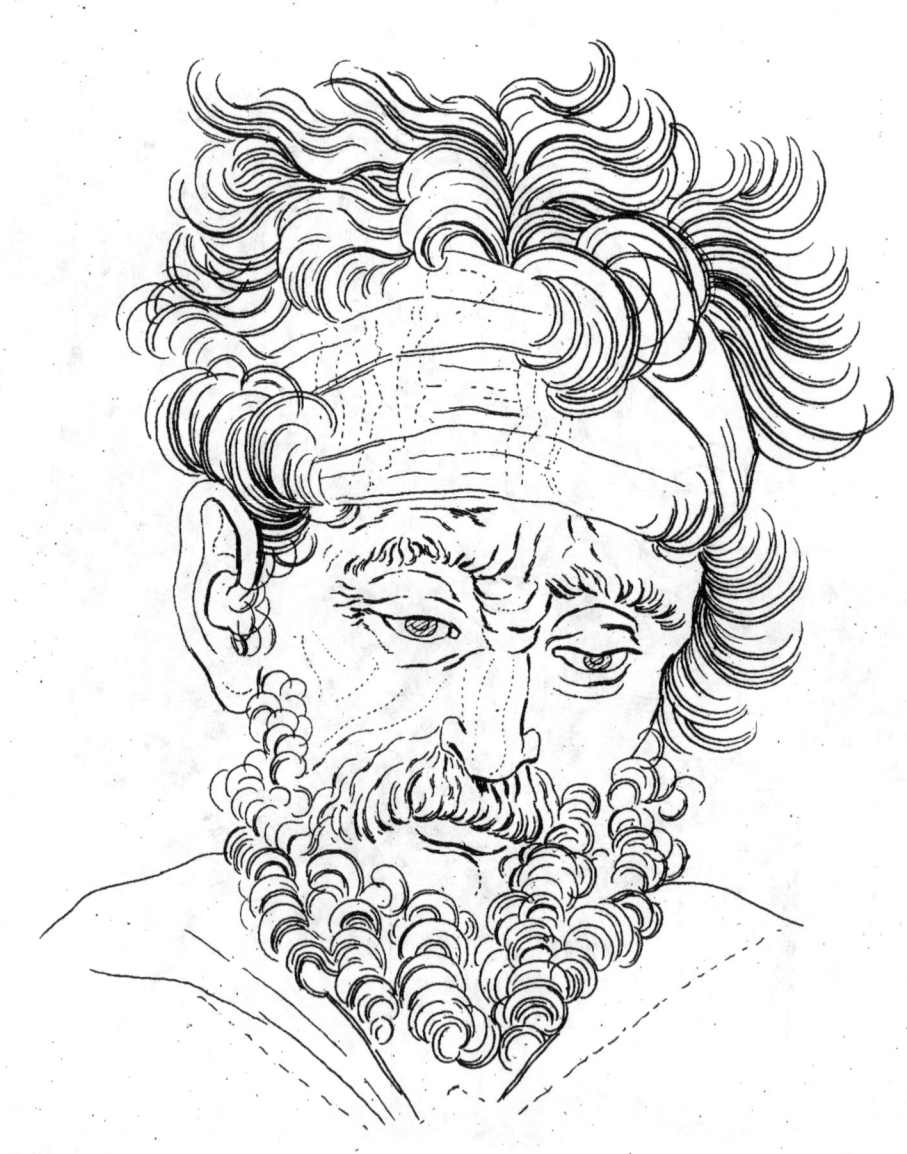

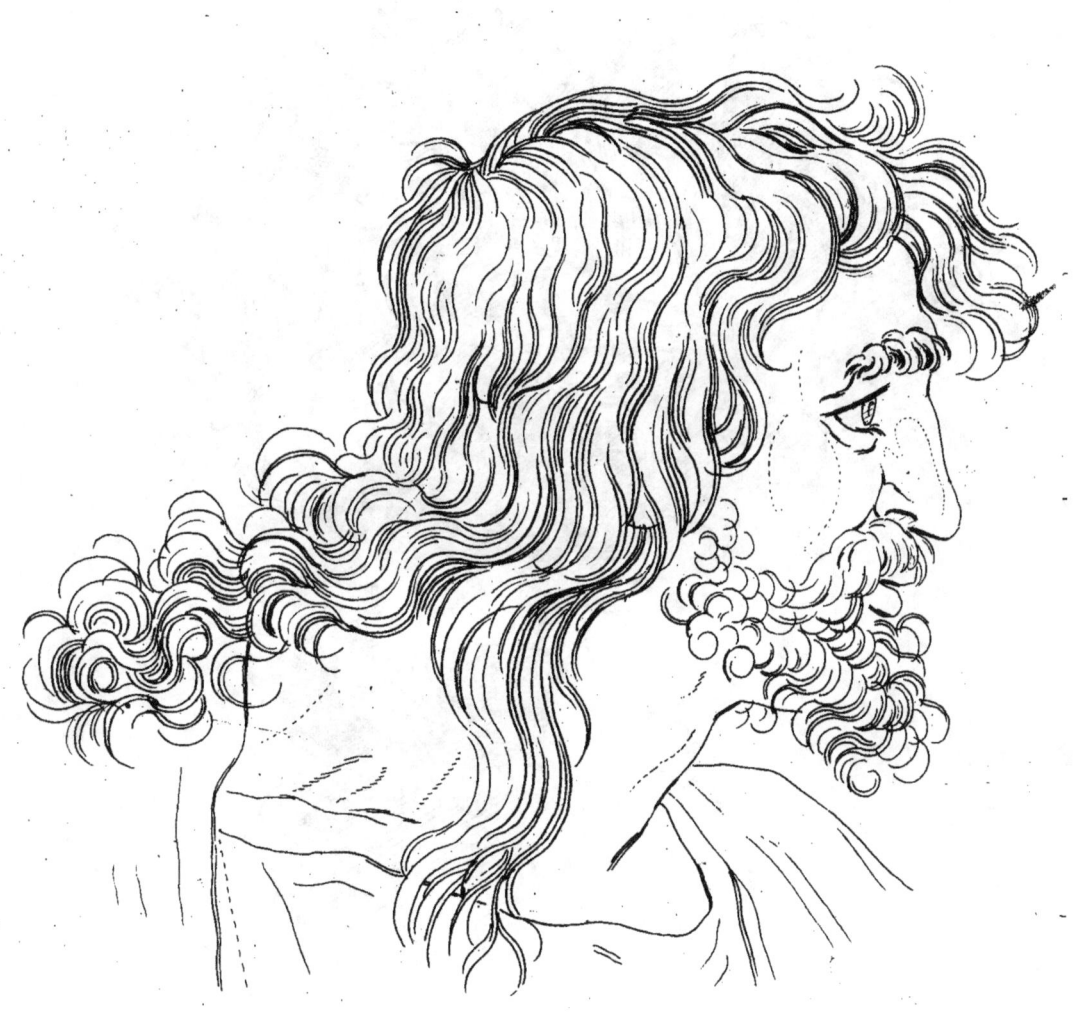

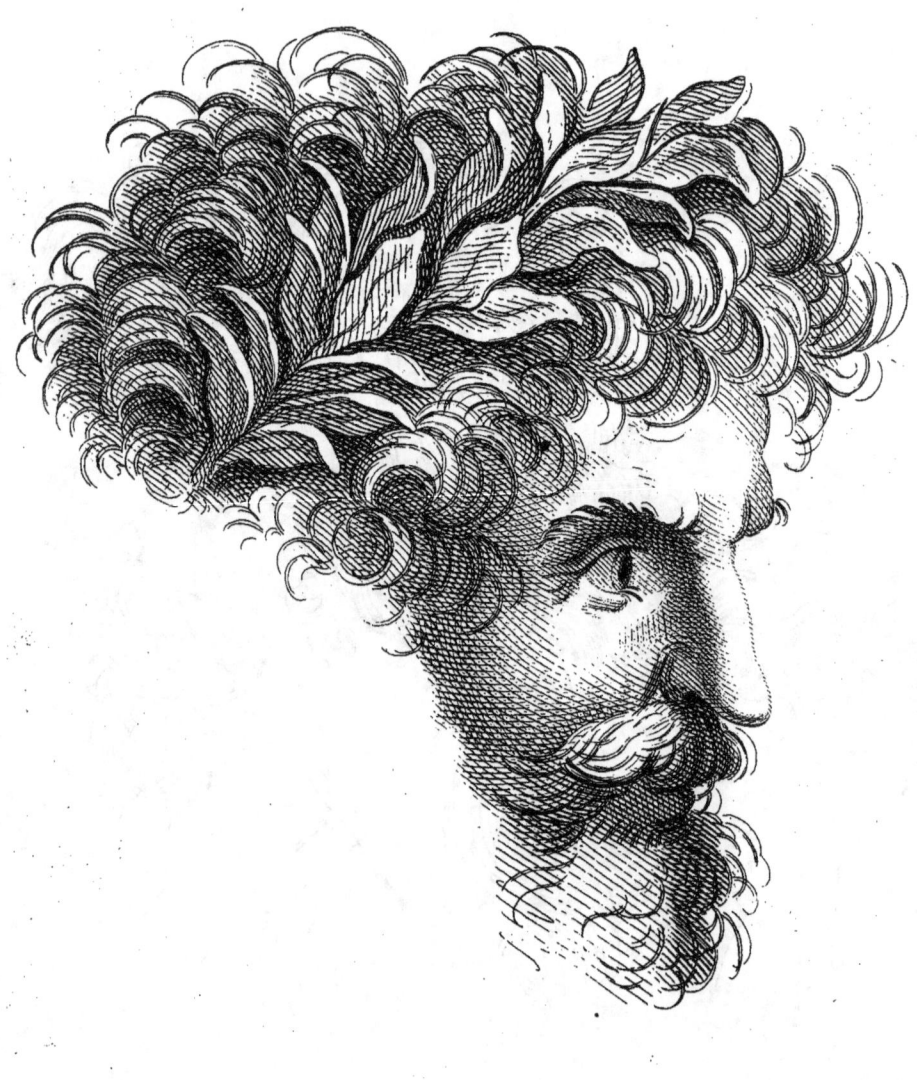

Raph. Vrb pinx .

Plate 6. I. - from Paul and Barnabas

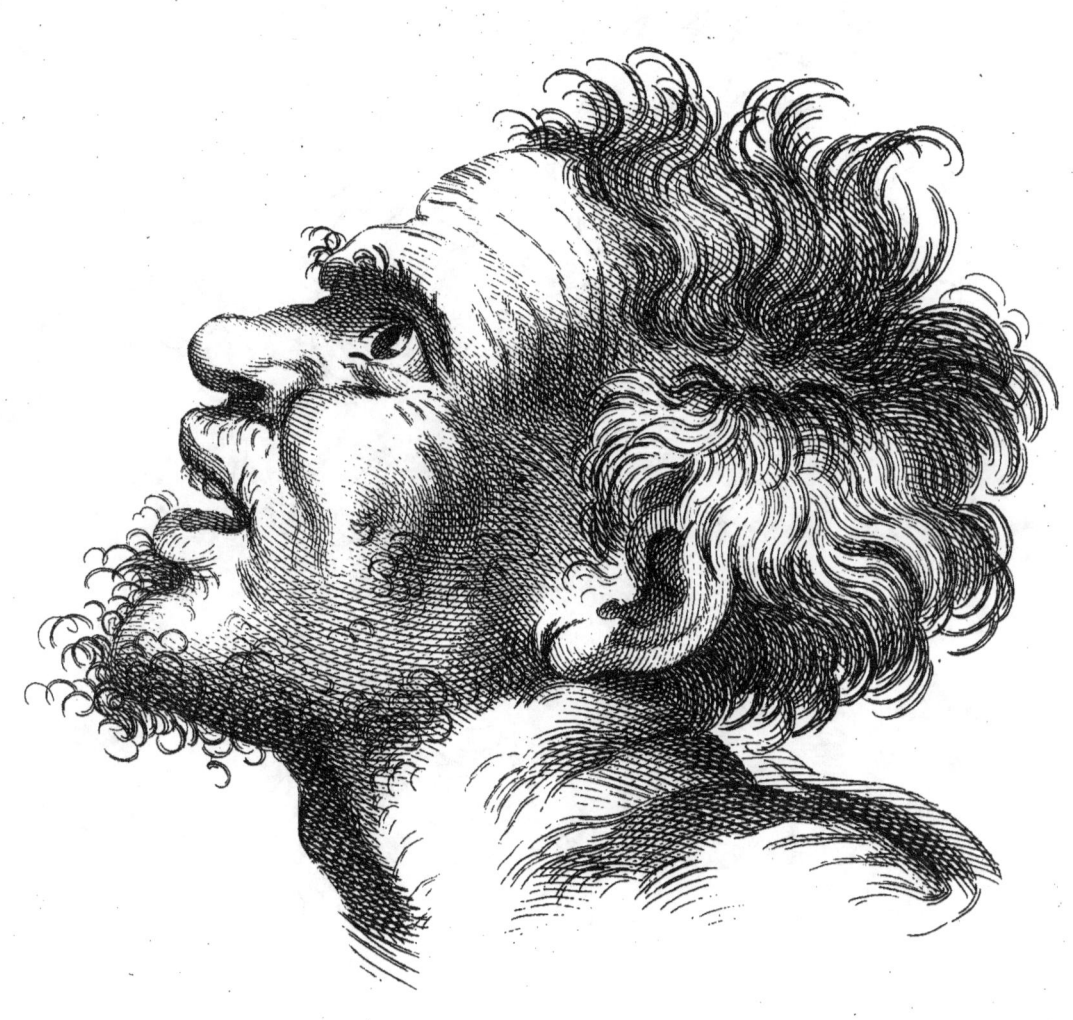

D . Beauvais sculp

Plate 6. II. - from The Lame Man Healed

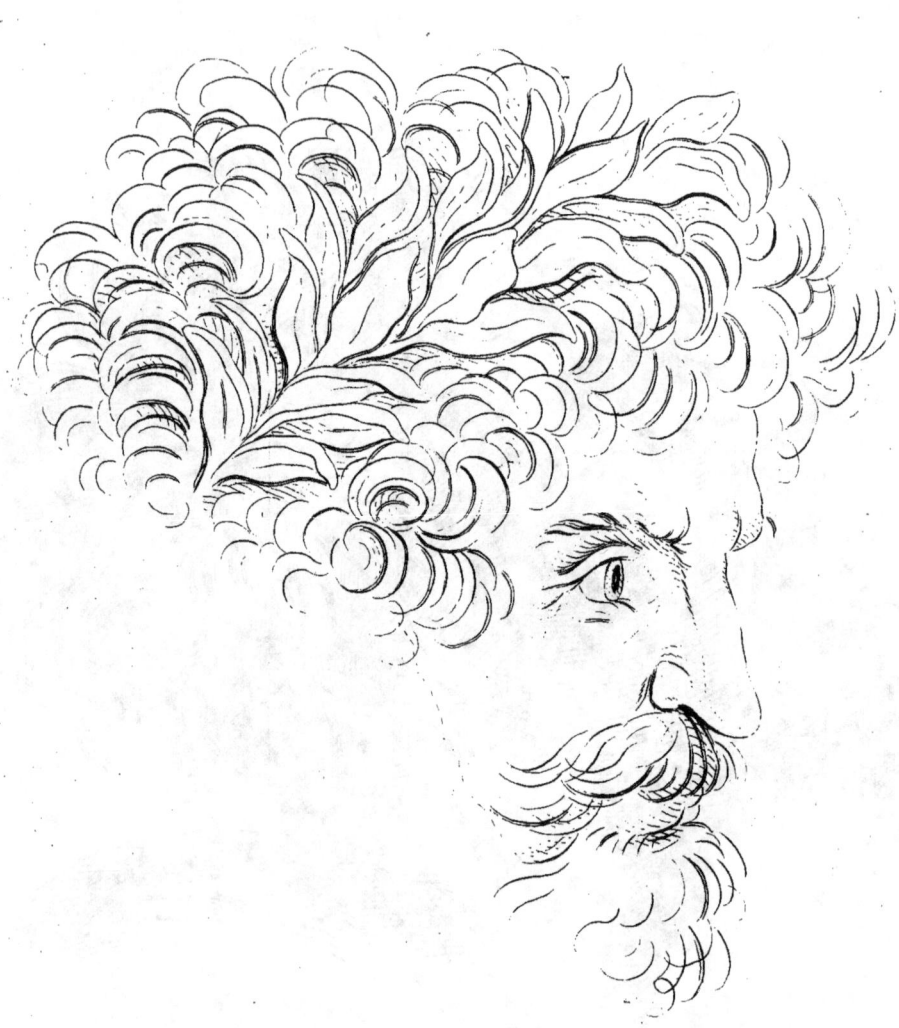

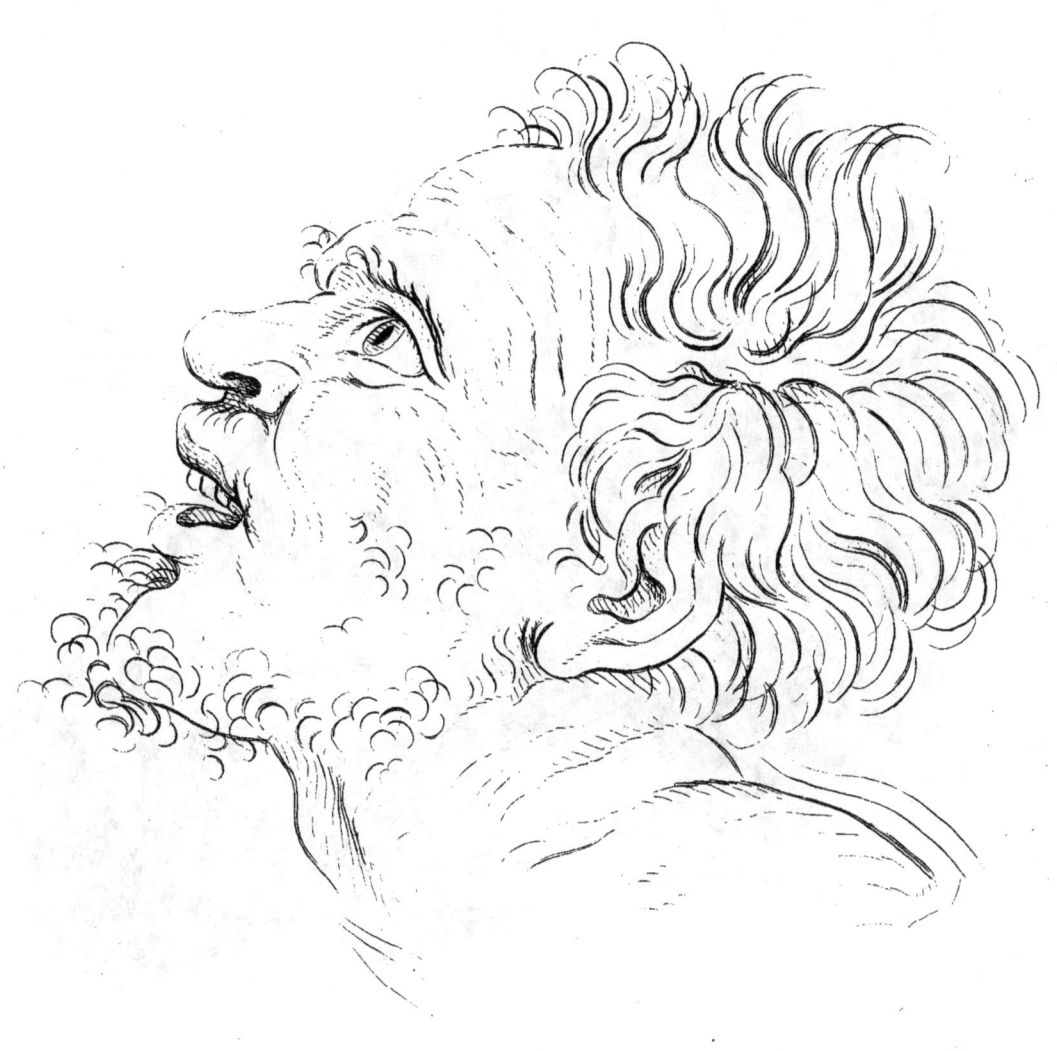

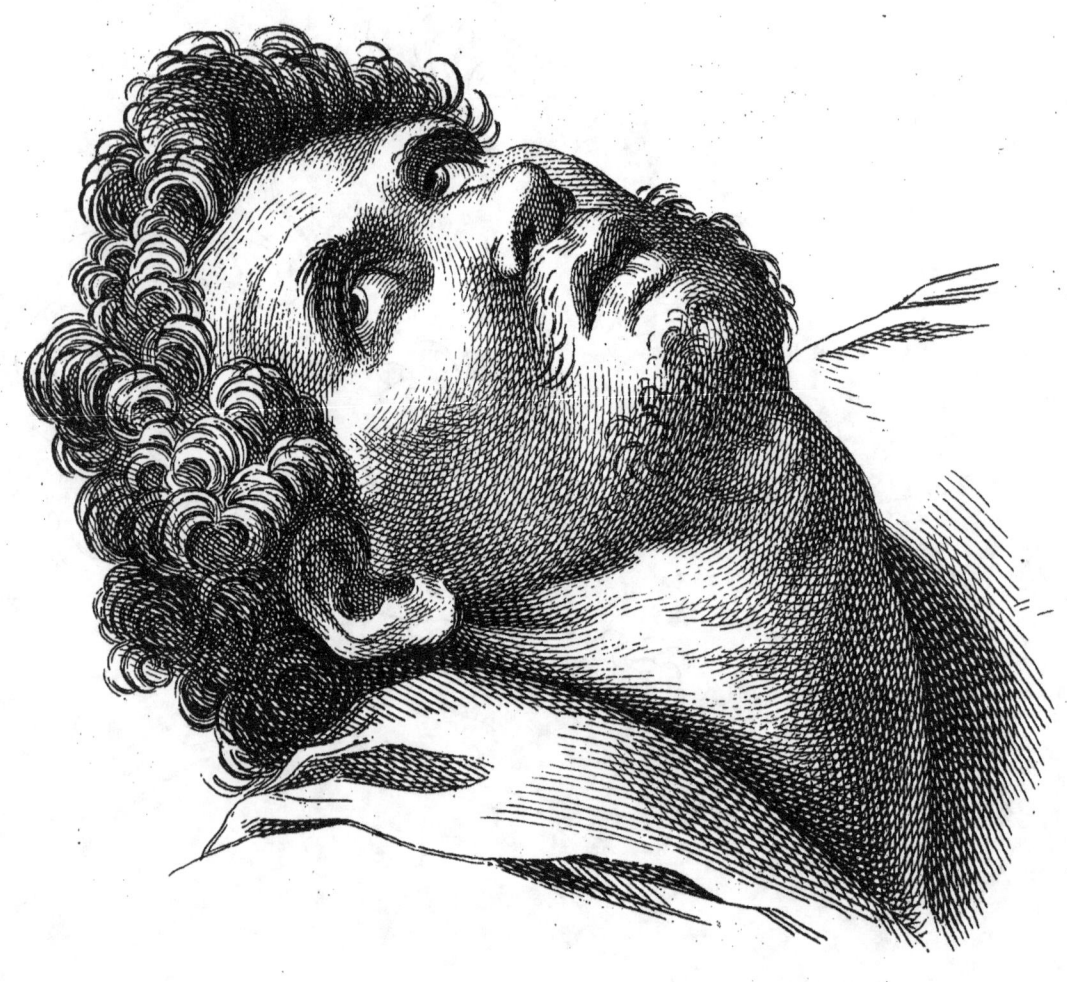

Raph. Vrb. pinx .

Plate 7. I. - from The Death of Ananias

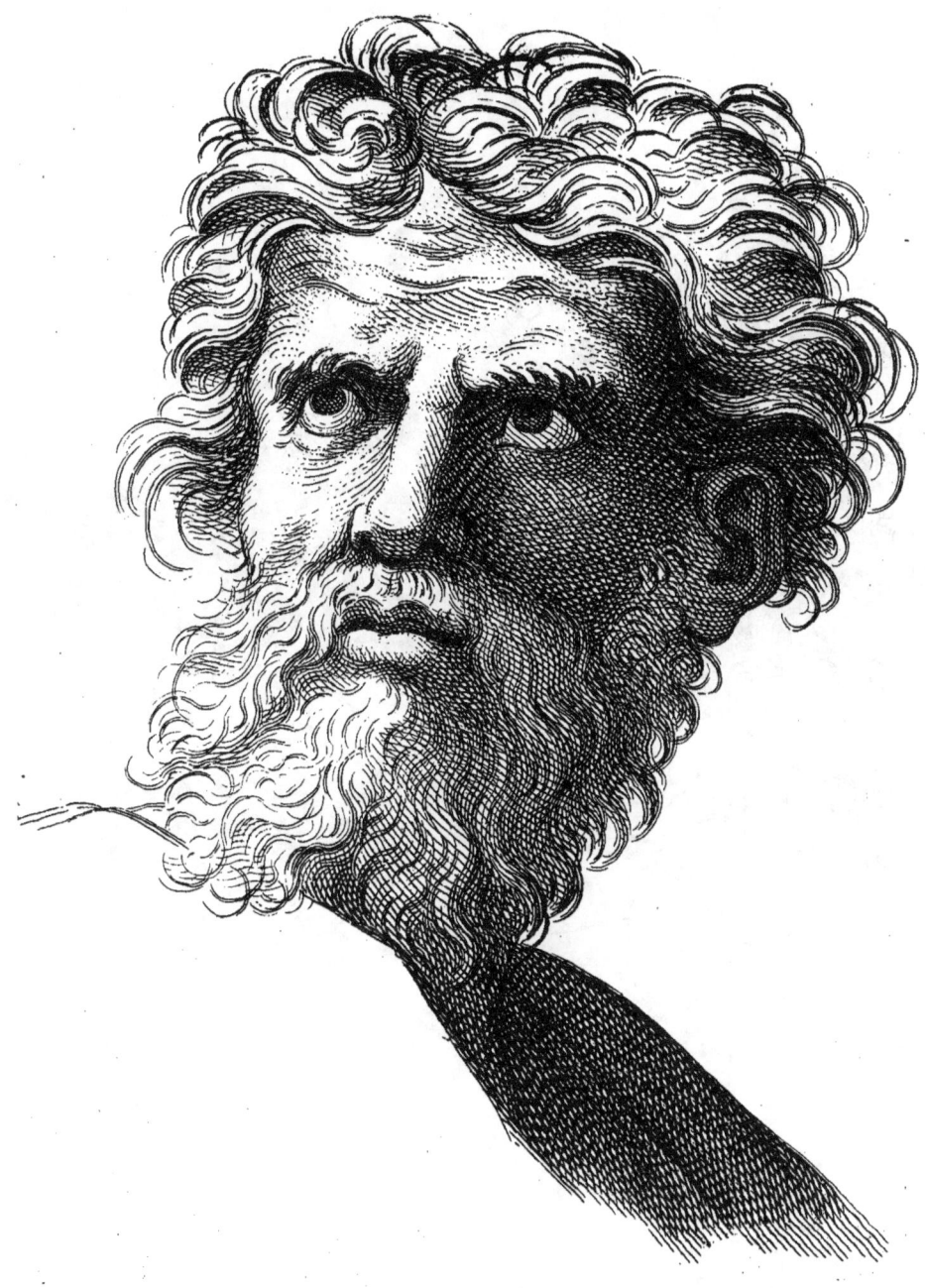

n. Dupuis sculp

Plate 7. II. - from The Death of Ananias

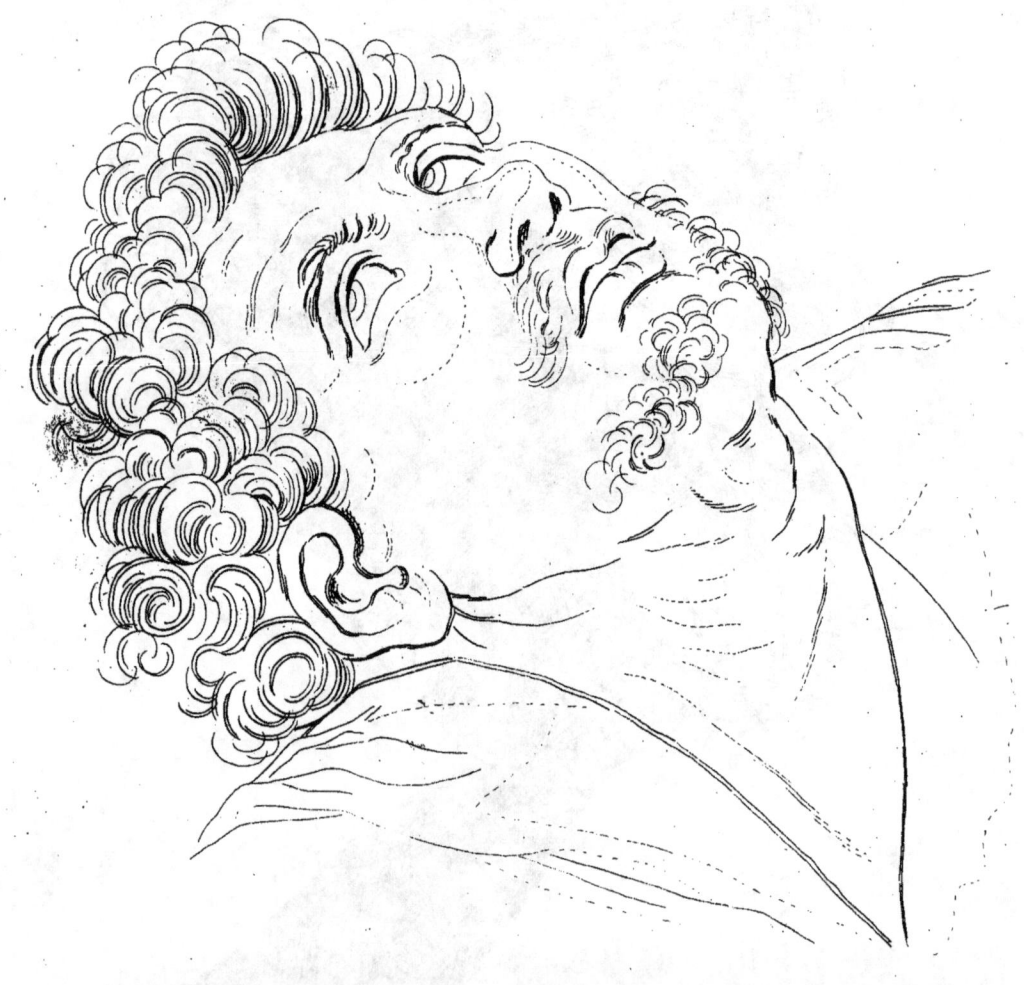

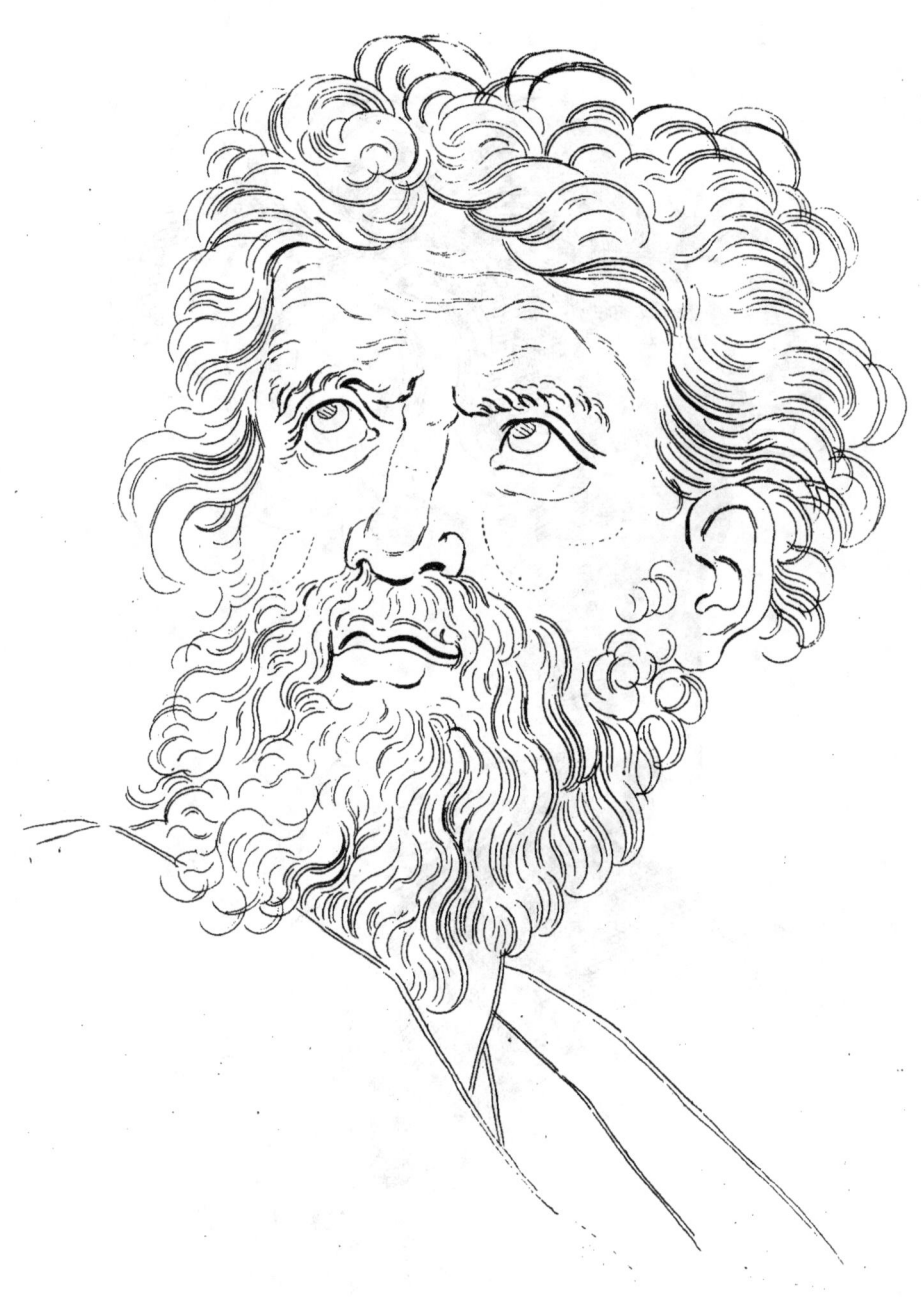

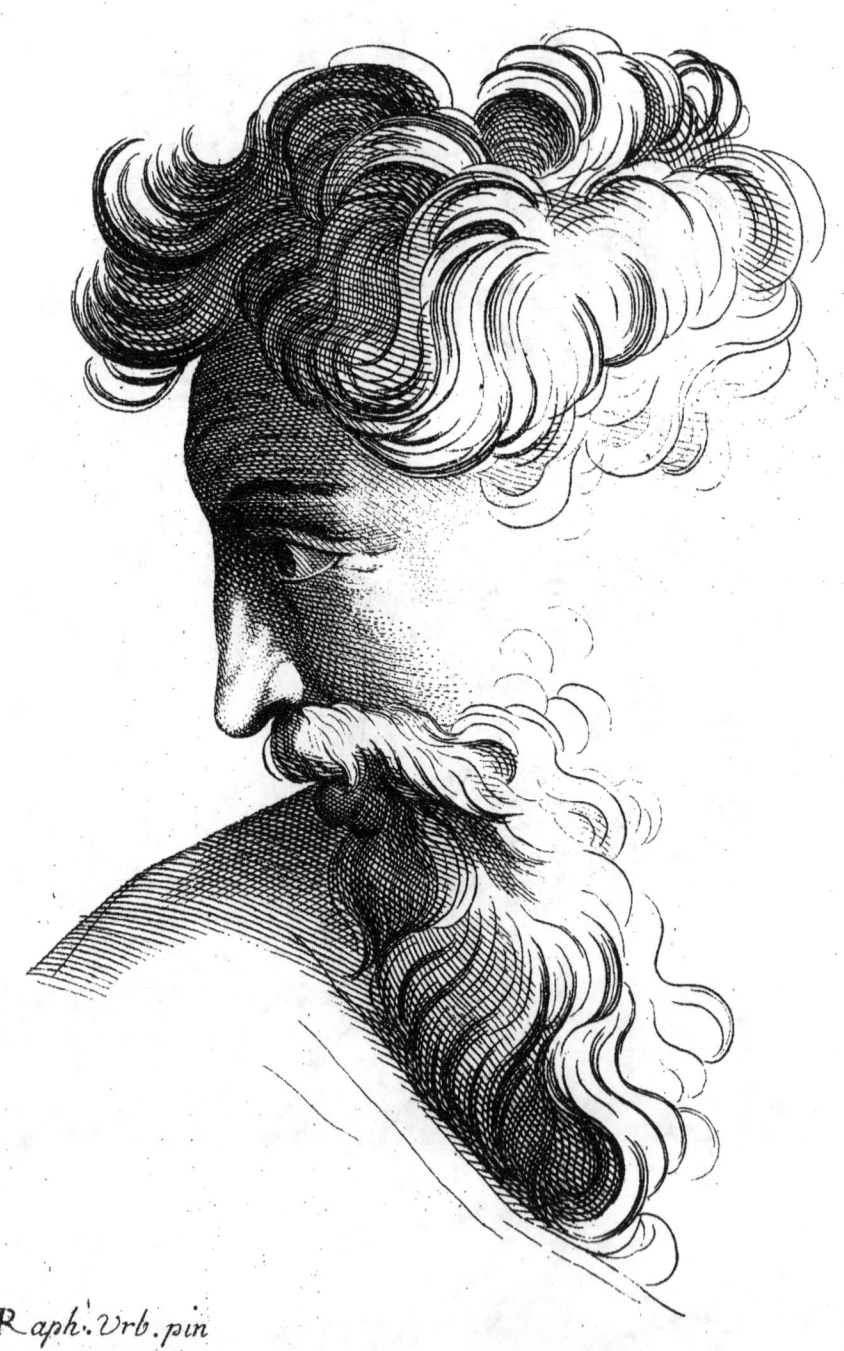

Raph.Vrb.pin

Plate 8. I. - from Paul Preaching

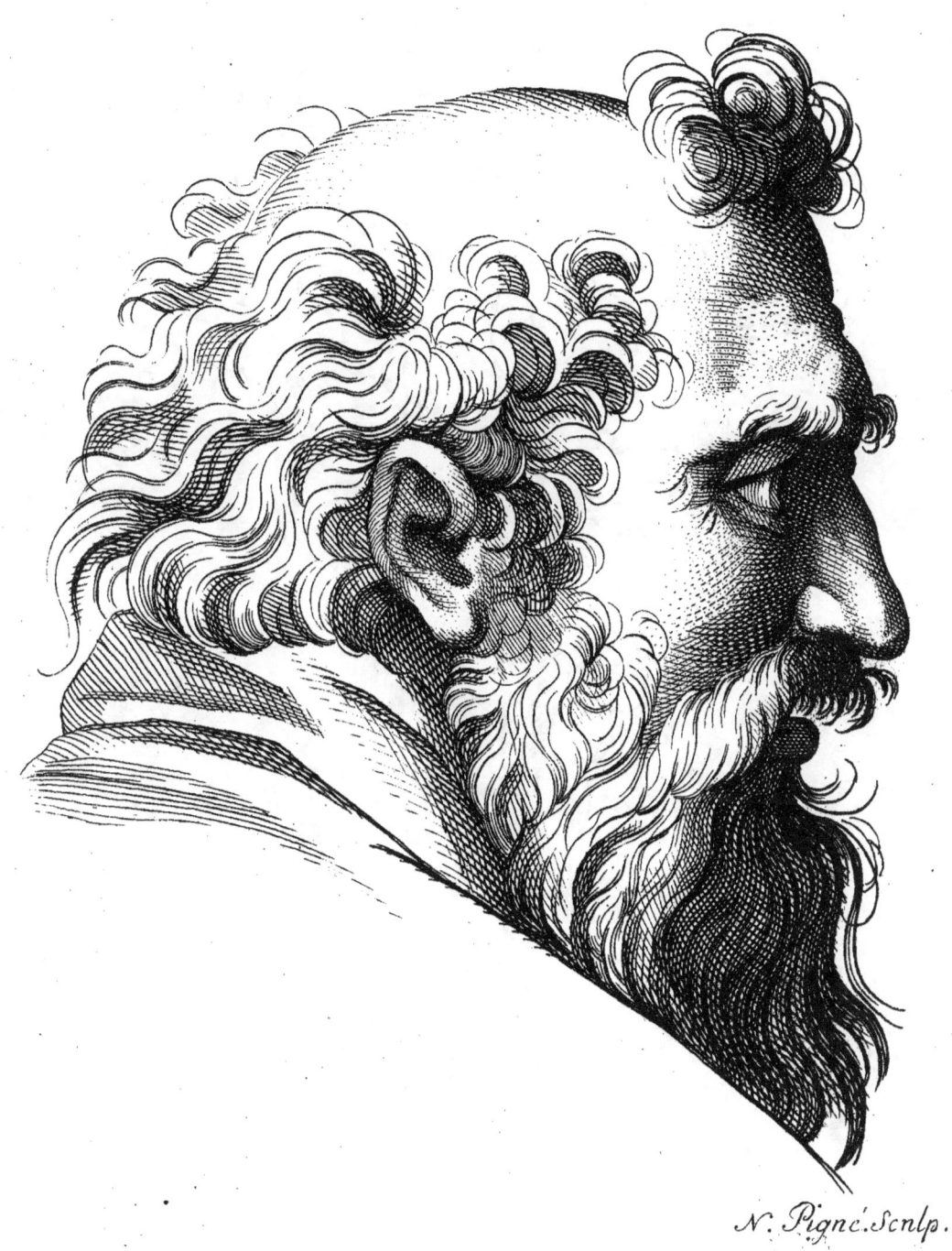

N. Pigne. Sculp.

Plate 8. II. - from Christ's Charge to Peter

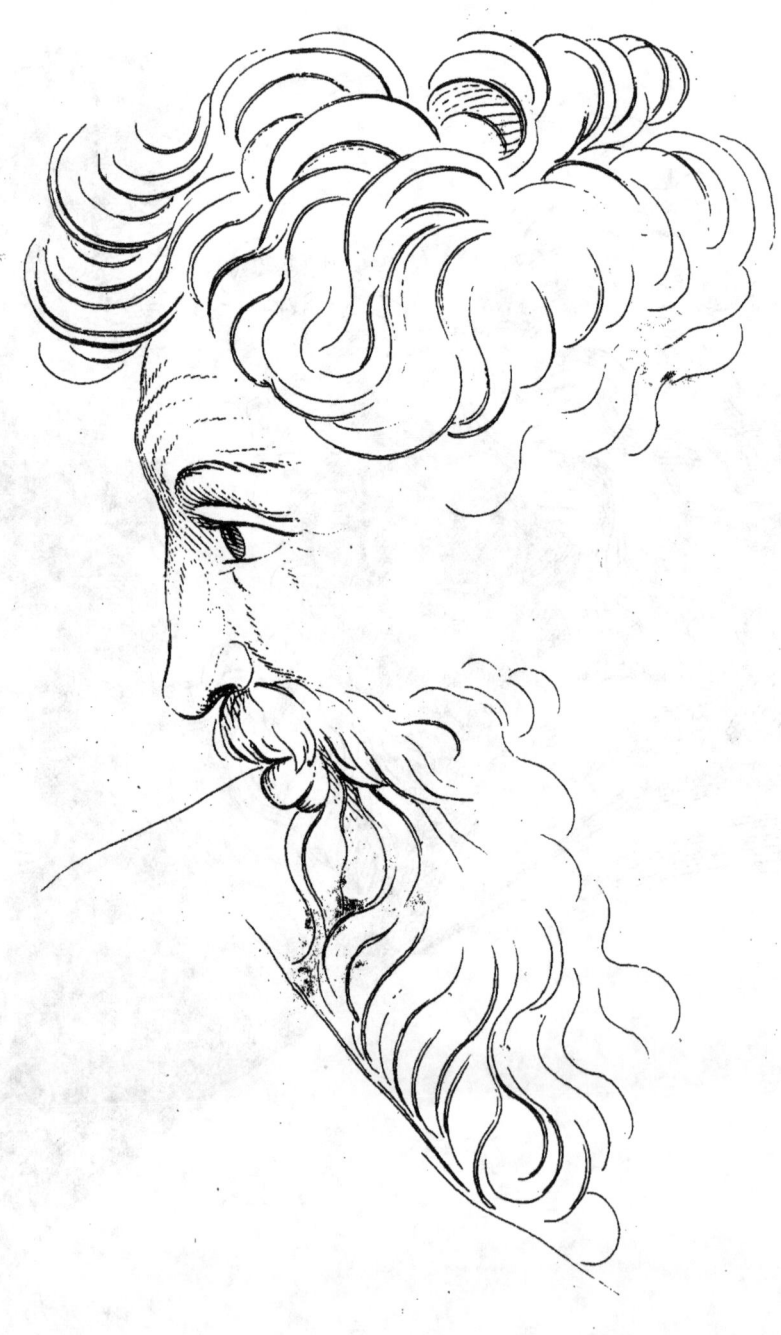

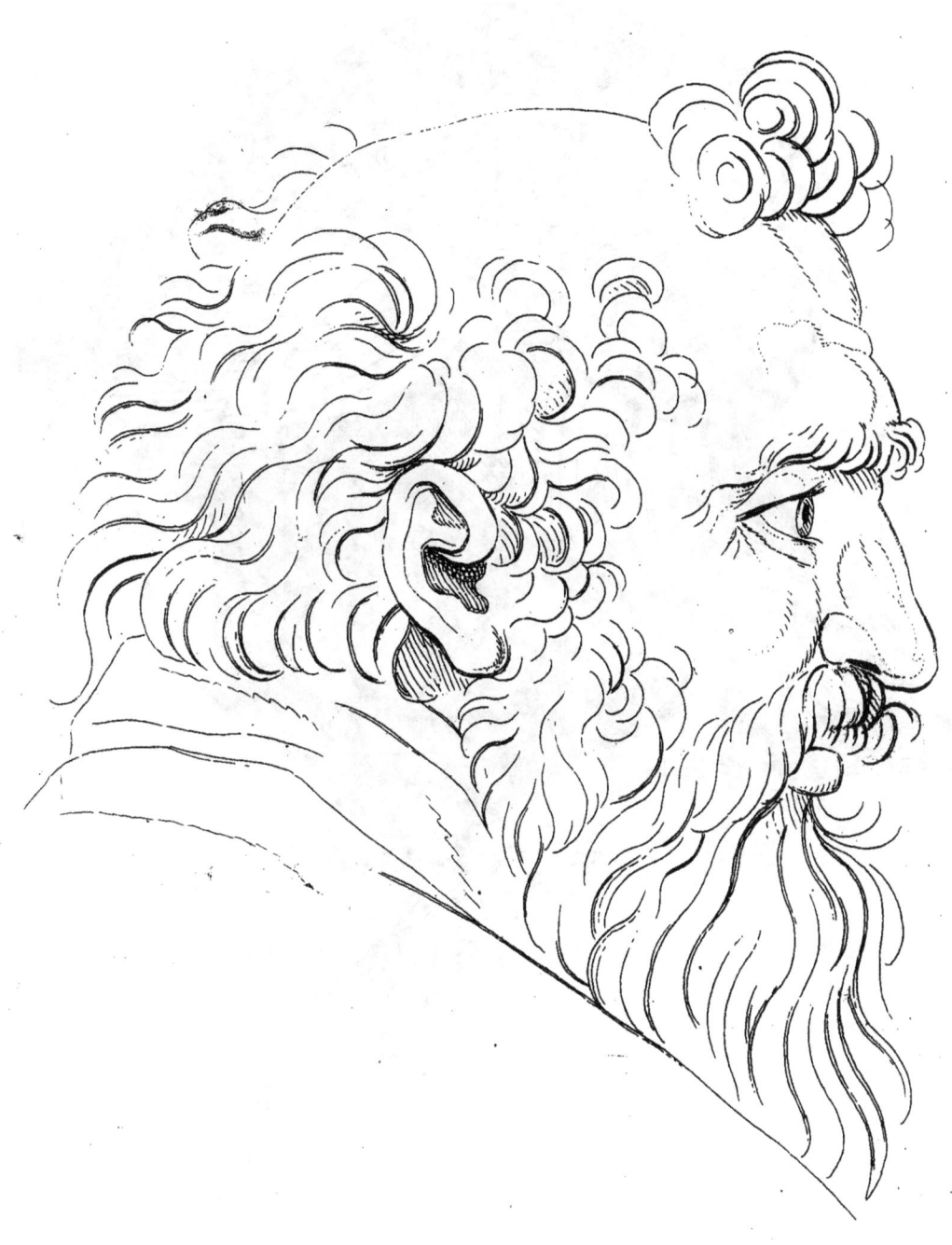

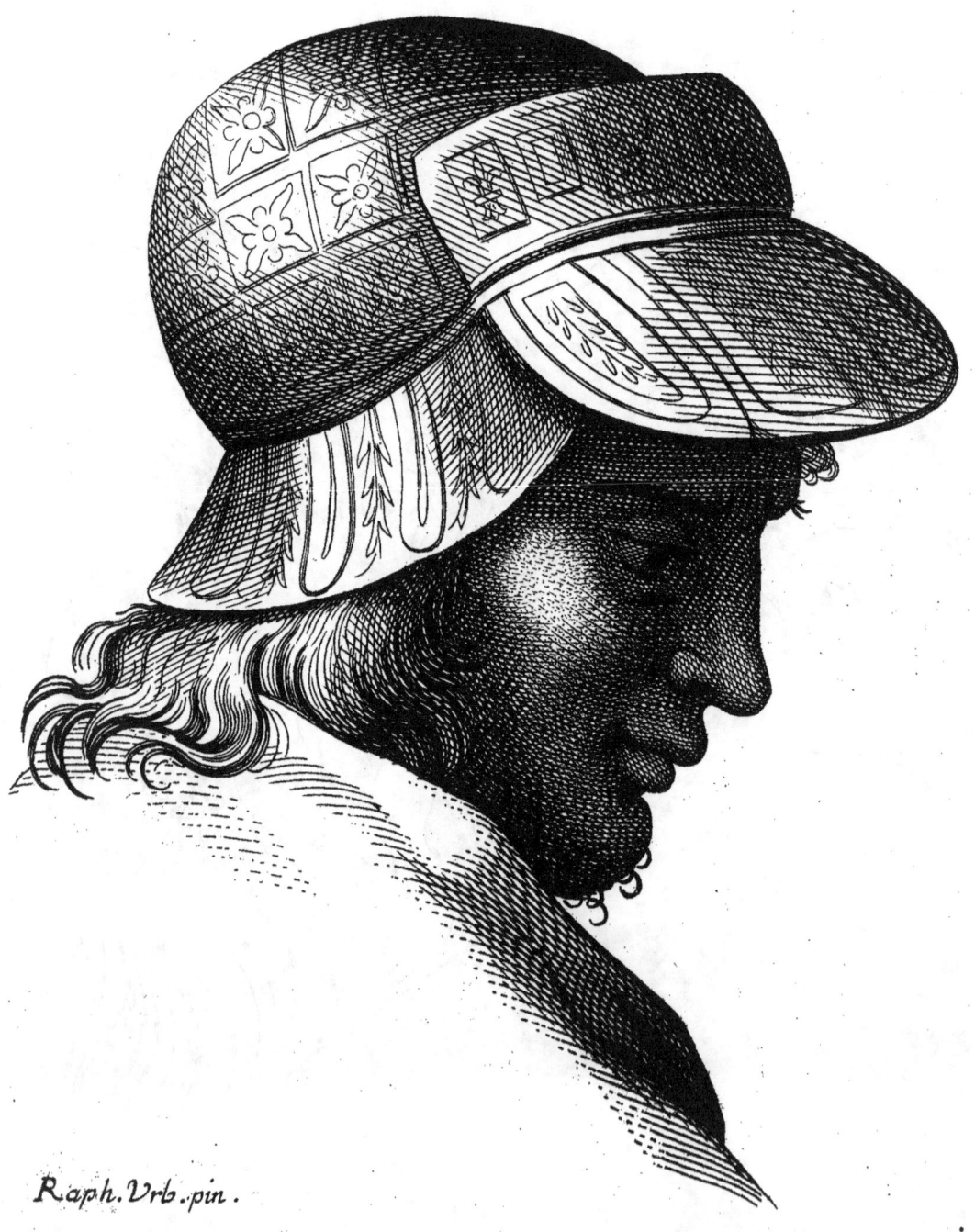

Raph. Vrb. pin.

Plate 9. I. - from The Death of Ananias

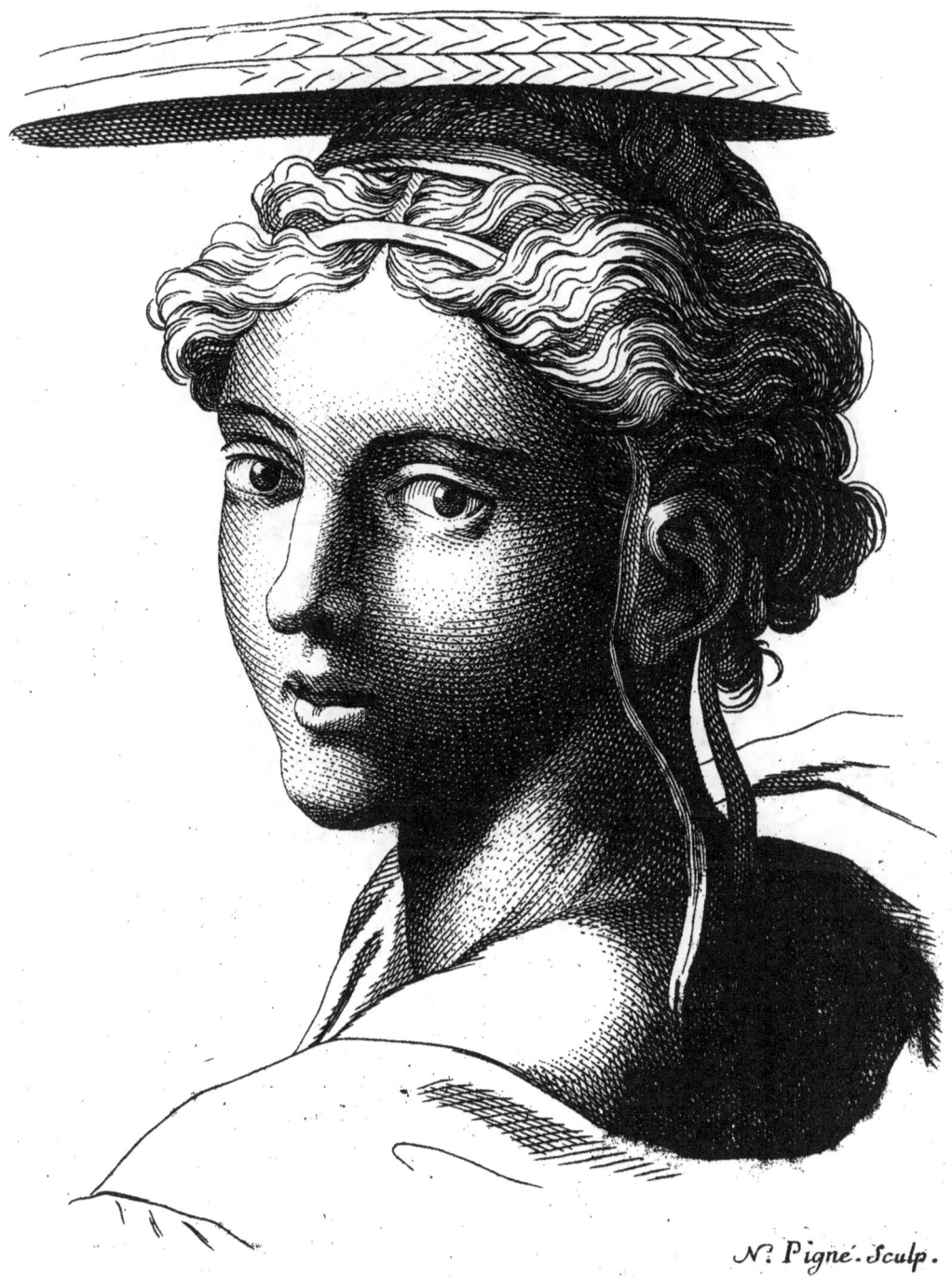

Plate 9. II. - from The Lame Man Healed

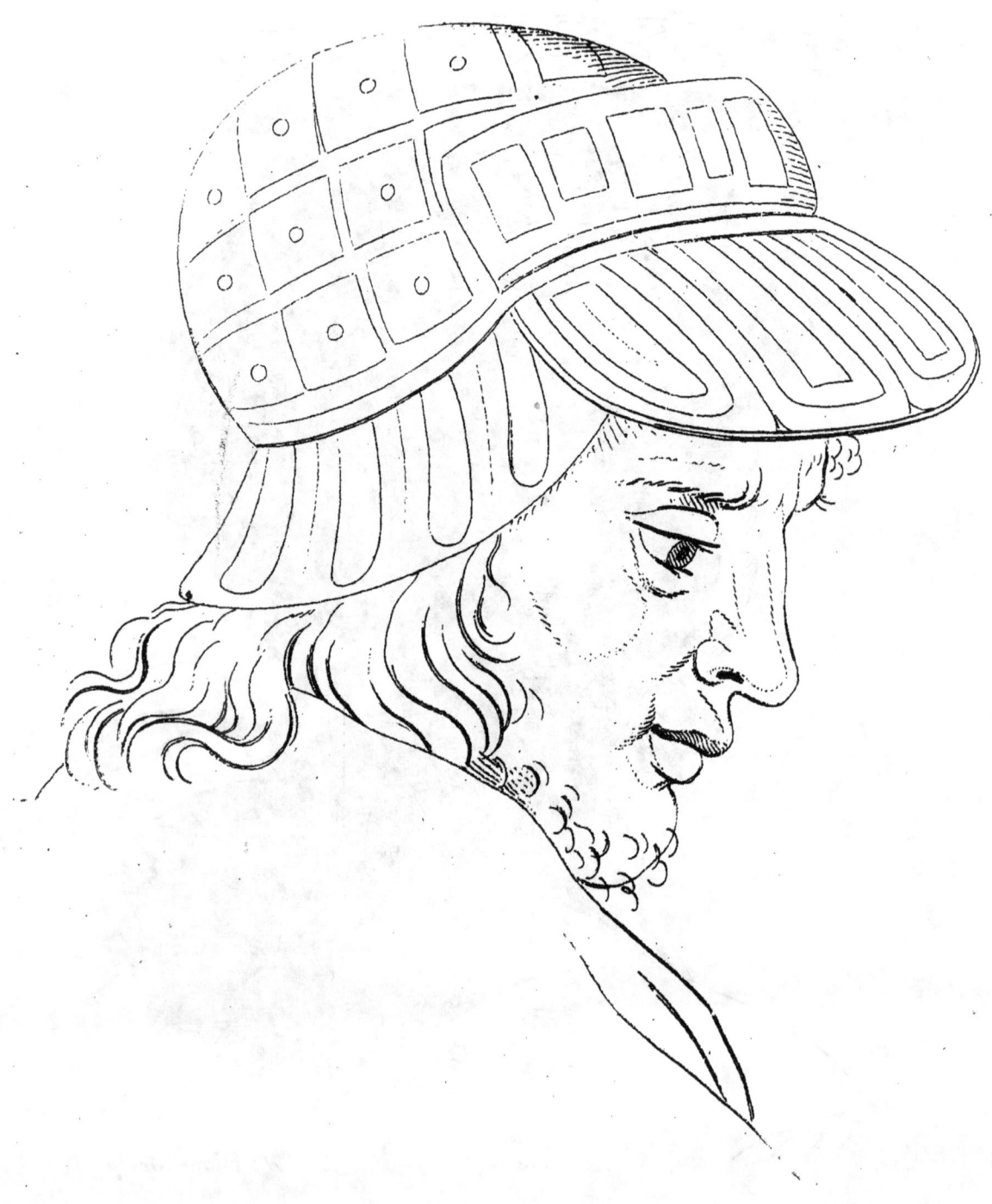

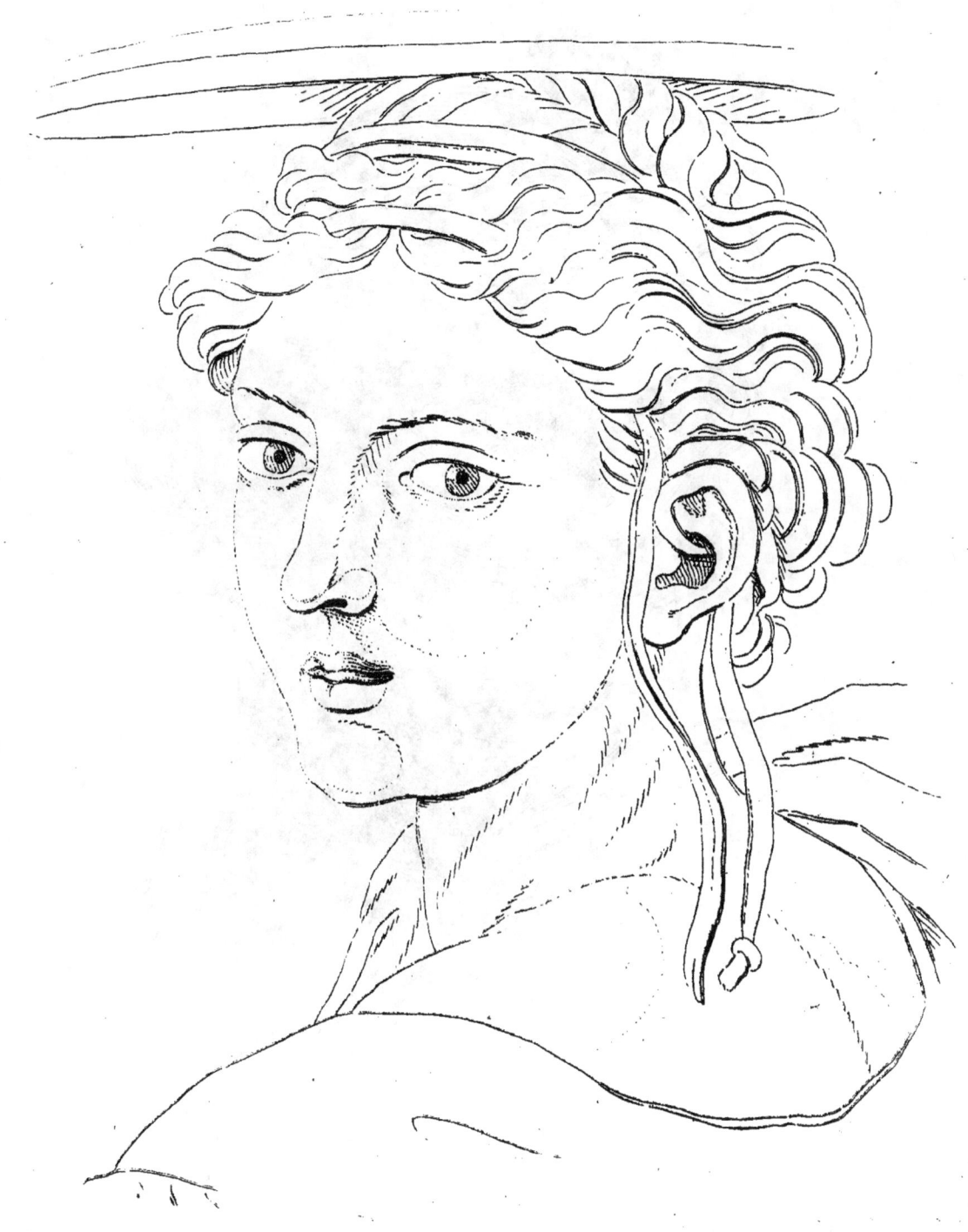

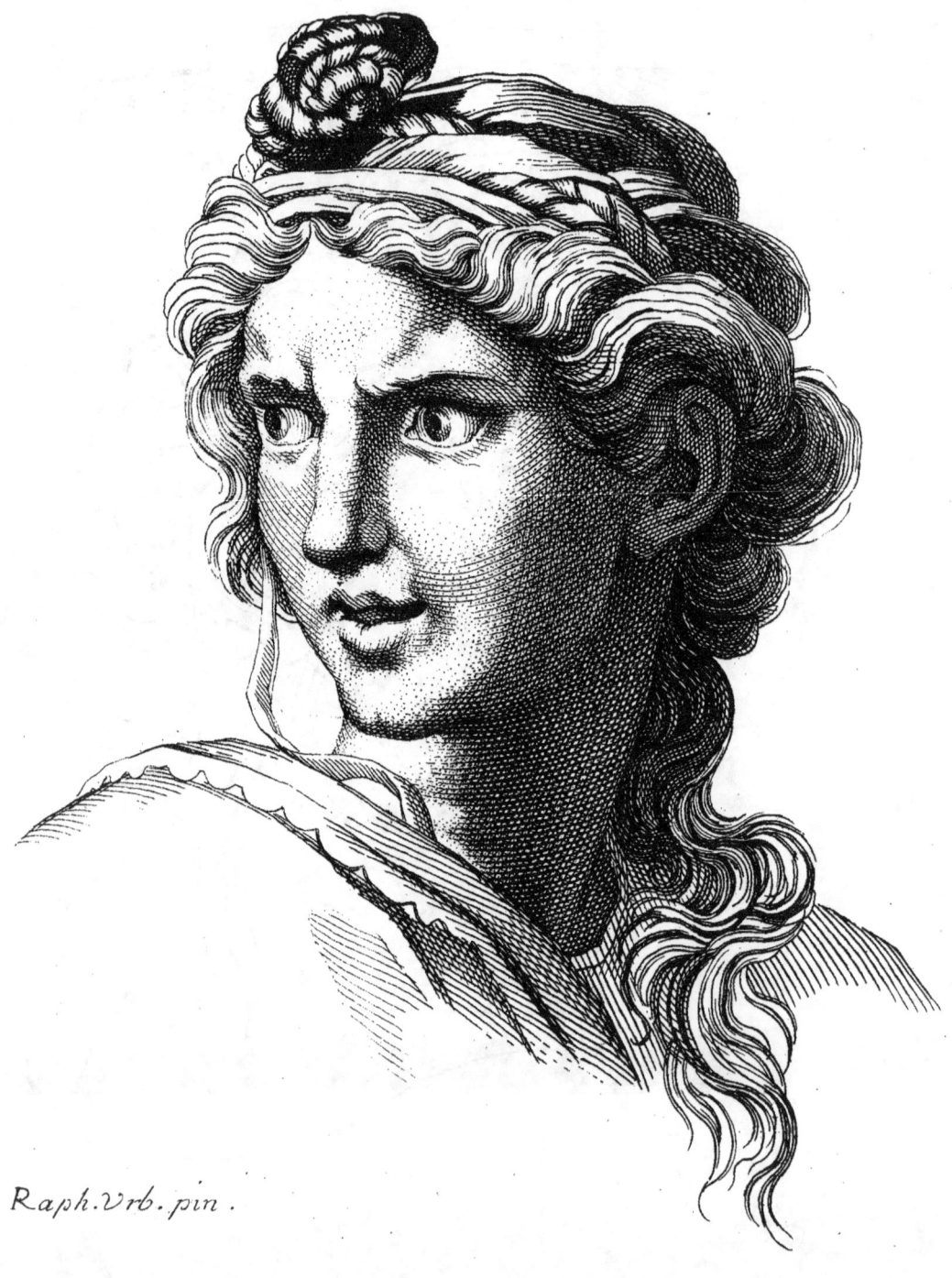

Raph.Vrb.pin.

Plate 10. I. - from The Death of Ananias

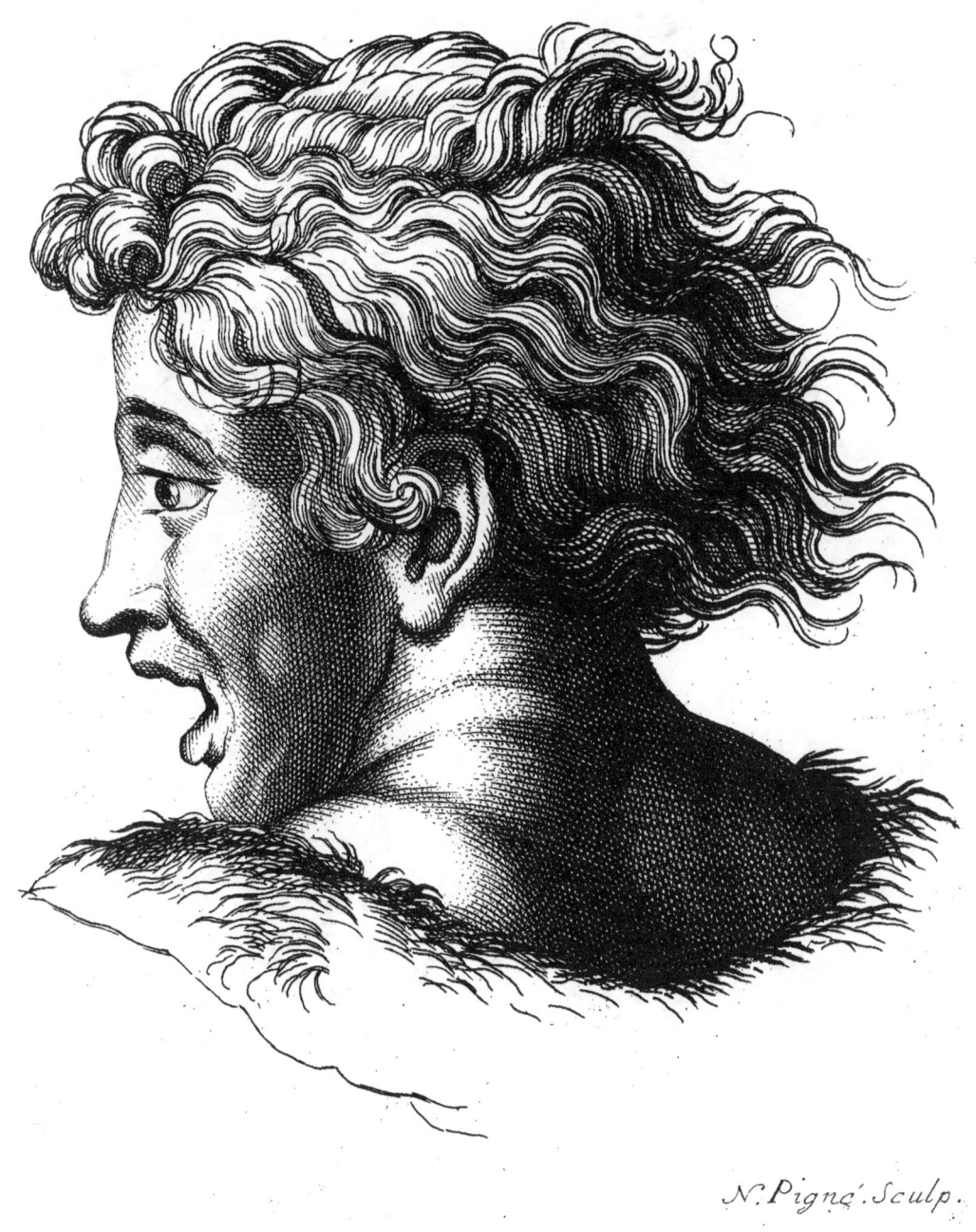

N. Pigné. Sculp.

Plate 10. II. - from The Death of Ananias

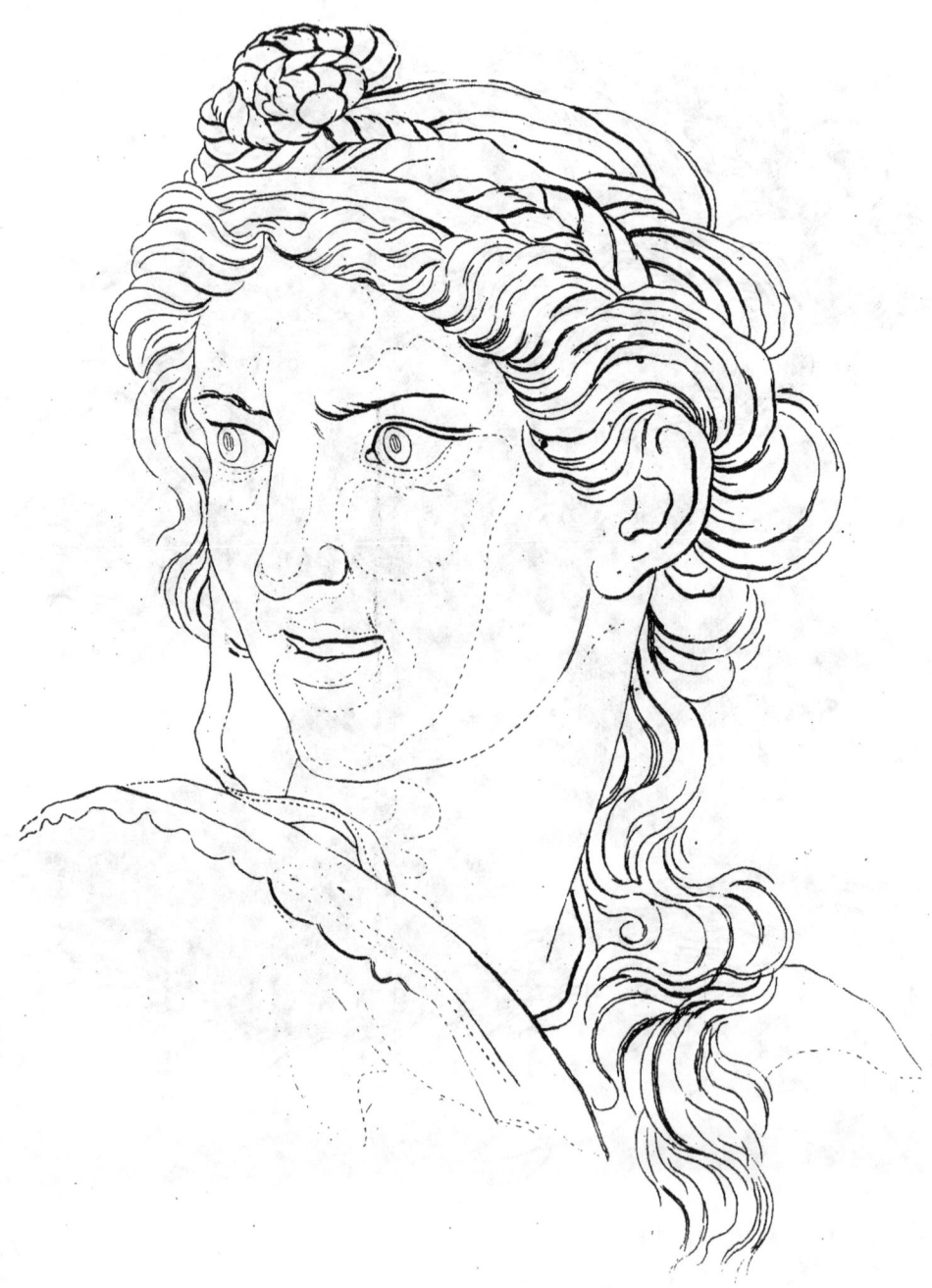

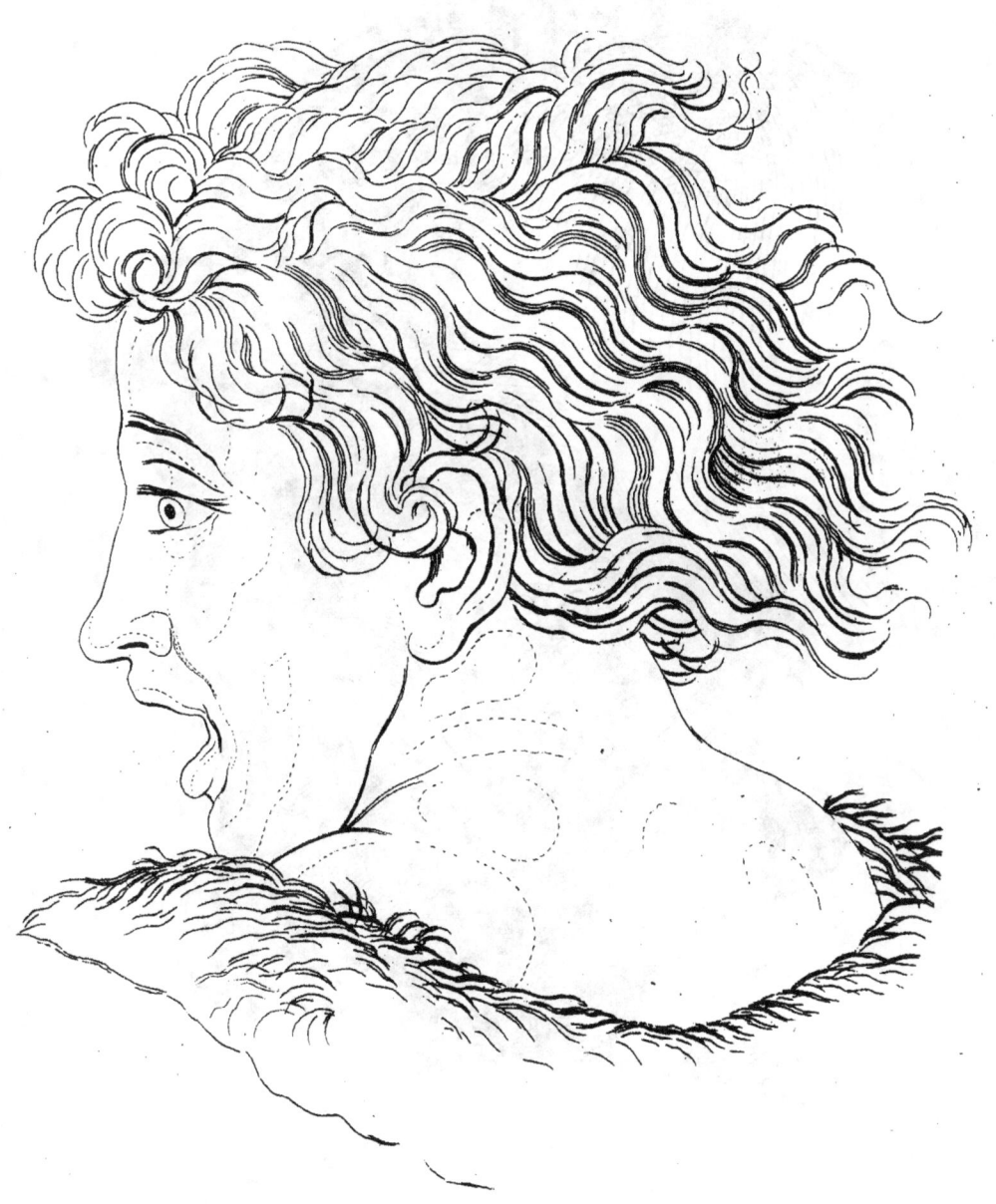

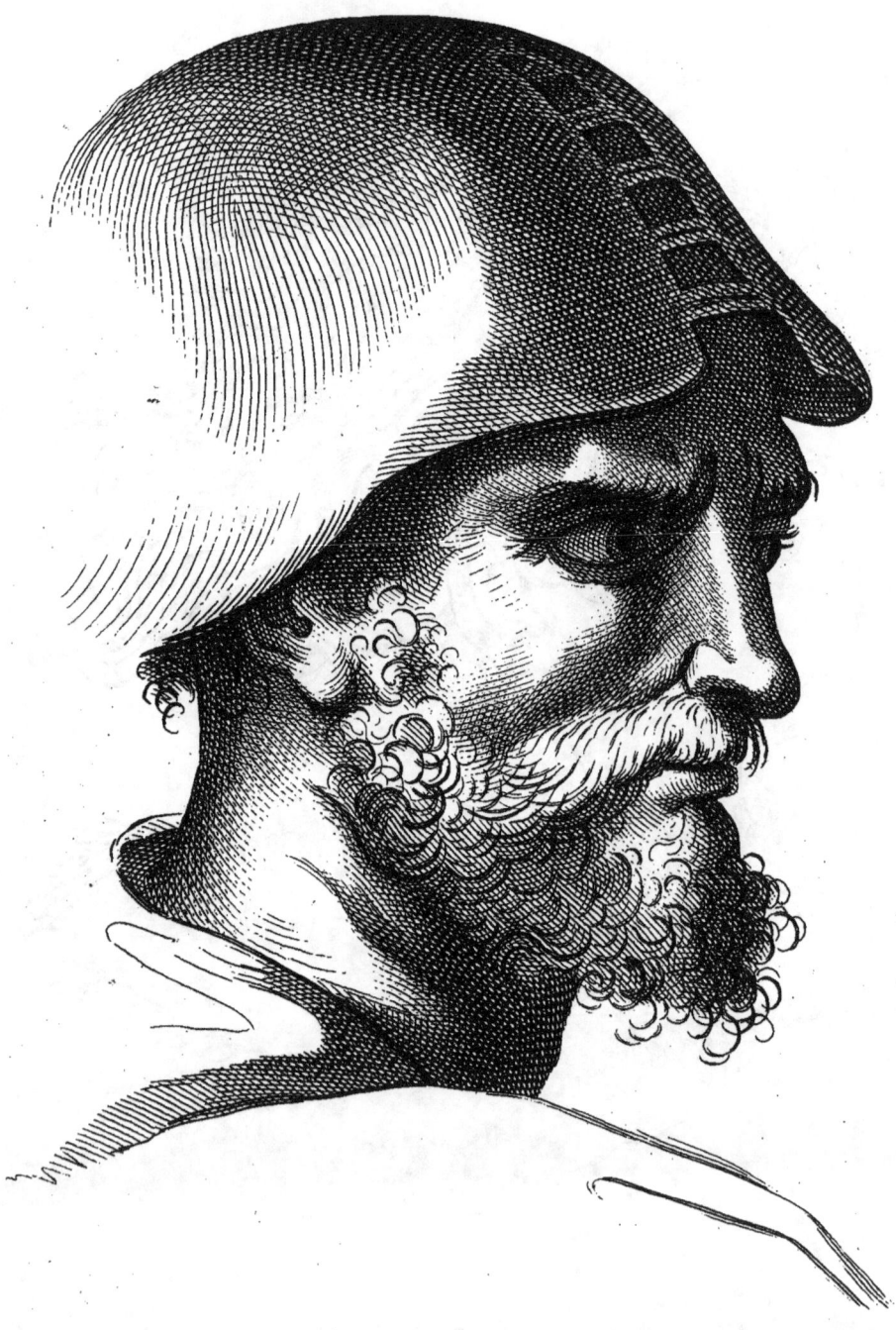

Raph. Vrb pinx.

Plate 11. I. - from The Lame Man Healed

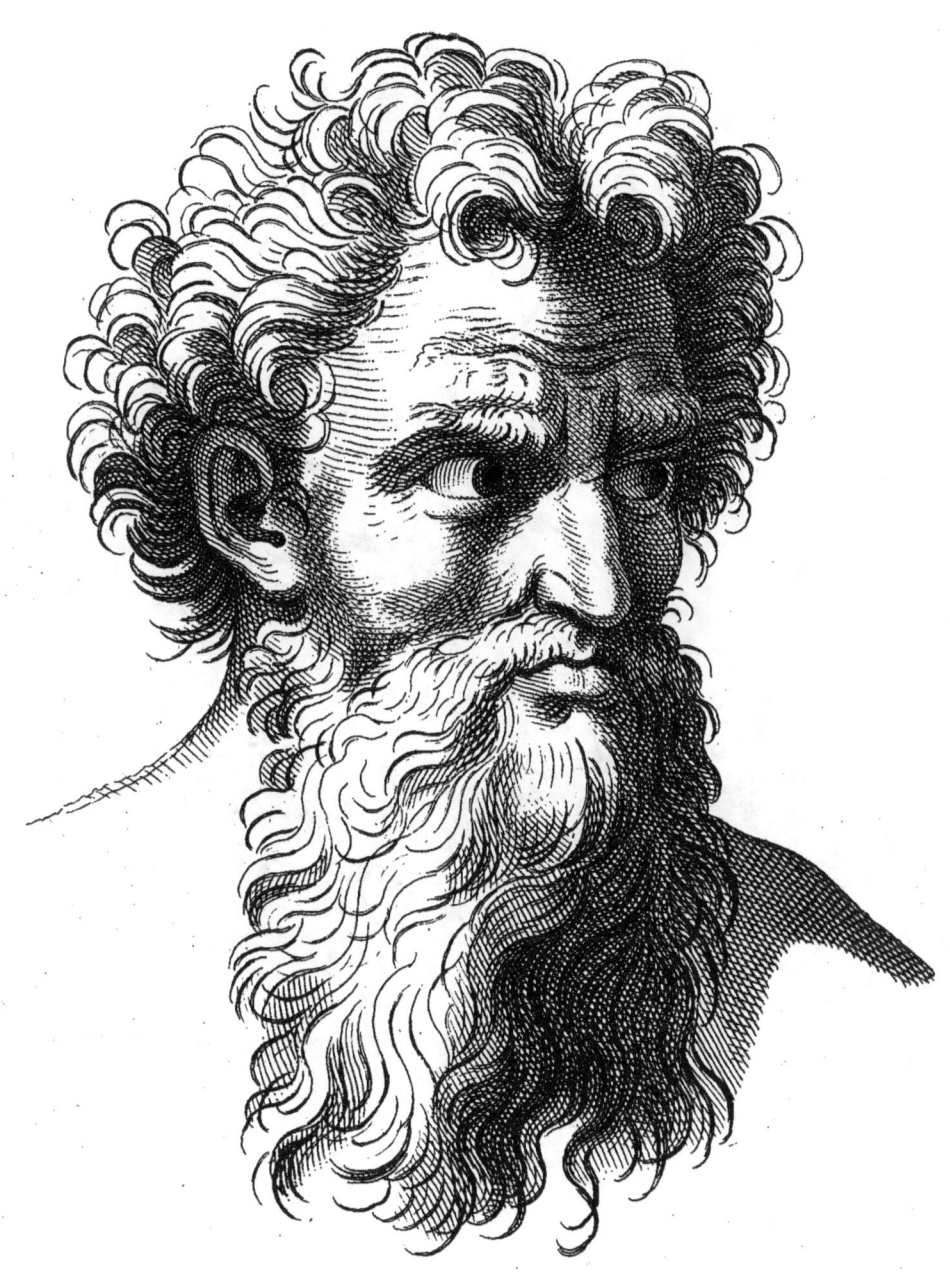

G. Duchange sculp.

Plate 11. II. - from Christ's Charge to Peter

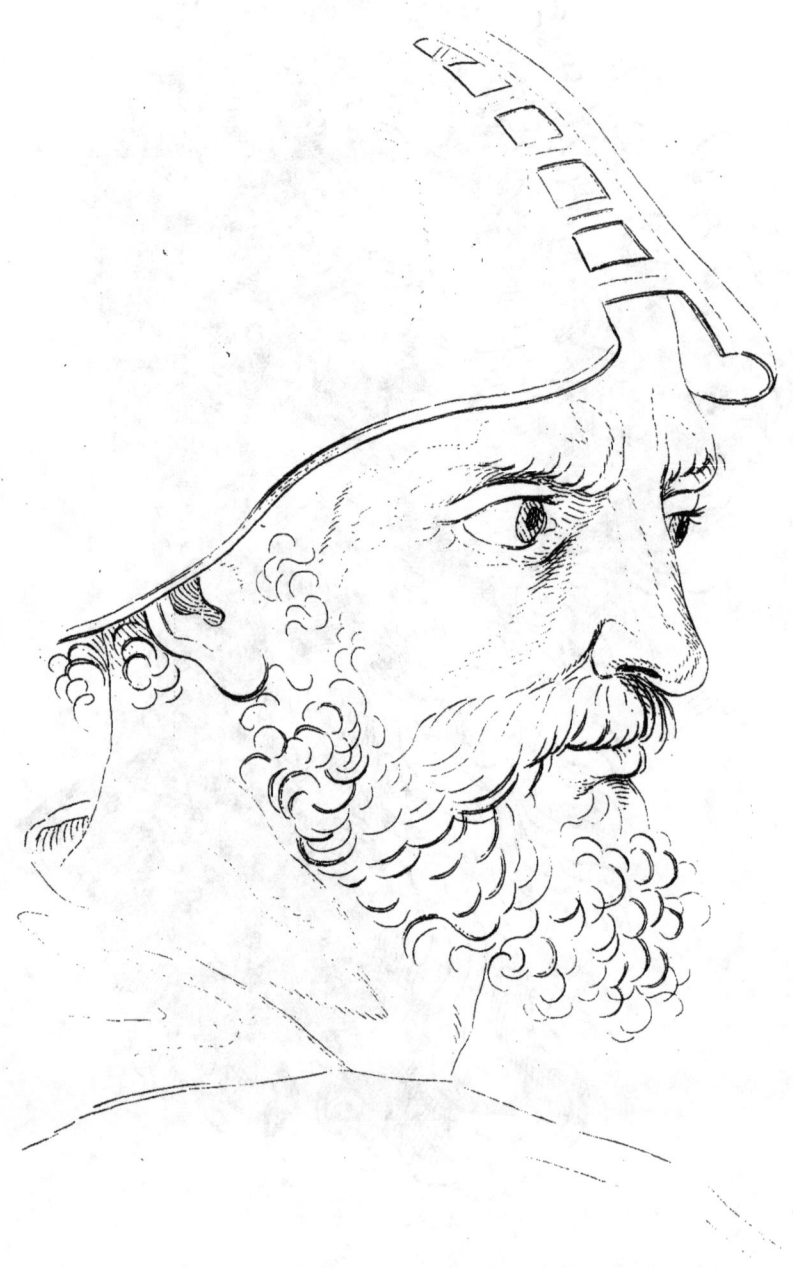

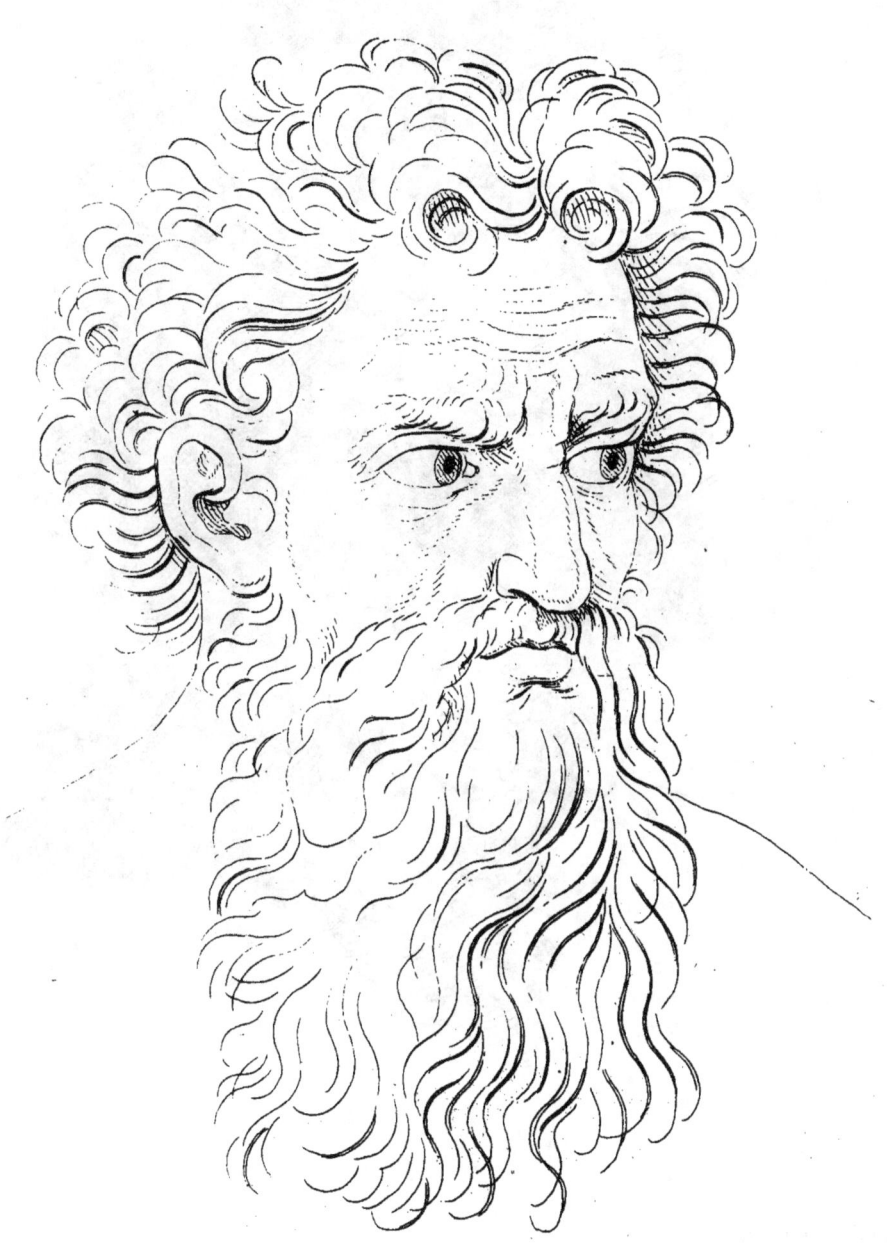

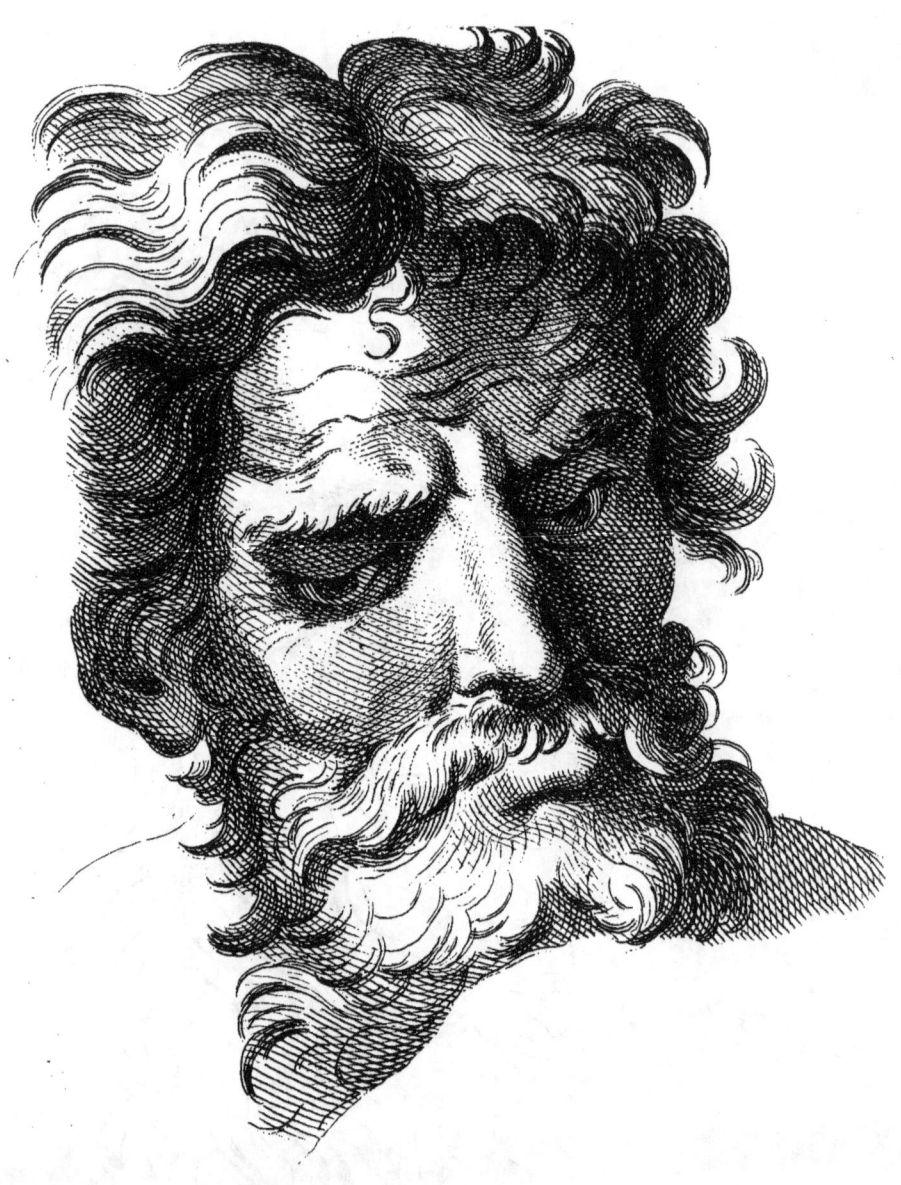

Raph . Vrb pinx .

Plate 12. I. - from Paul Preaching

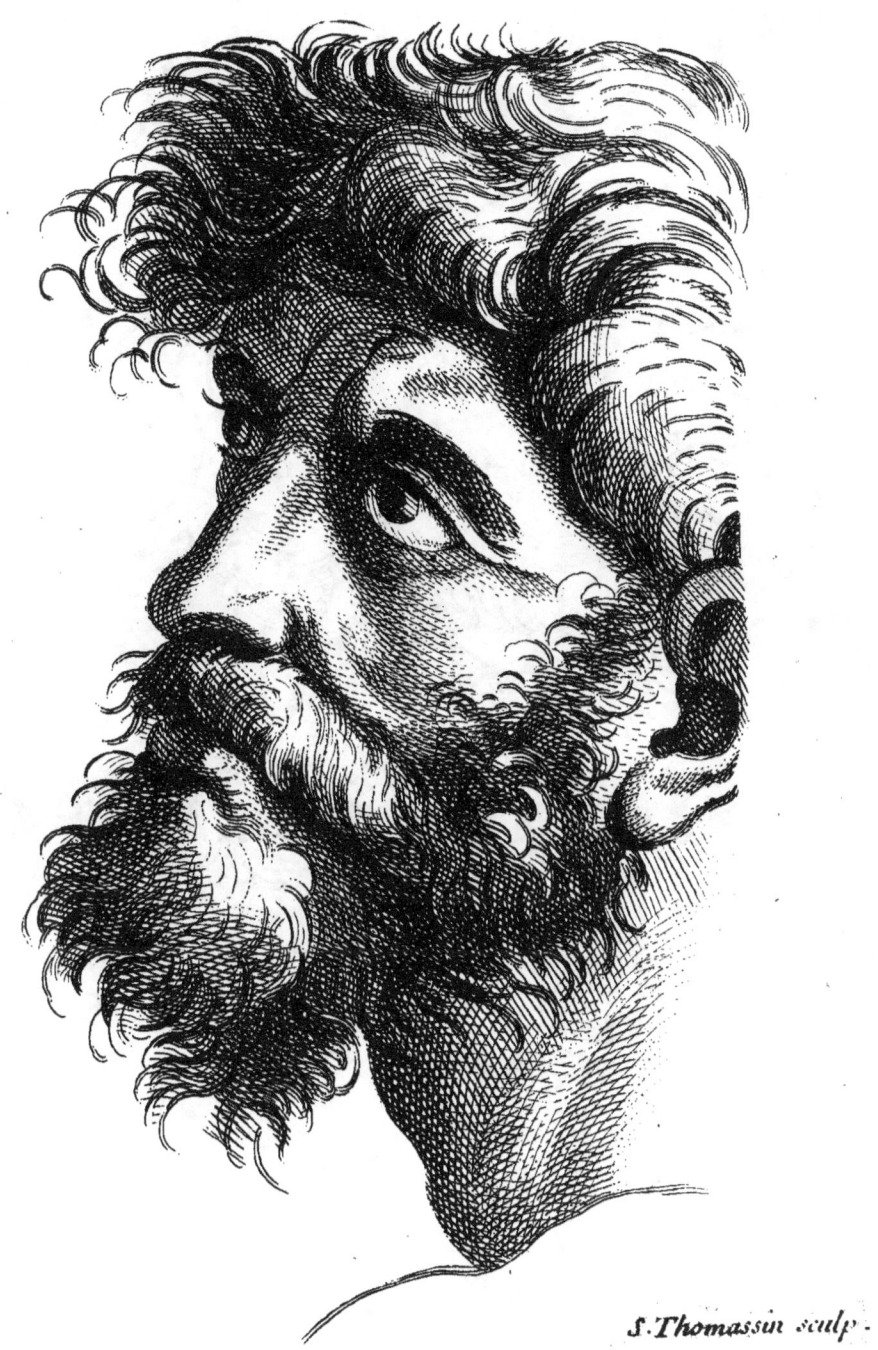

Plate 12. II - from Elymas the Sorcerer

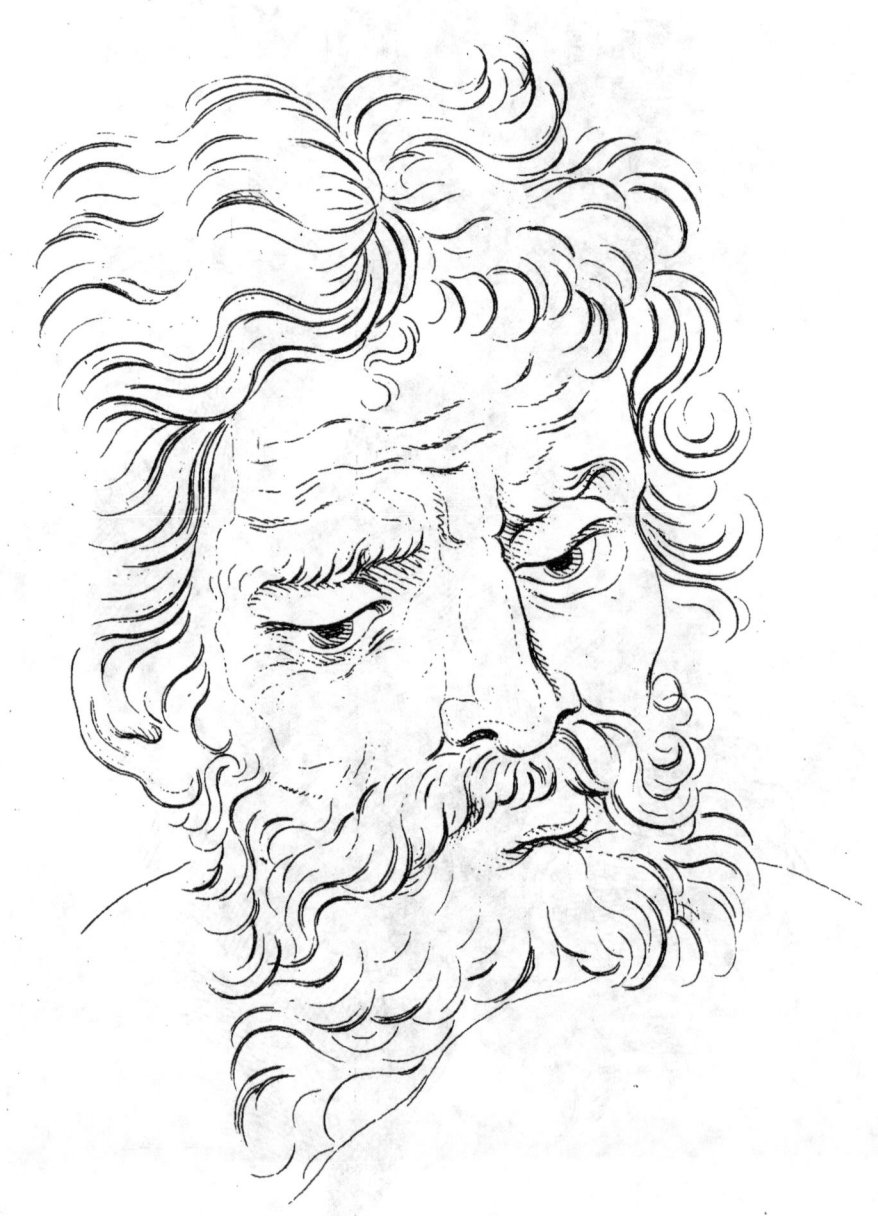

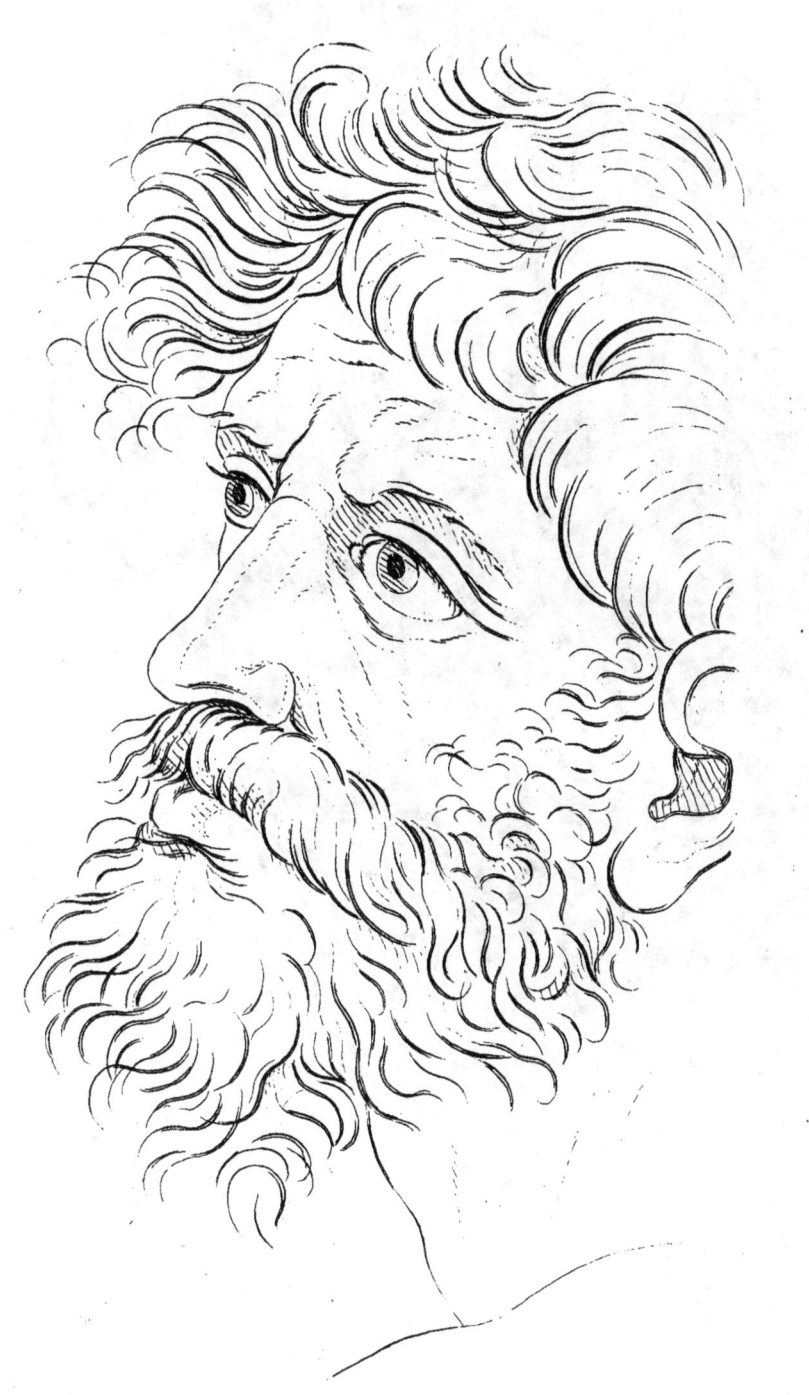

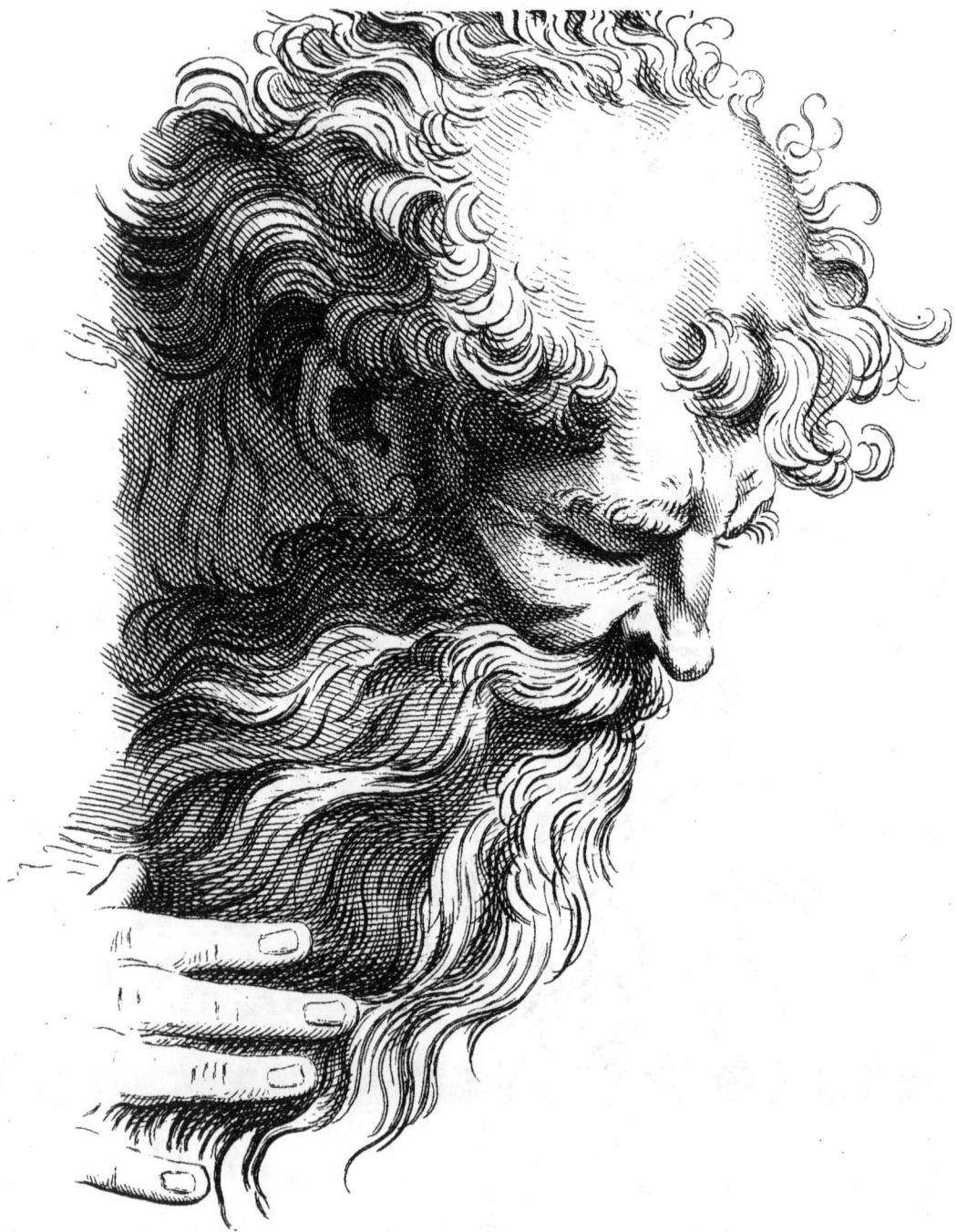

Raph . Vrb . pinx .

Plate 13. I. - from Paul and Barnabas

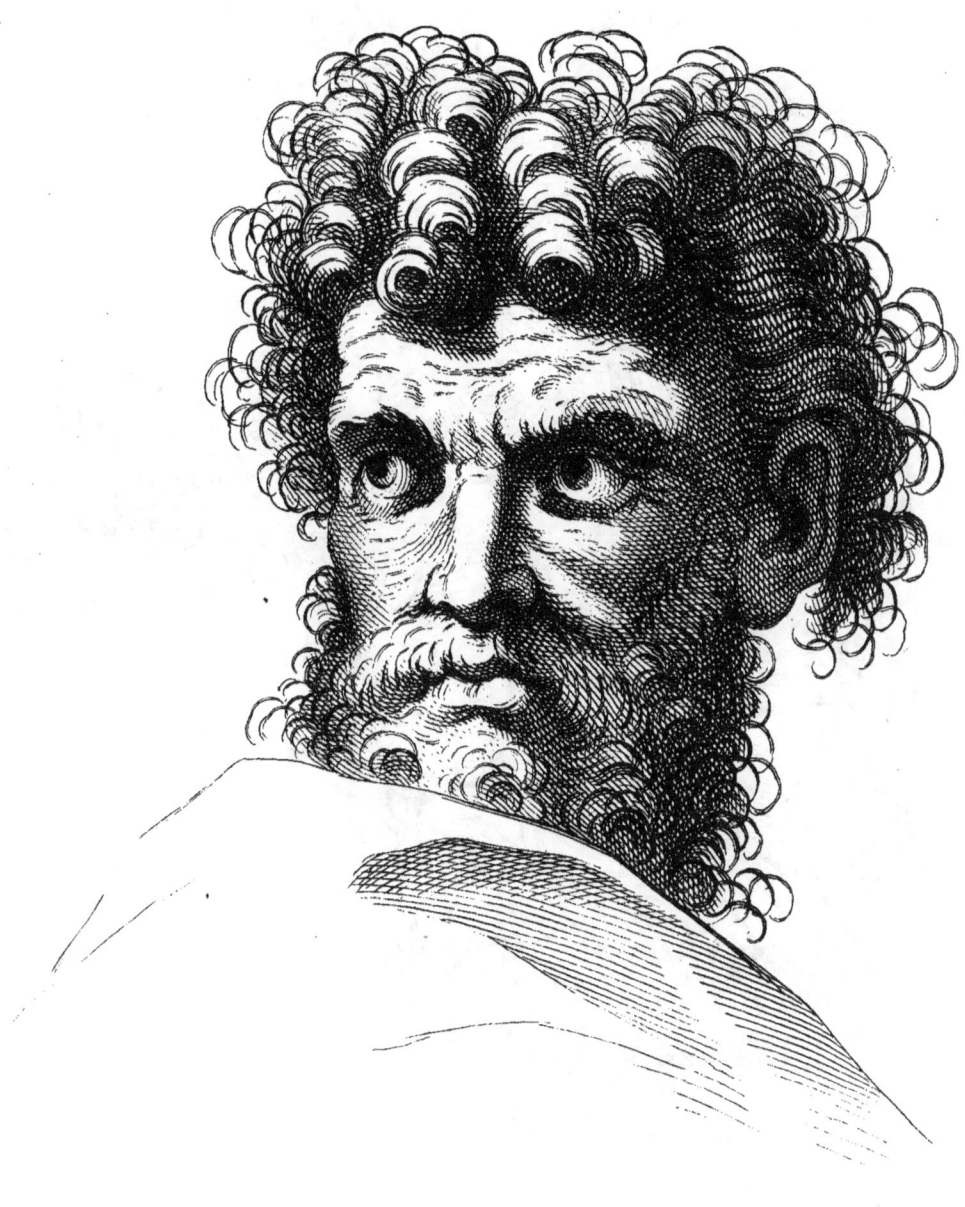

G. Duchange sculp.

Plate 13. II - from Christ's Charge to Peter

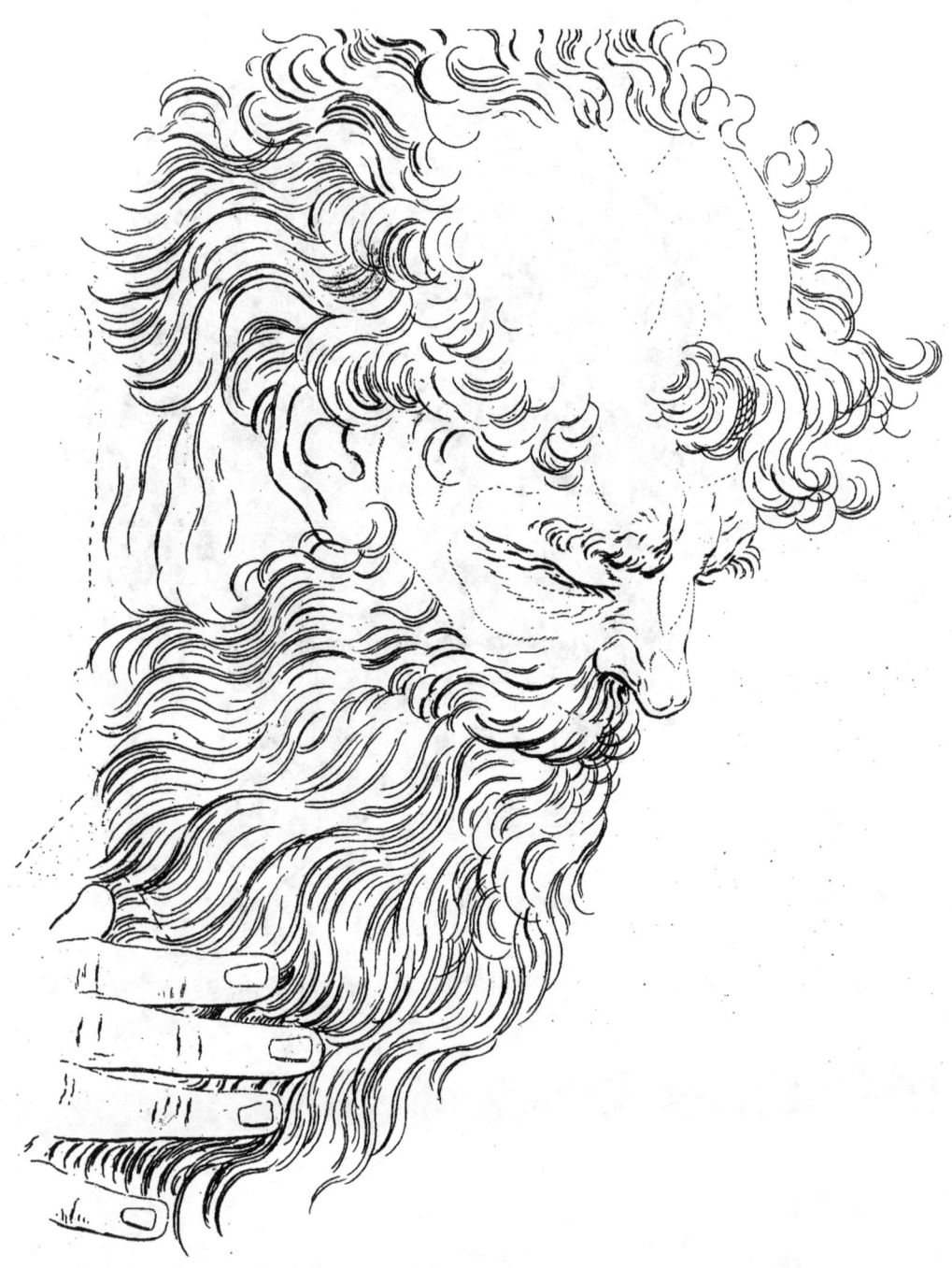

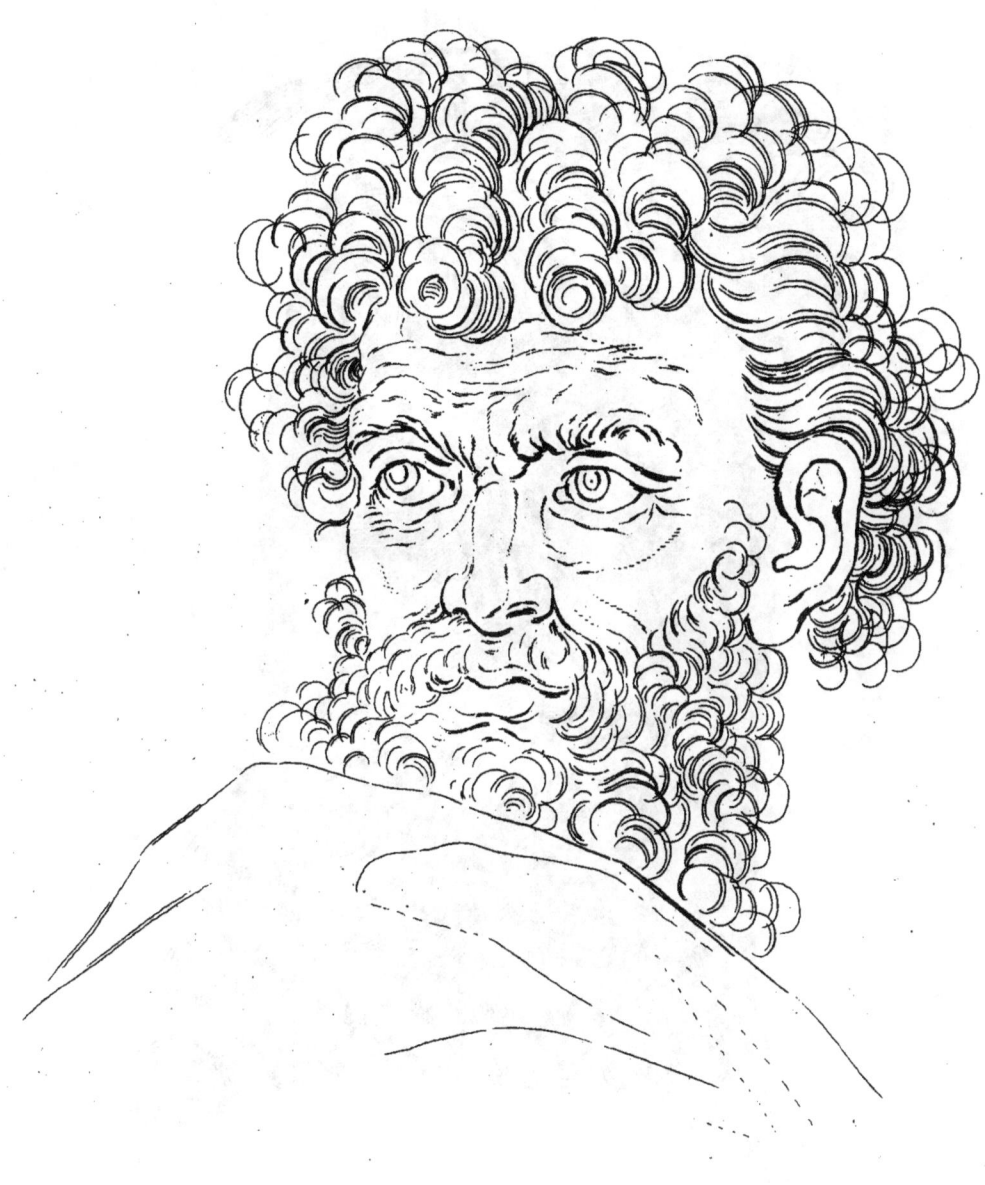

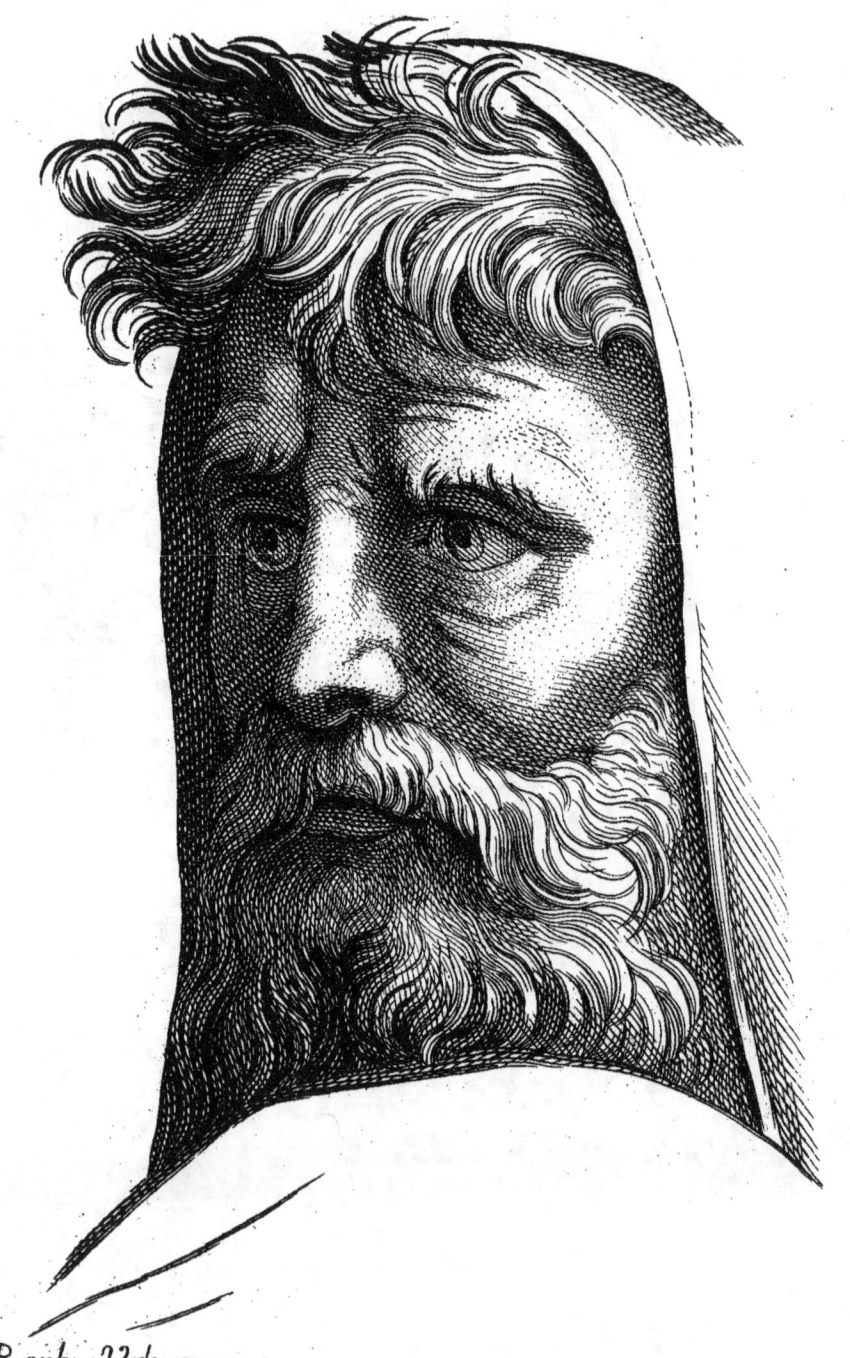

Plate 14. I. - from Elymas the Sorcerer

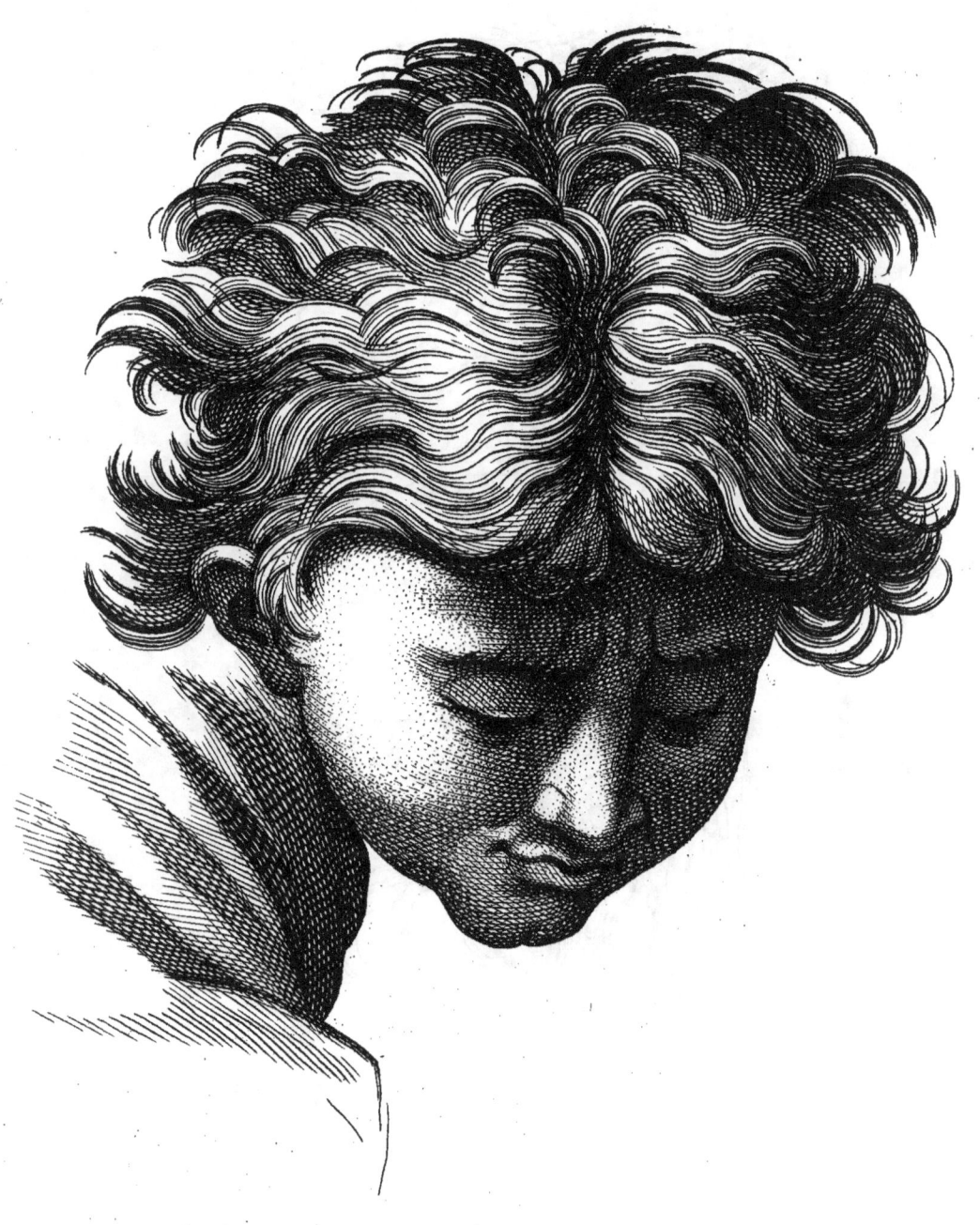

N? Pigné. Sculp.

Plate 14. II. - from The Death of Ananias

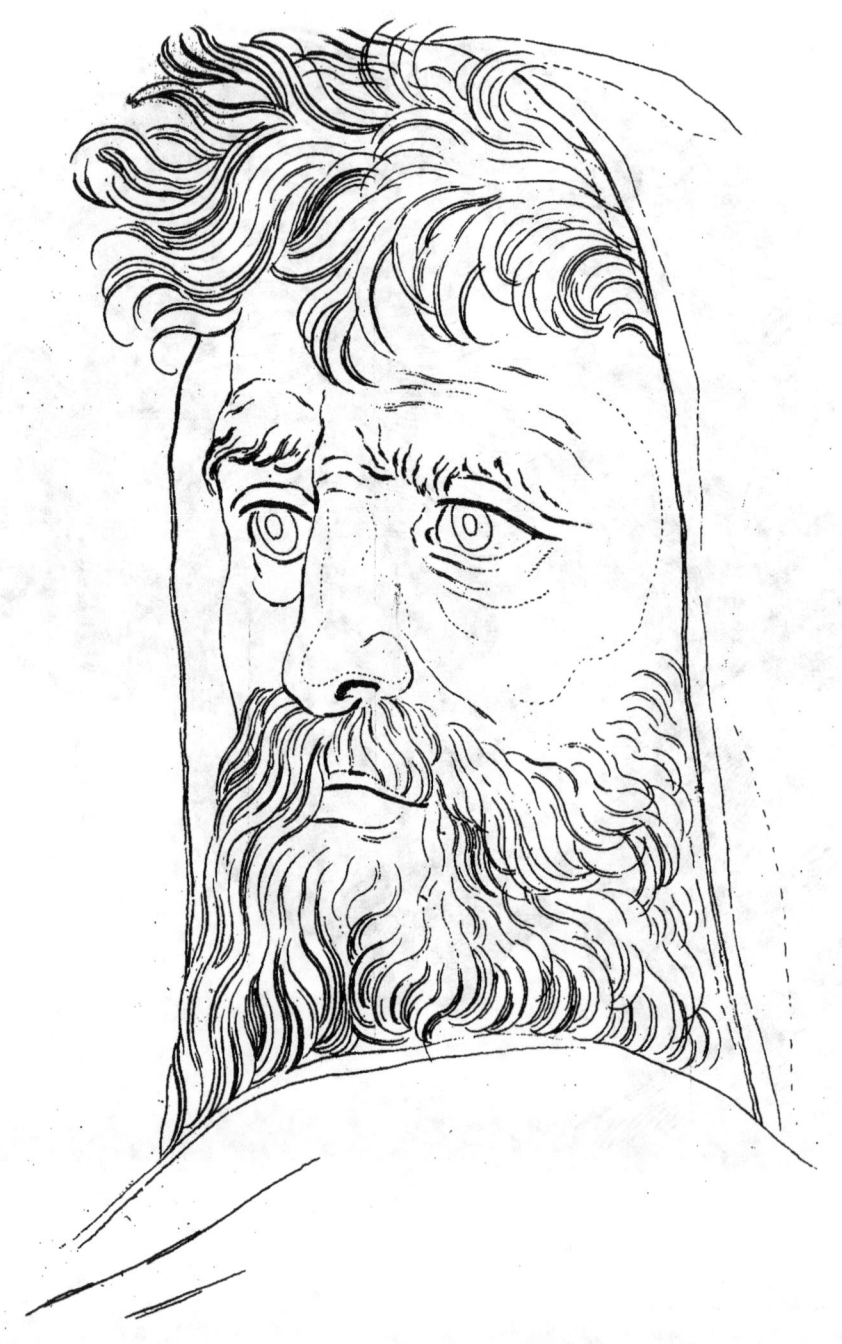

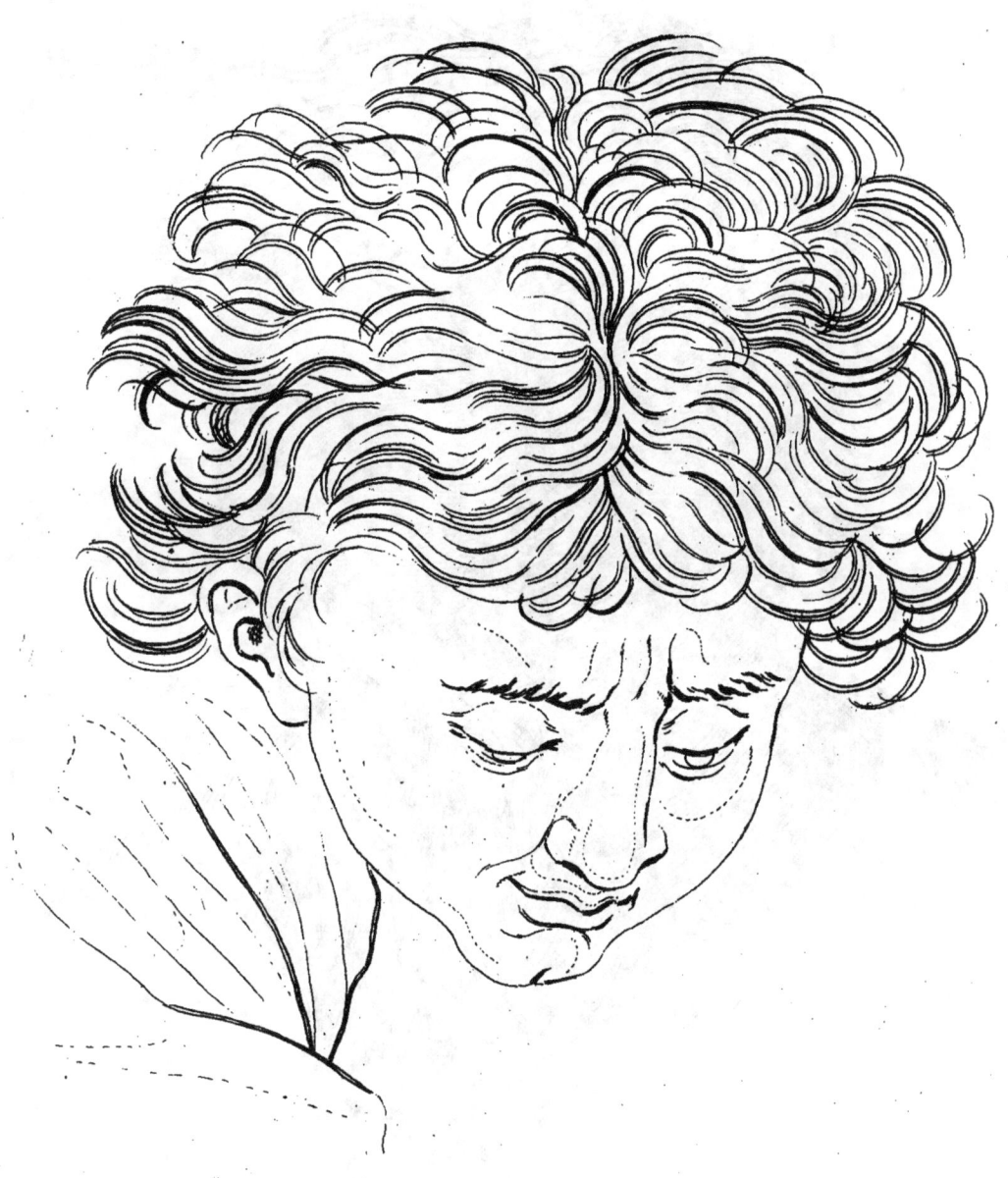

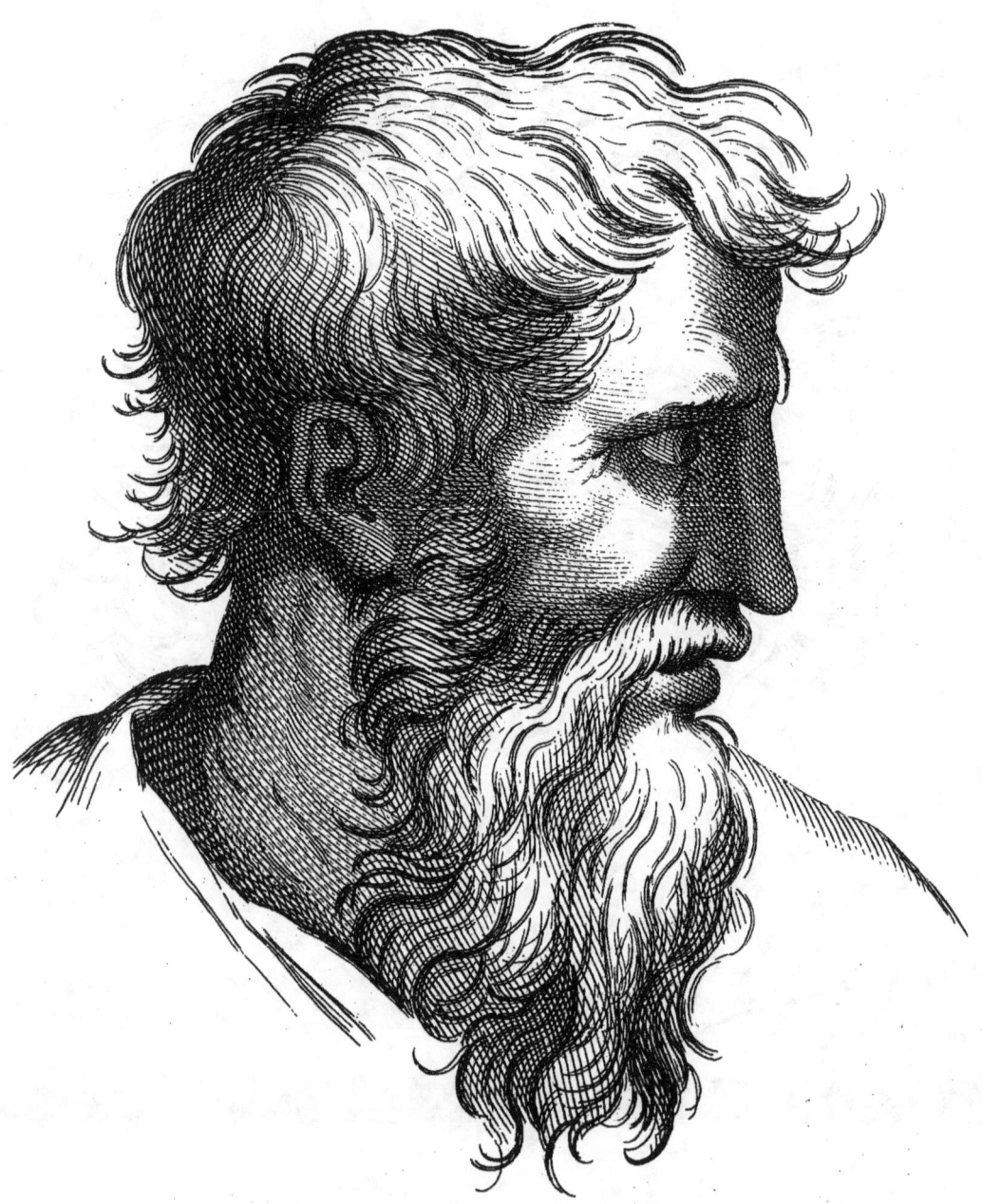

R'aph. Vrb. pinx .

Plate 15. I. - from Paul Preaching

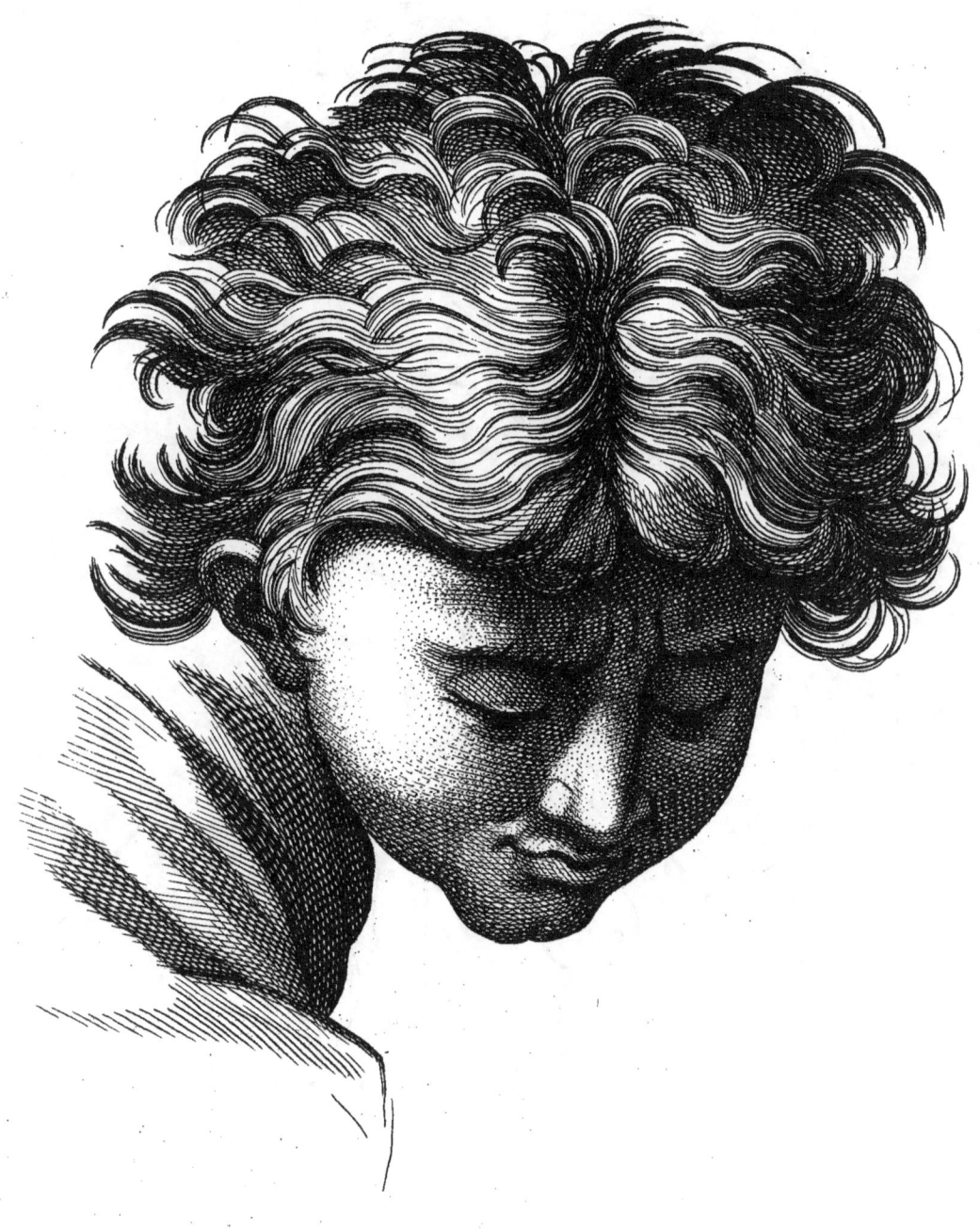

N. Pigné. Sculp.

Plate 15. II. - fromThe Lame Man Healed

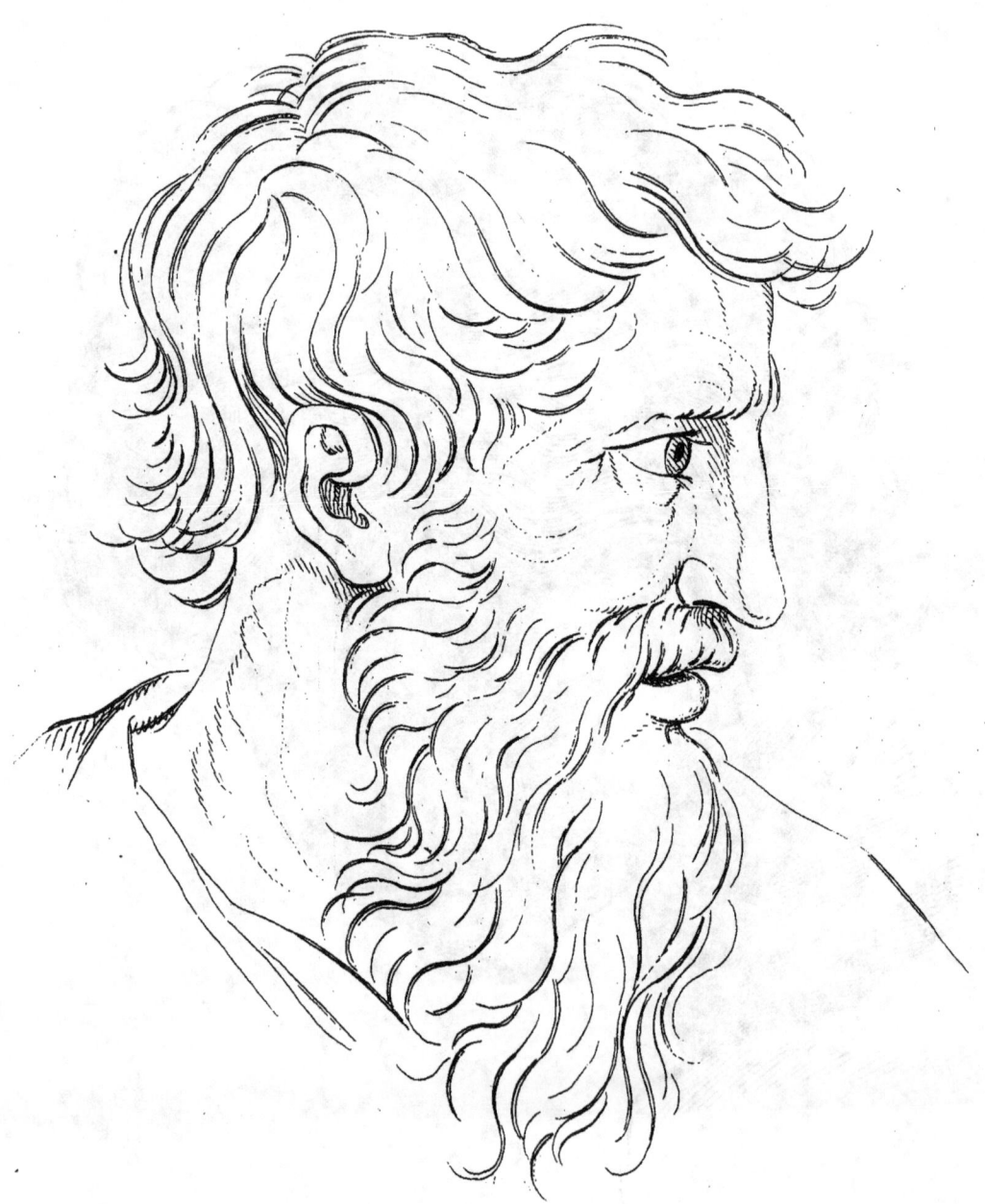

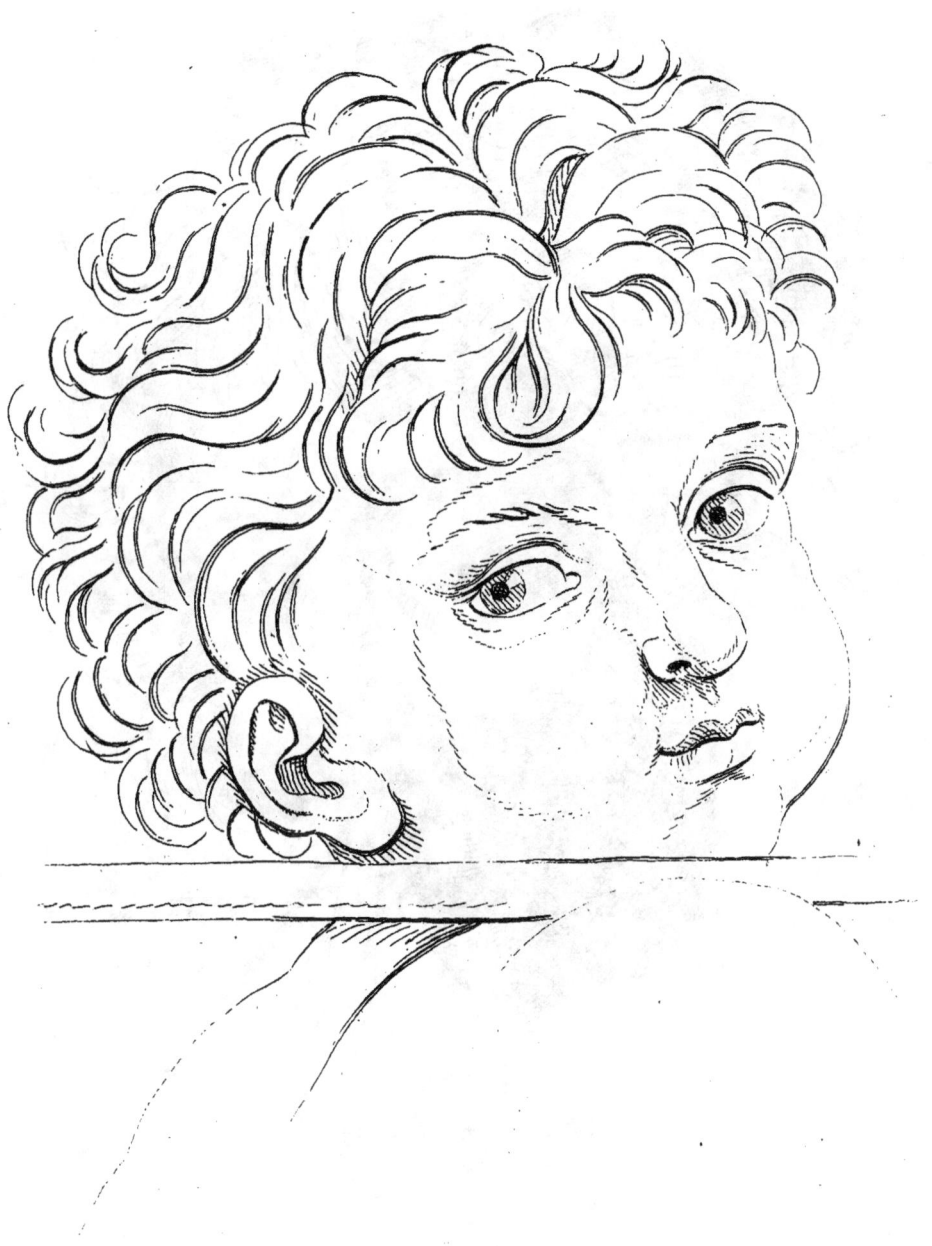

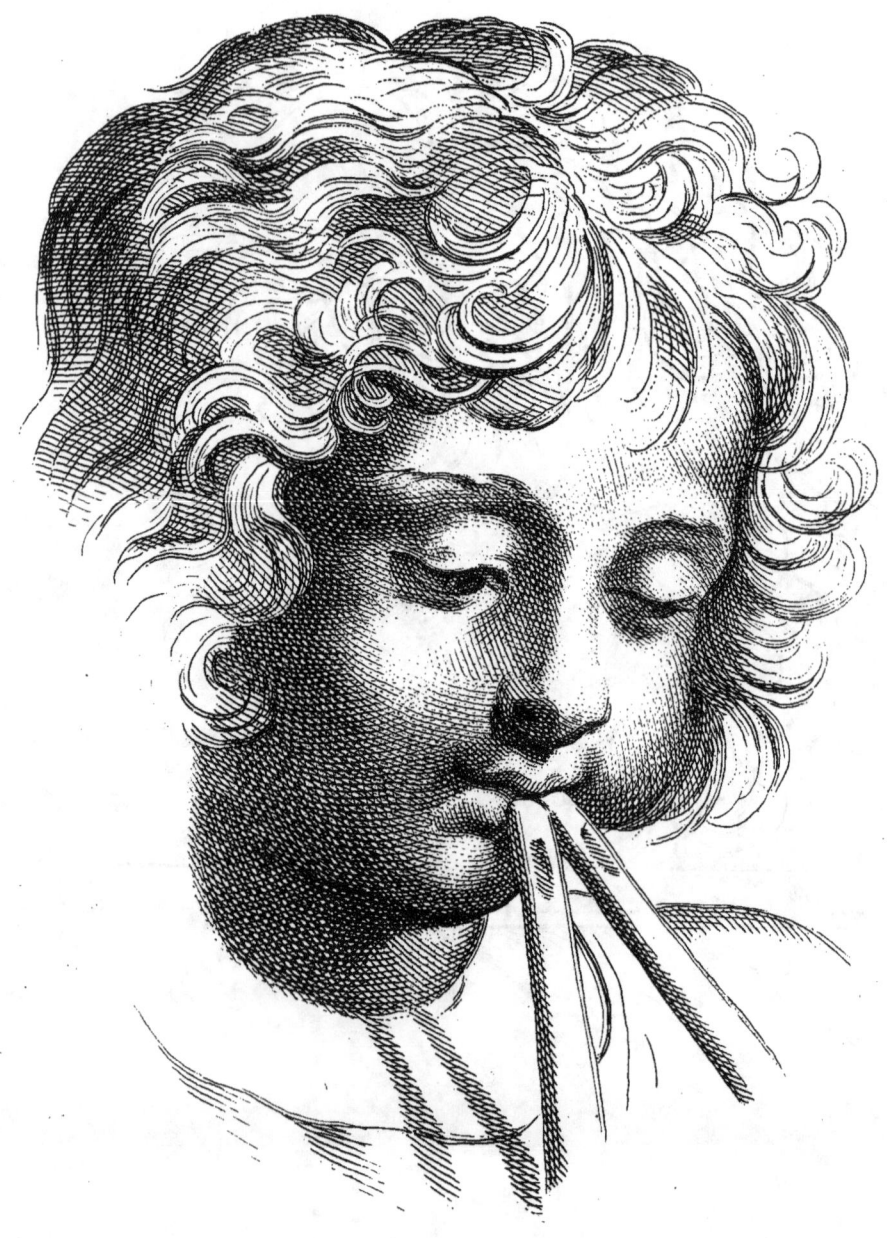

Raph . Vrb . pinx

Plat 16. I. - from Paul and Barnabas

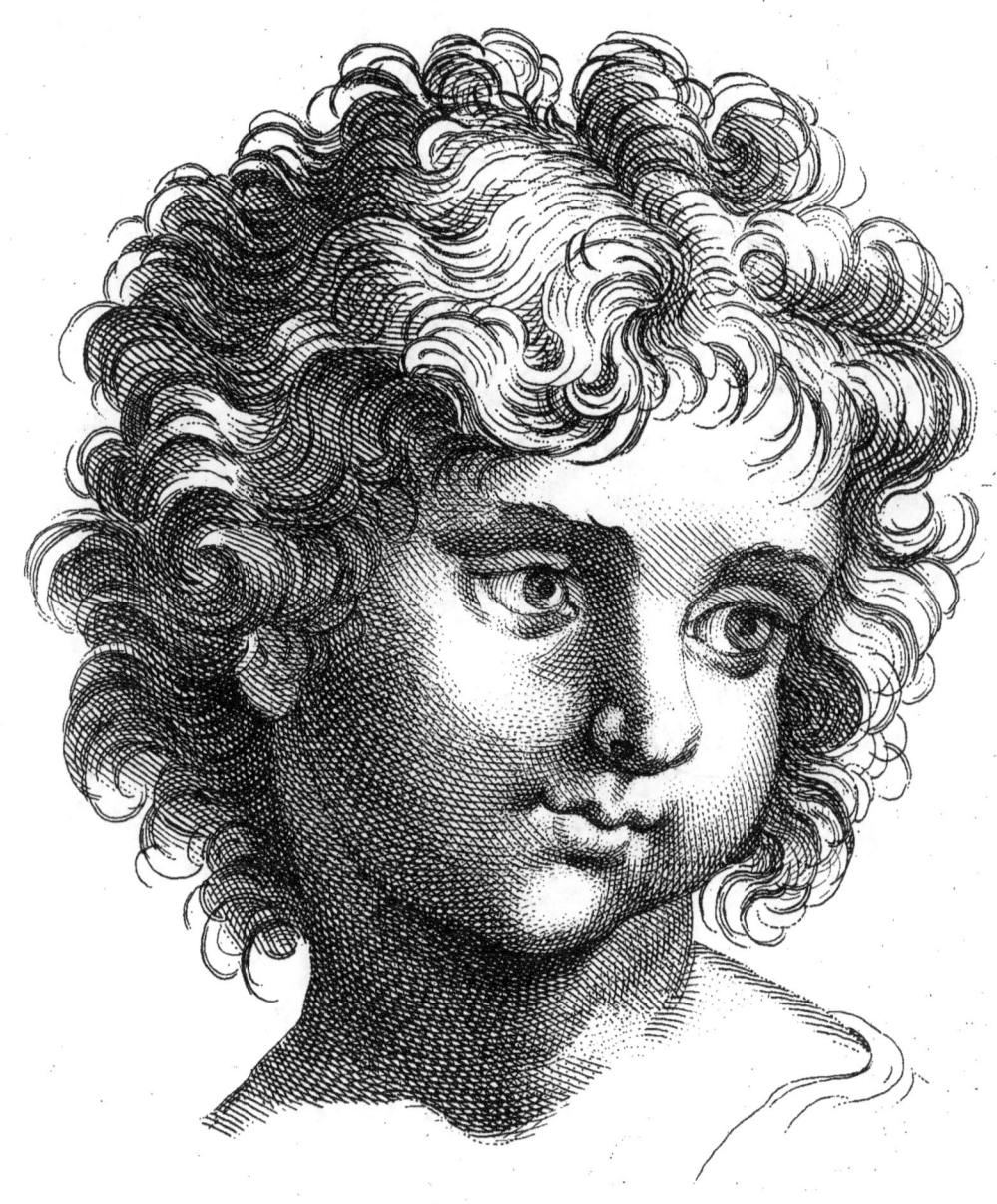

S.Thomassin sculp.

Plate 16. II. - from Paul and Barnabus

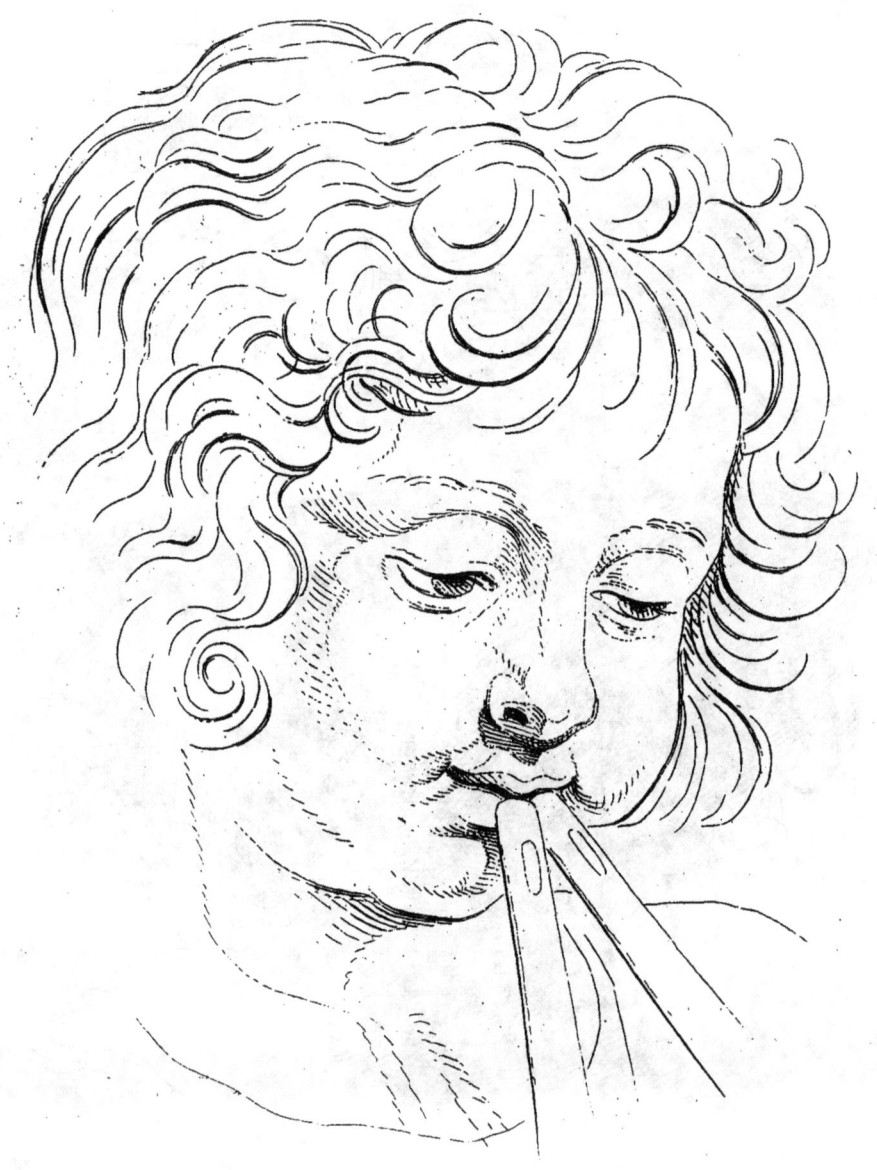

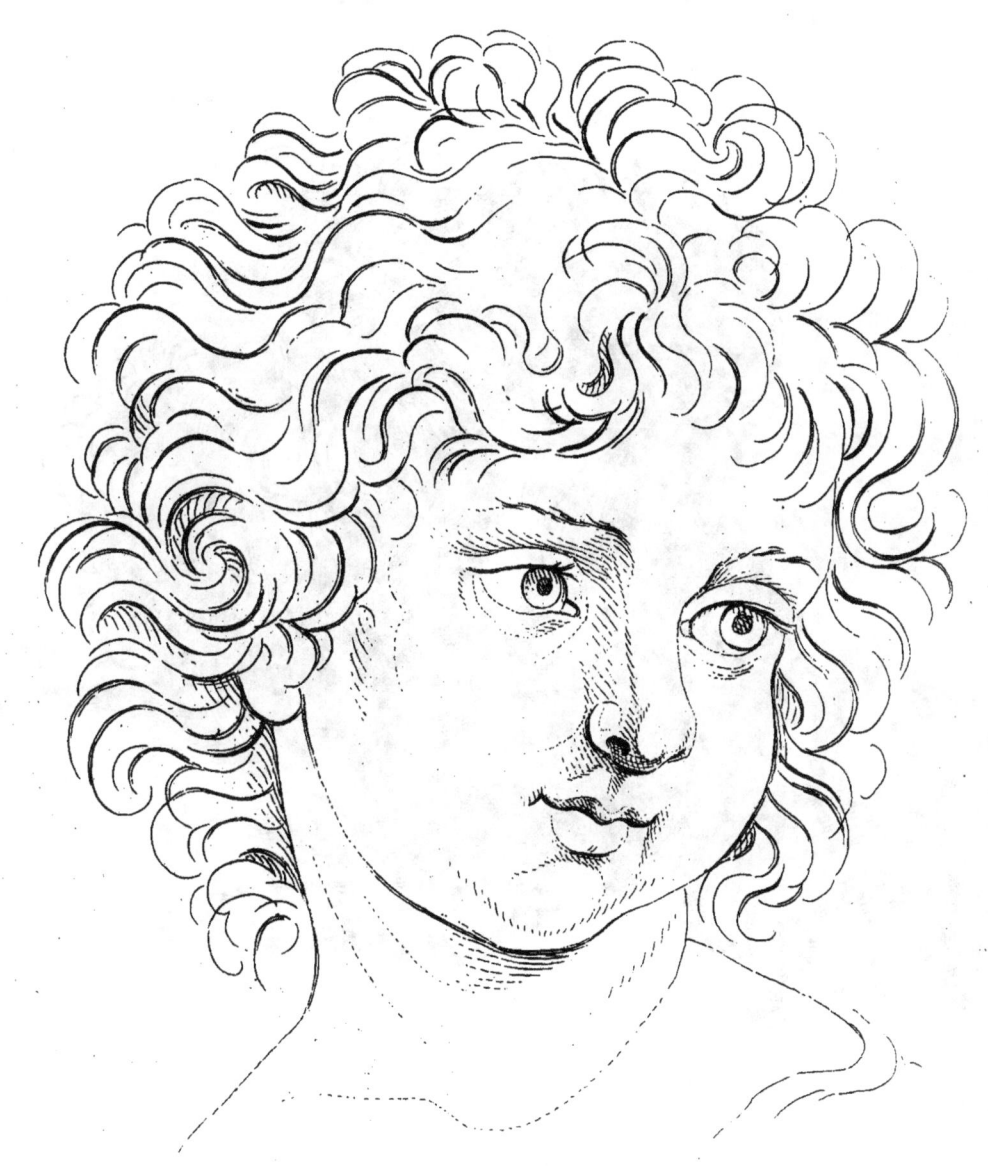

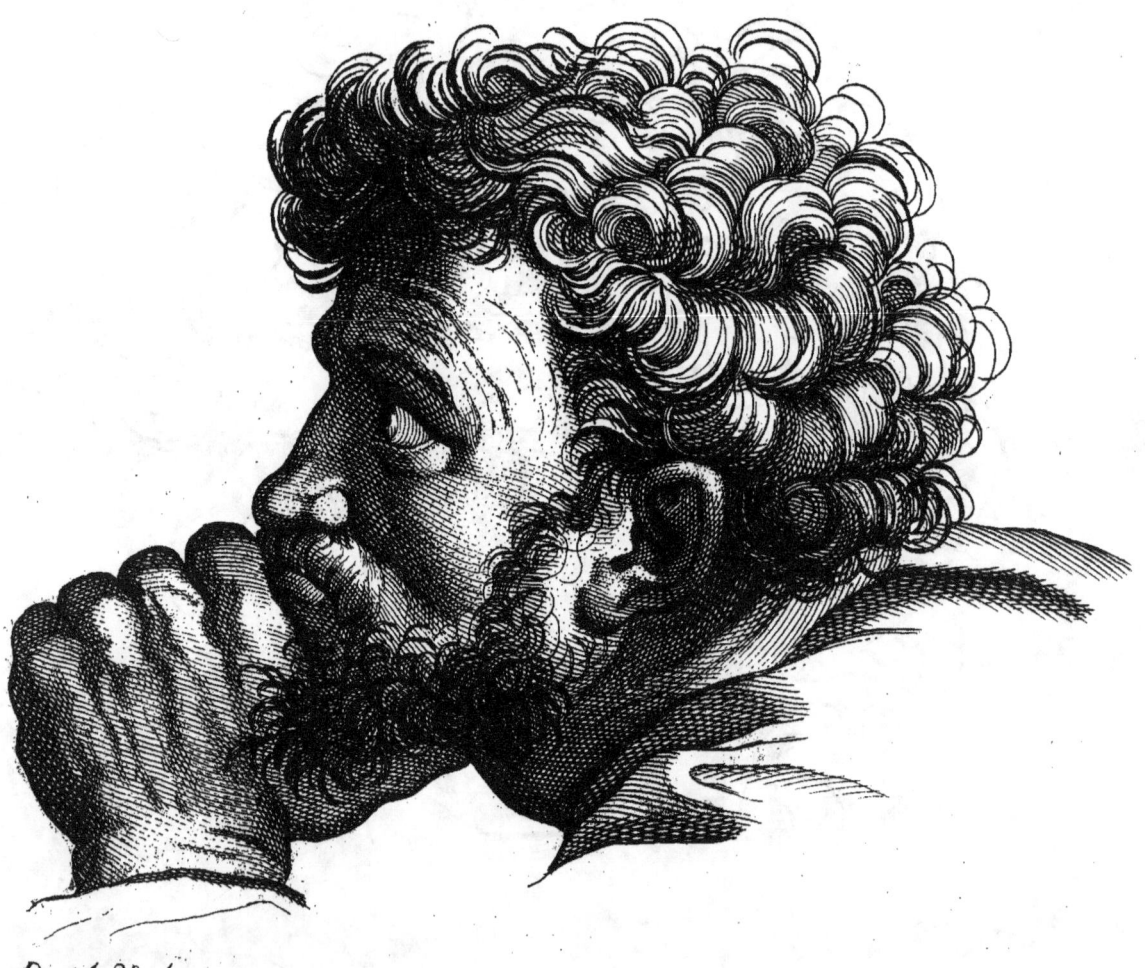

Raph. Urb. pin.

Plate 17. I. - from The Lame Man Healed

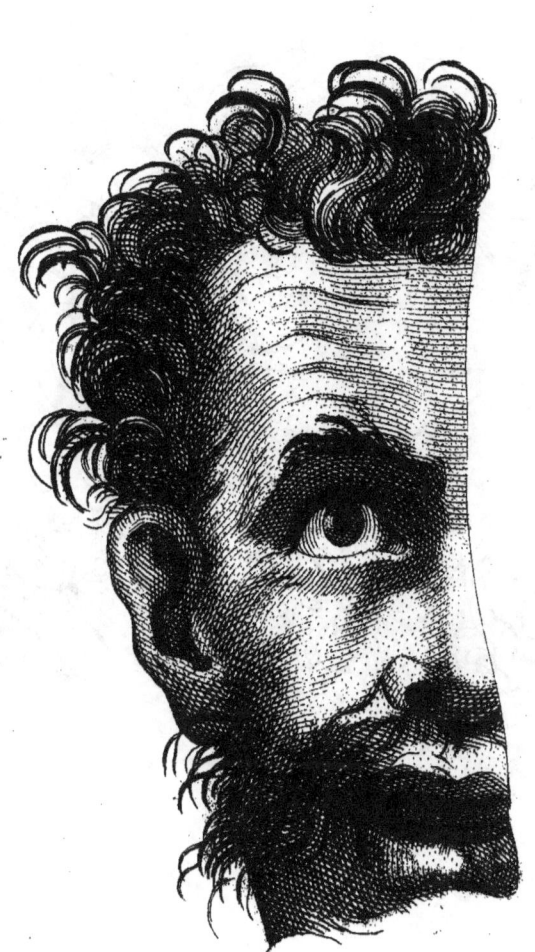

N. Pigne. Sculp.

Plate 17. II. - from The Lame Man Healed

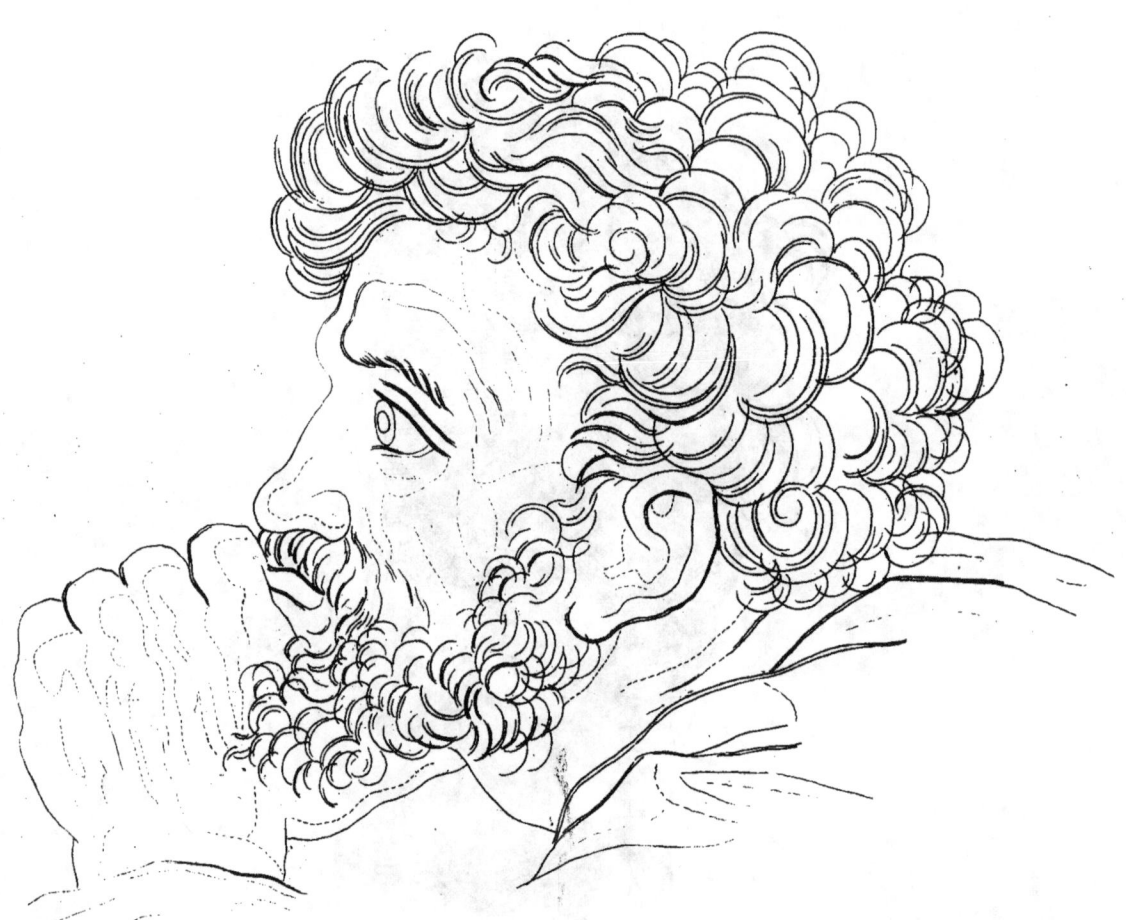

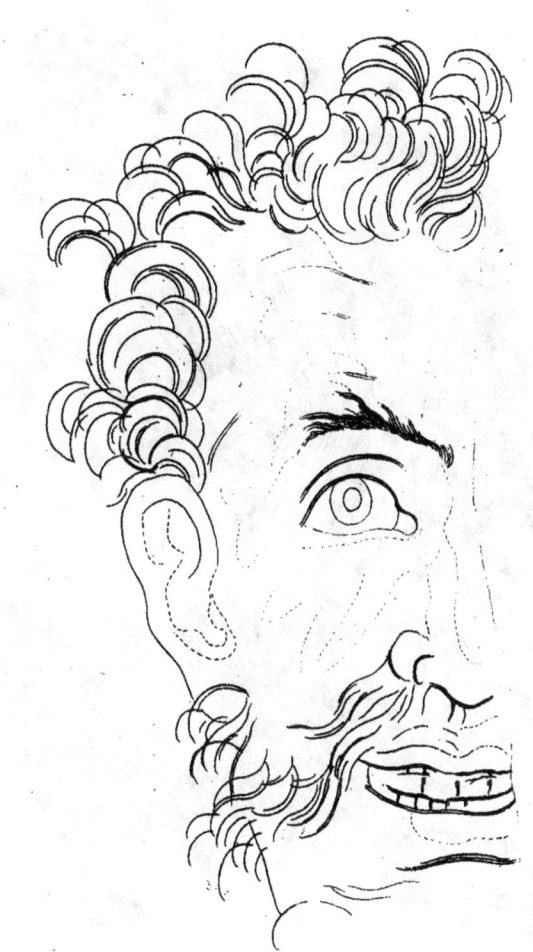

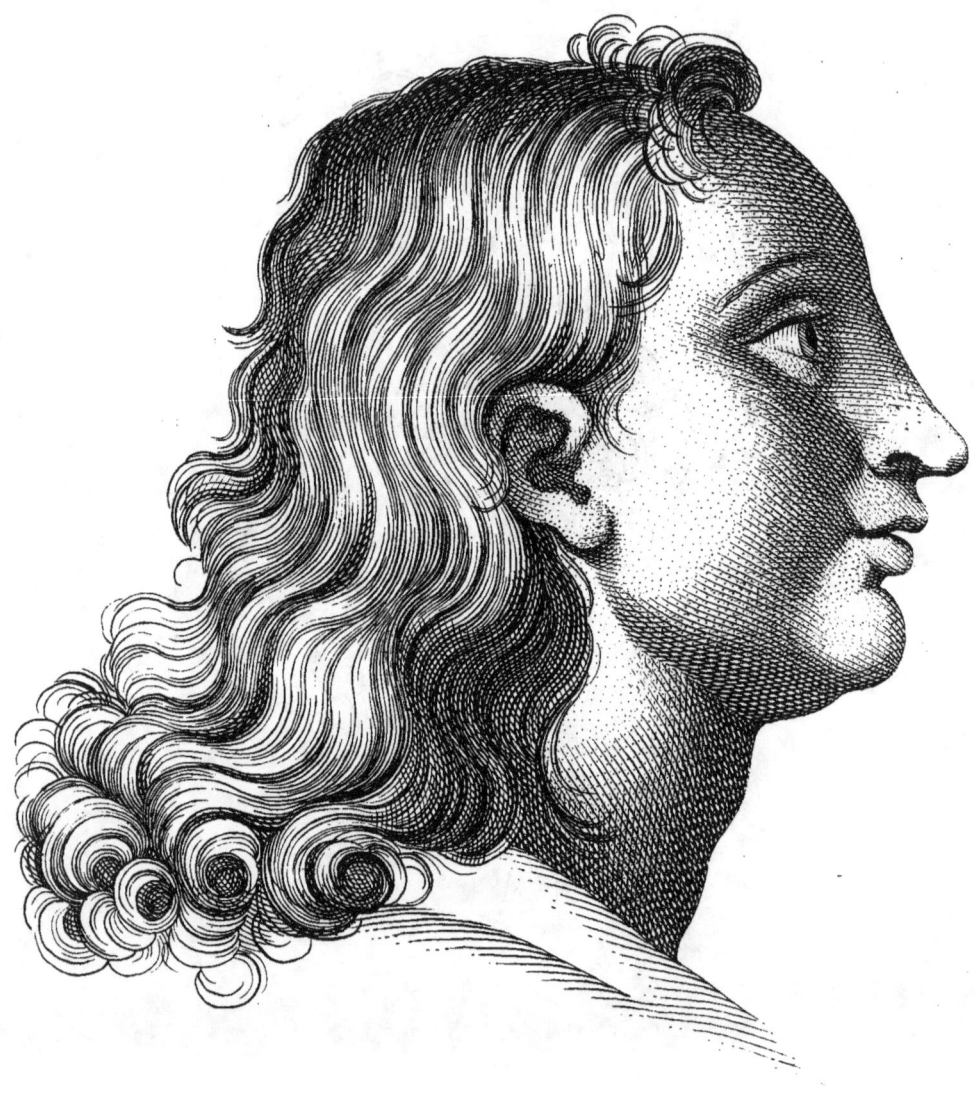

Raph . Vrb pinx .

Plate 18. I. - from Christ's Charge to Peter

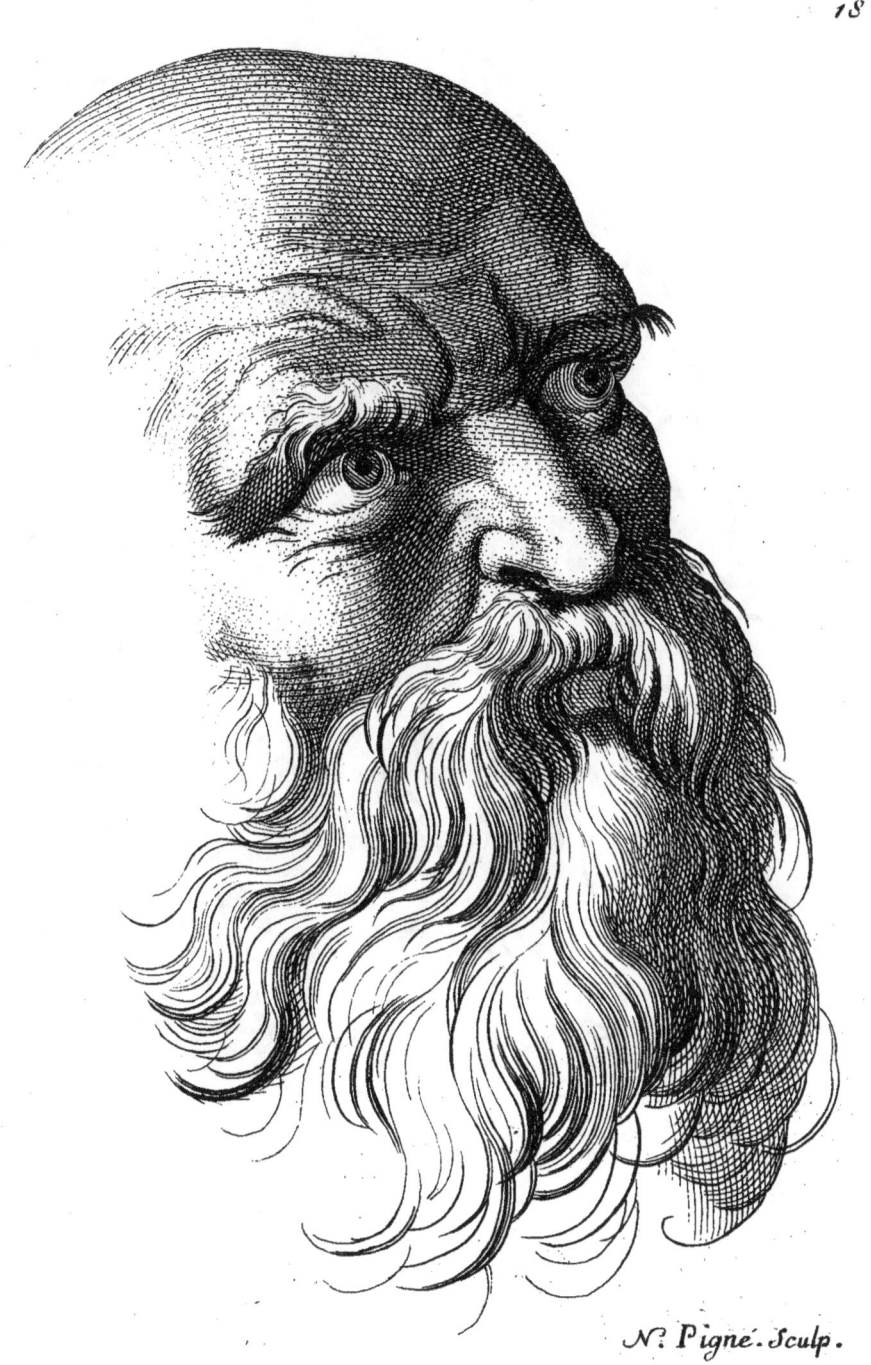

18

N. Pigné. Sculp.

Plate 18. II. - from Christ's Charge to Peter

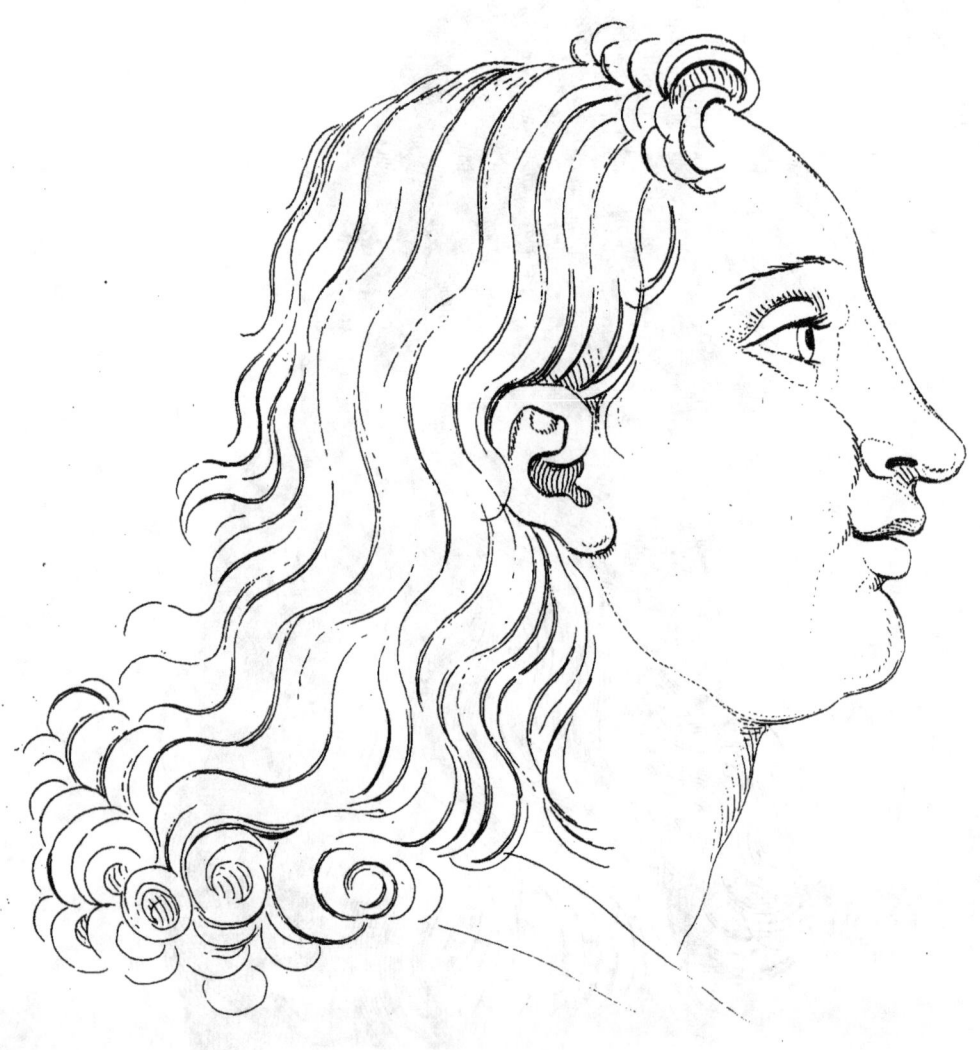

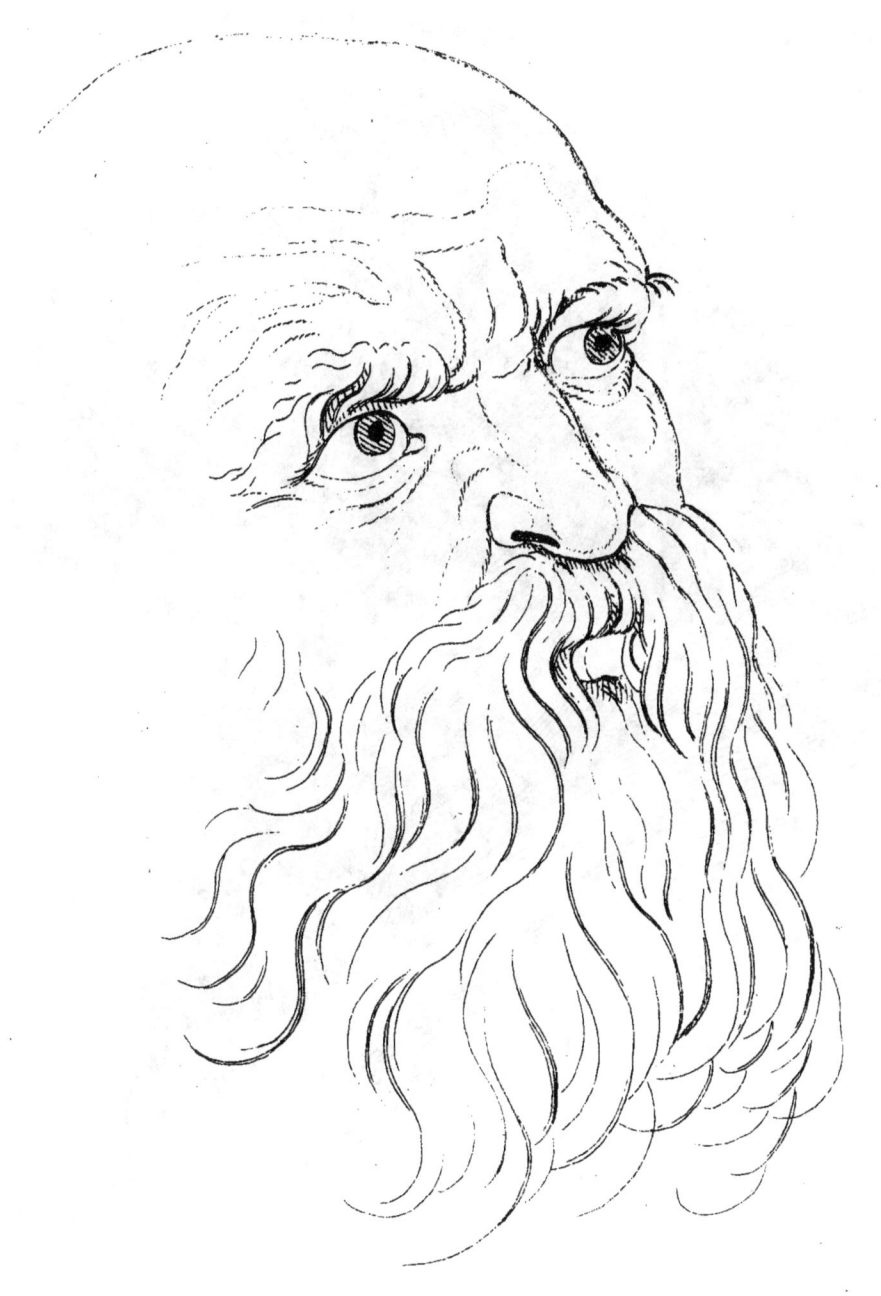

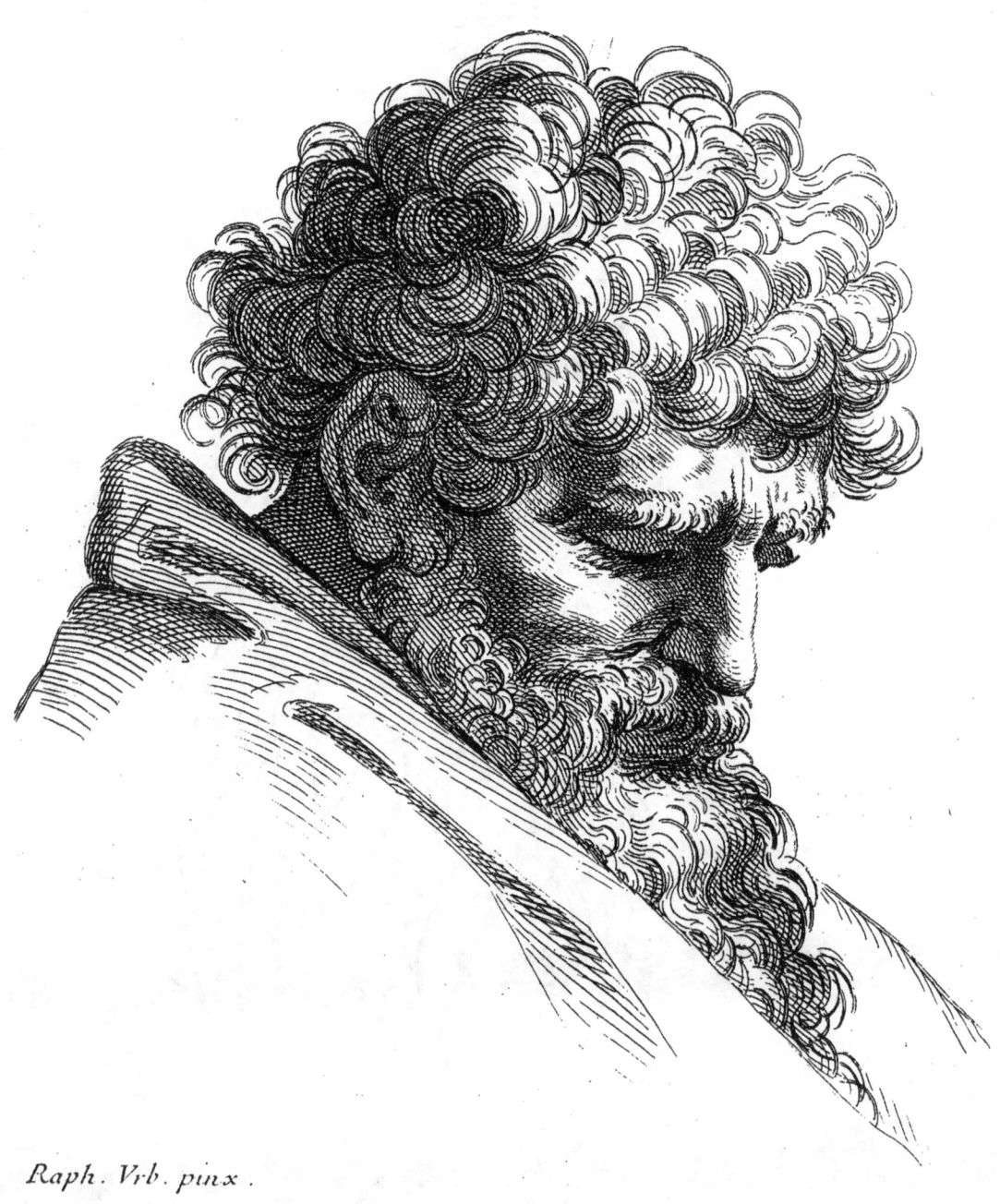

Raph . Vrb . pinx .

Plate 19. I. - from Paul Preaching

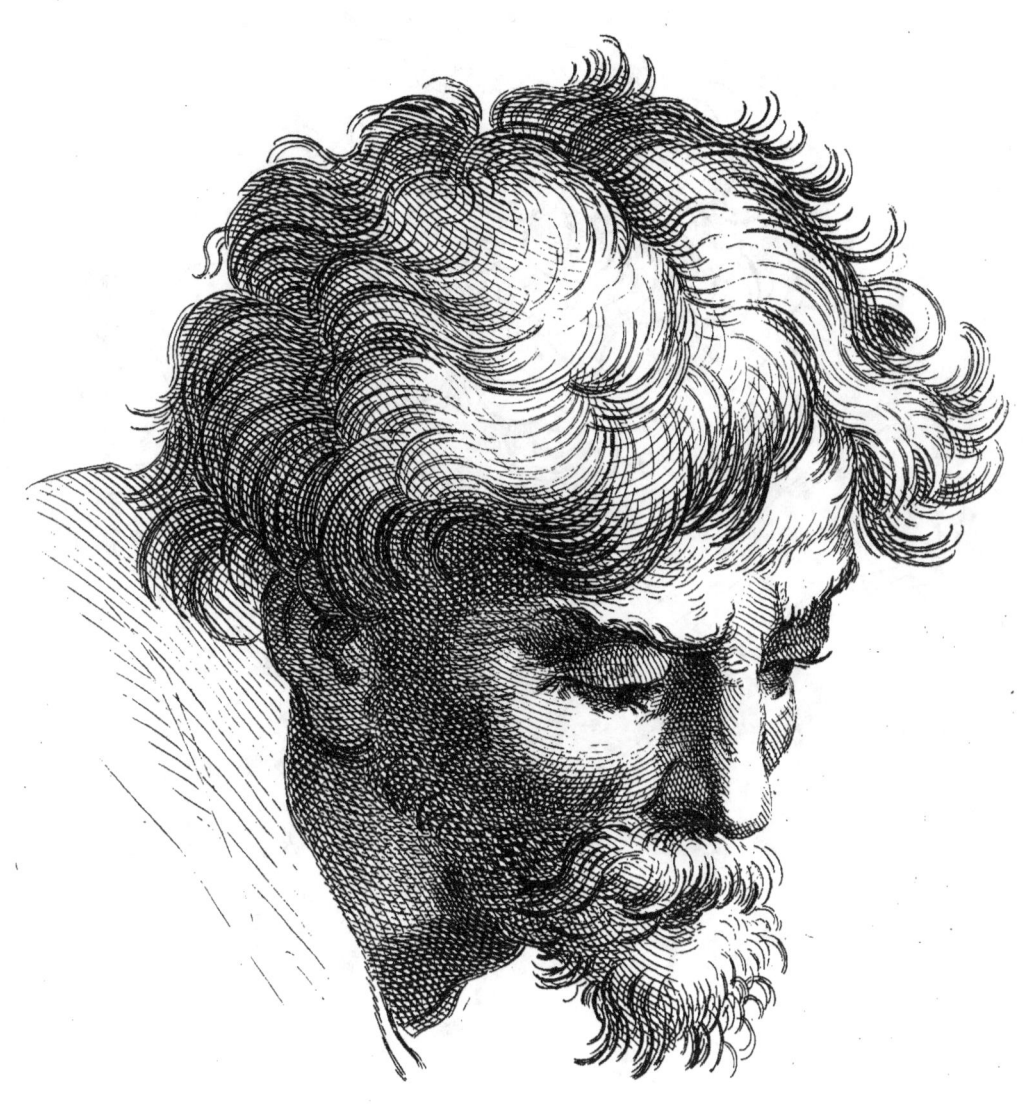

L. Desplaces scul.

Plate 19. II. - from Paul and Barnabus

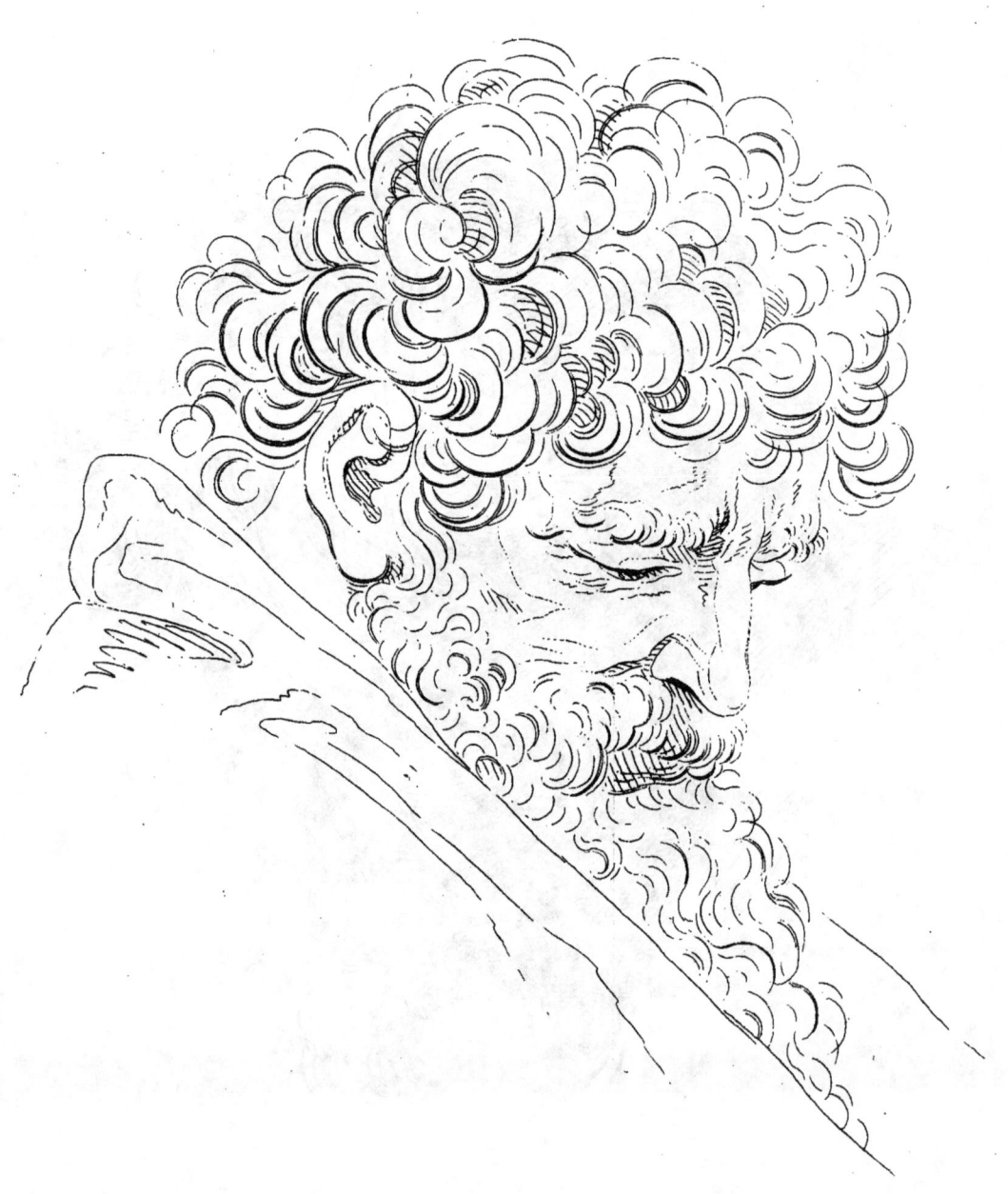

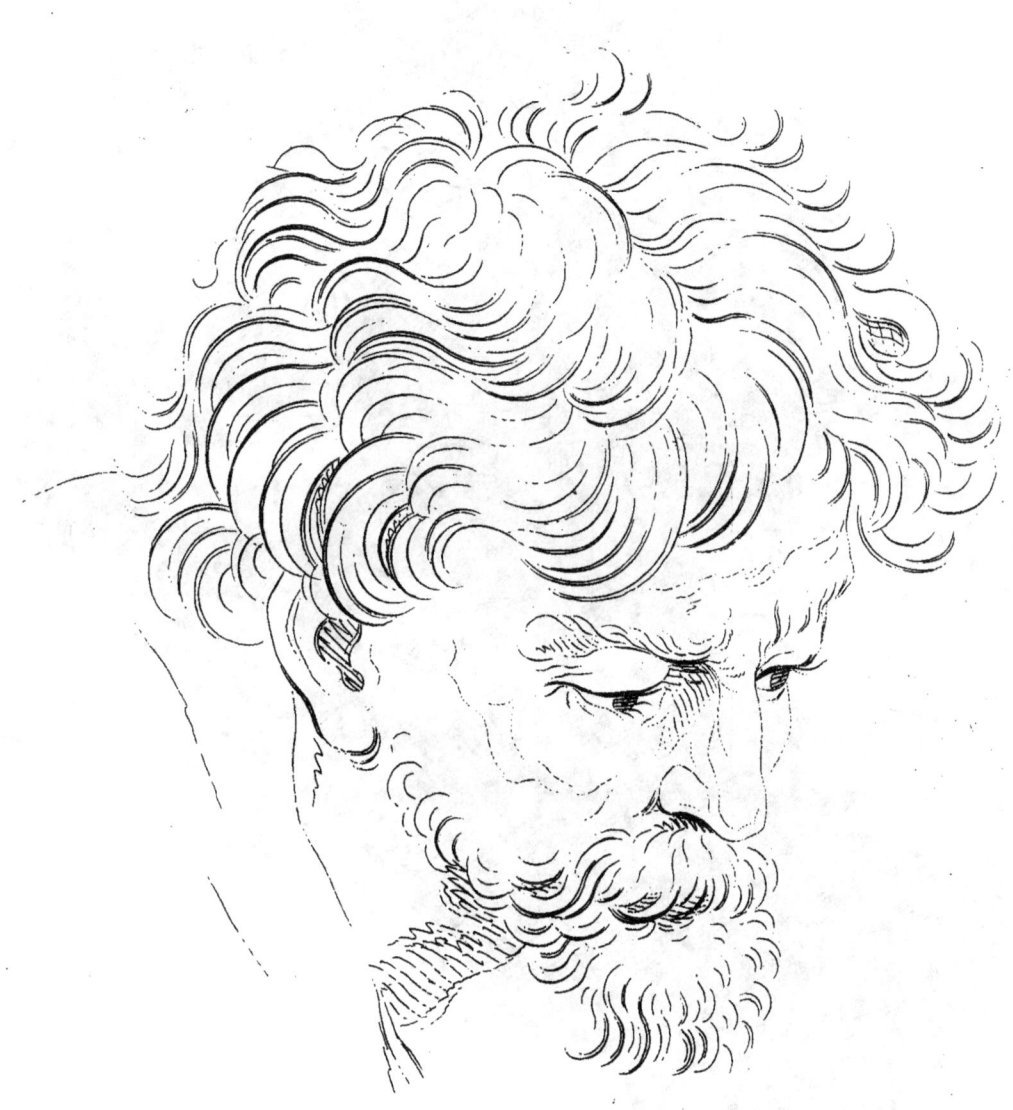

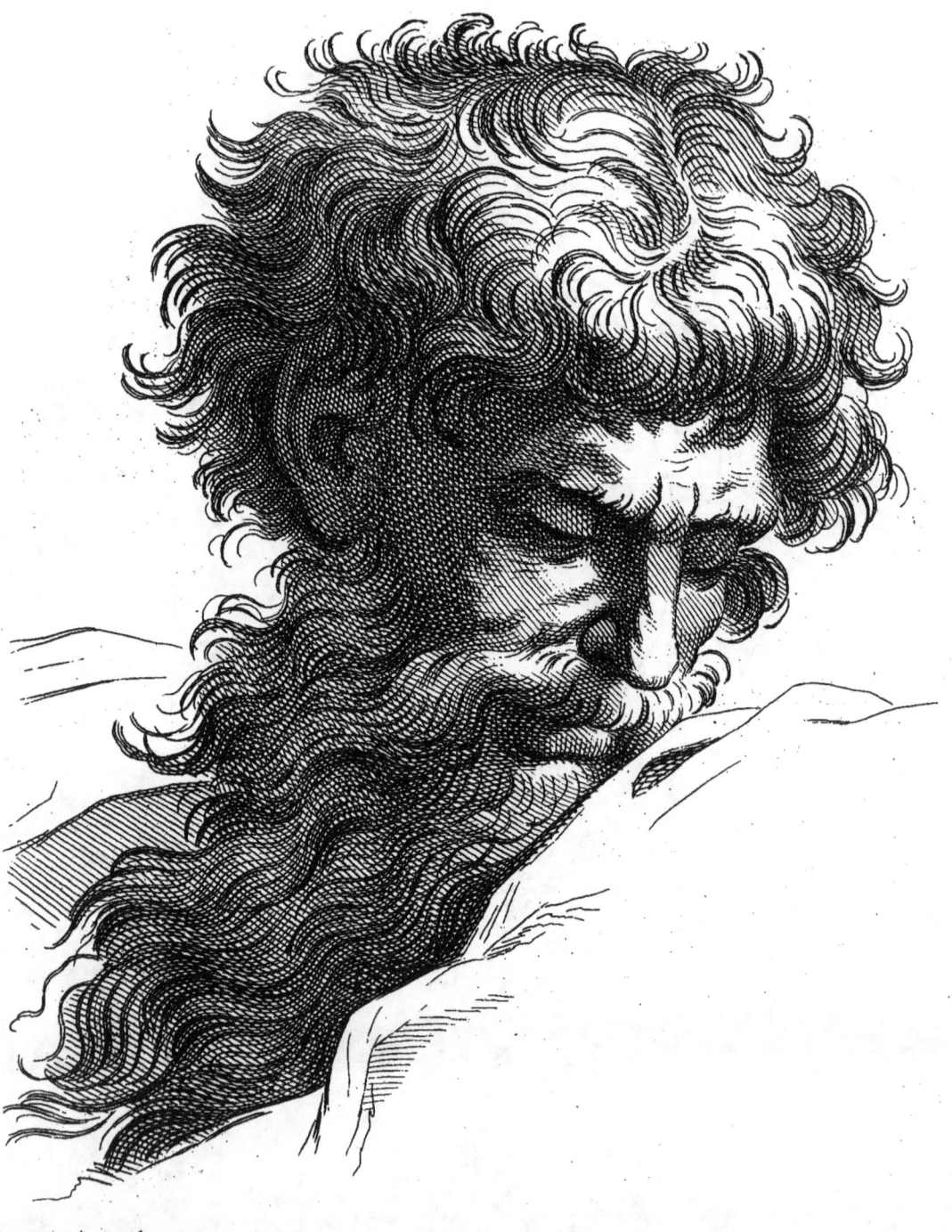

Raph. Vrb. pinx .

Plate 20. I. - from Paul and Barnabus

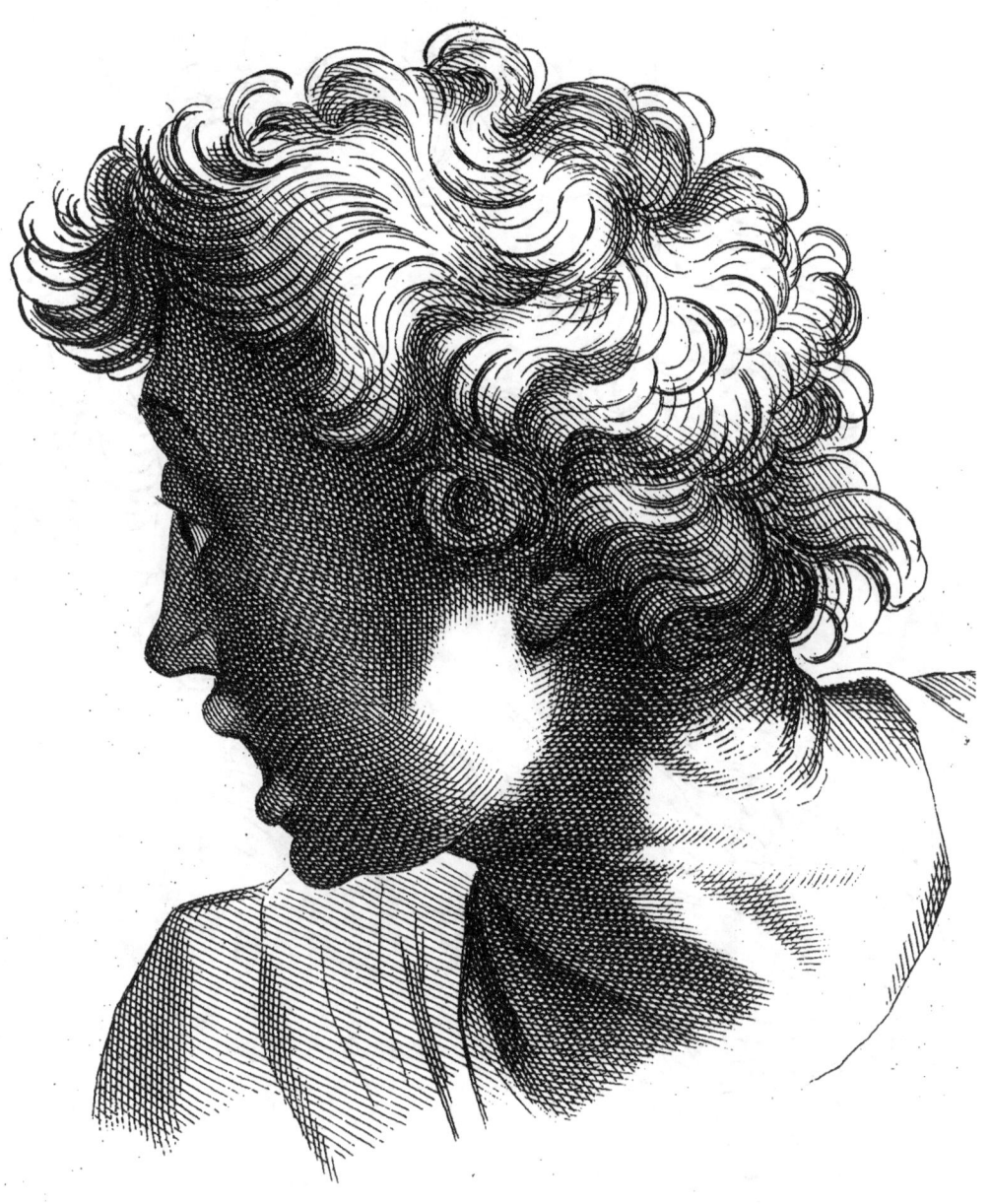

G. Duchange scul.

Plate 20. II. - from Paul Preaching at Athens

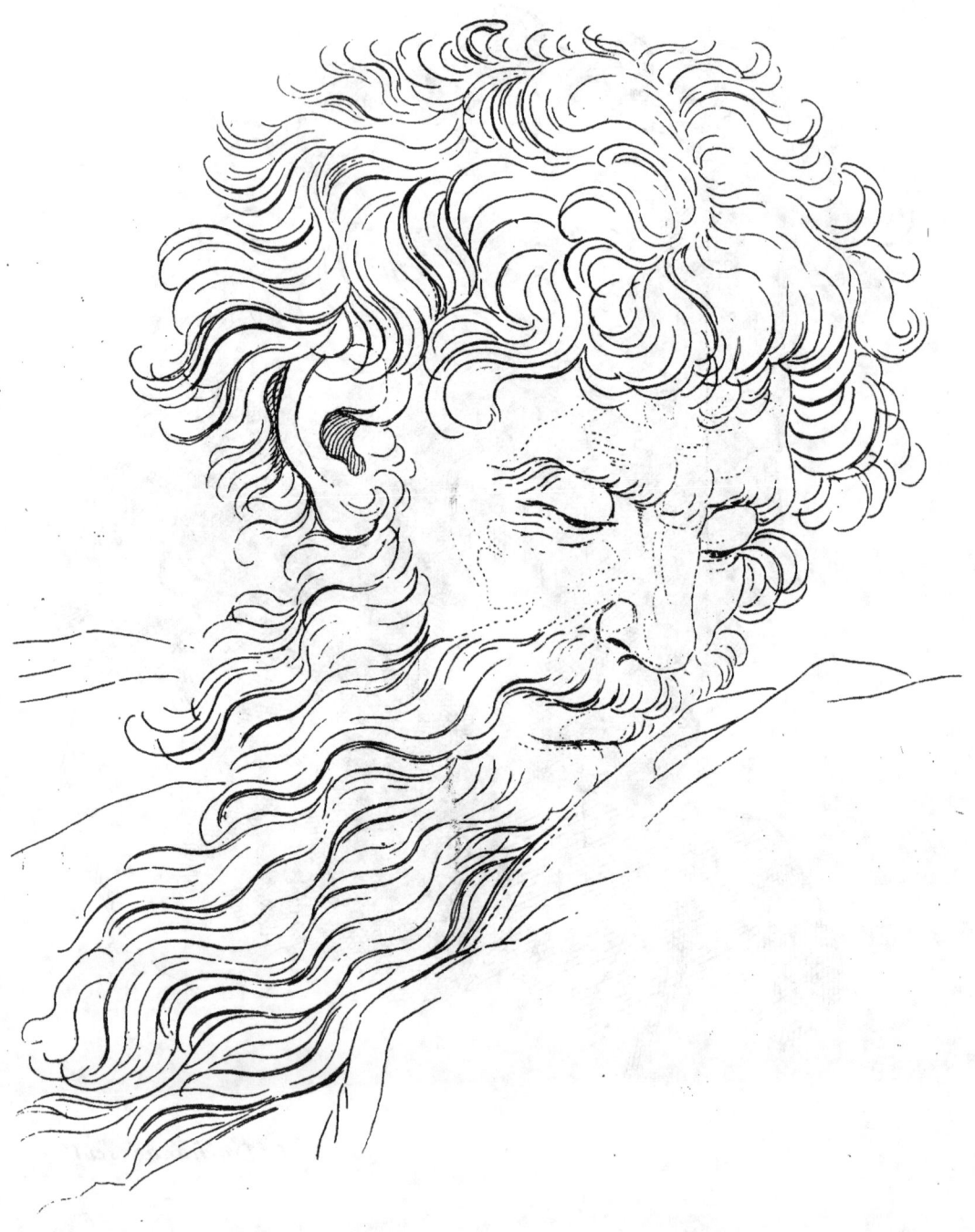

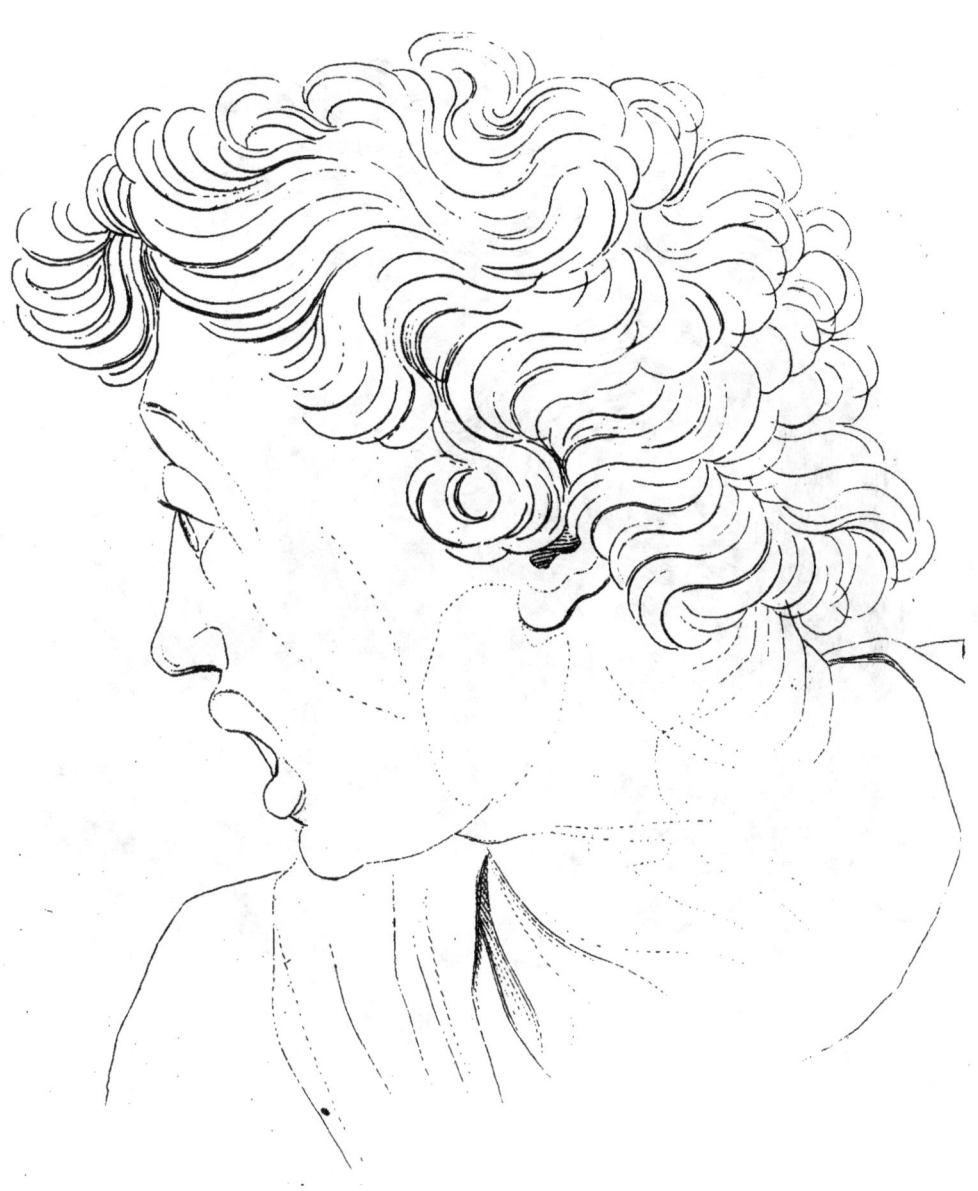

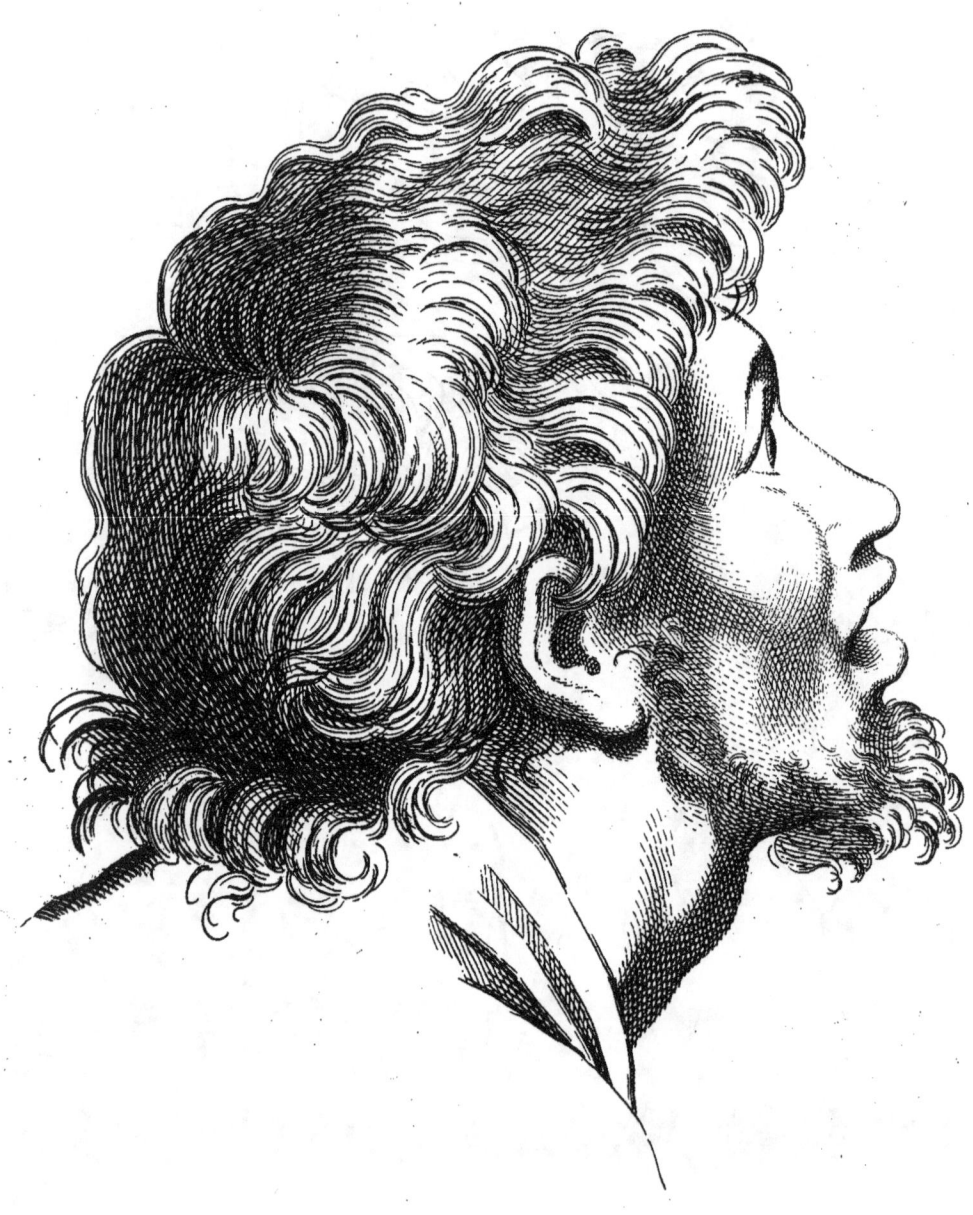

Raph. Vrb. pinx

Plate 21. I. - from The Death of Ananias

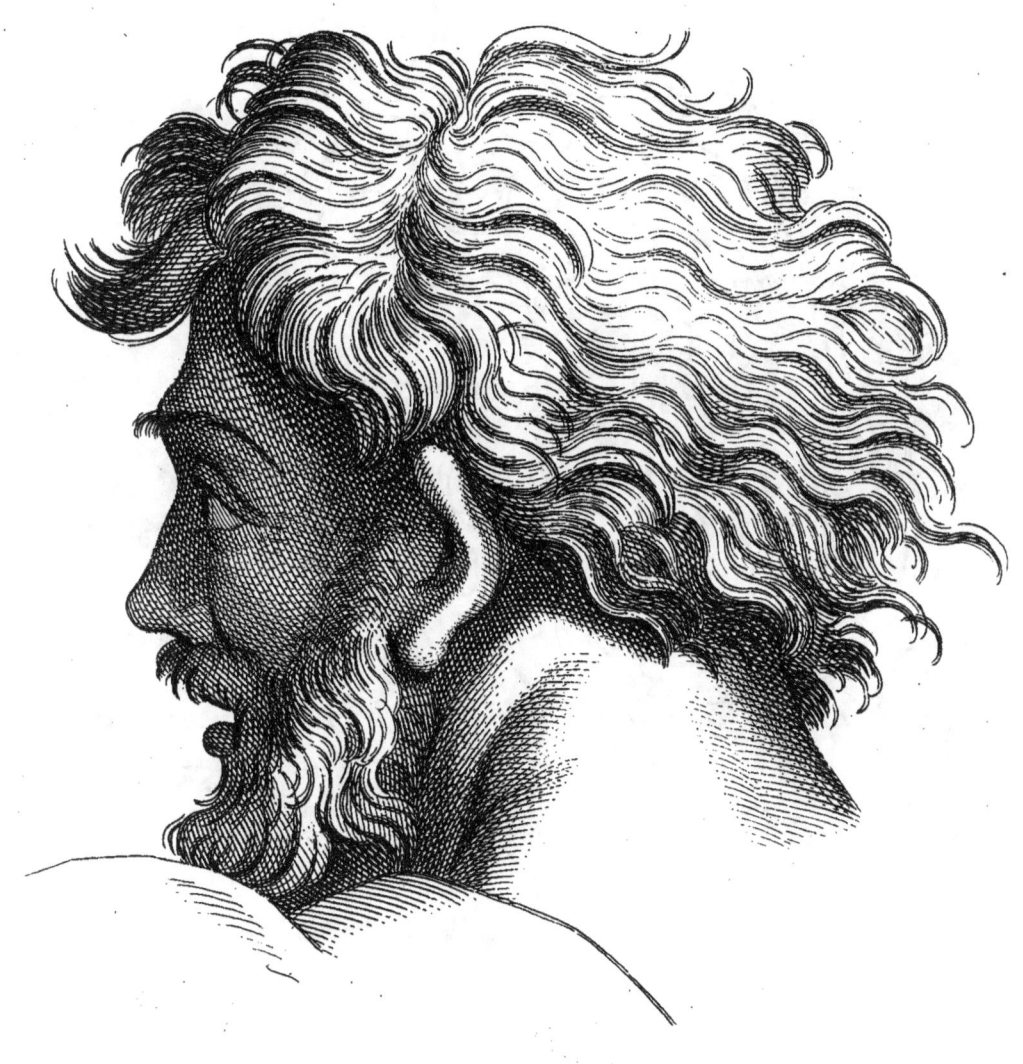

D · Beauvais scul .

Plate 21. II. - from Elymas the Sorcerer

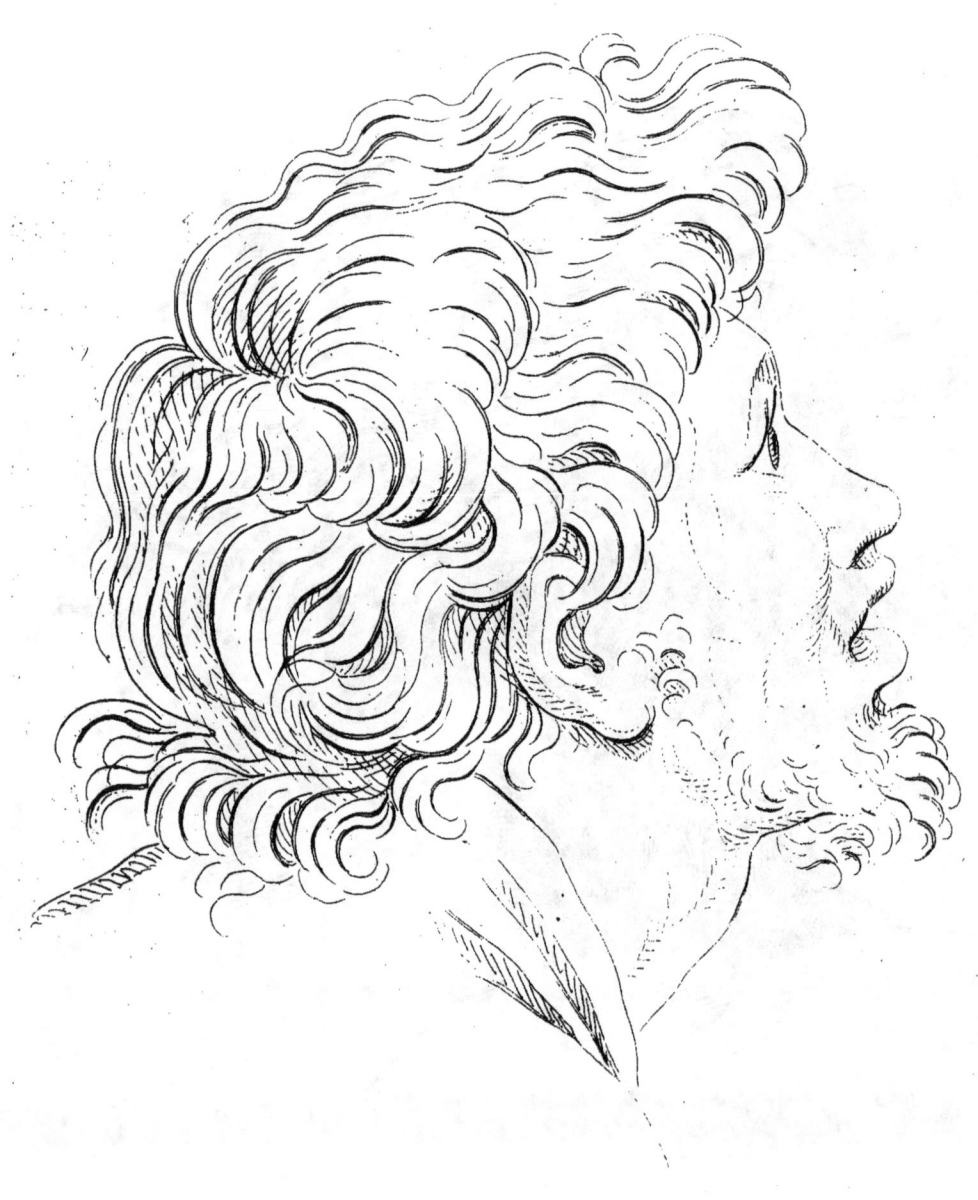

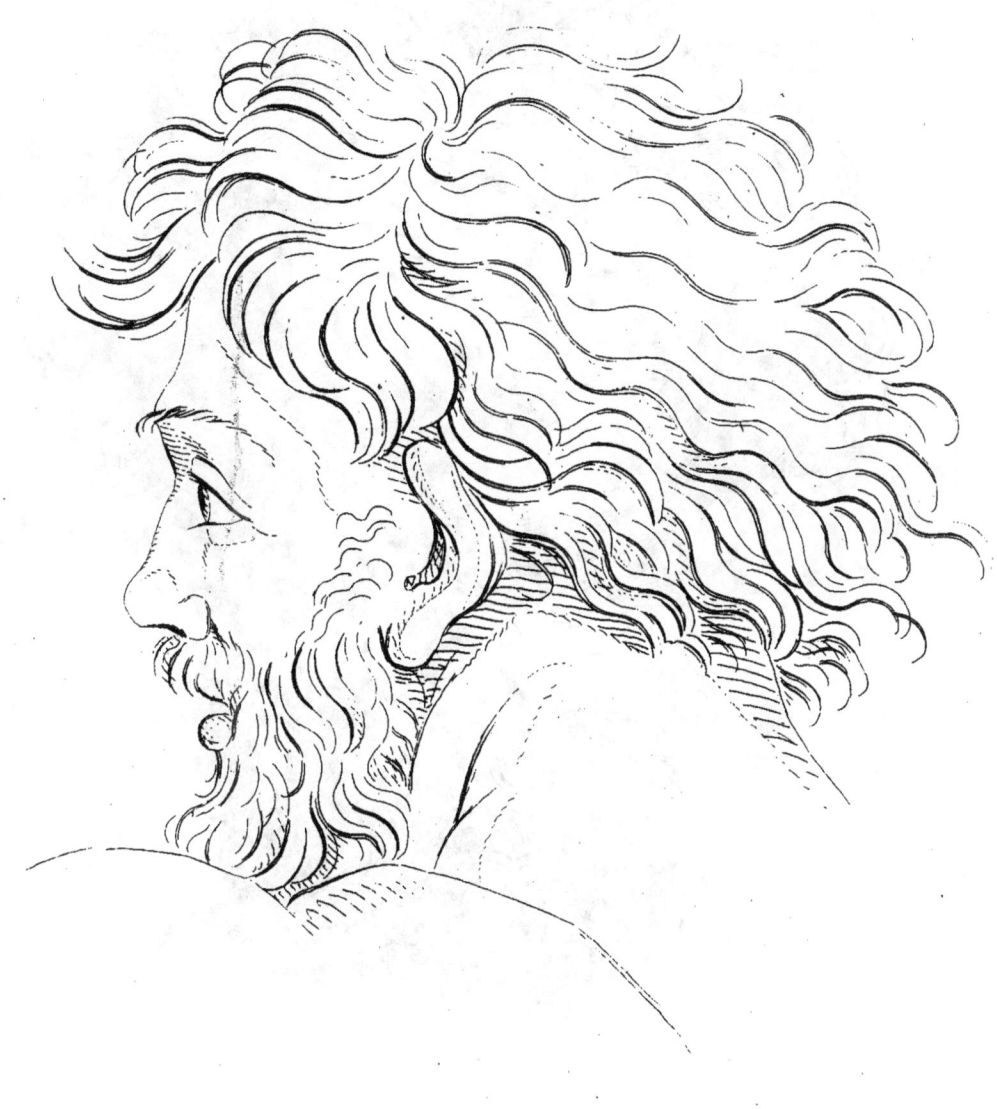

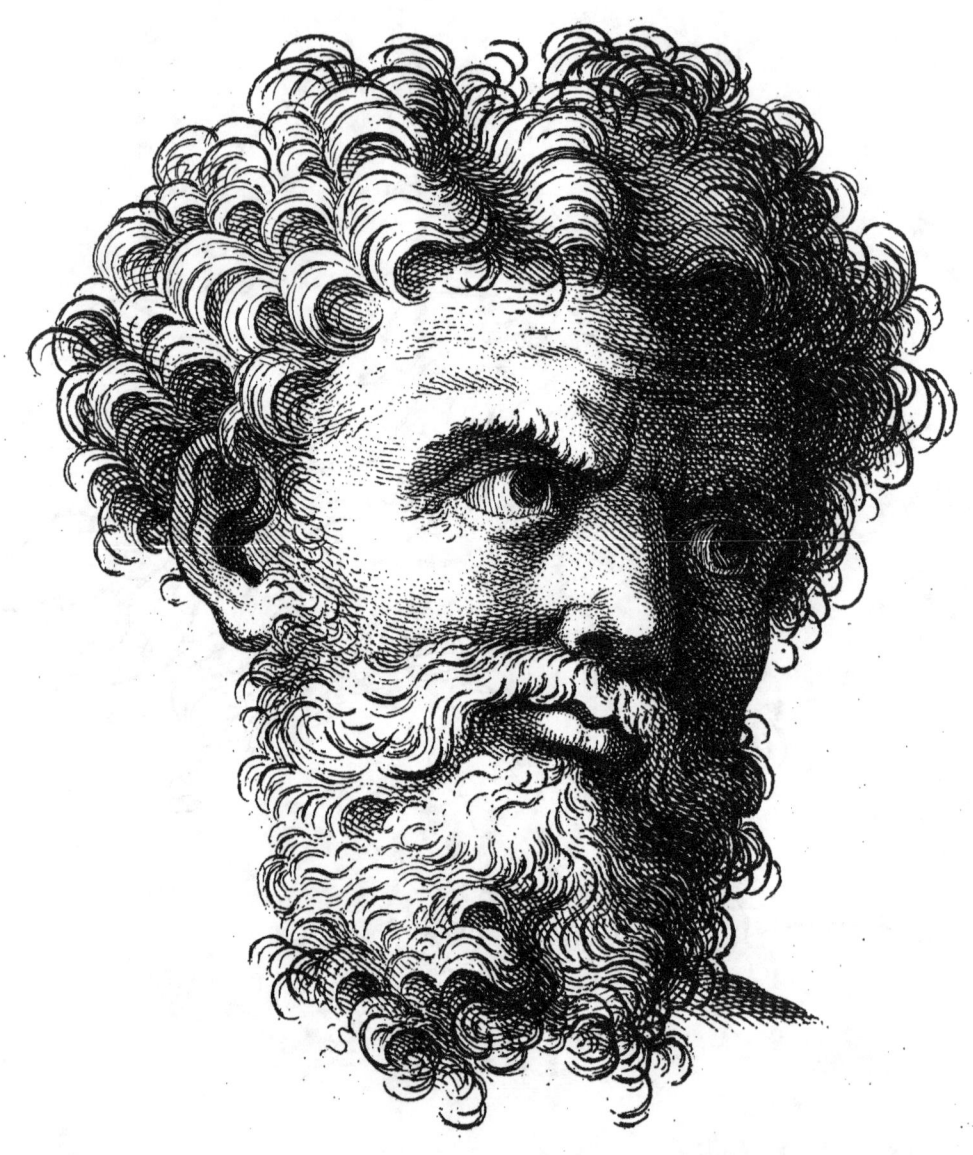

Raph . Vrb . pinx .

Plate 22. I. - Christ's Charge to Peter

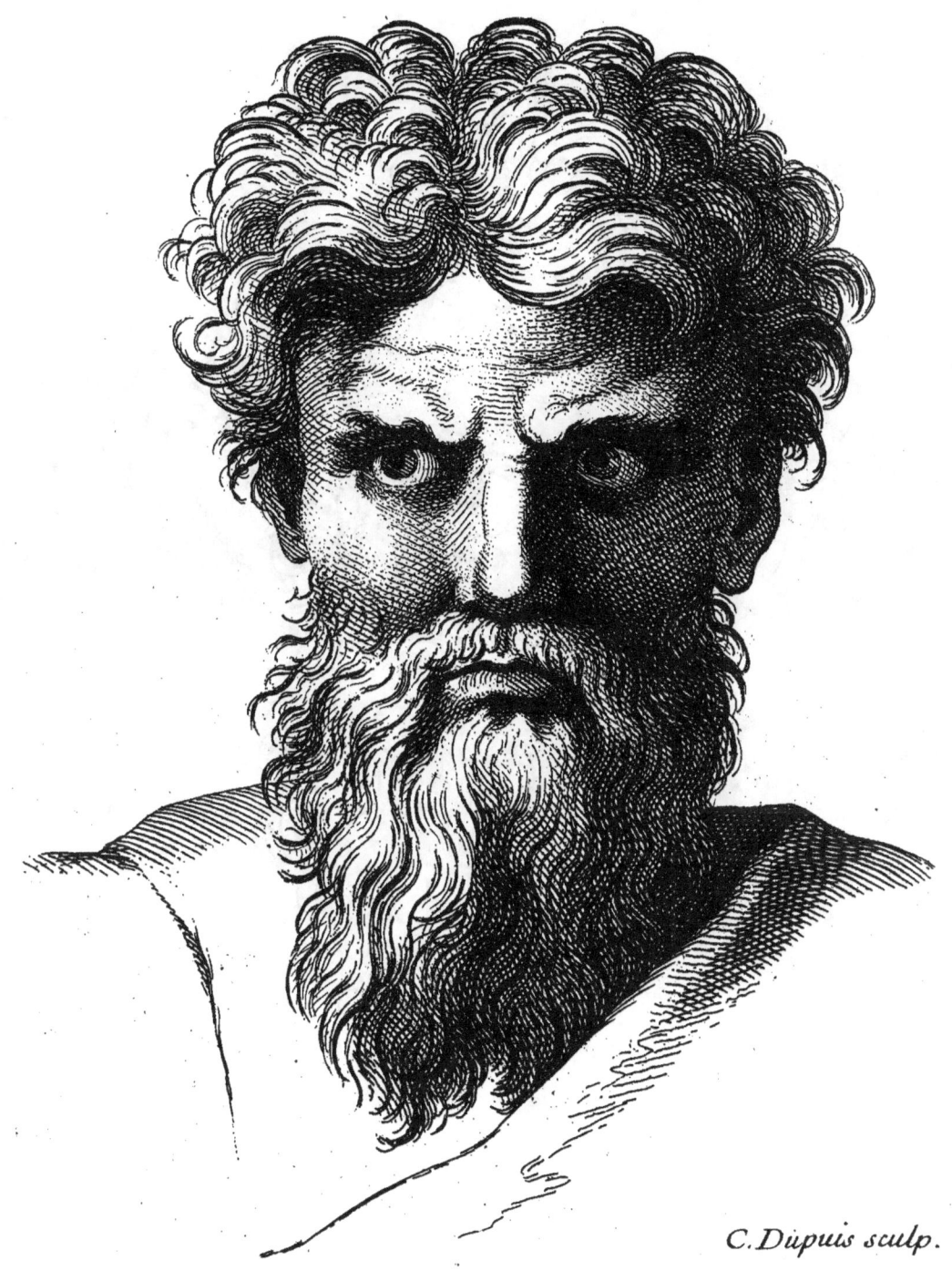

Plate 22. II. - The Death of Ananias

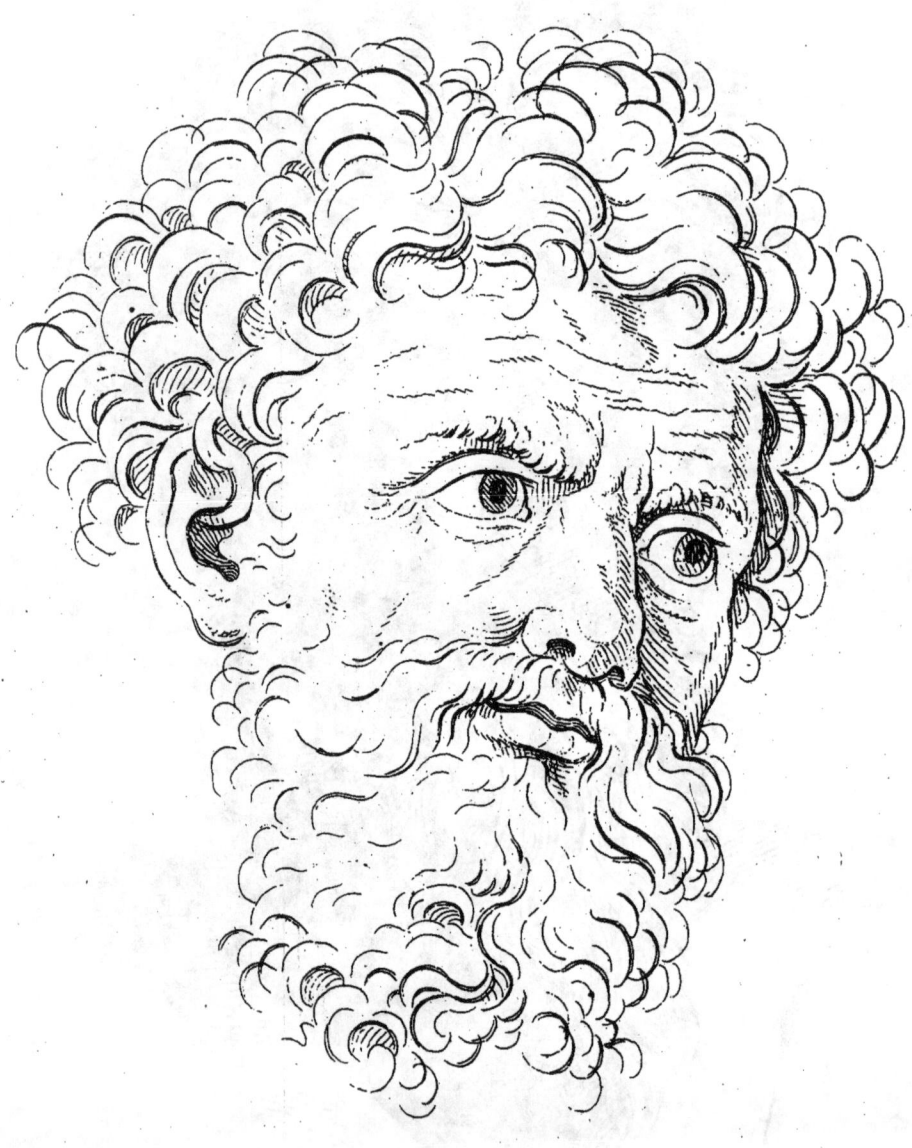

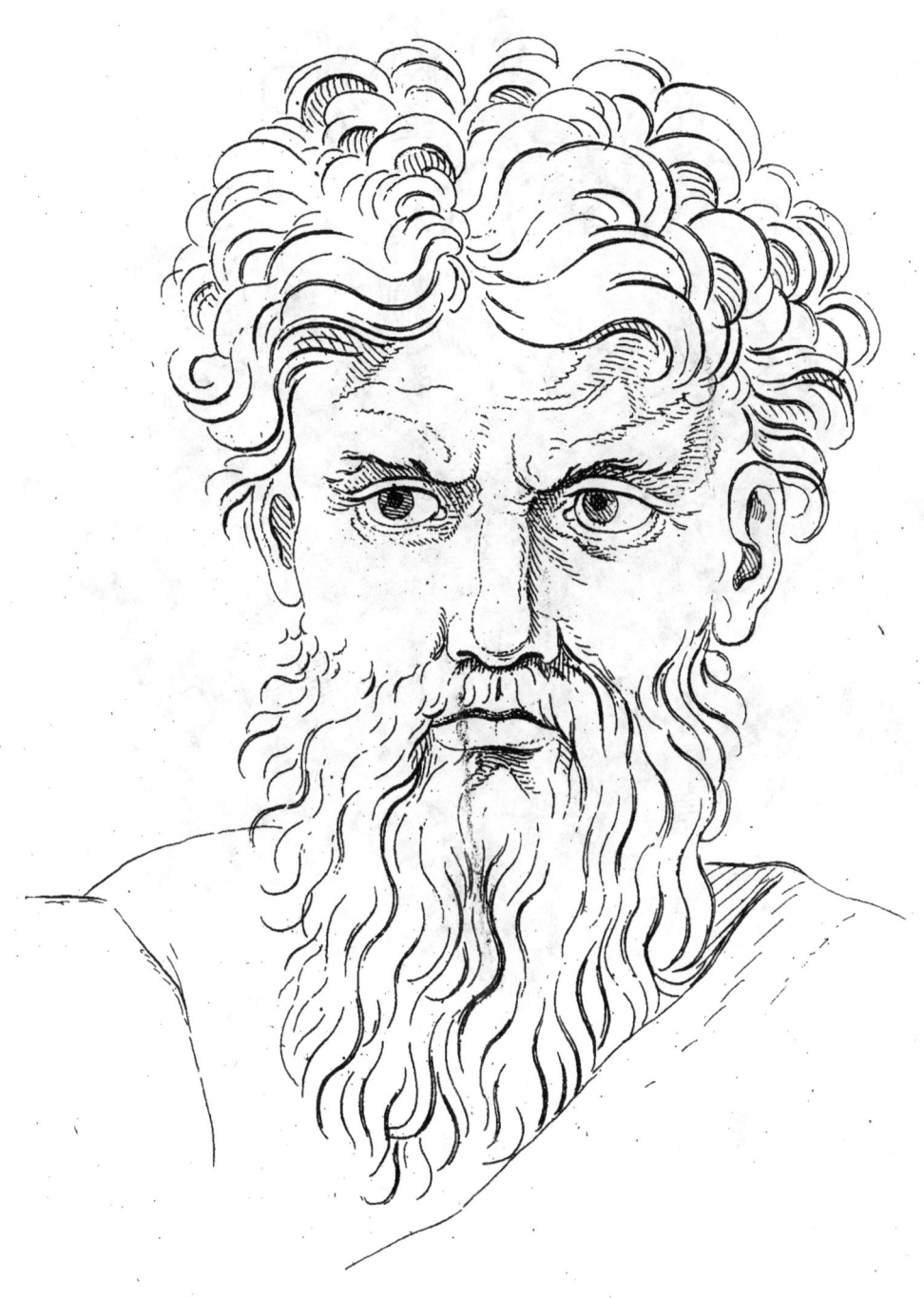

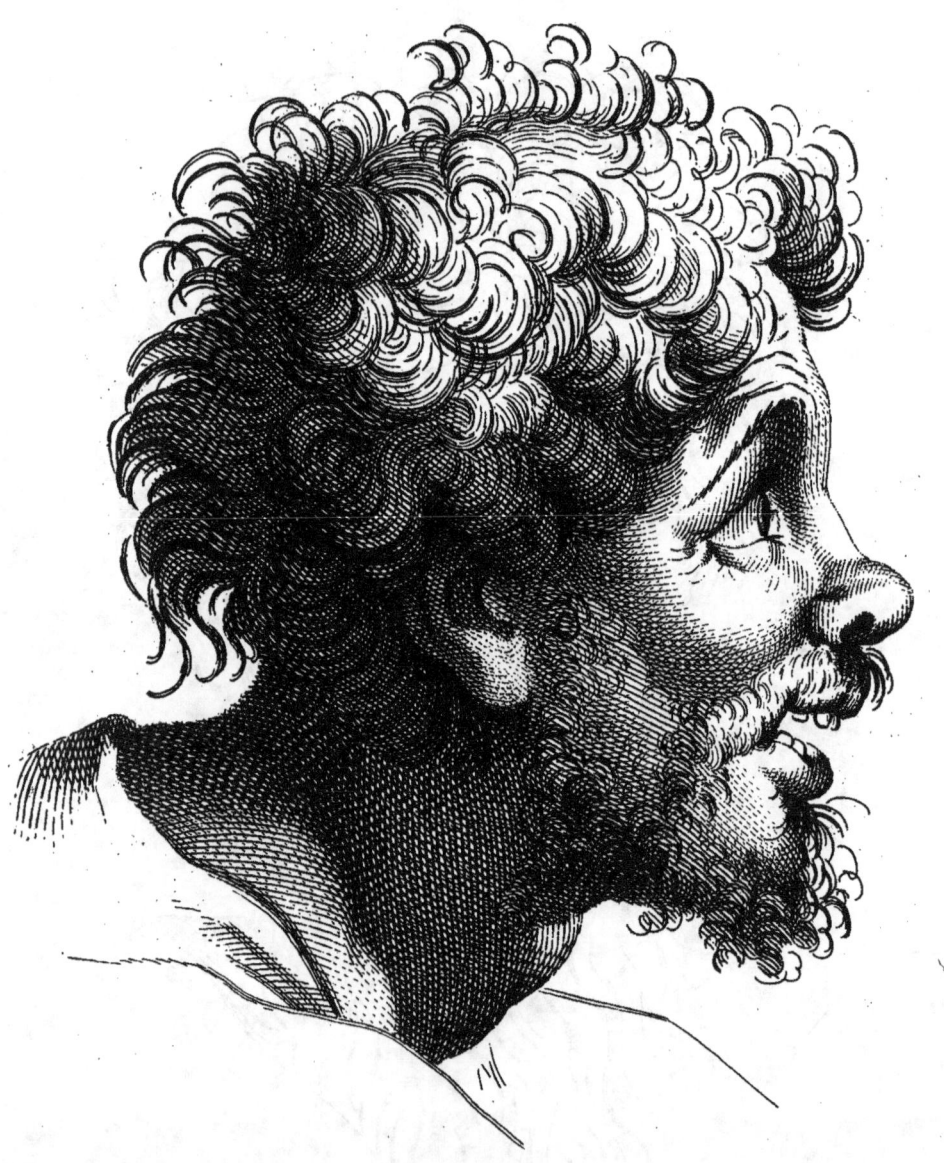

Raphael Vrb. pinxit

Plate 23. I. - from Paul and Barnabas

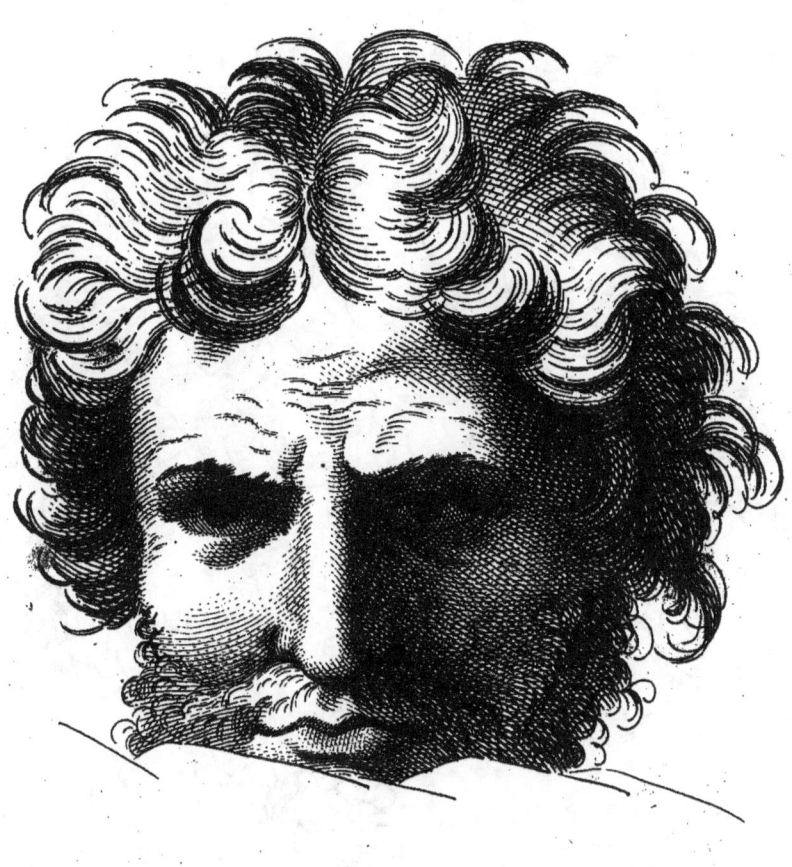

D. Beauvais sculp.

Plate 23. II. - from The Death of Ananias

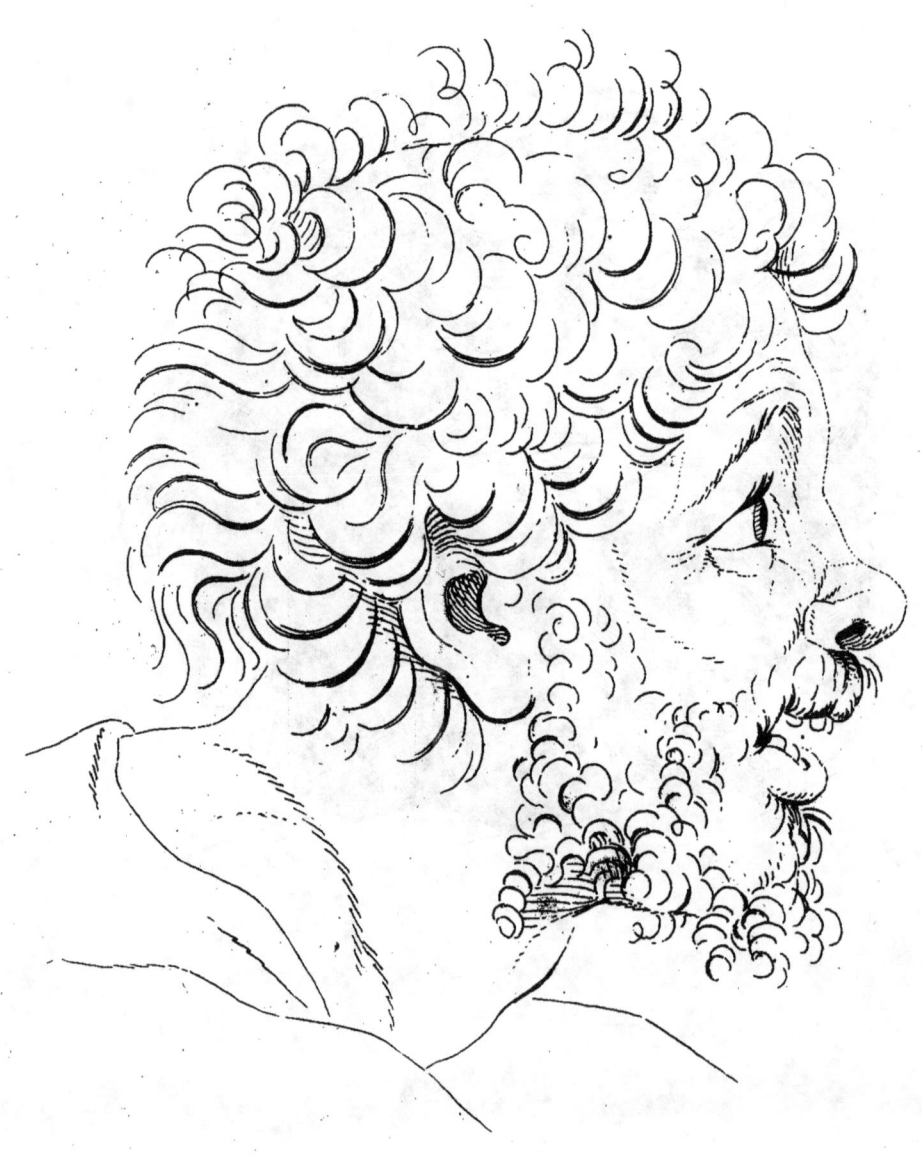

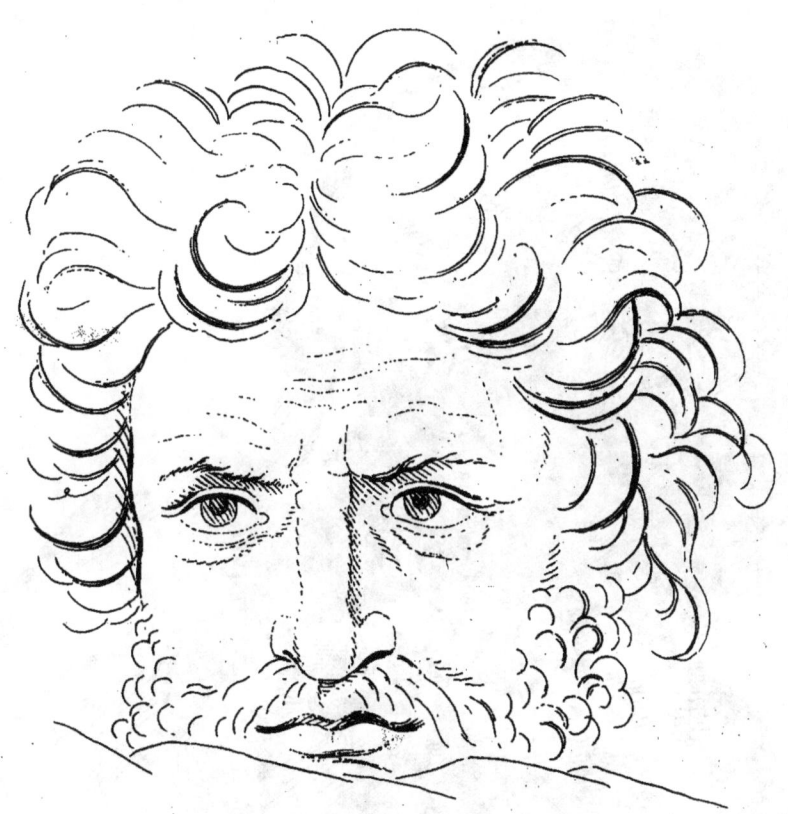

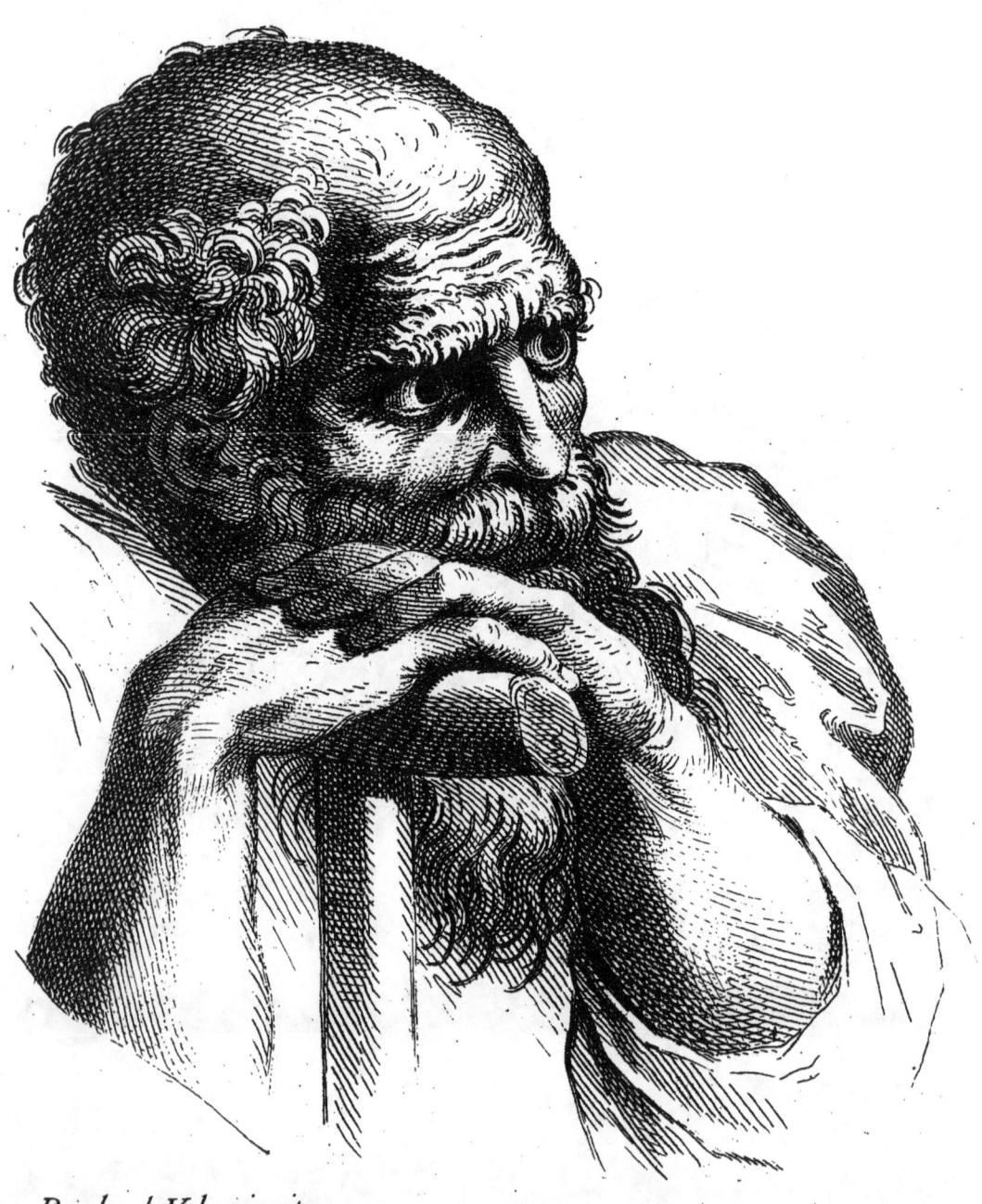

Raphael Vrb. pinxit

Plate 24. I. - from Paul Preaching

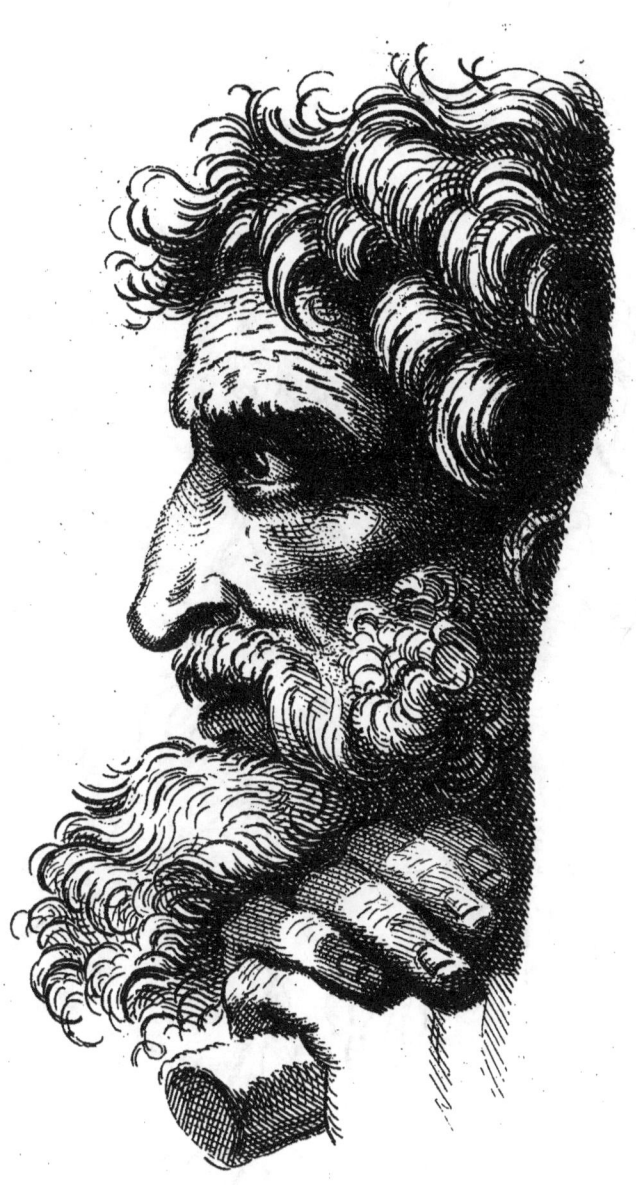

L. Desplaces sculp.

Plate 24. II. - from The Lame Man Healed

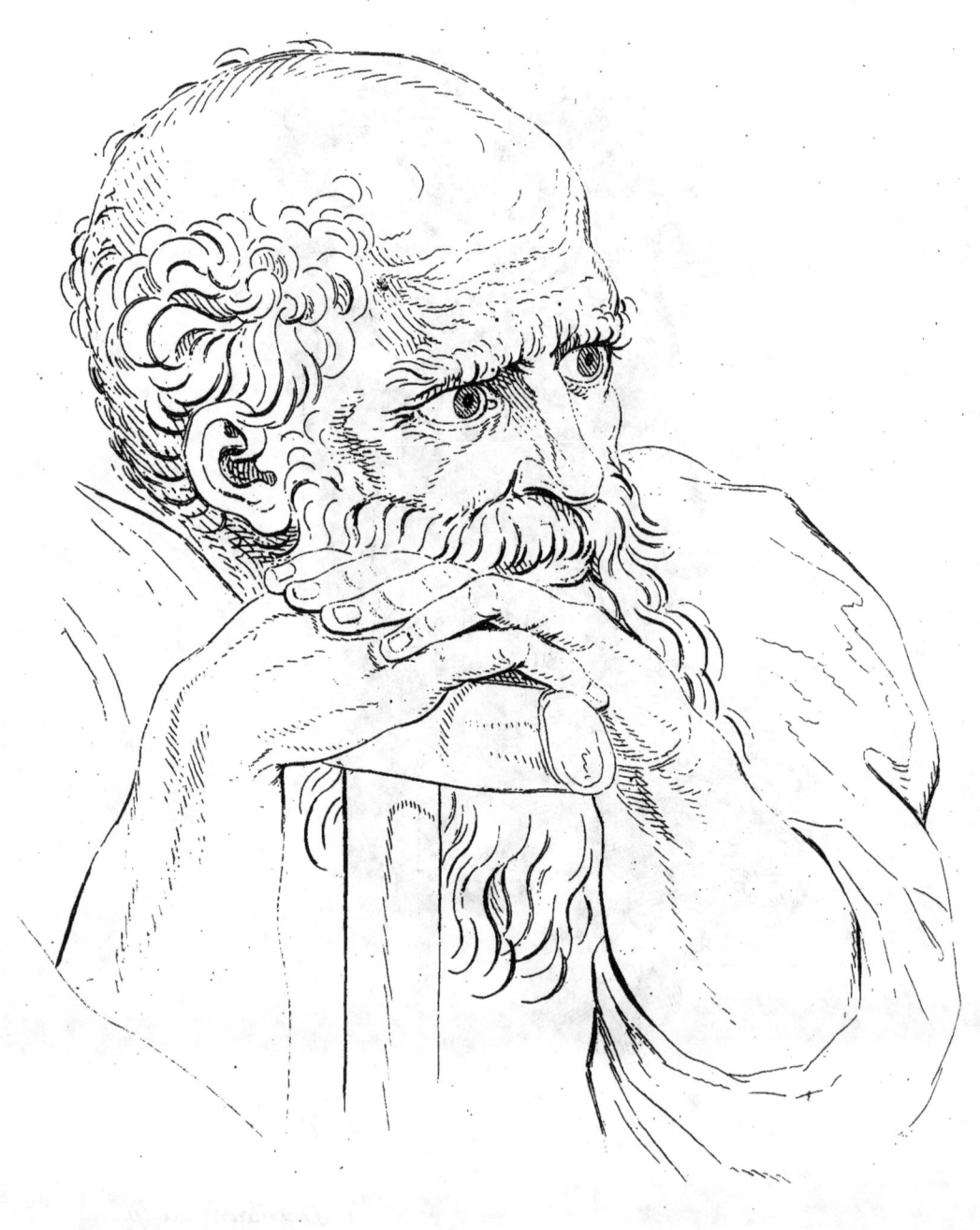

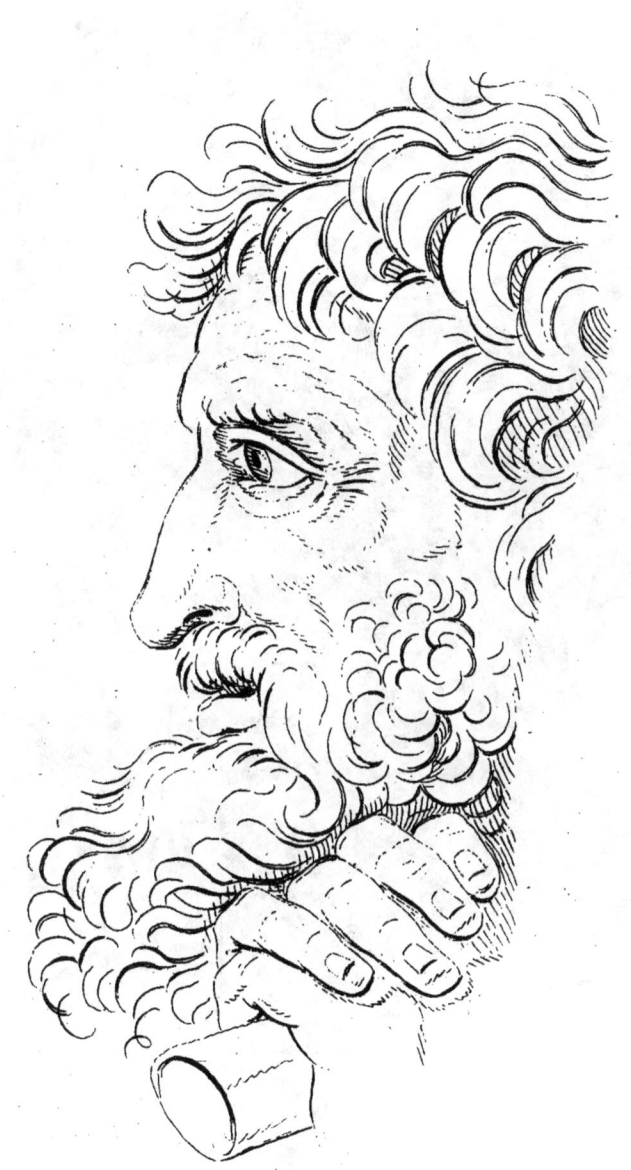

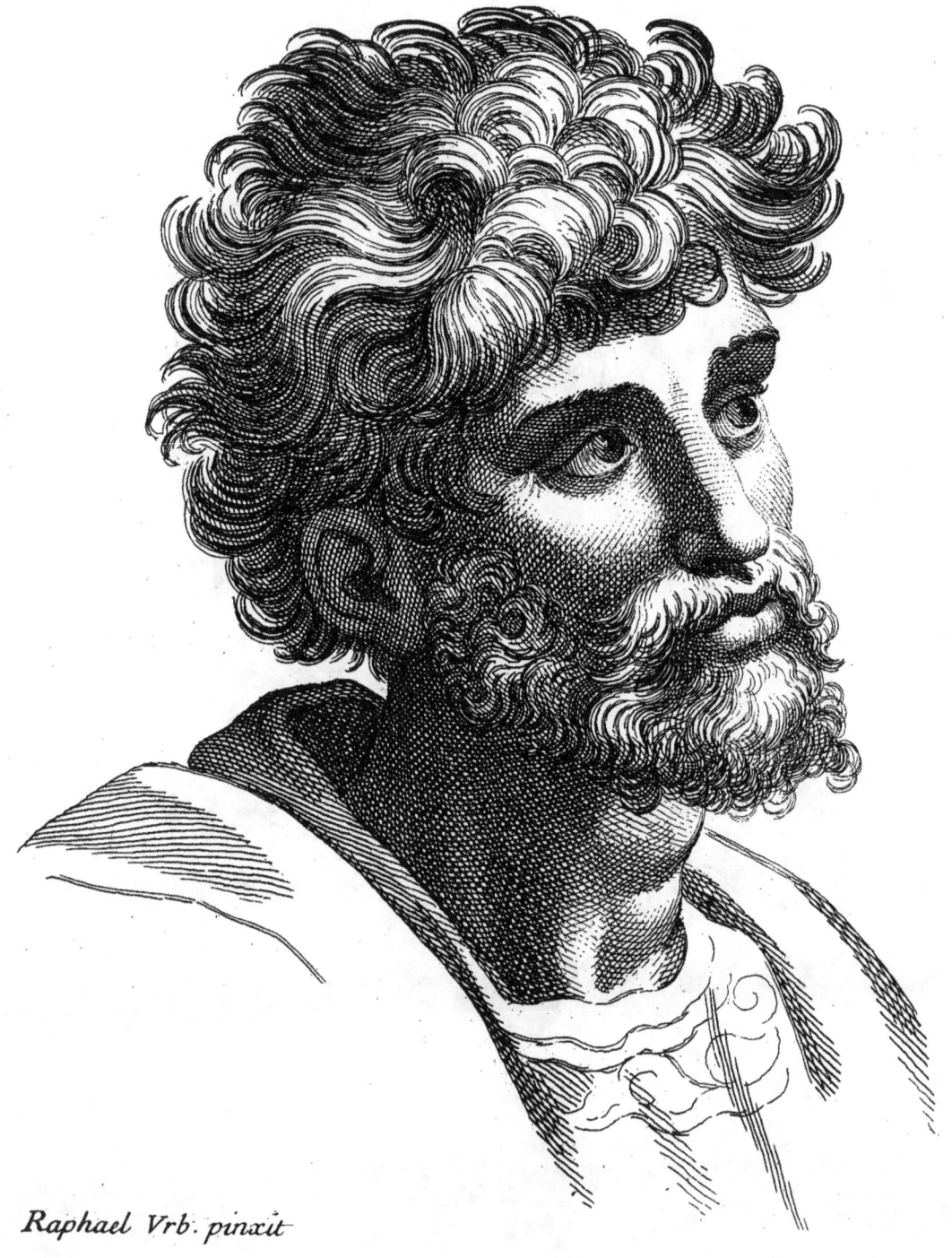

Raphael Vrb. pinxit

Plate 25. I. - from Paul Preaching

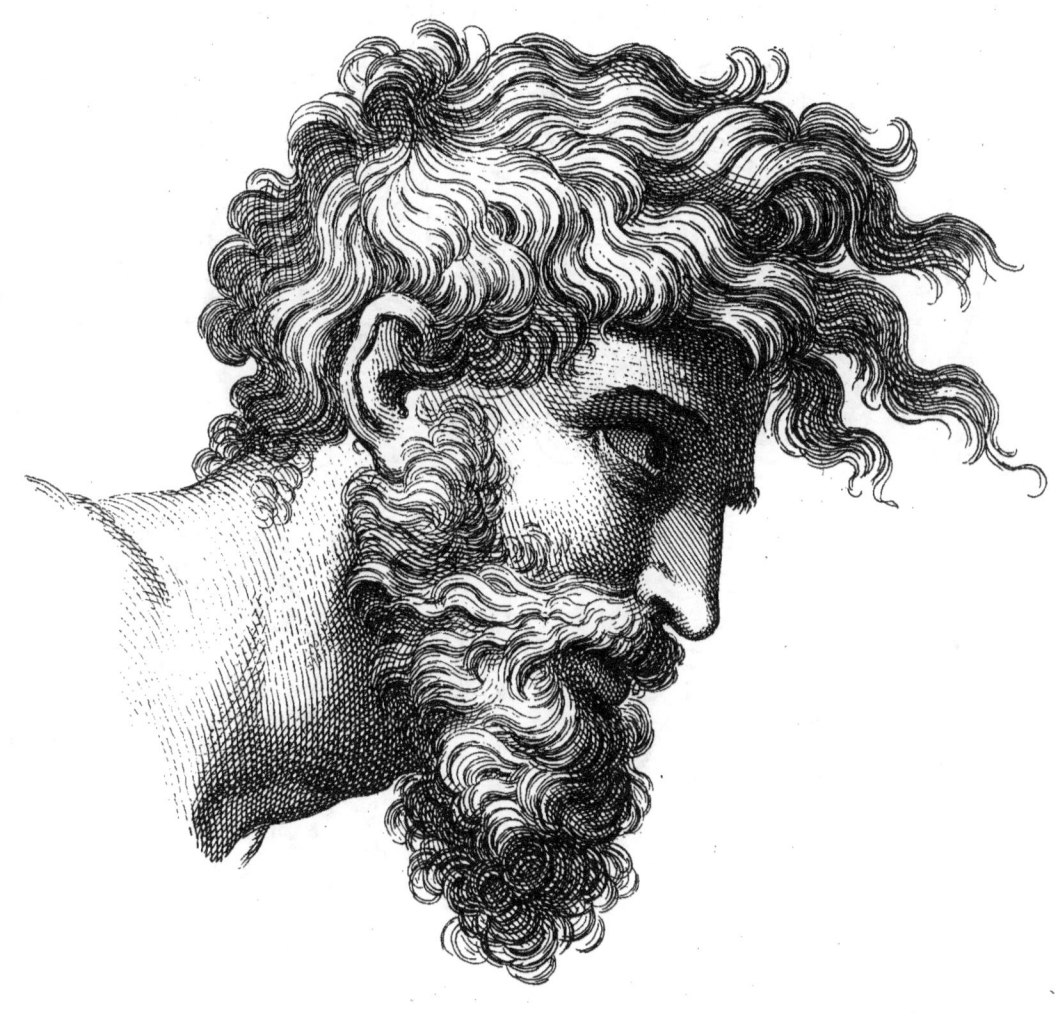

n. Tardieu sculp.

Plate 25. II. - from The Miraculous Draught of Fishes

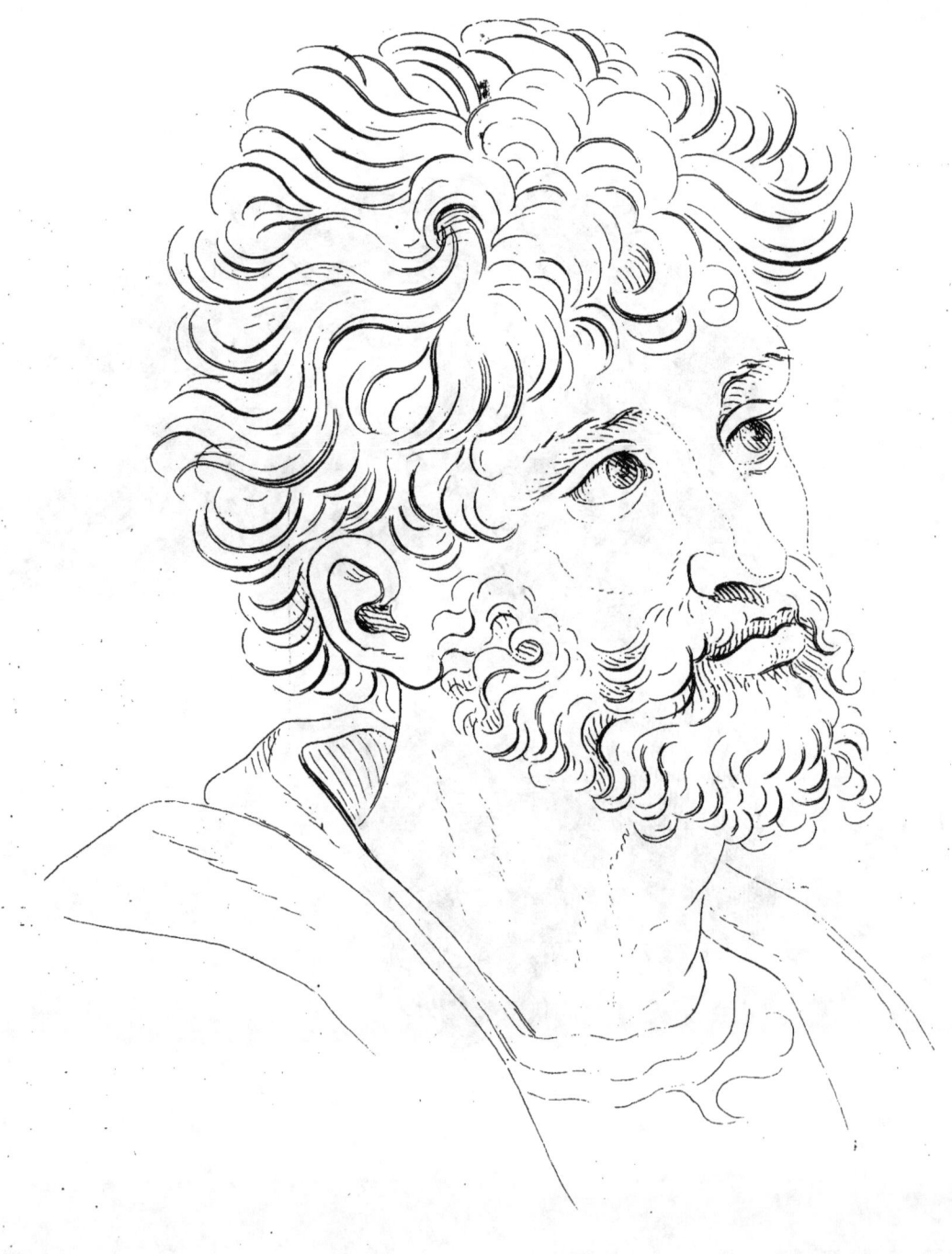

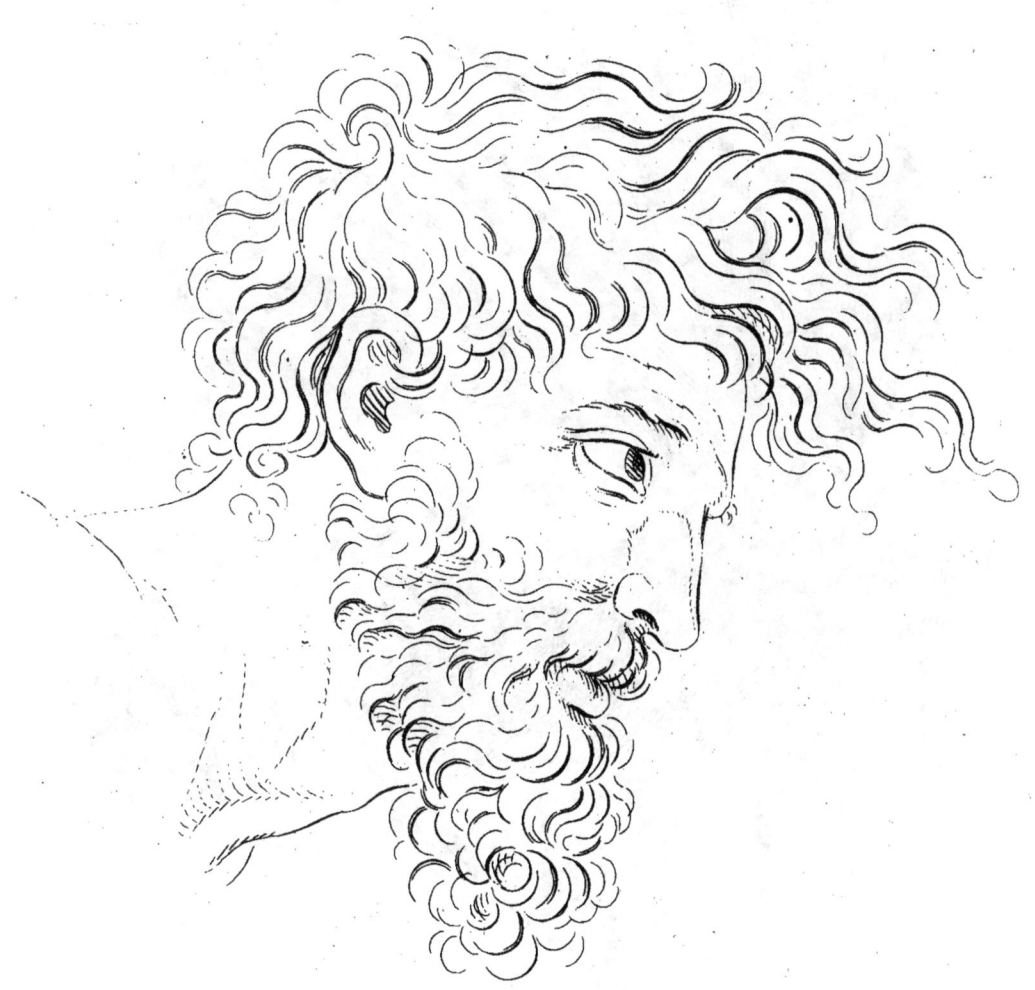

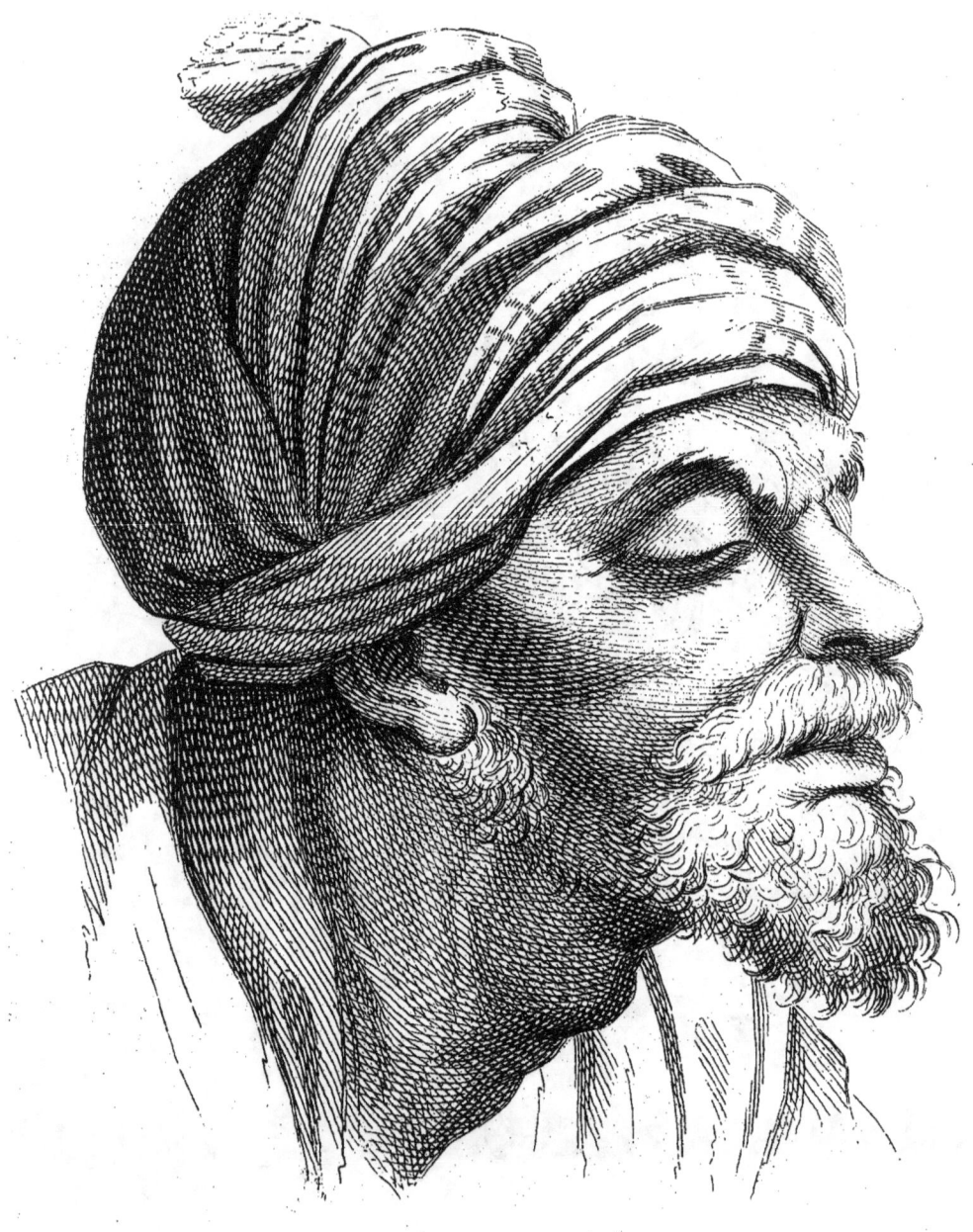

Raph . Vrb . pinx .

Plate 26. I. - from Elymas the Sorcerer

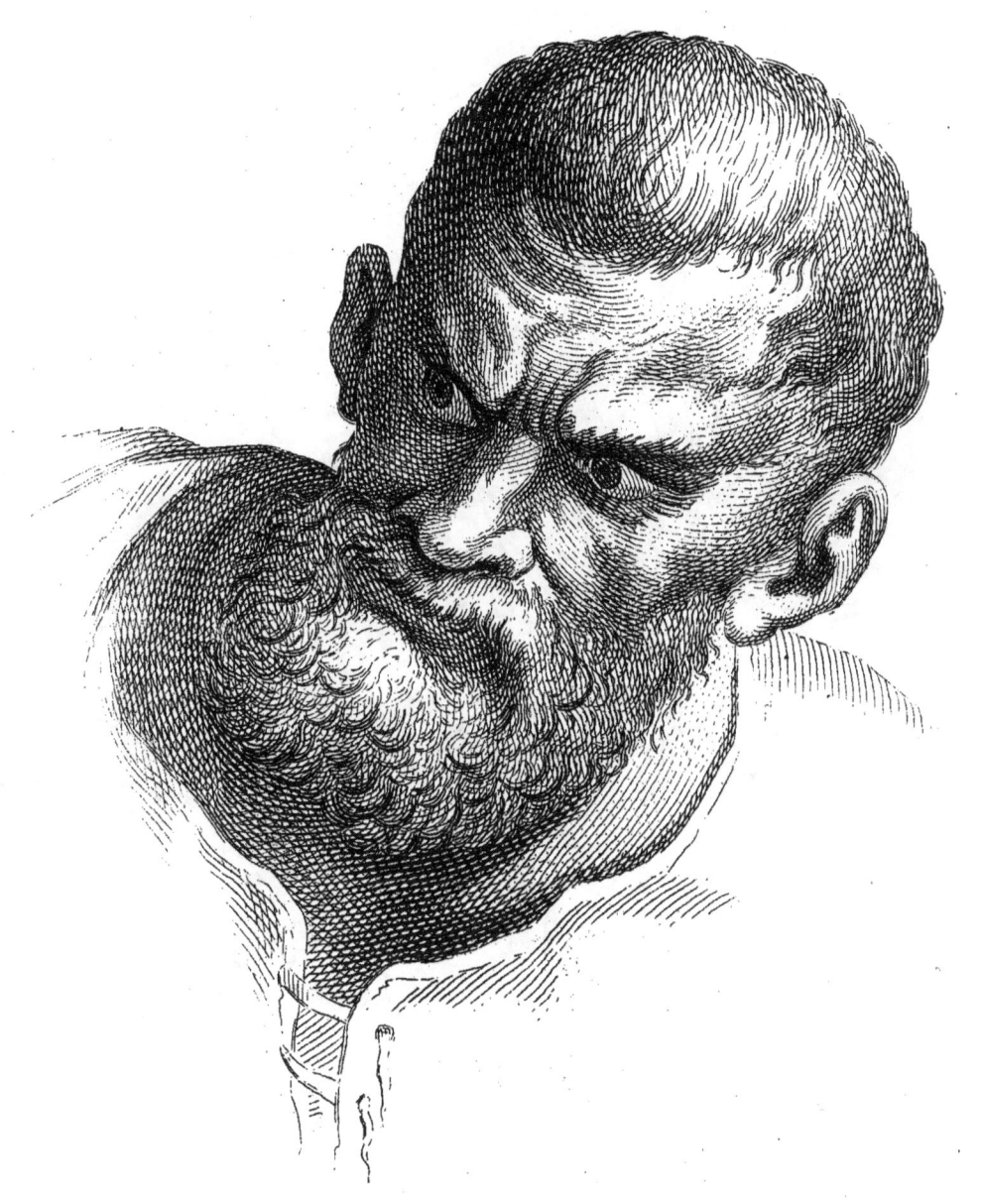

n. Dupuis sculp.

Plate 26. II. - from Elymas the Sorcerer

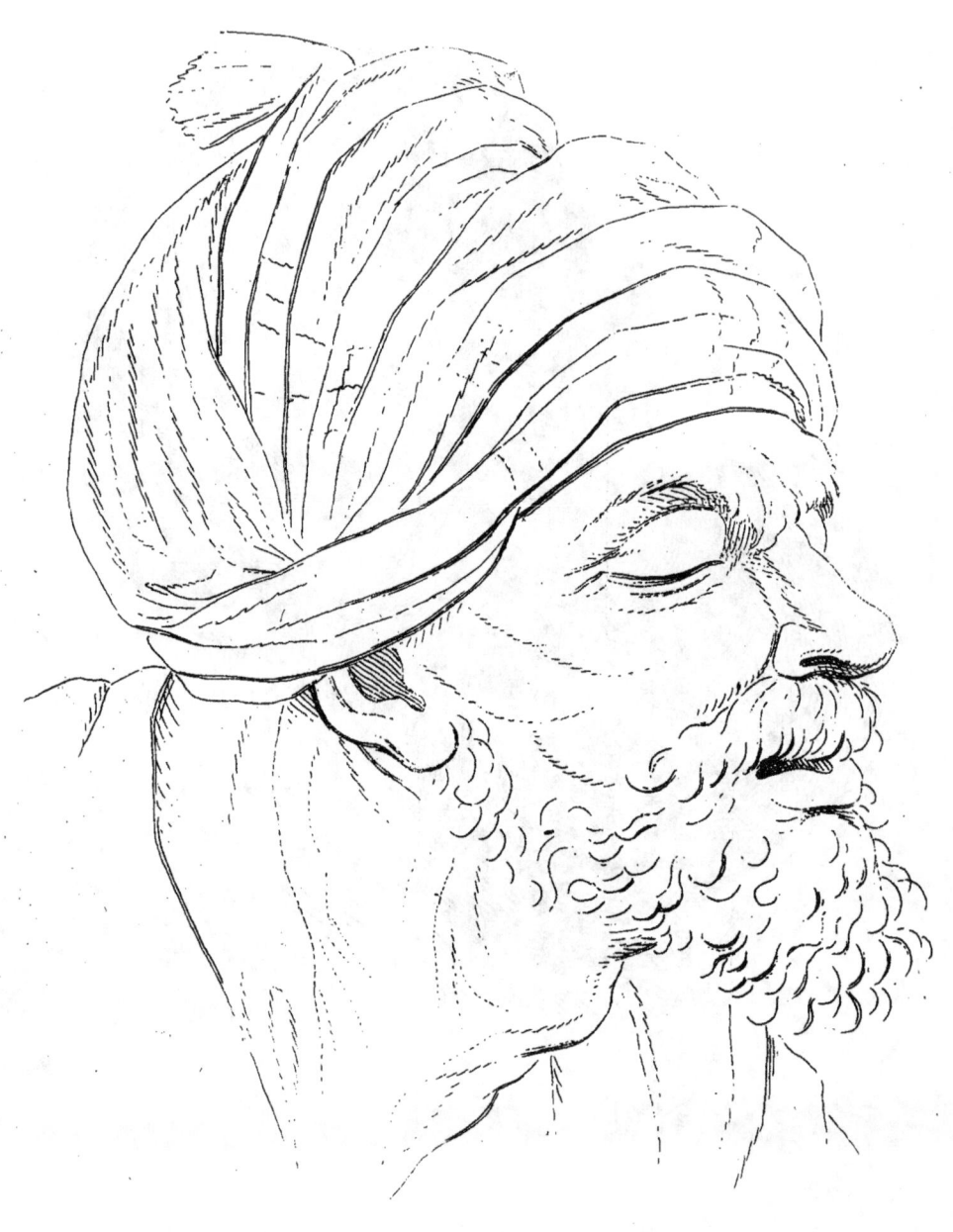

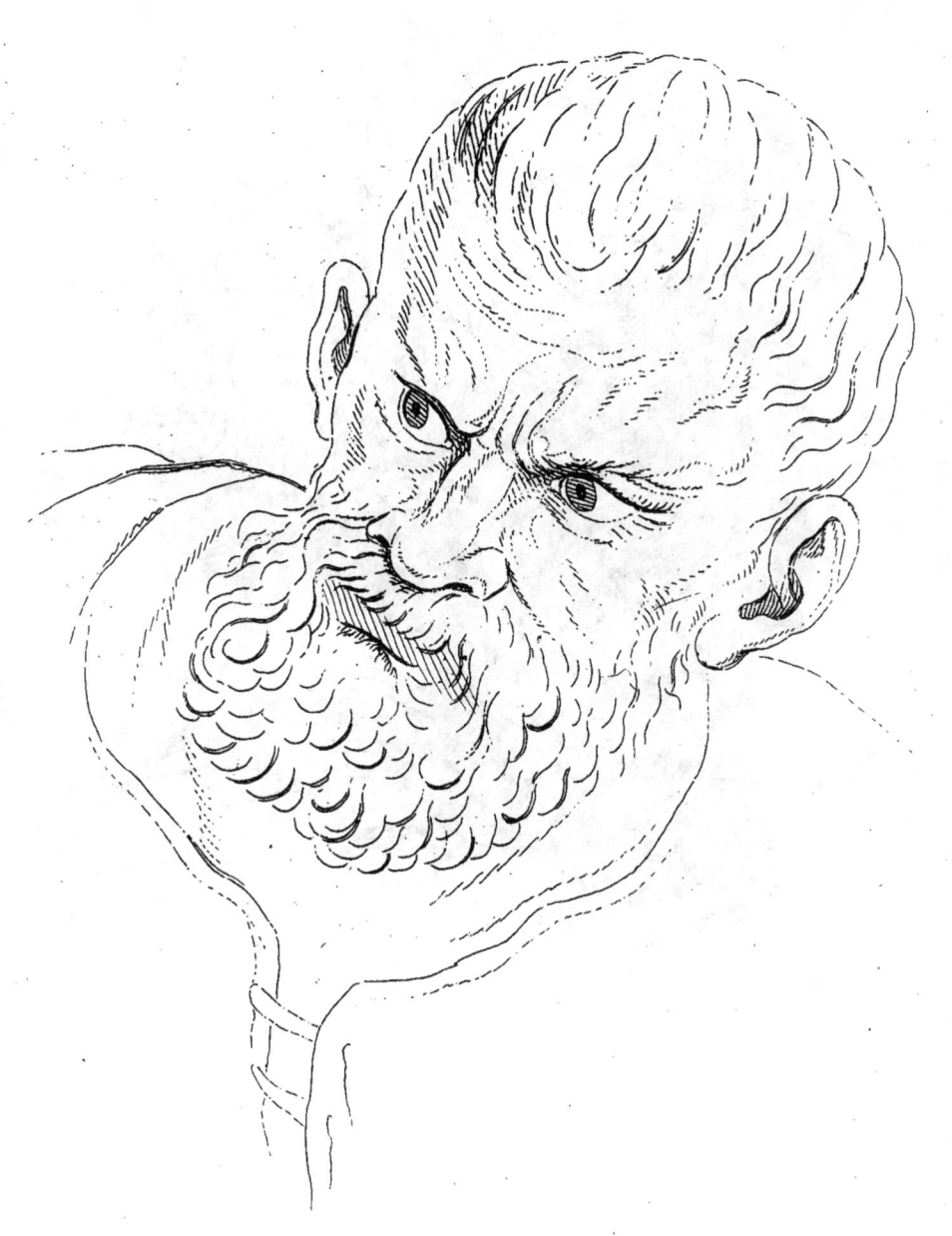

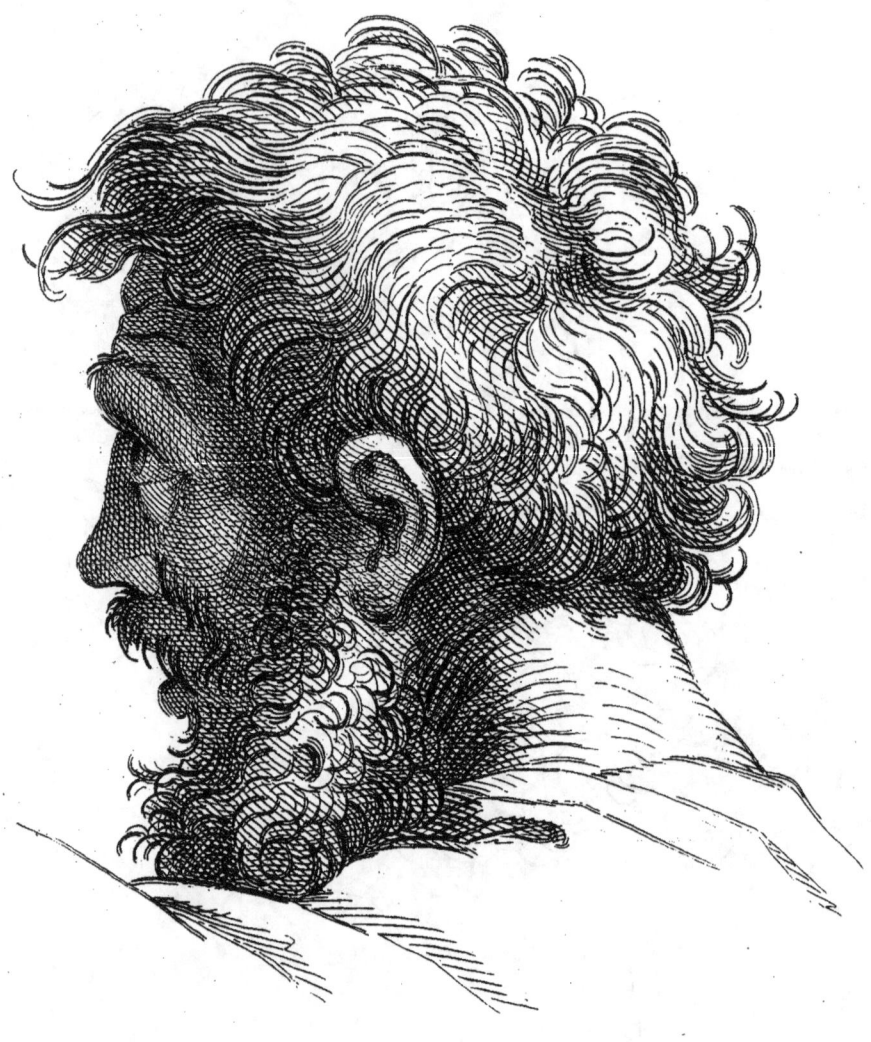

Raph. Vrb. pinx .

Plate 27. I. - from Paul Preaching at Athens

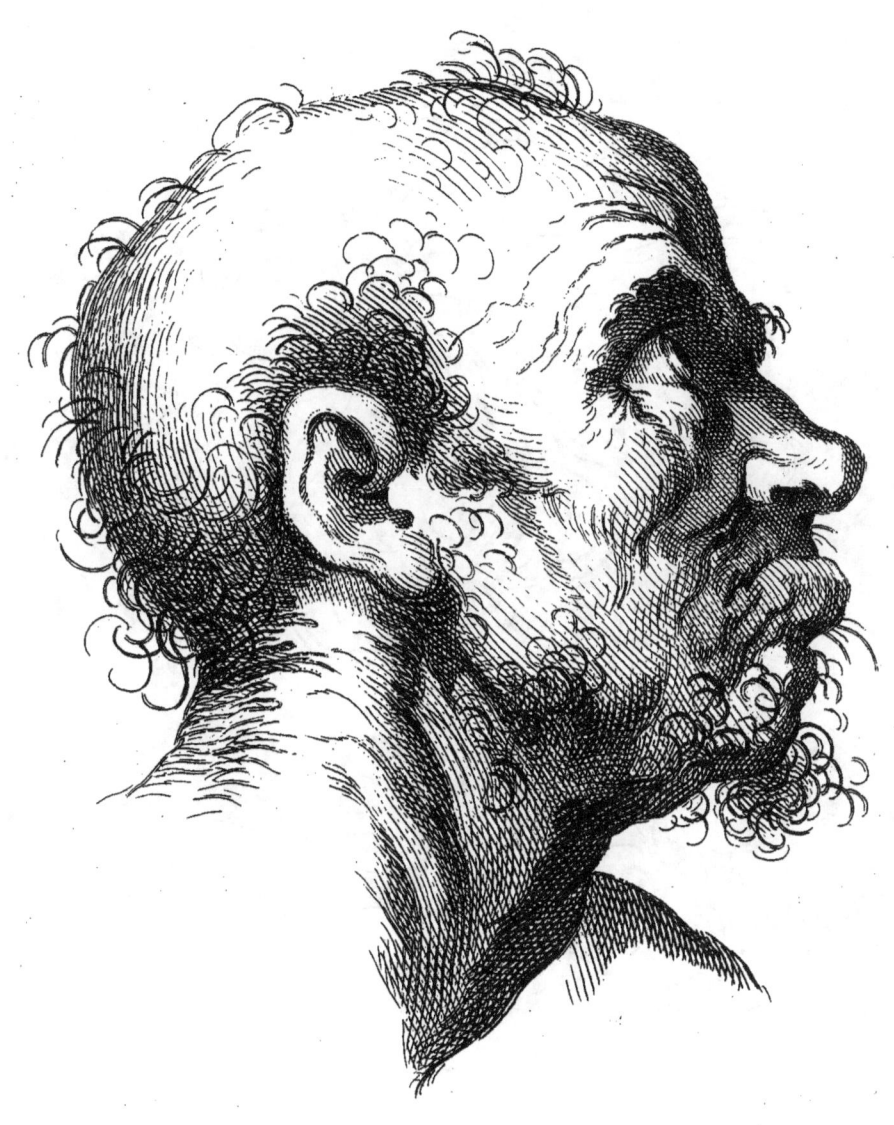

L. Desplaces scul.

Plate 27. II. - from The Lame Man Healed

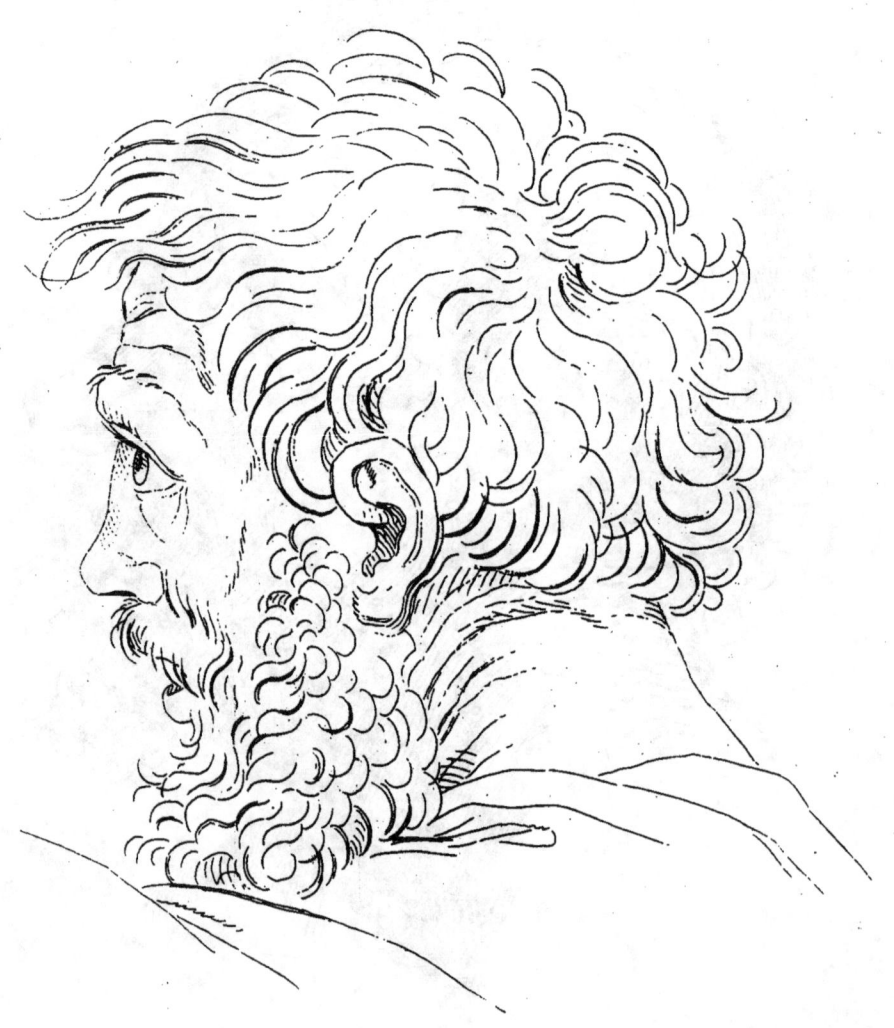

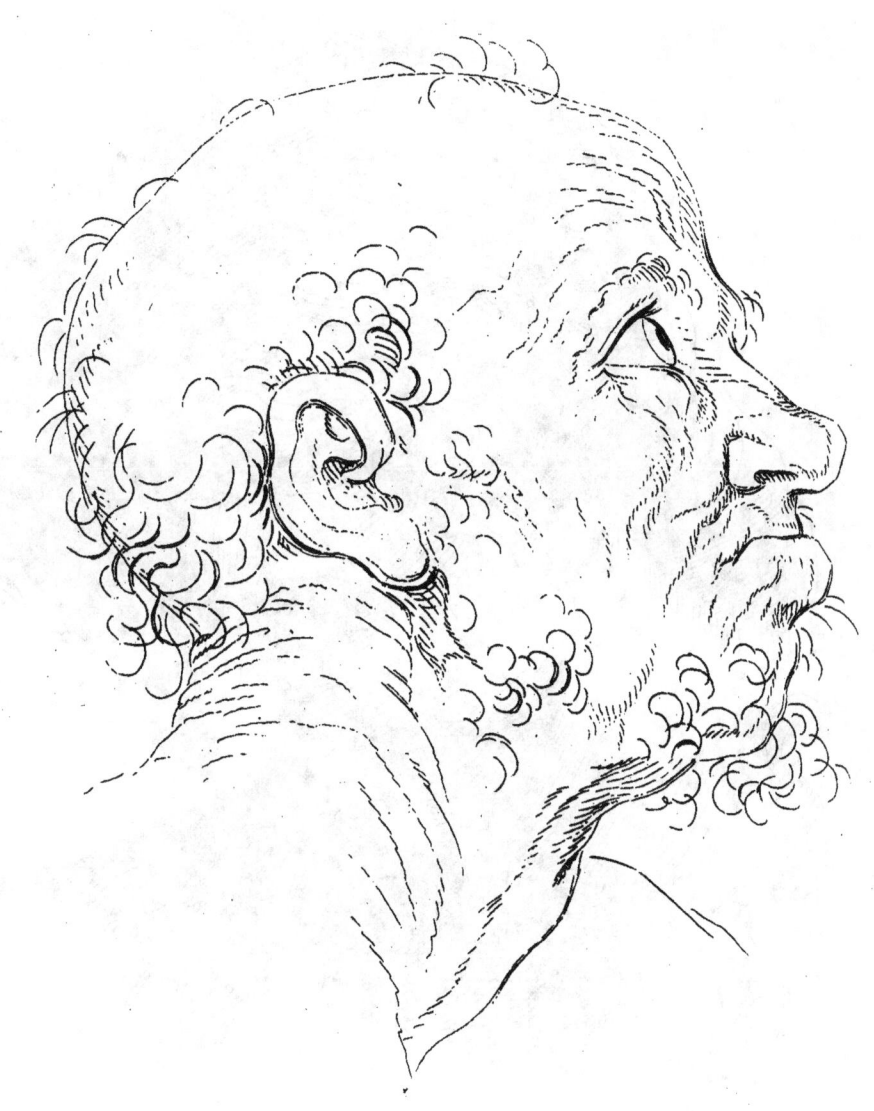

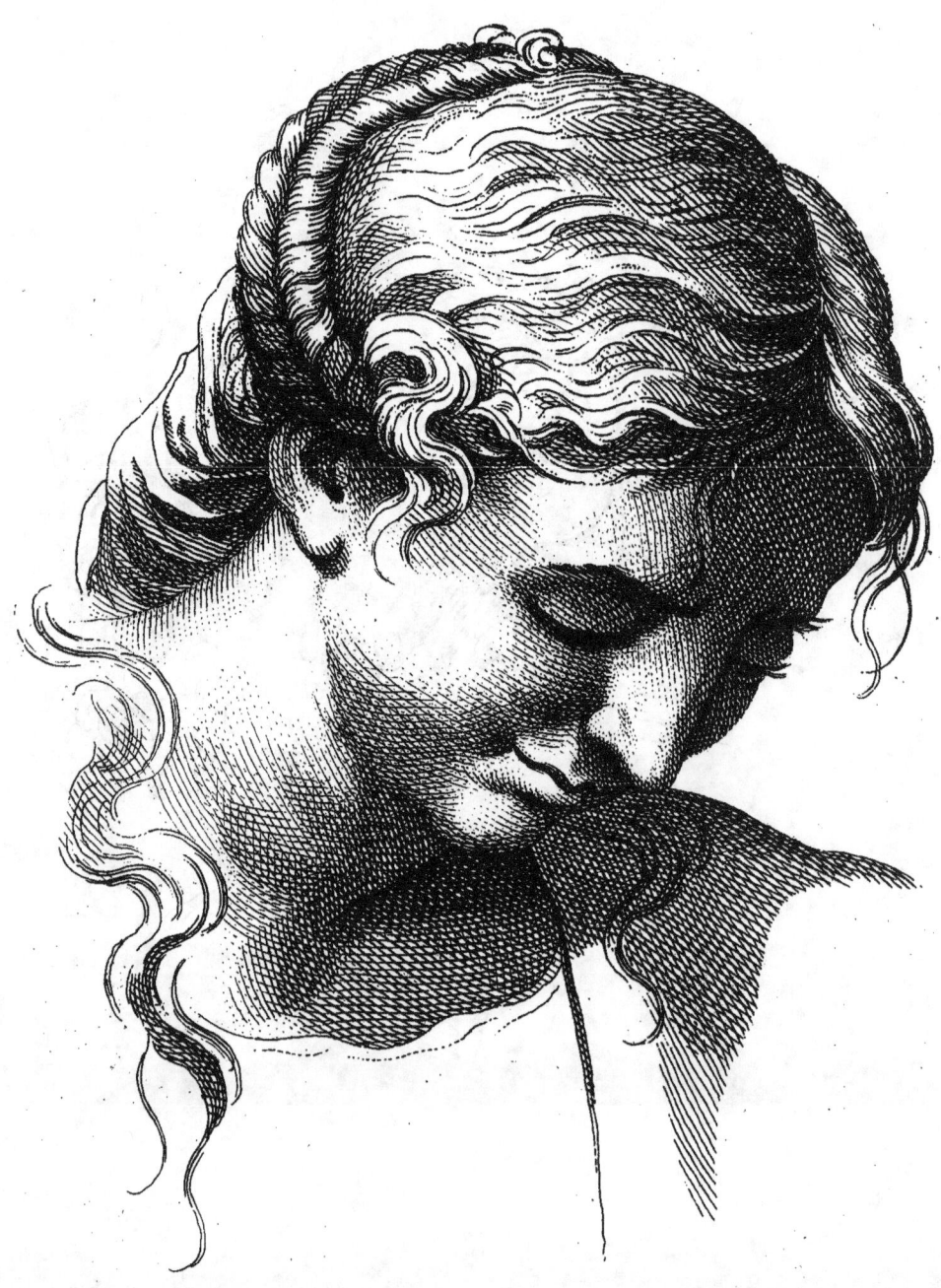

Raph. Vrb. pinx .

Plate 28. I. - from The Death of Ananias

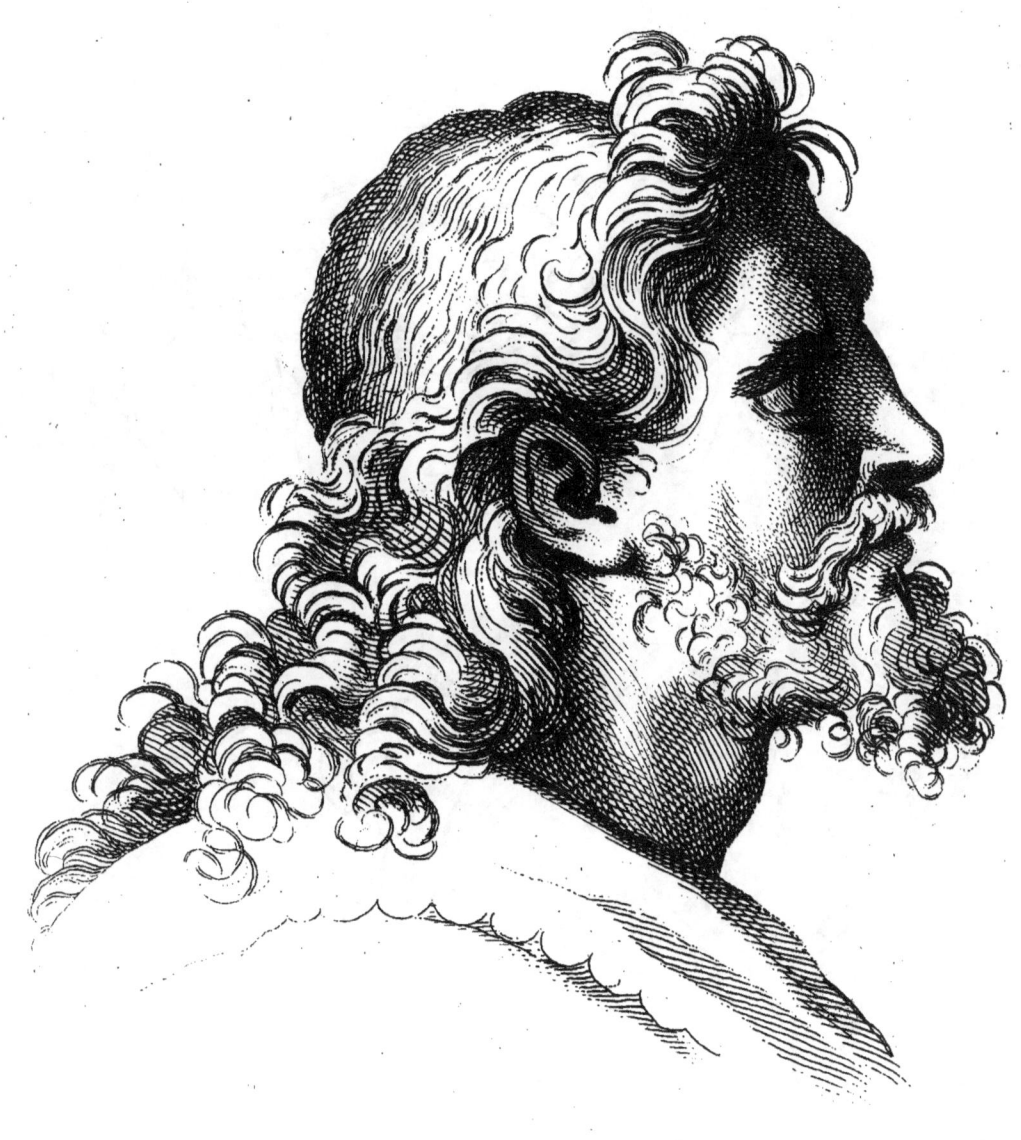

S. Thomassin scul.

Plate 28. II. - from Christ's Charge to Peter

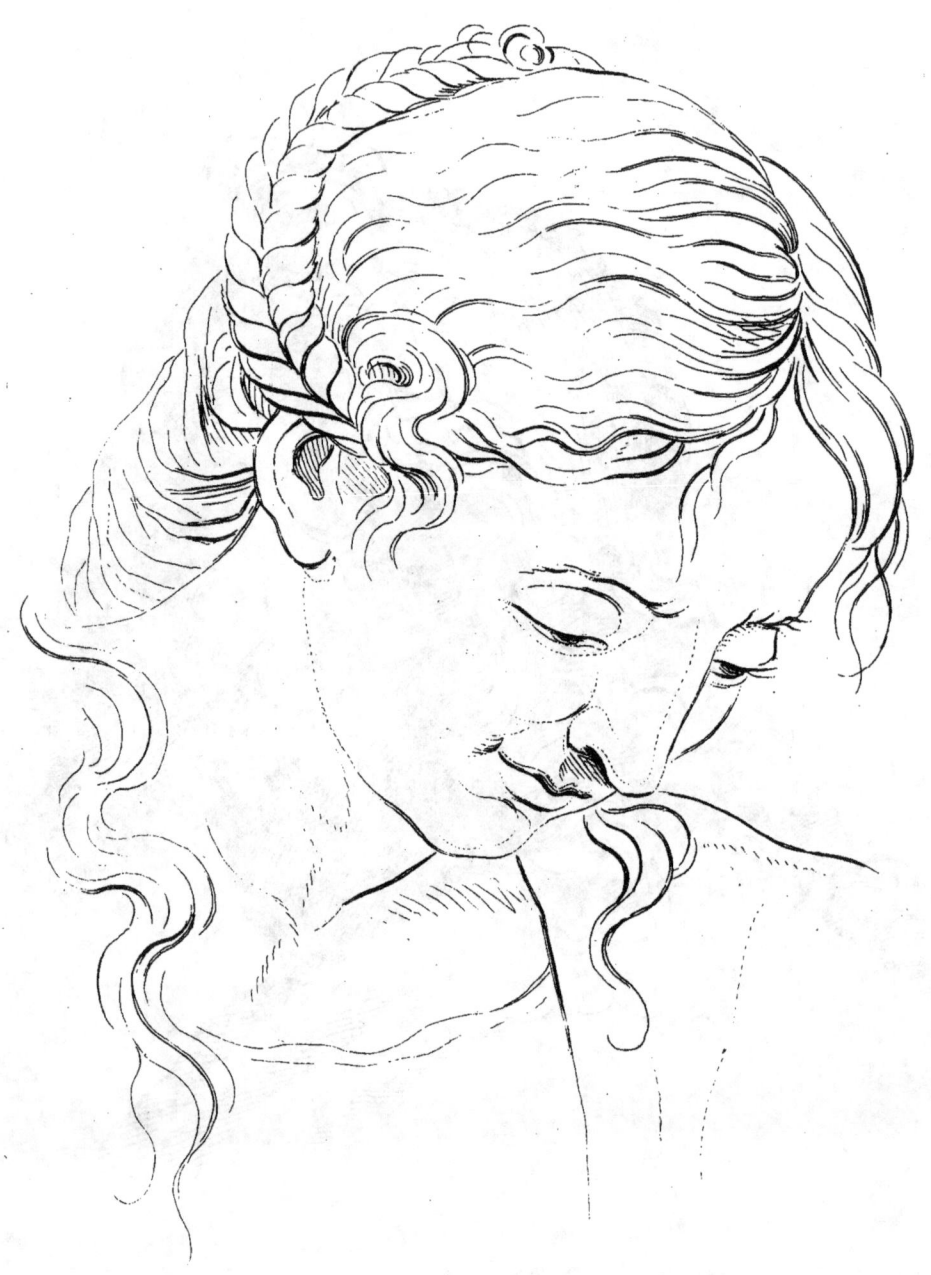

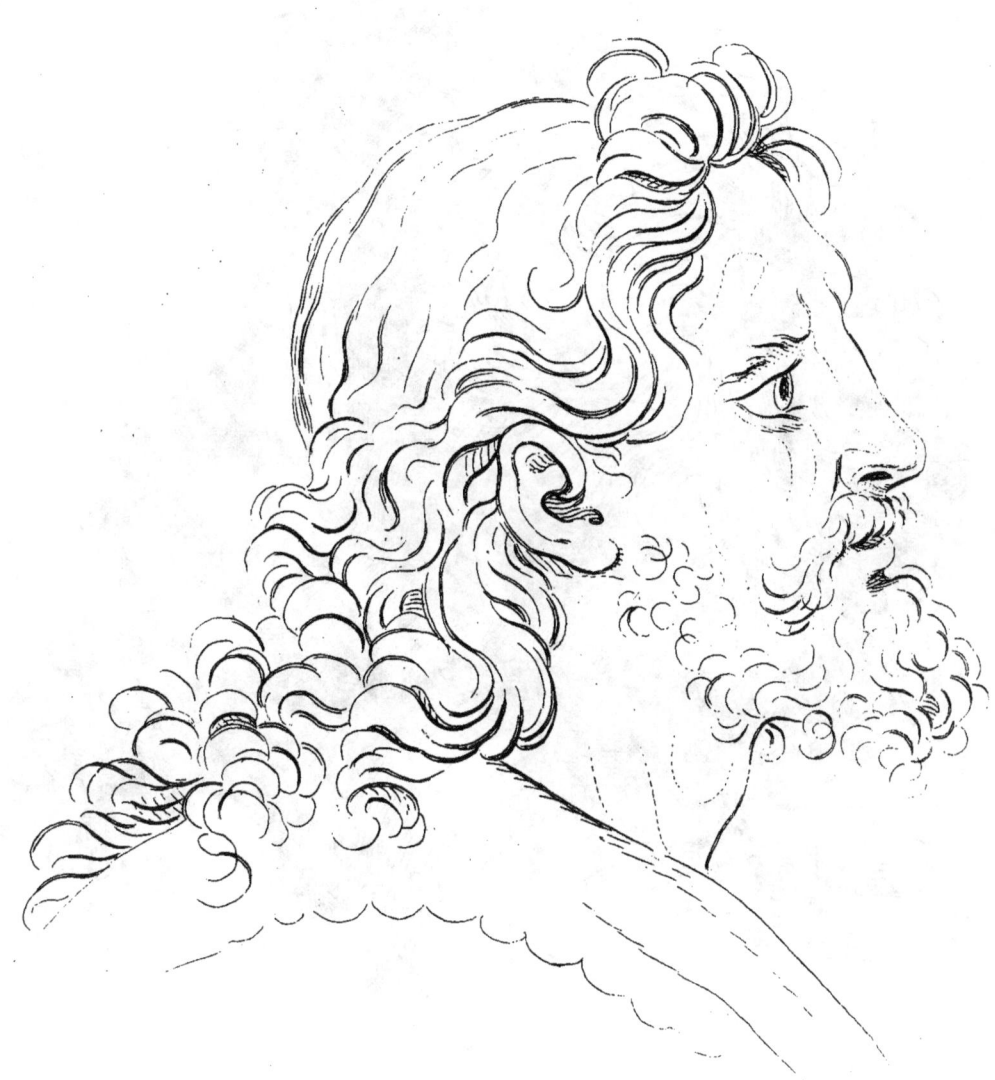

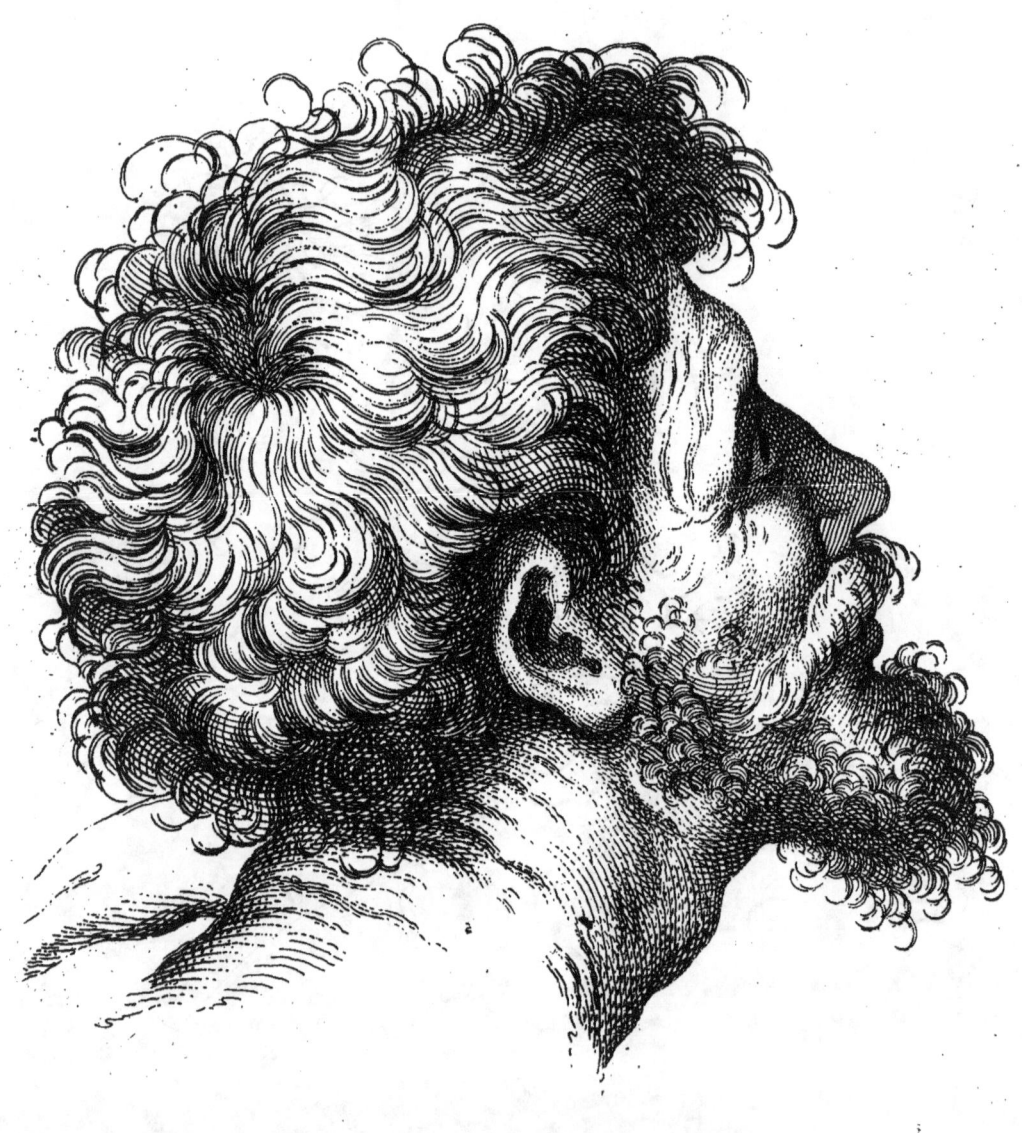

Raph.Vrb.pinx .

Plate 29. I. - from Christ's Charge to Peter

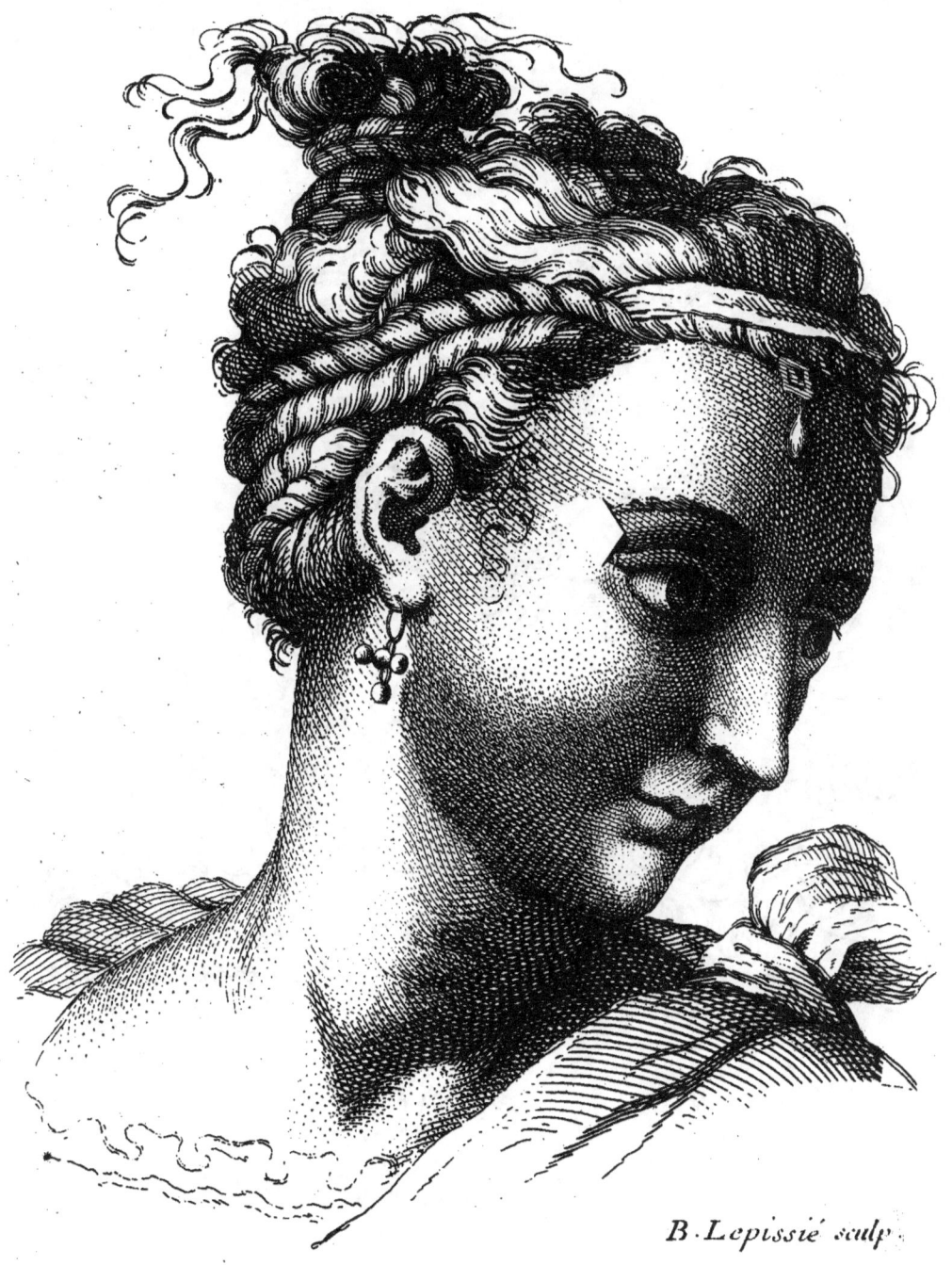

B. Lepissié sculp.

Plate 29. II. - from The Lame Man Healed

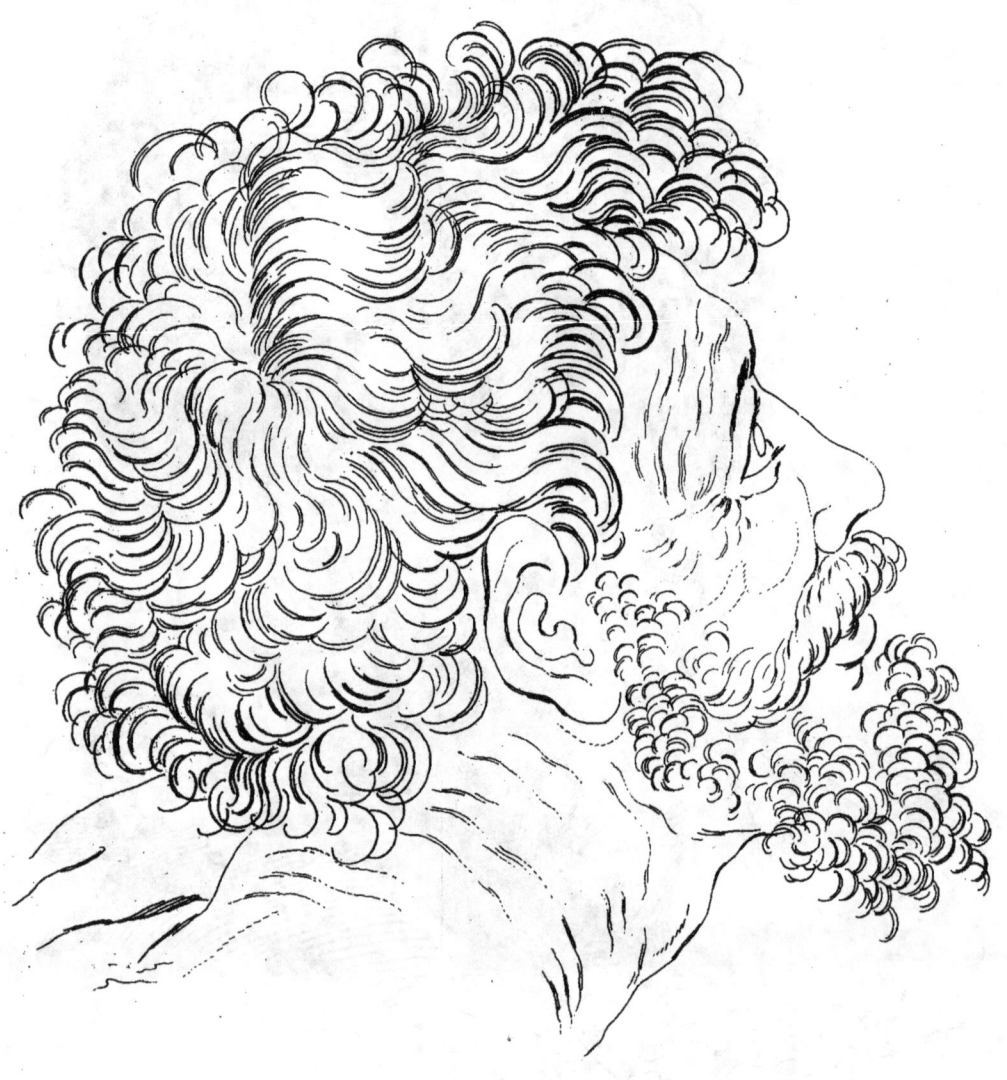

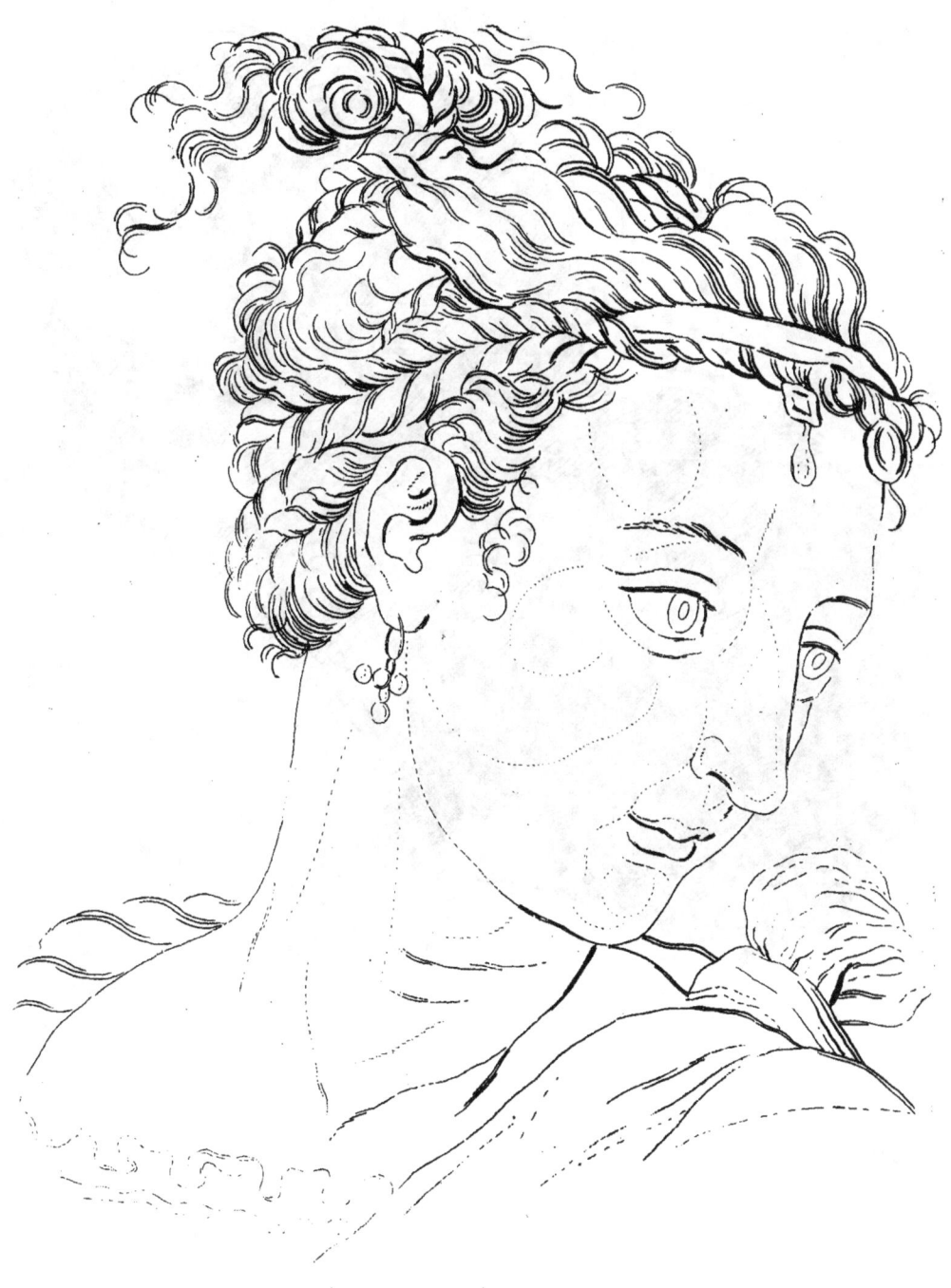

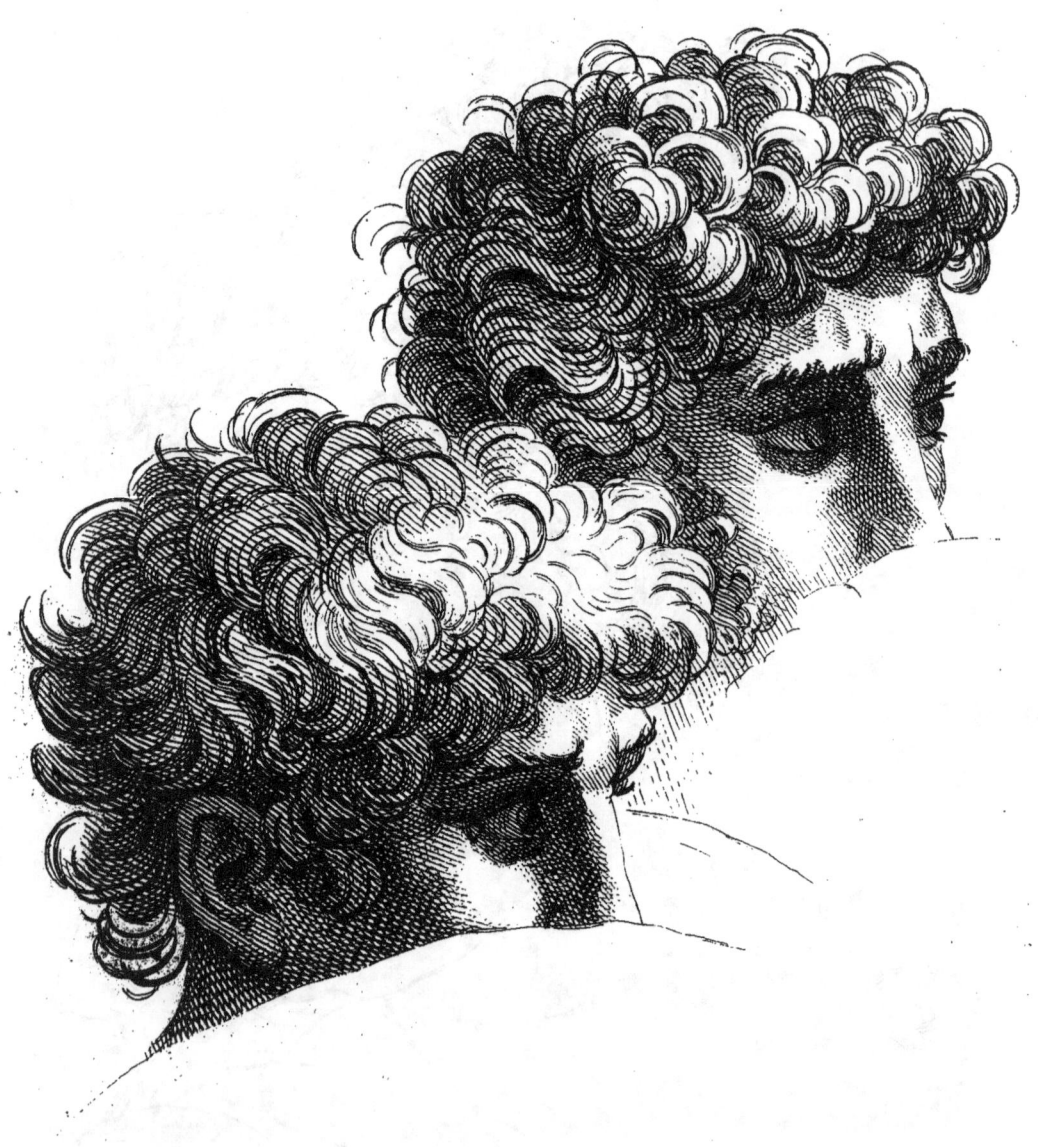

Raph. Vrb. pinx.

Plate 30. I. - from Paul Preaching

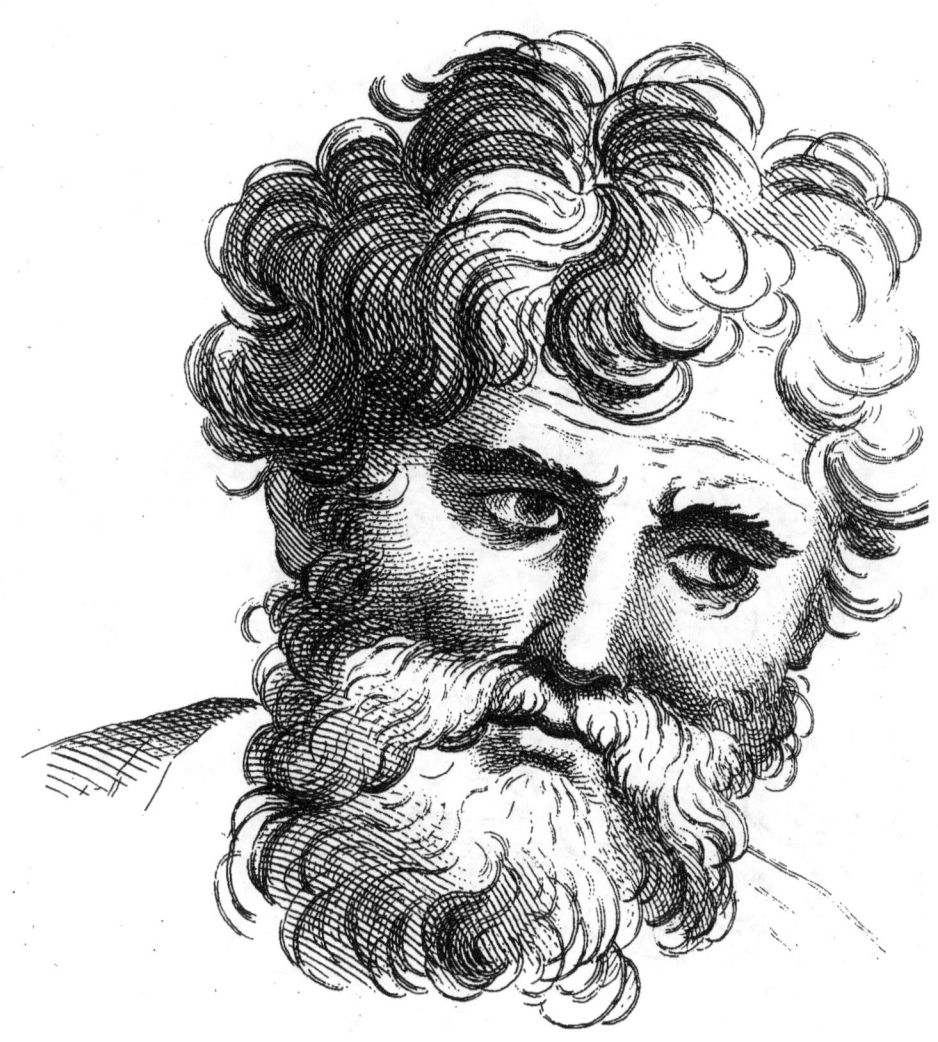

S. Thomassin sculp.

Plate 30. I. - from Paul Preaching

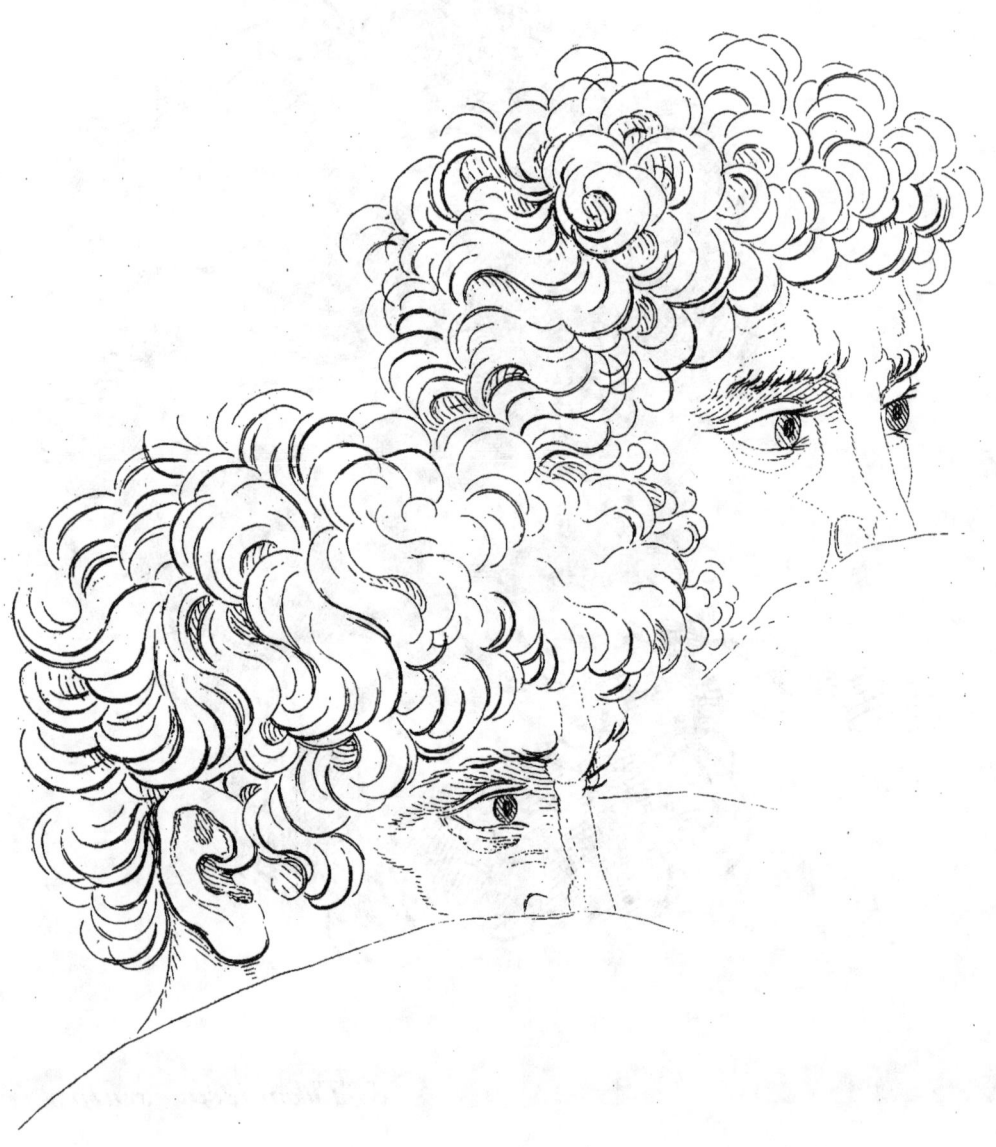

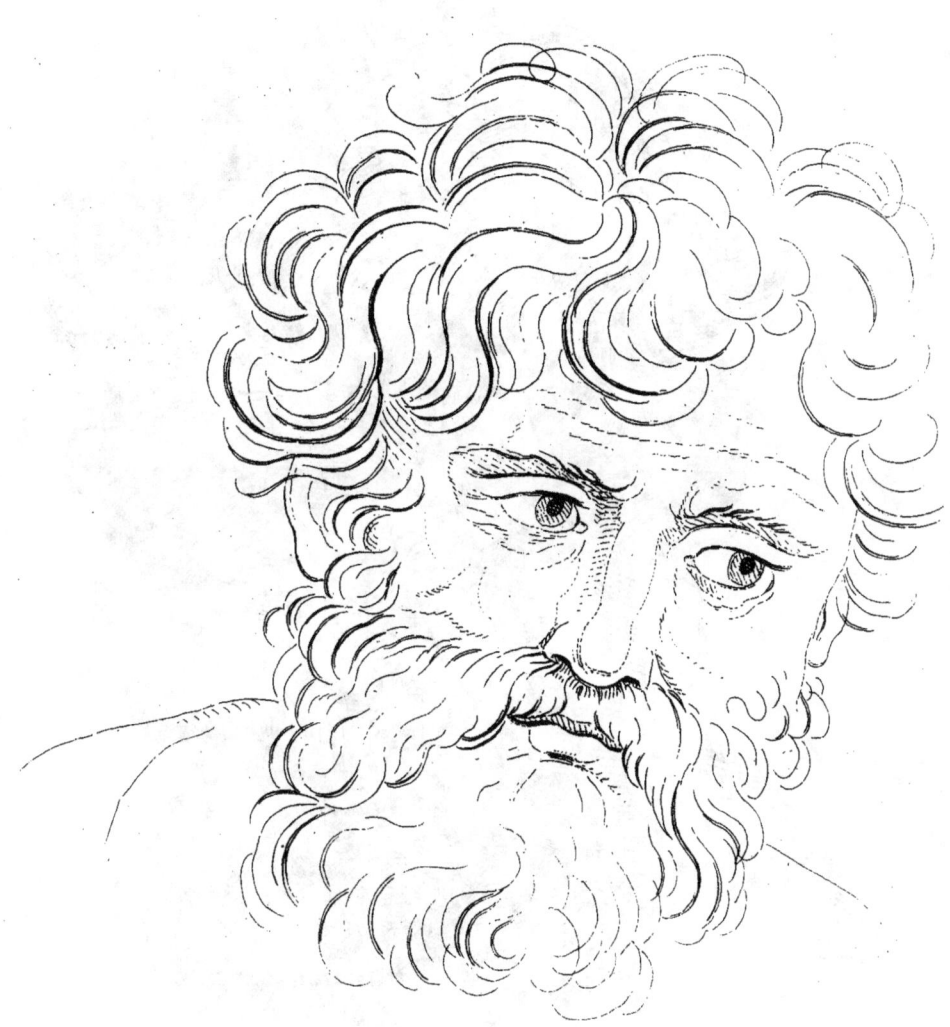

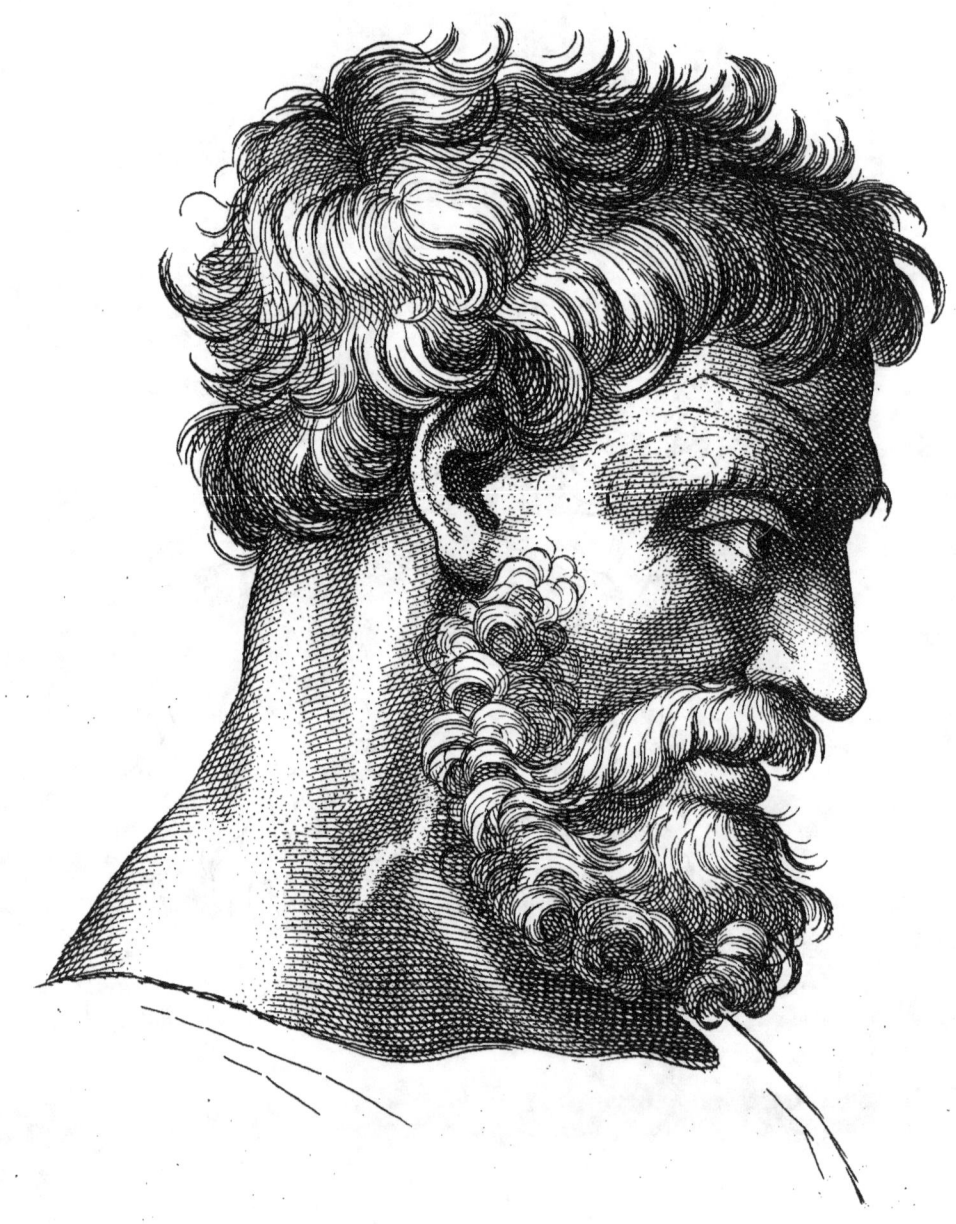

Raph . Urb.pin.

Plate 31. I. - from The Lame Man Healed

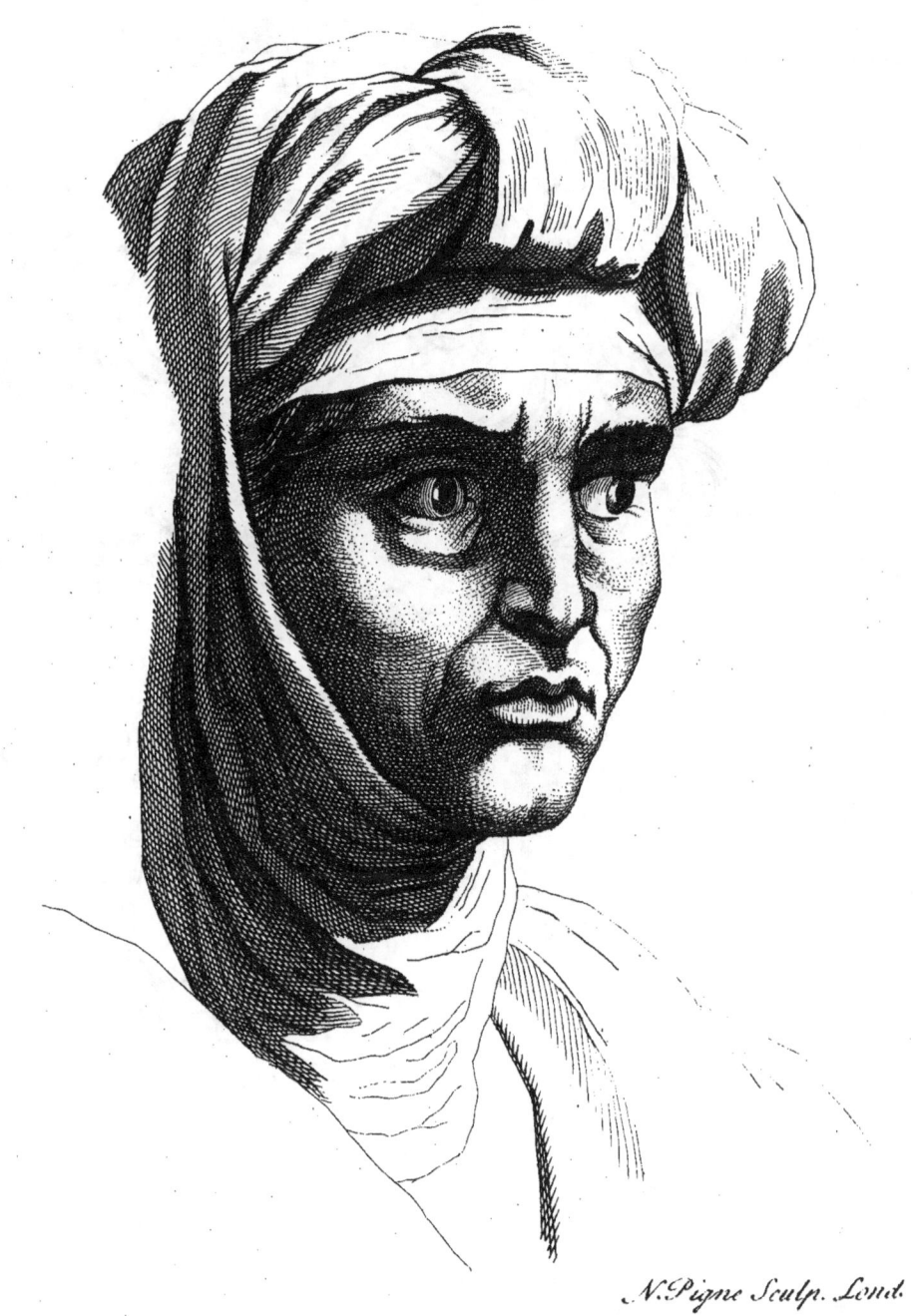

N. Pigne Sculp. Lond.

Plate 31. II. - from The Lame Man Healed

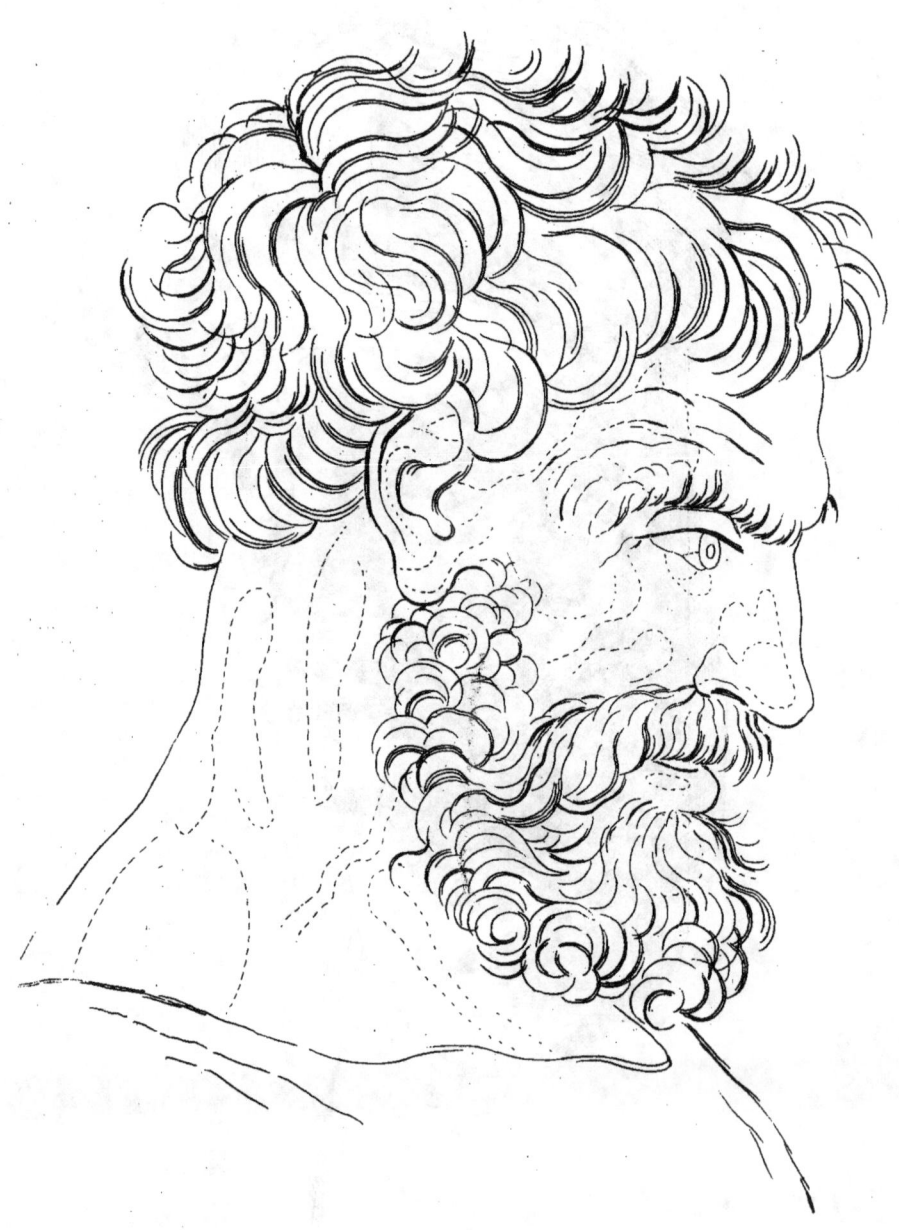

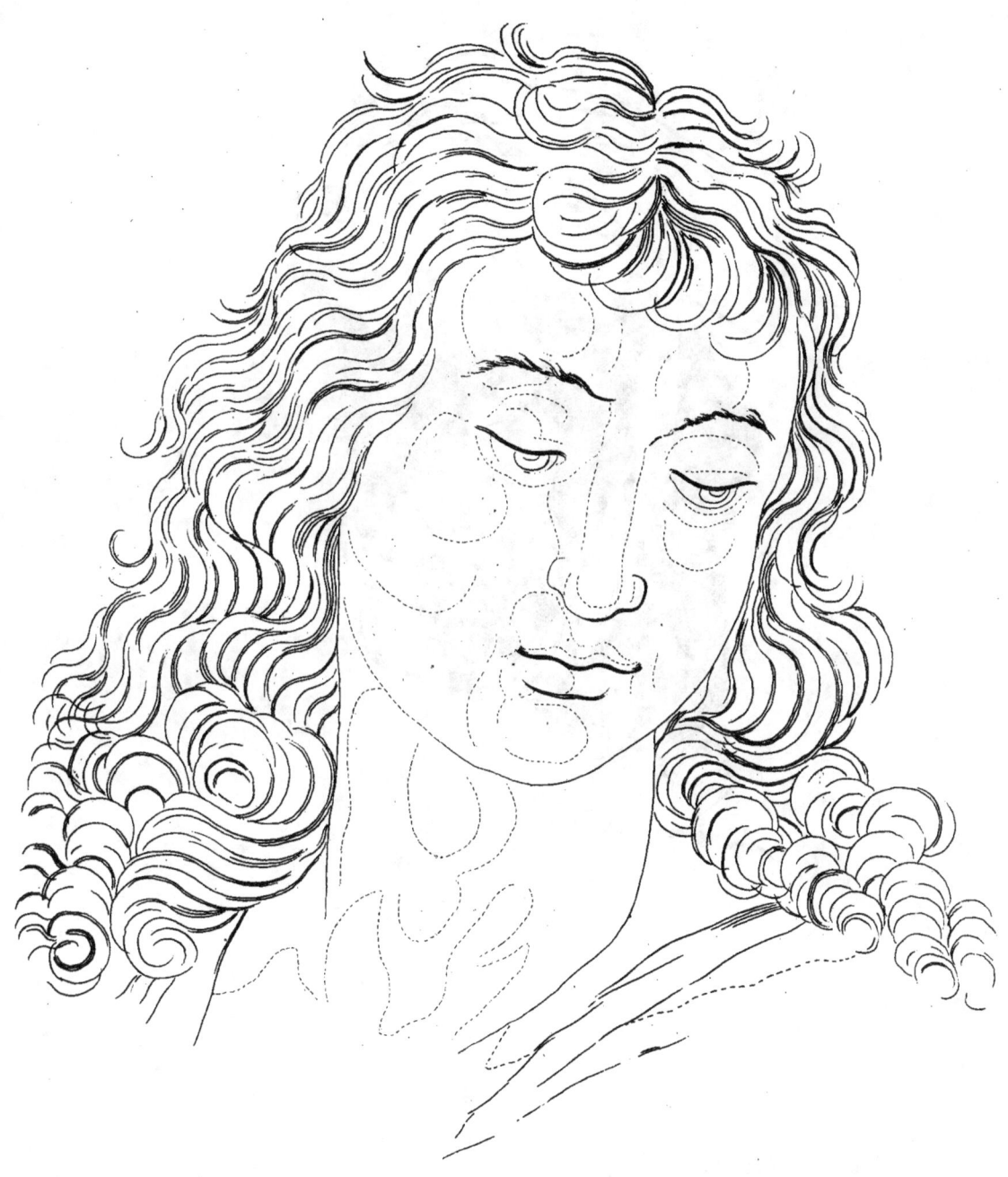

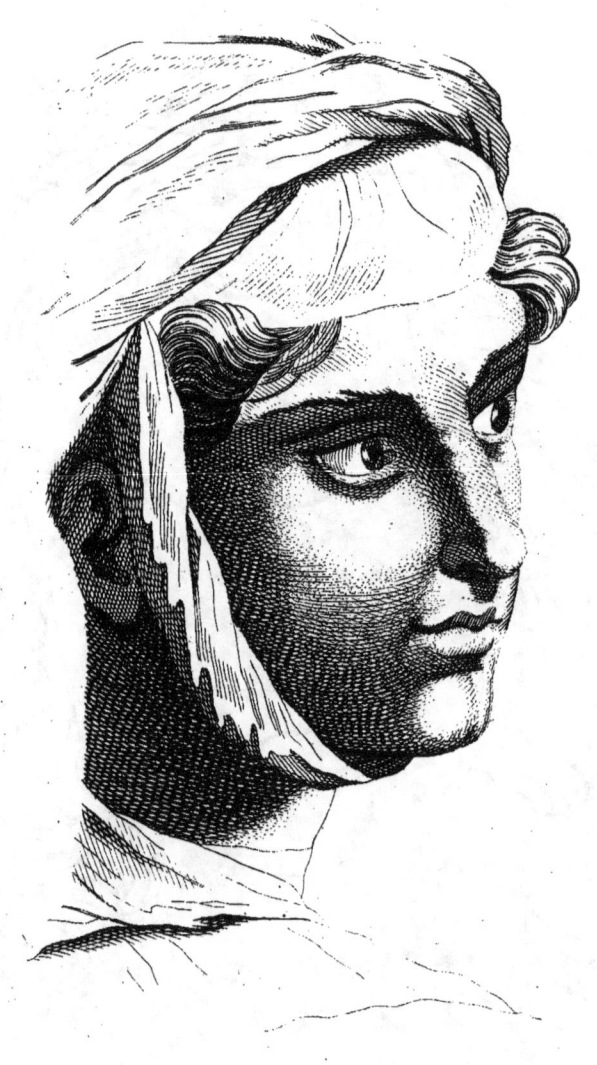

Raph: Urb: Pinx.t

Plate 32. I. - from The Death of Ananias

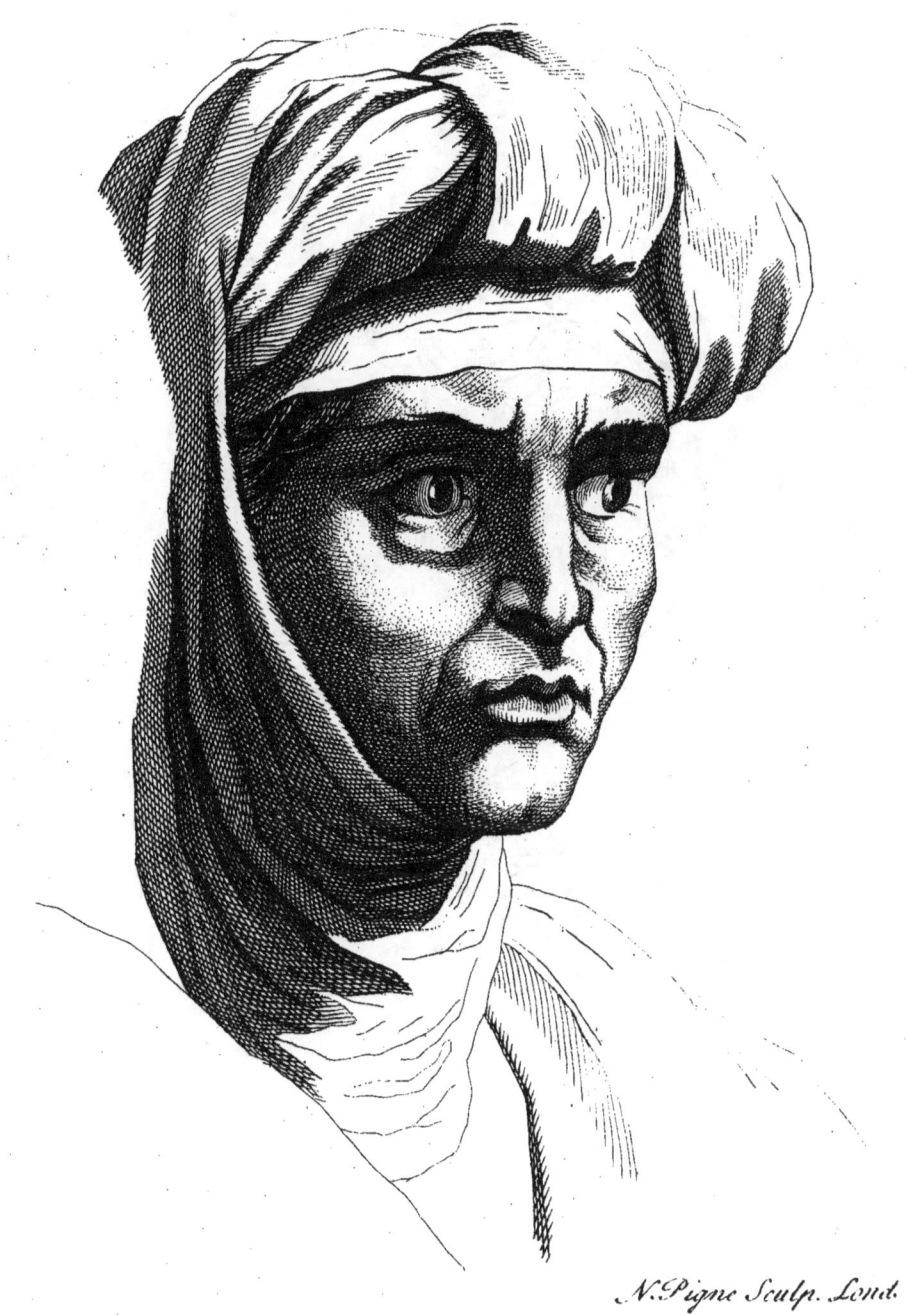

Plate 32. II. - from The Death of Ananias

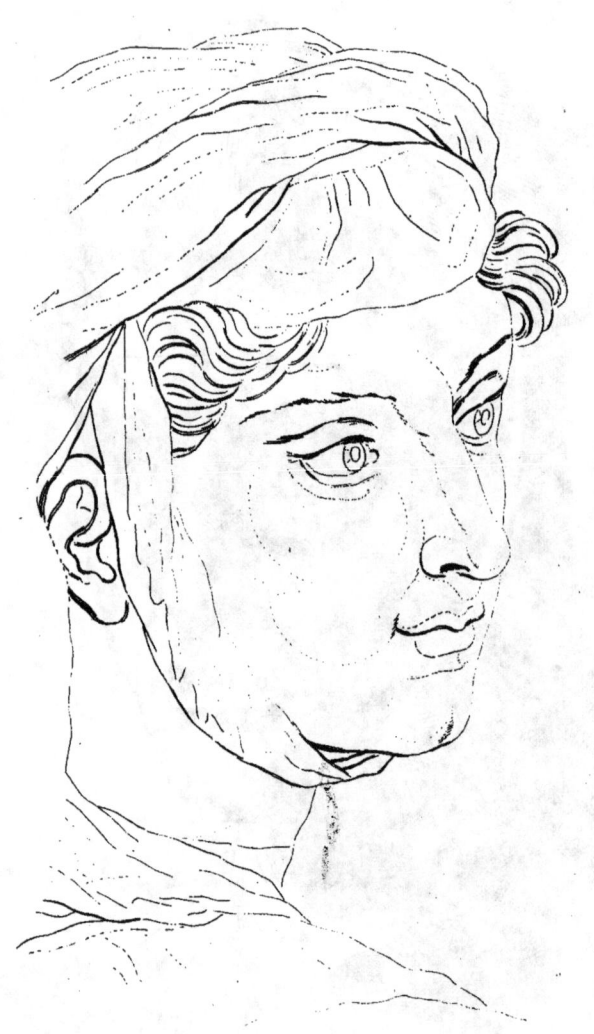

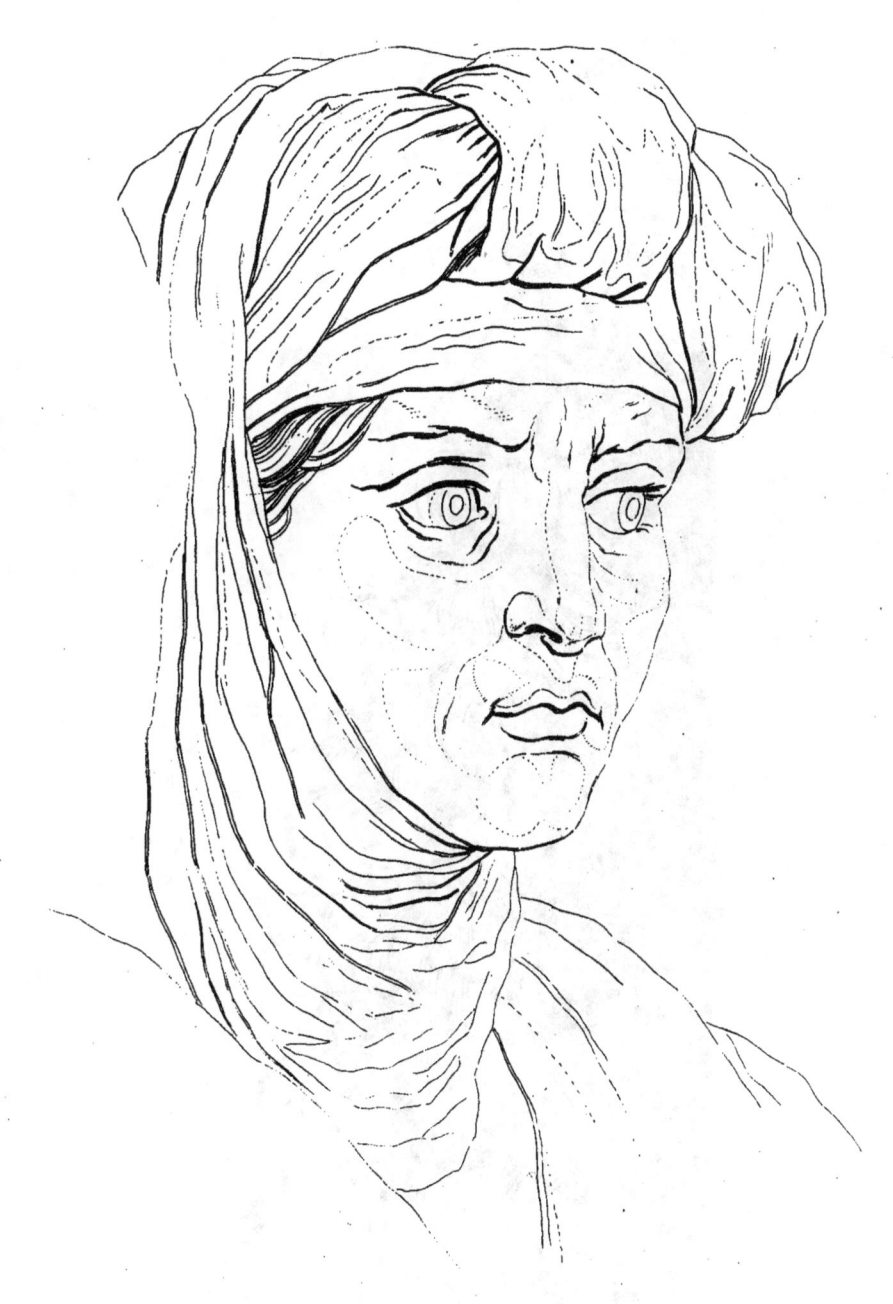

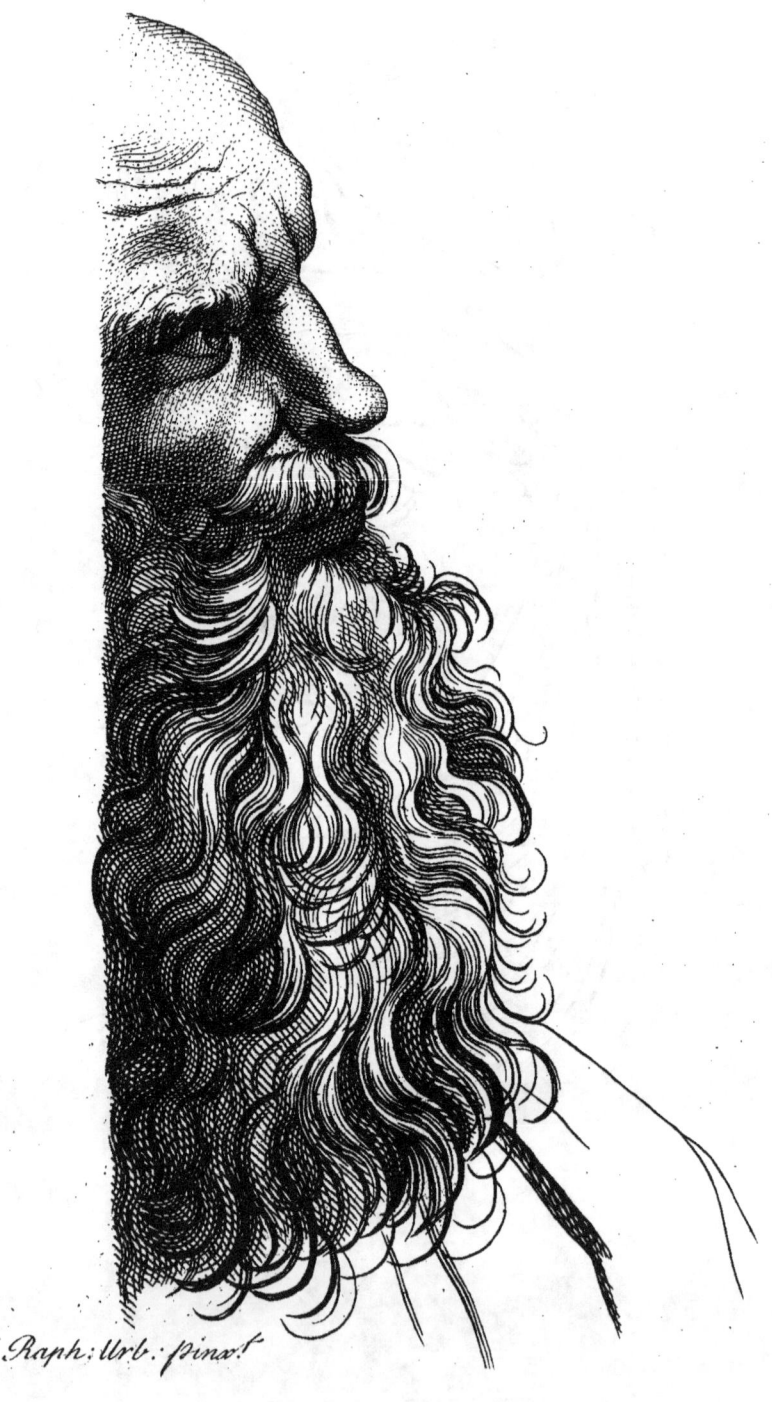

Raph: Urb: pinx.t

Plate 33. I. - from Paul and Barnabas

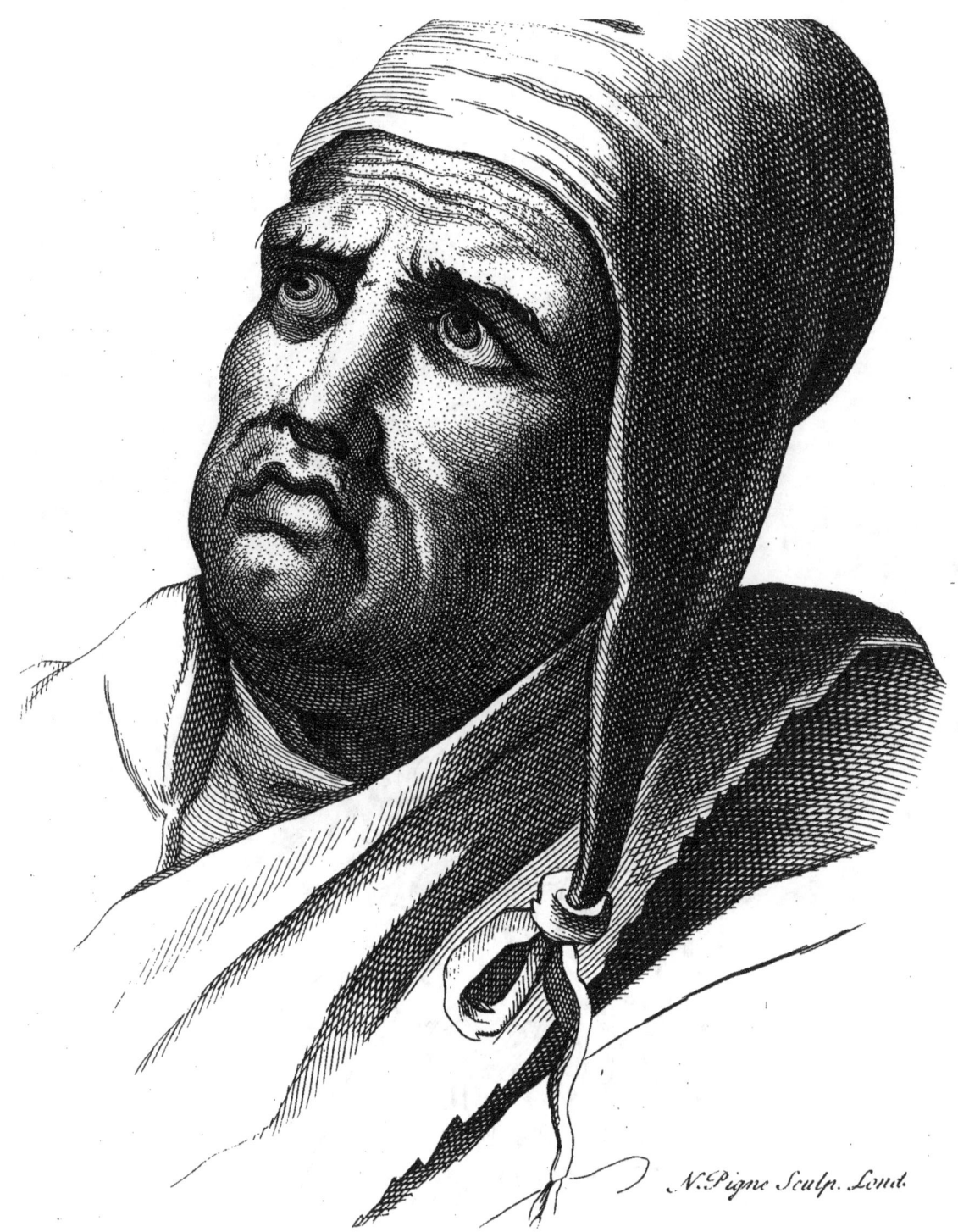

Plate 33. II. - from Paul Preaching

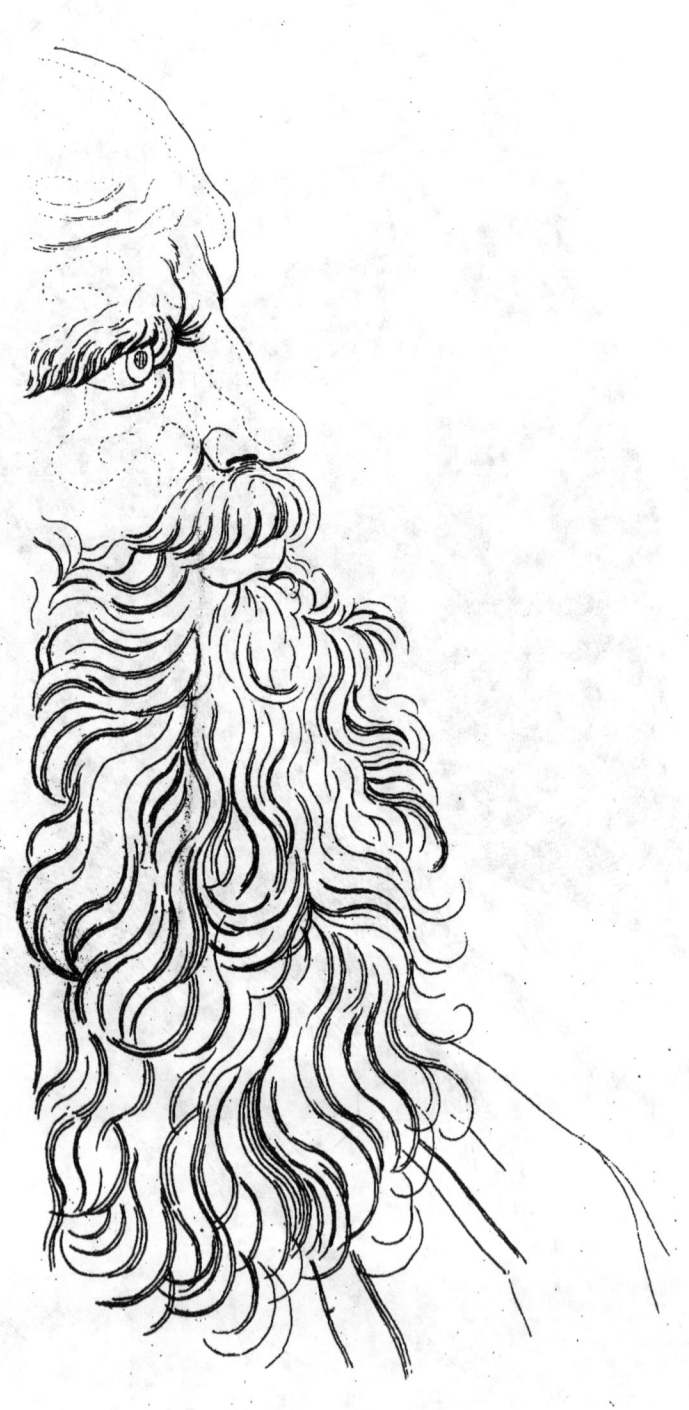

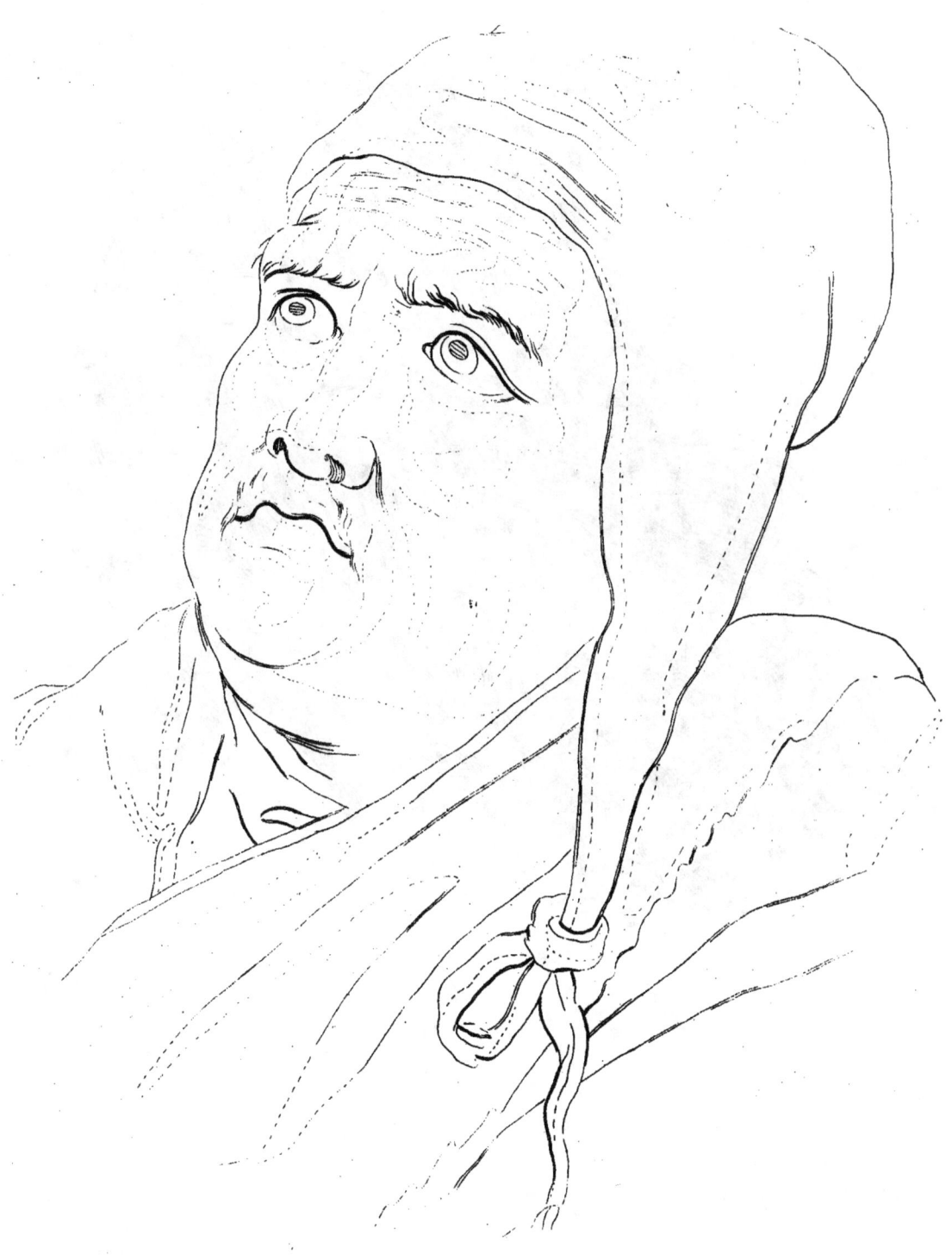

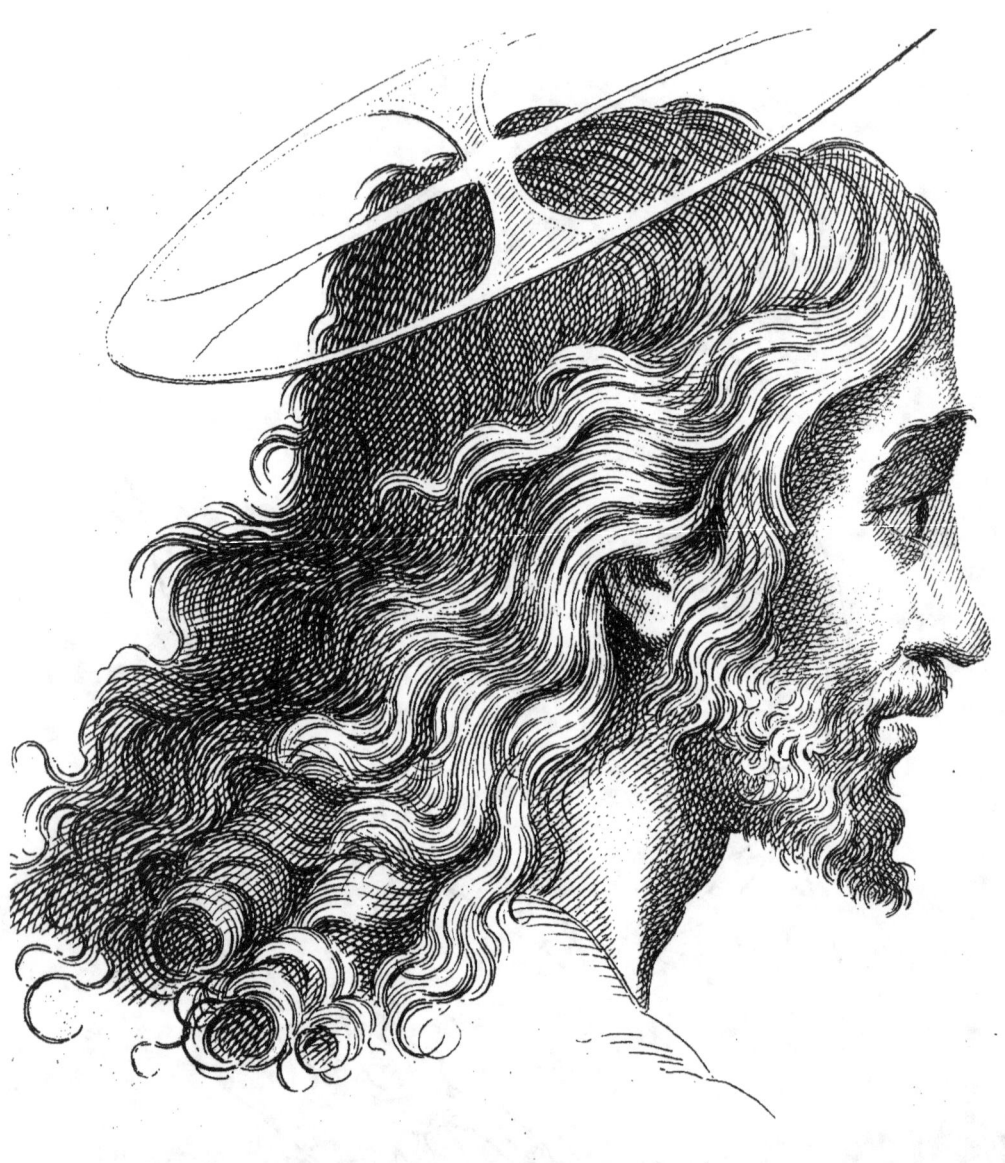

Raph. Vrb pinx.

Plate 34.I. - from The Miraculous Draught of Fishes

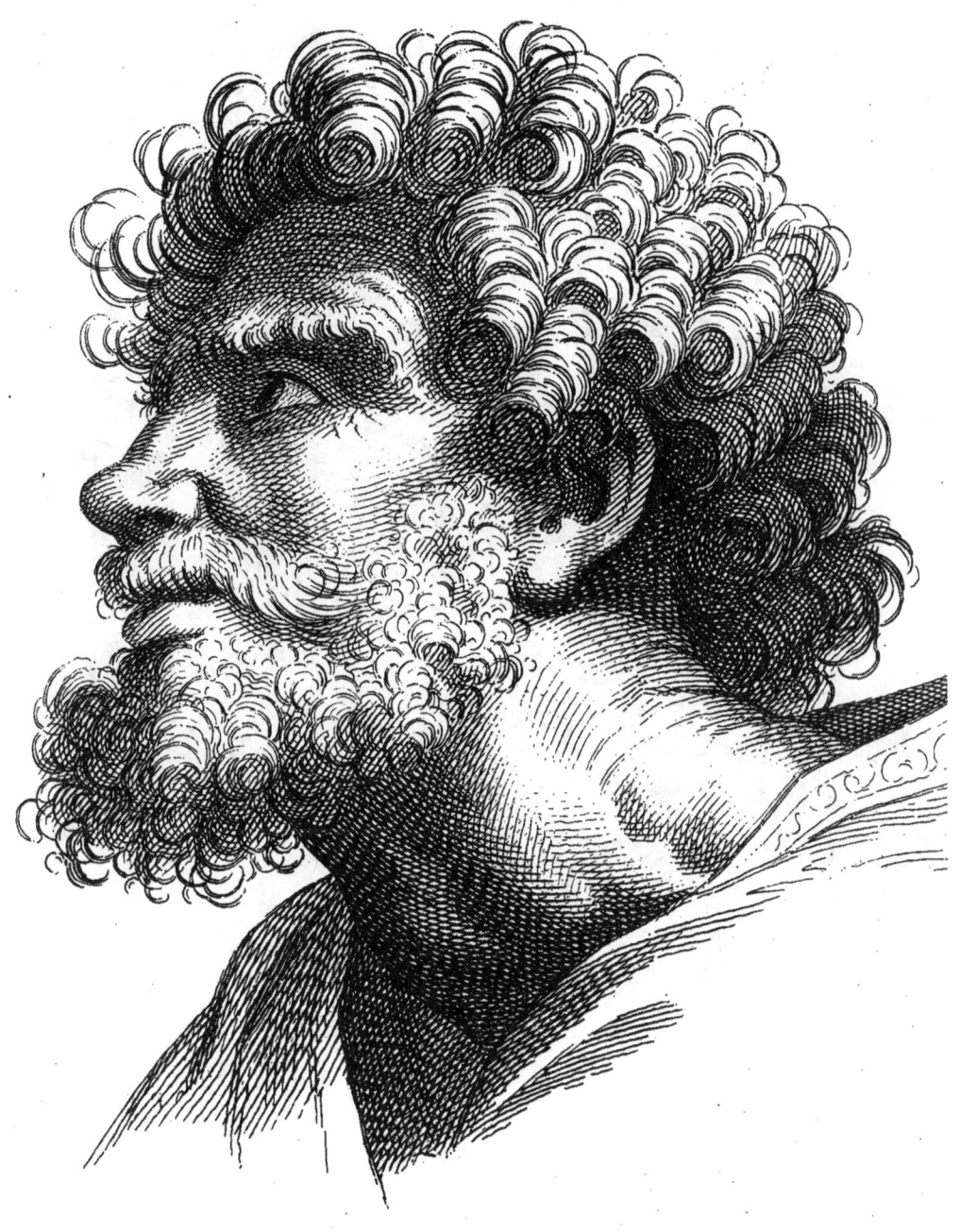

n. Dupuis sculp.

Plate 34.II. - from The Miraculous Draught of Fishes

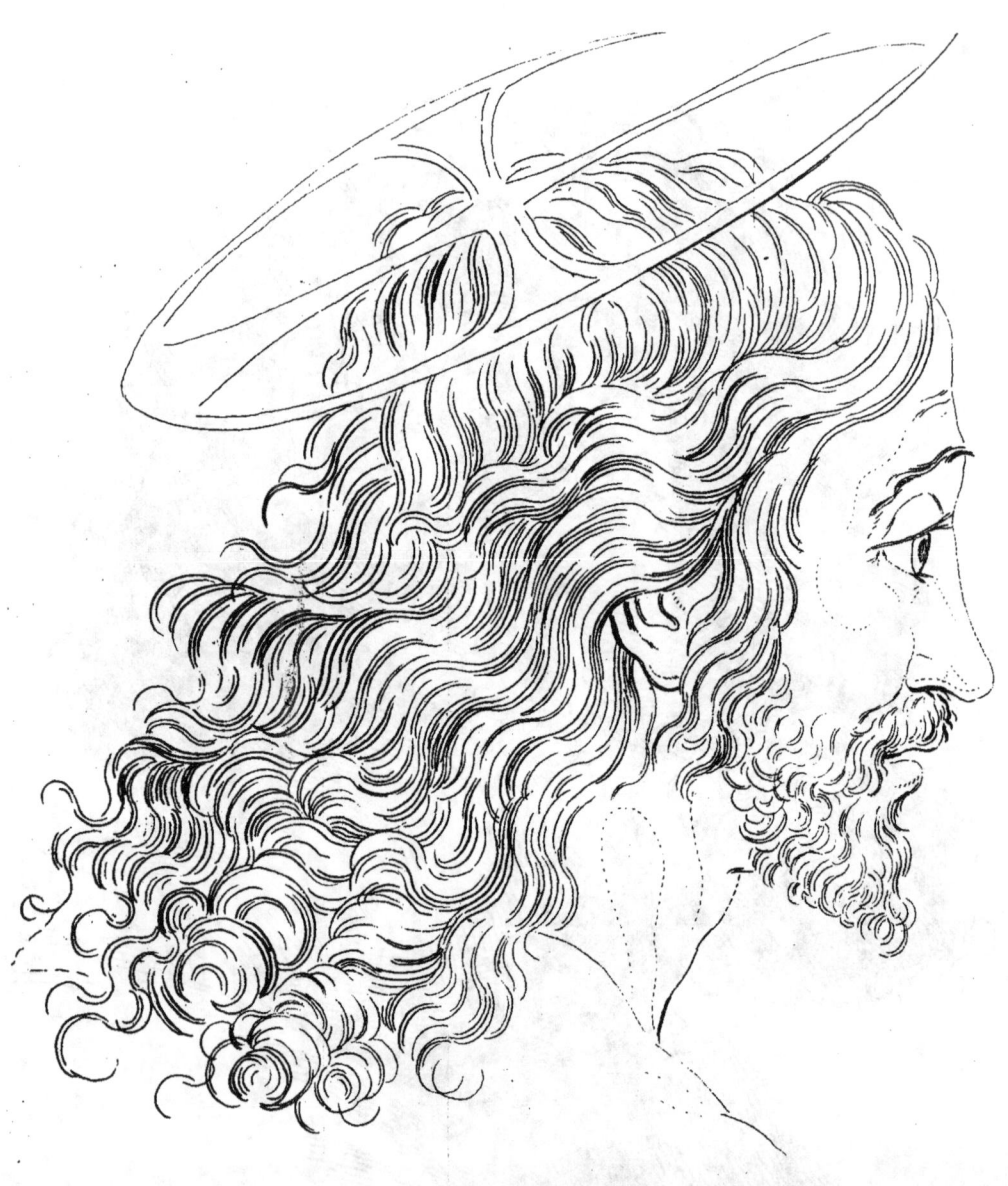

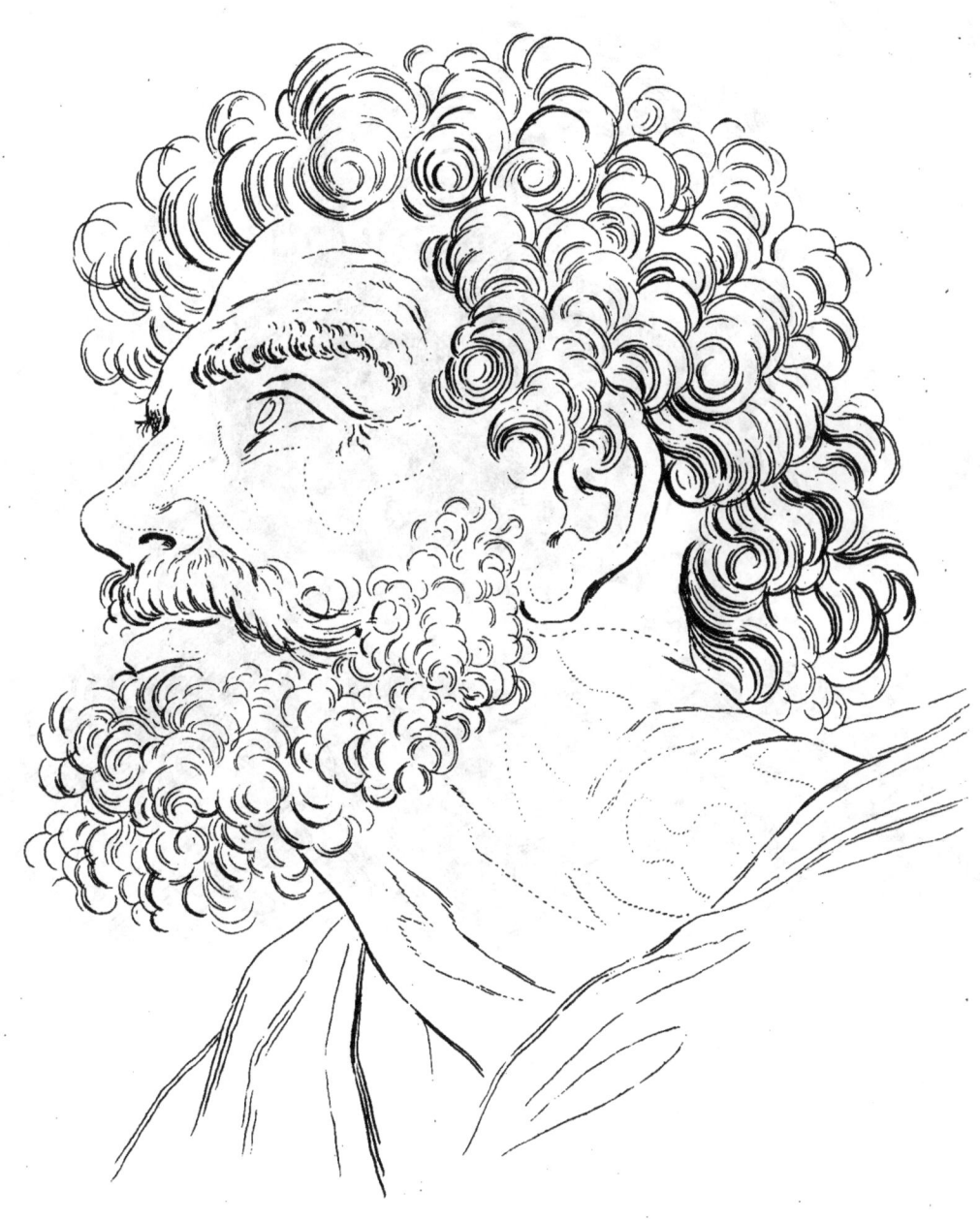

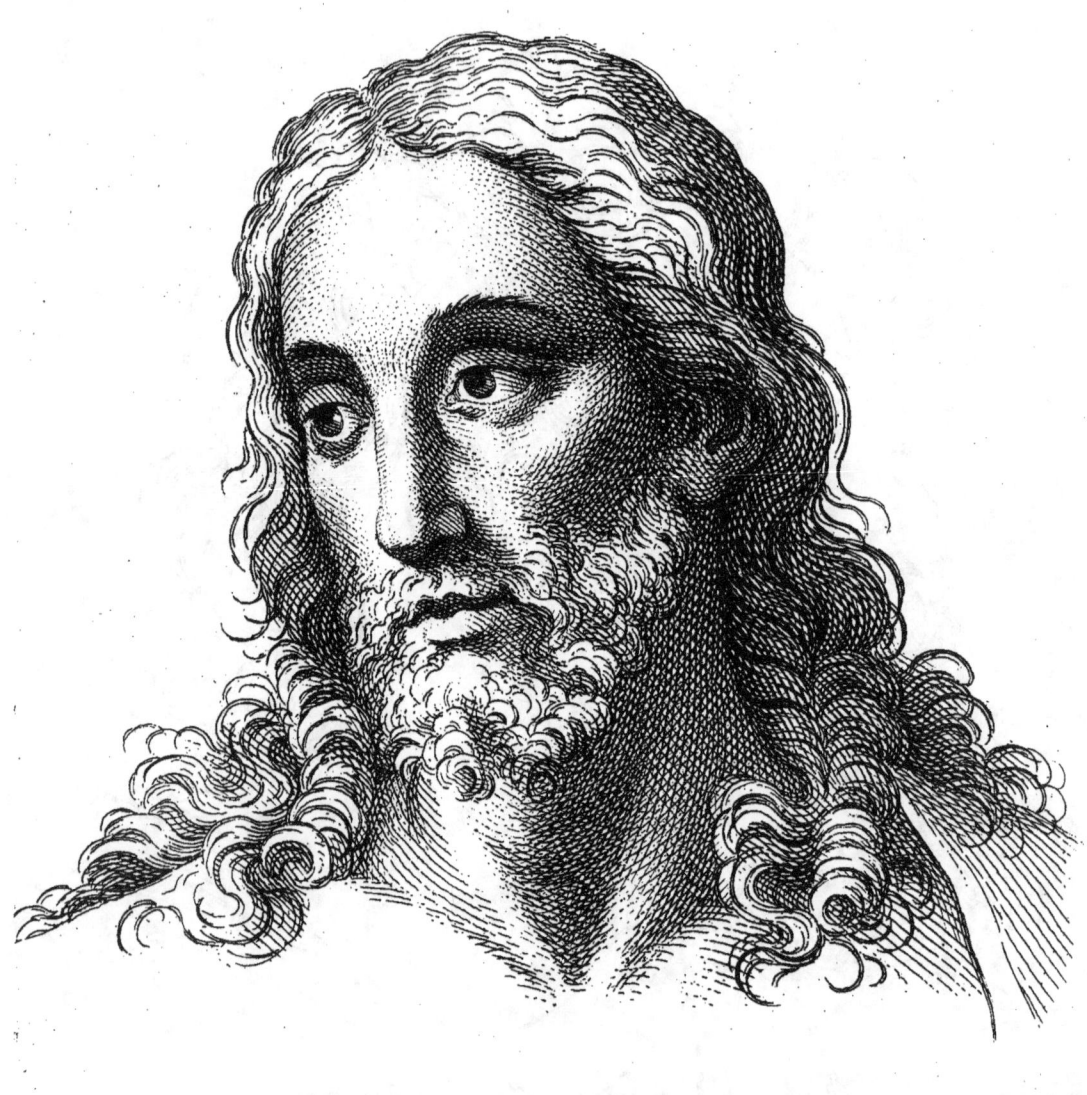

Raph . Vrb pinx .

Plate 35.I. - from Christ's Charge to Peter

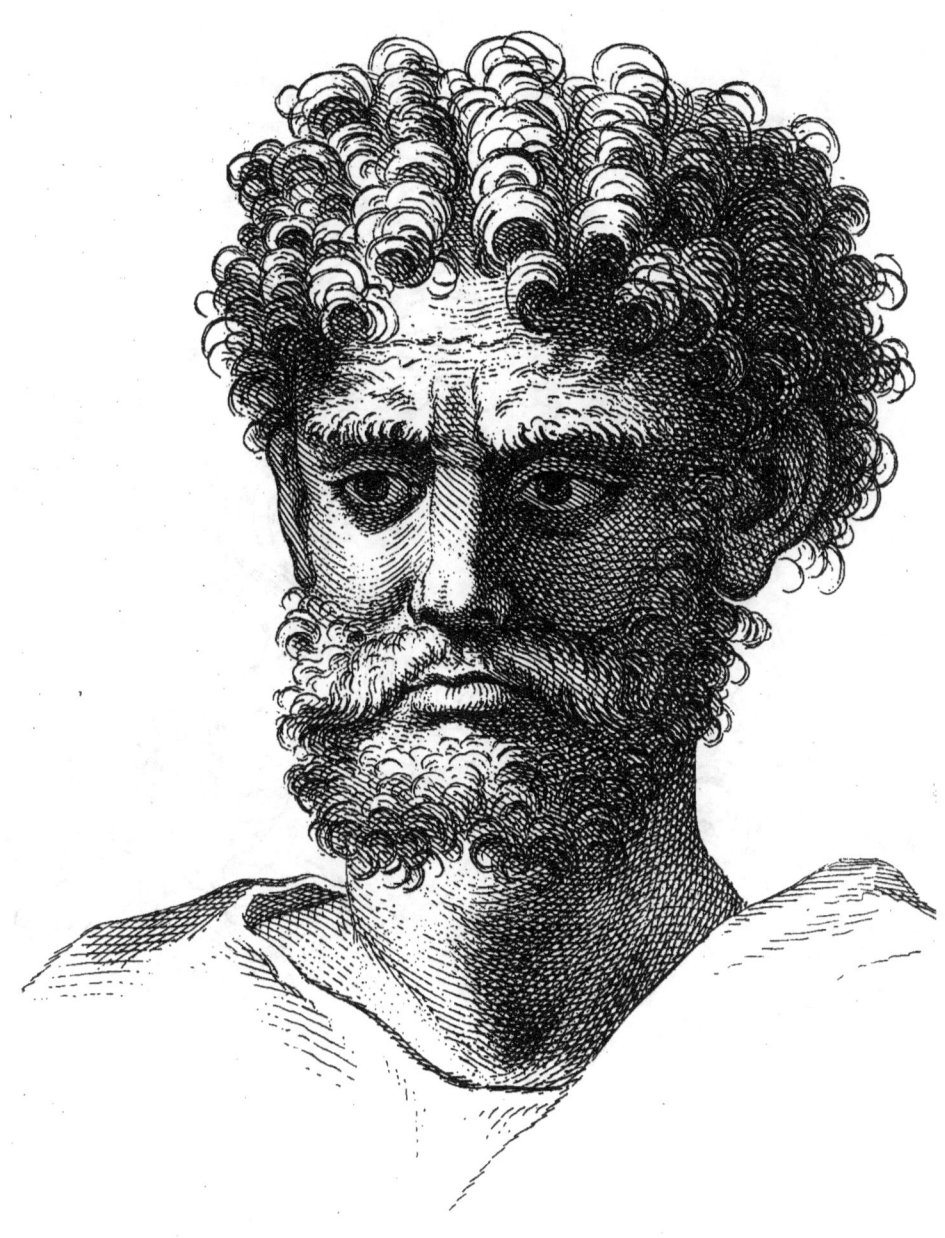

C. Dupuis sculp

Plate 35.II. - from The Death of Ananias

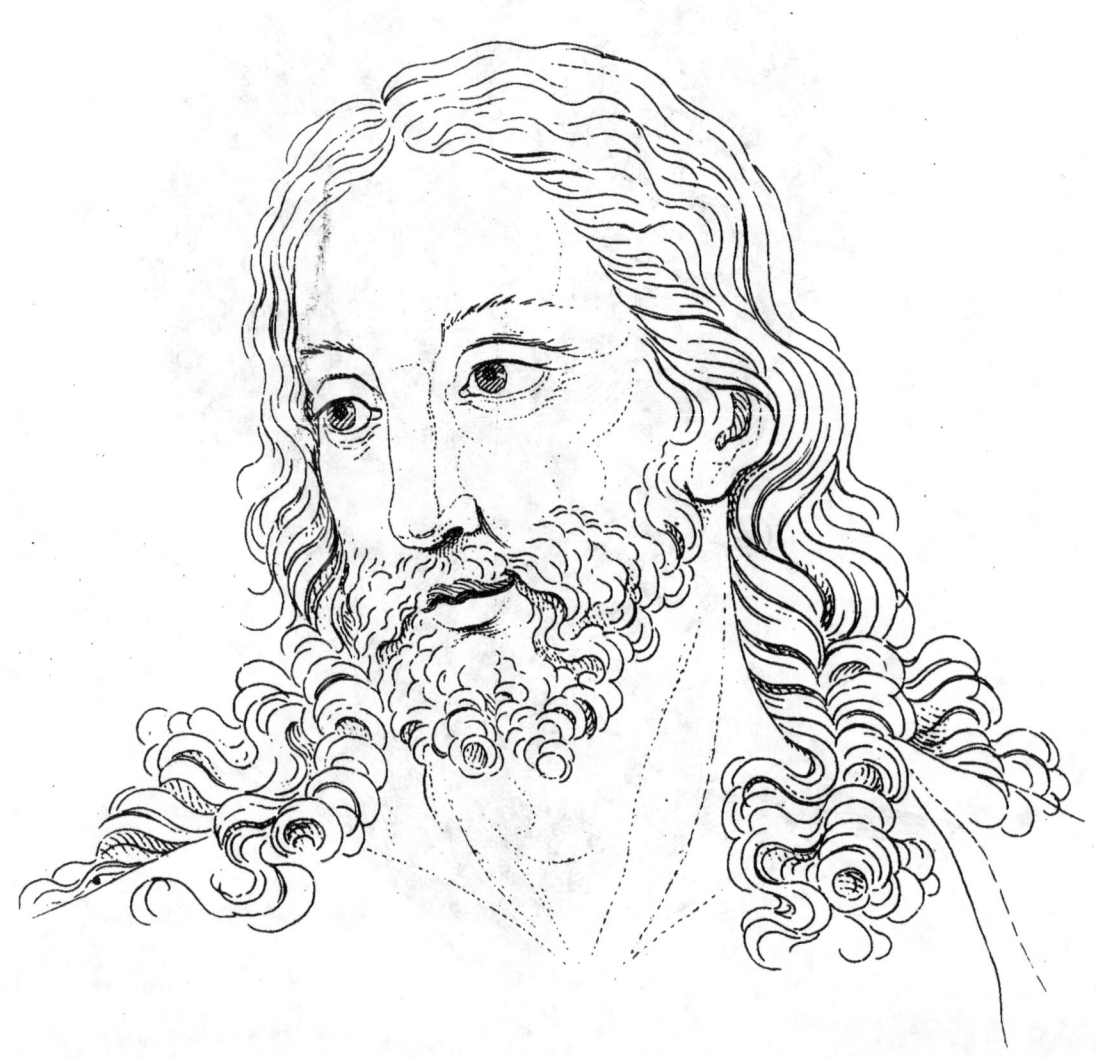

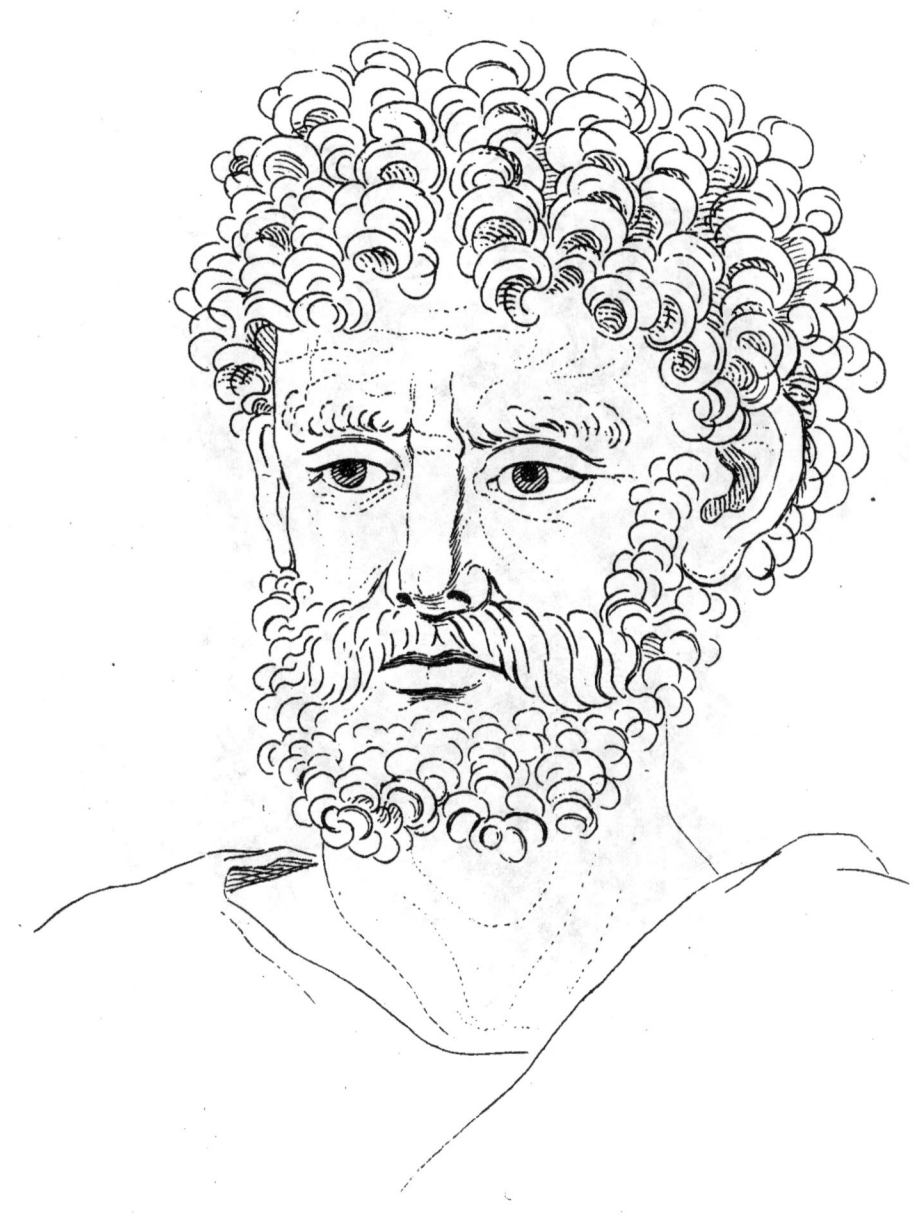

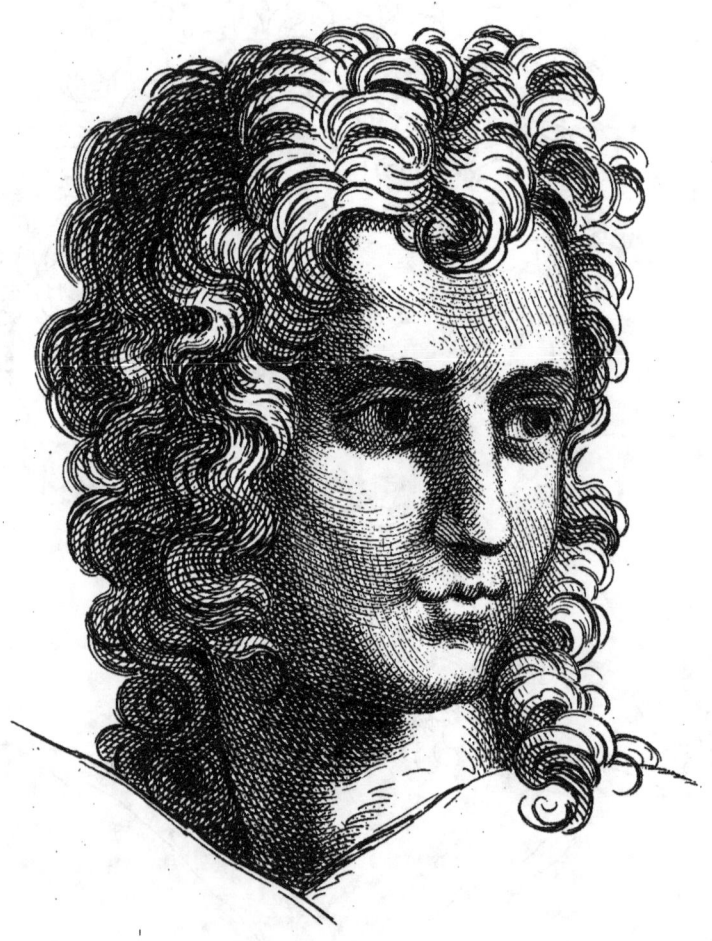

Raph . Vrb pinx .

Plate 36.I. - from The Death of Ananias

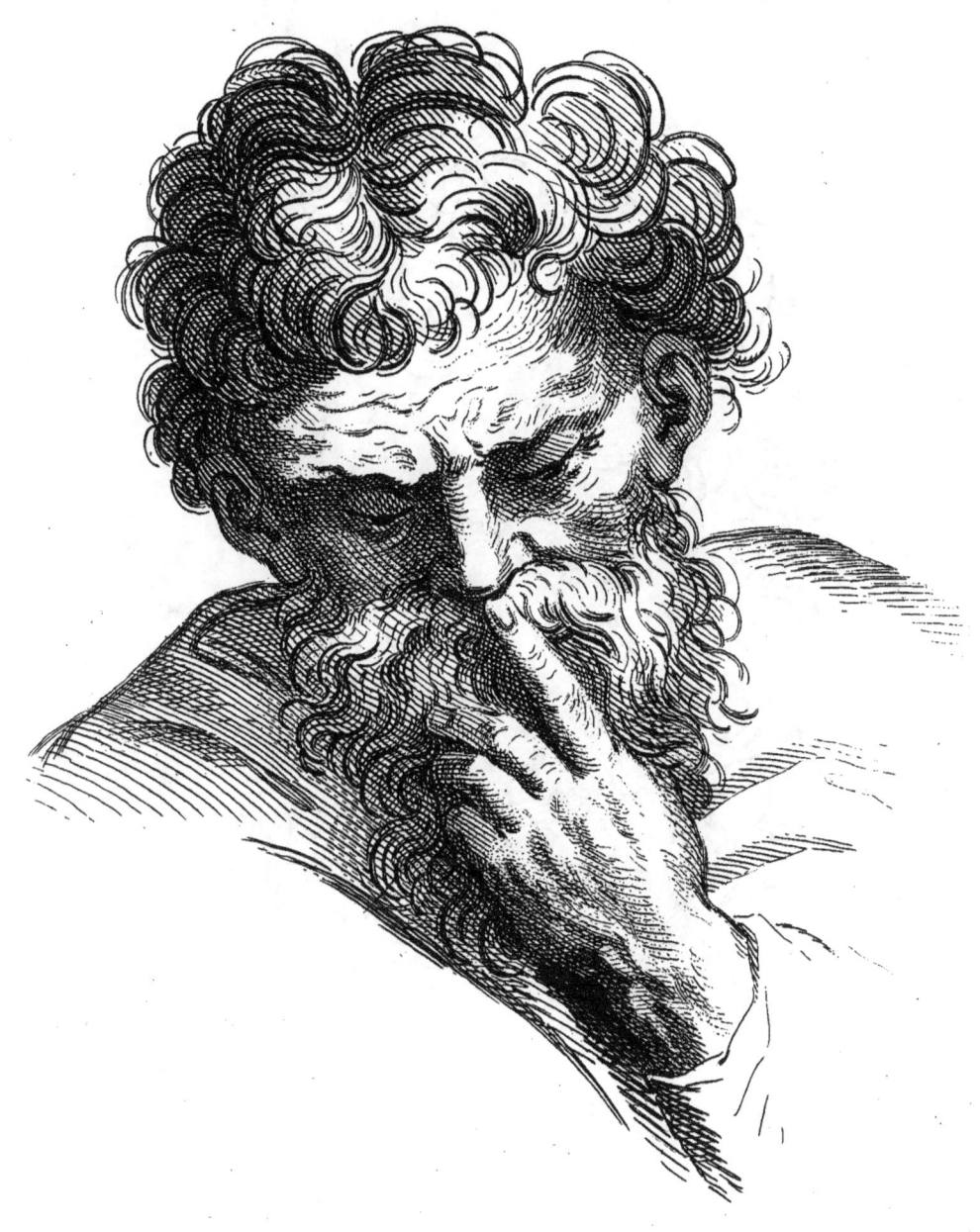

L. Desplaces sculp.

Plate 36.II. - from Paul Preaching

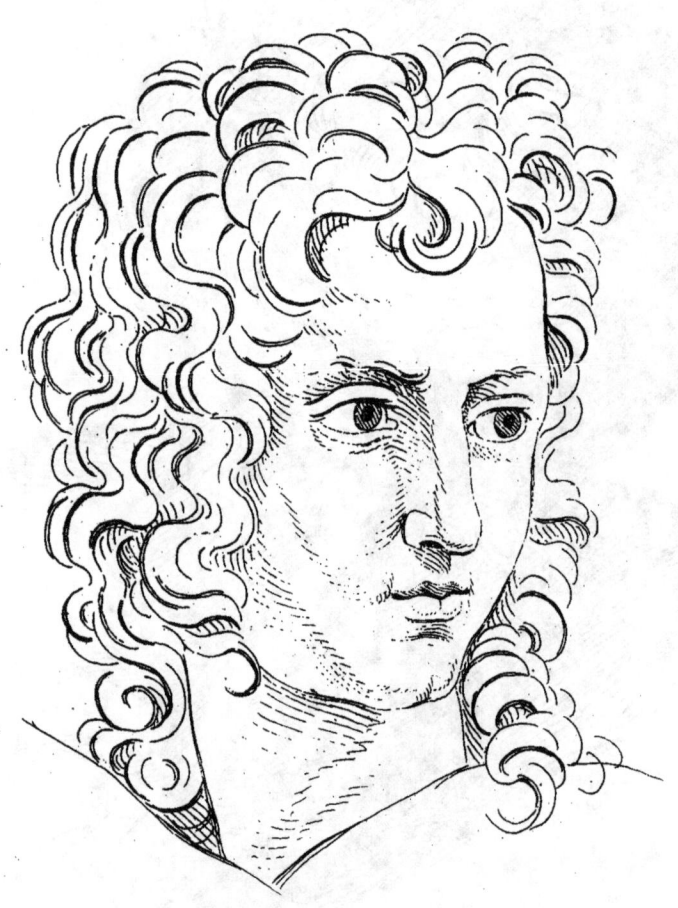

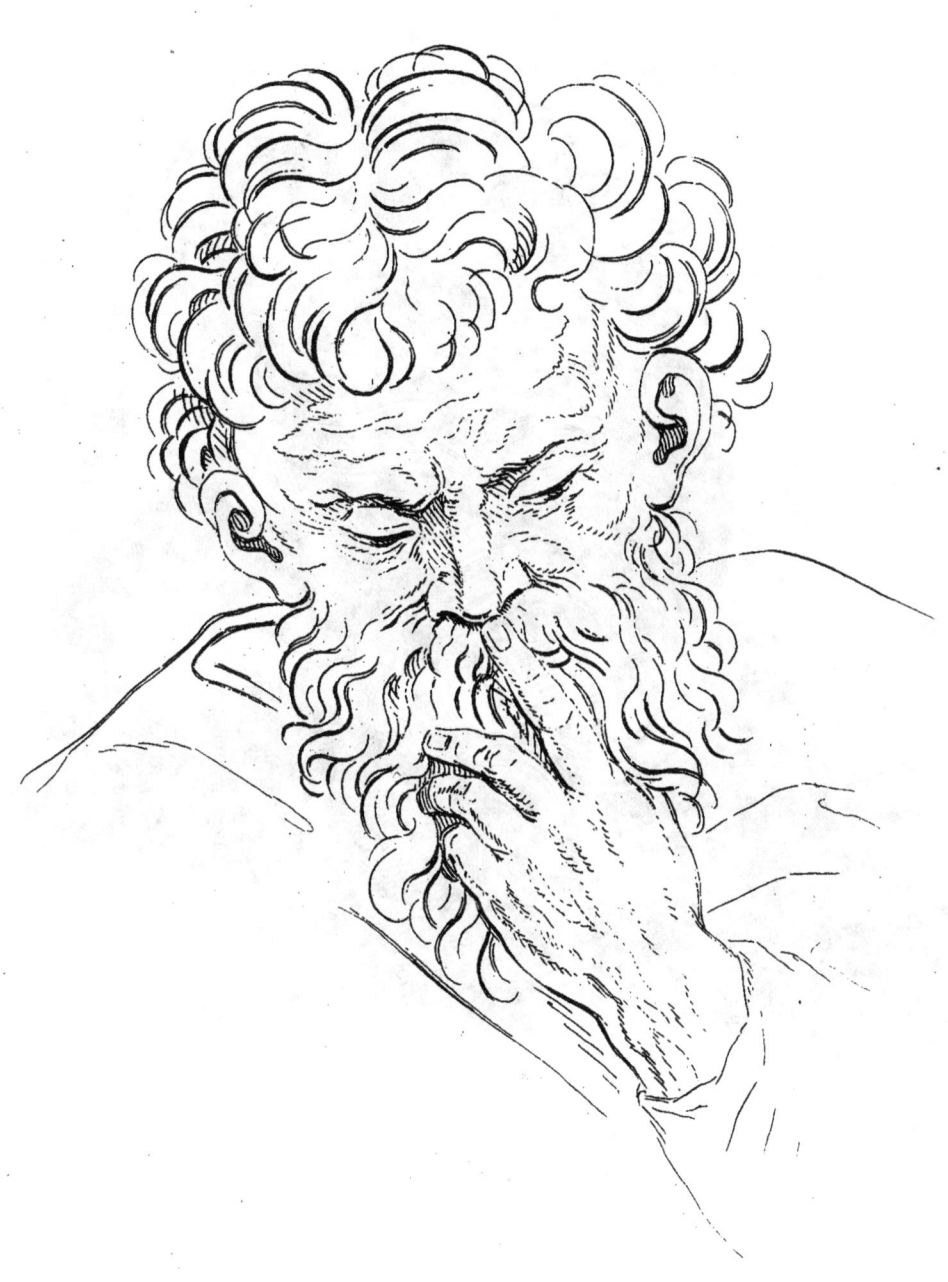

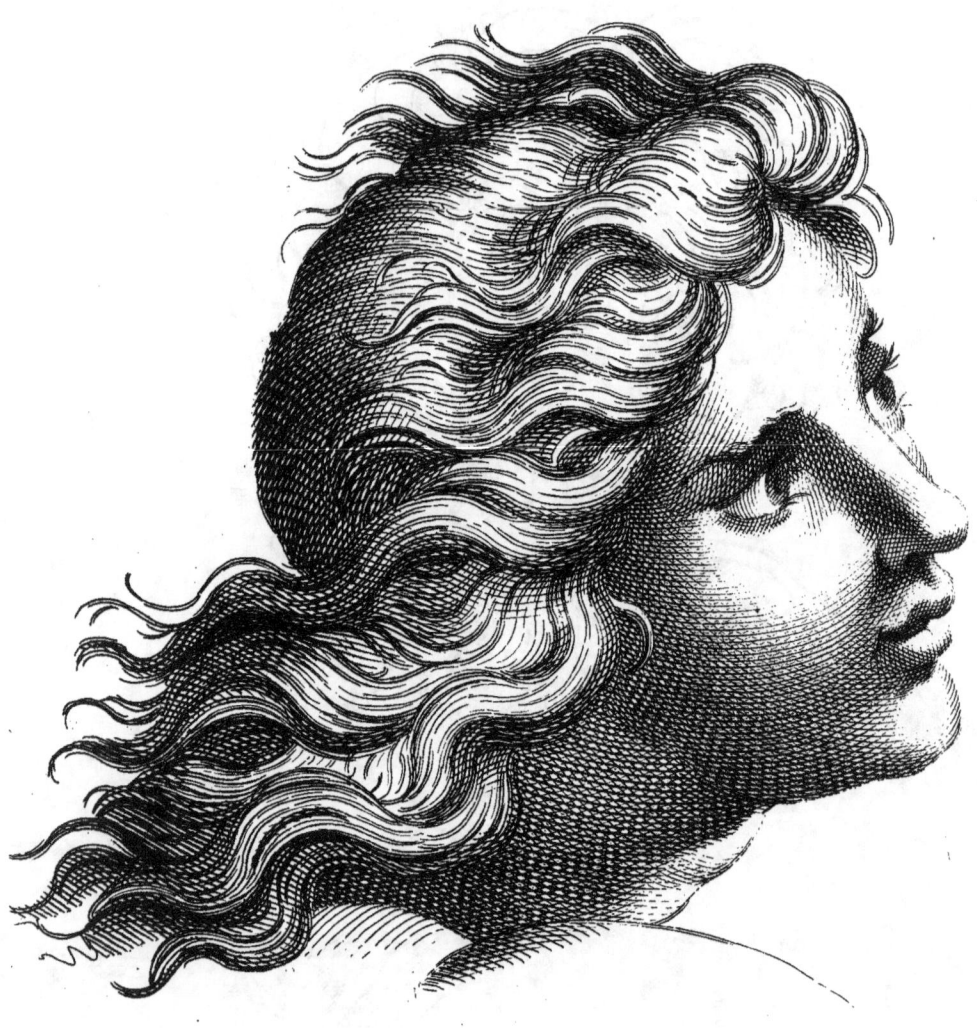

Raph . Vrb pinx .

Plate 37.I. - from Paul and Barnabas

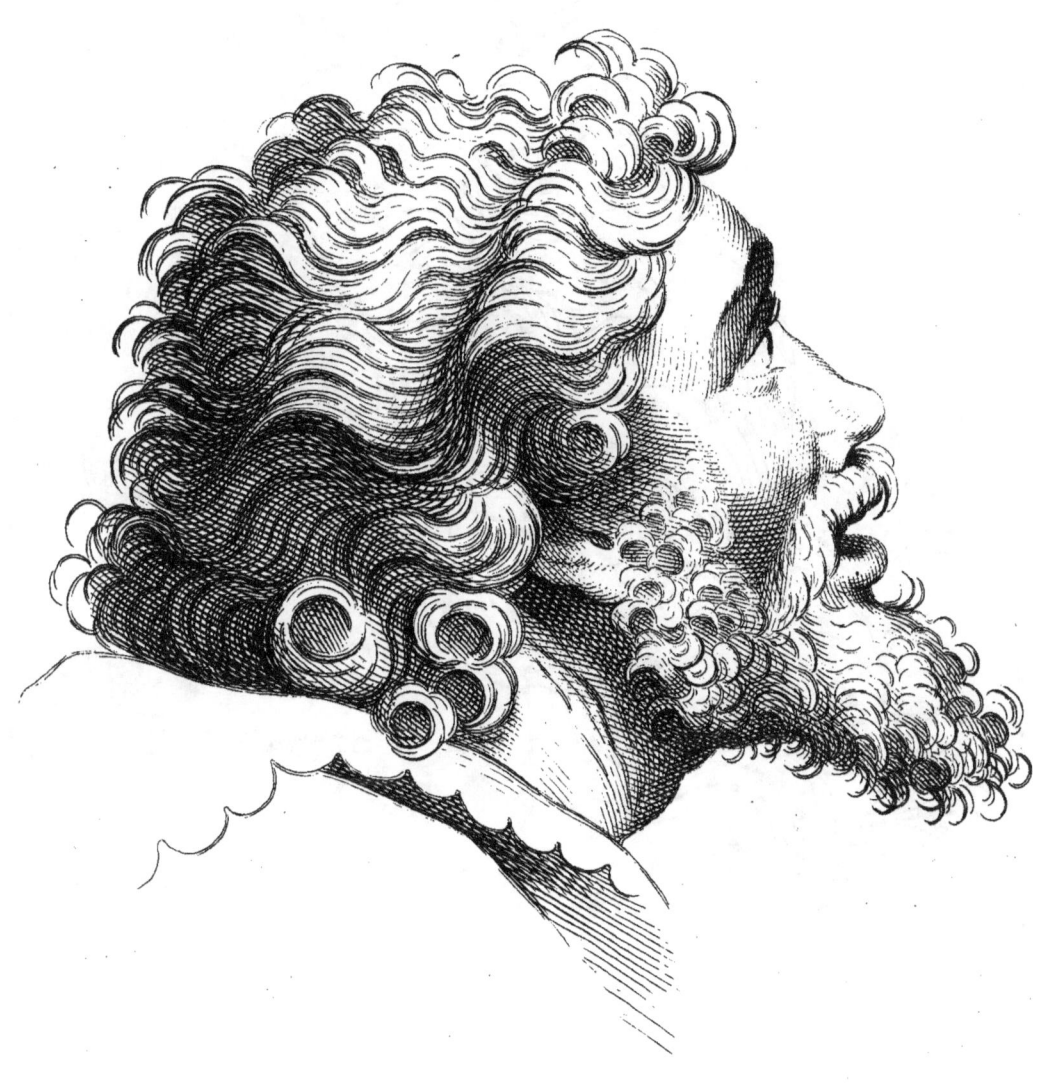

D. Beauvais sculp

Plate 37.II. - from Paul Preaching

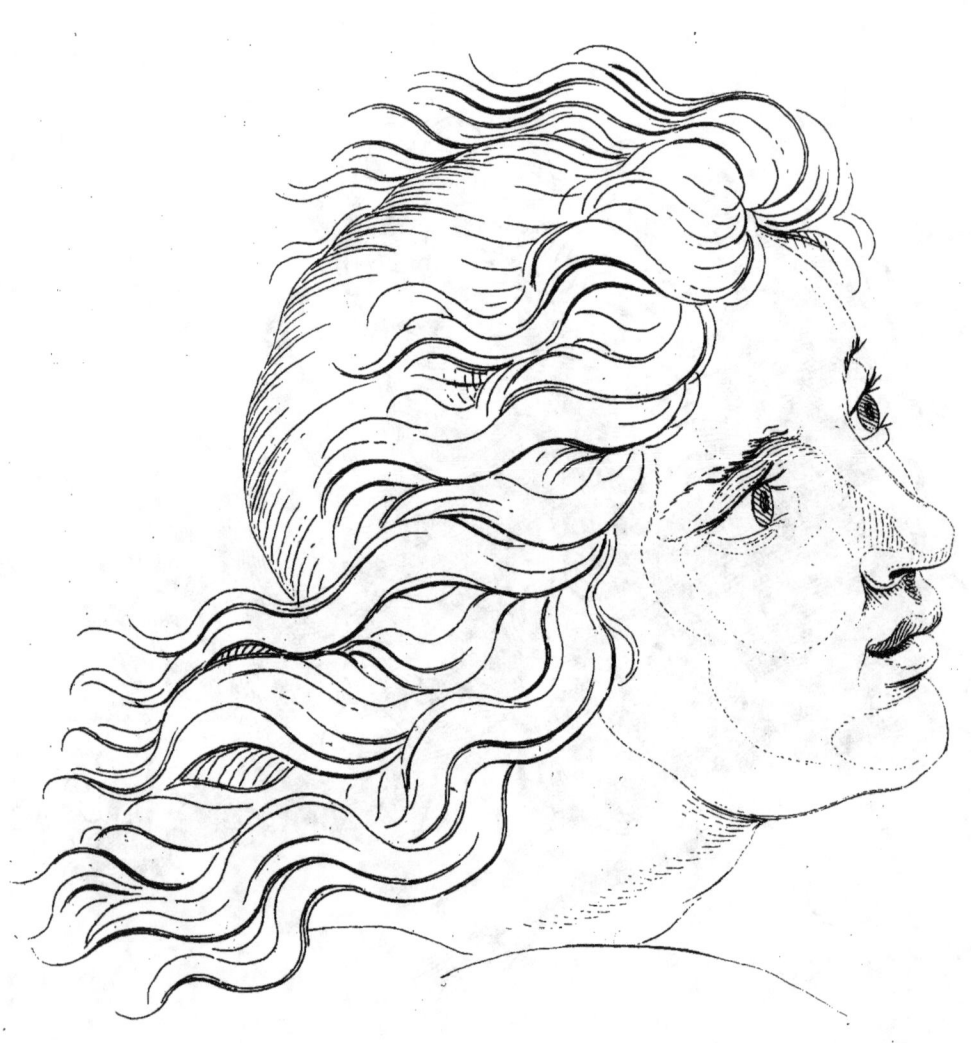

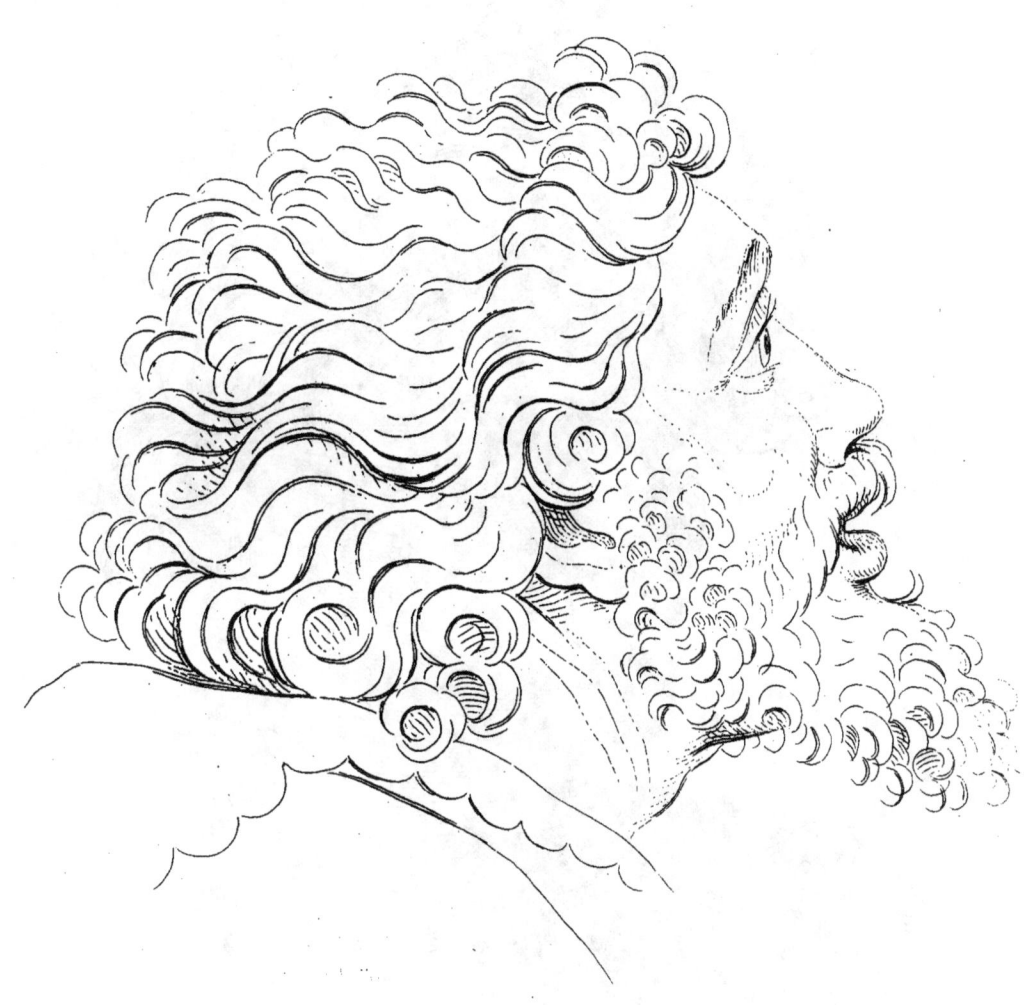

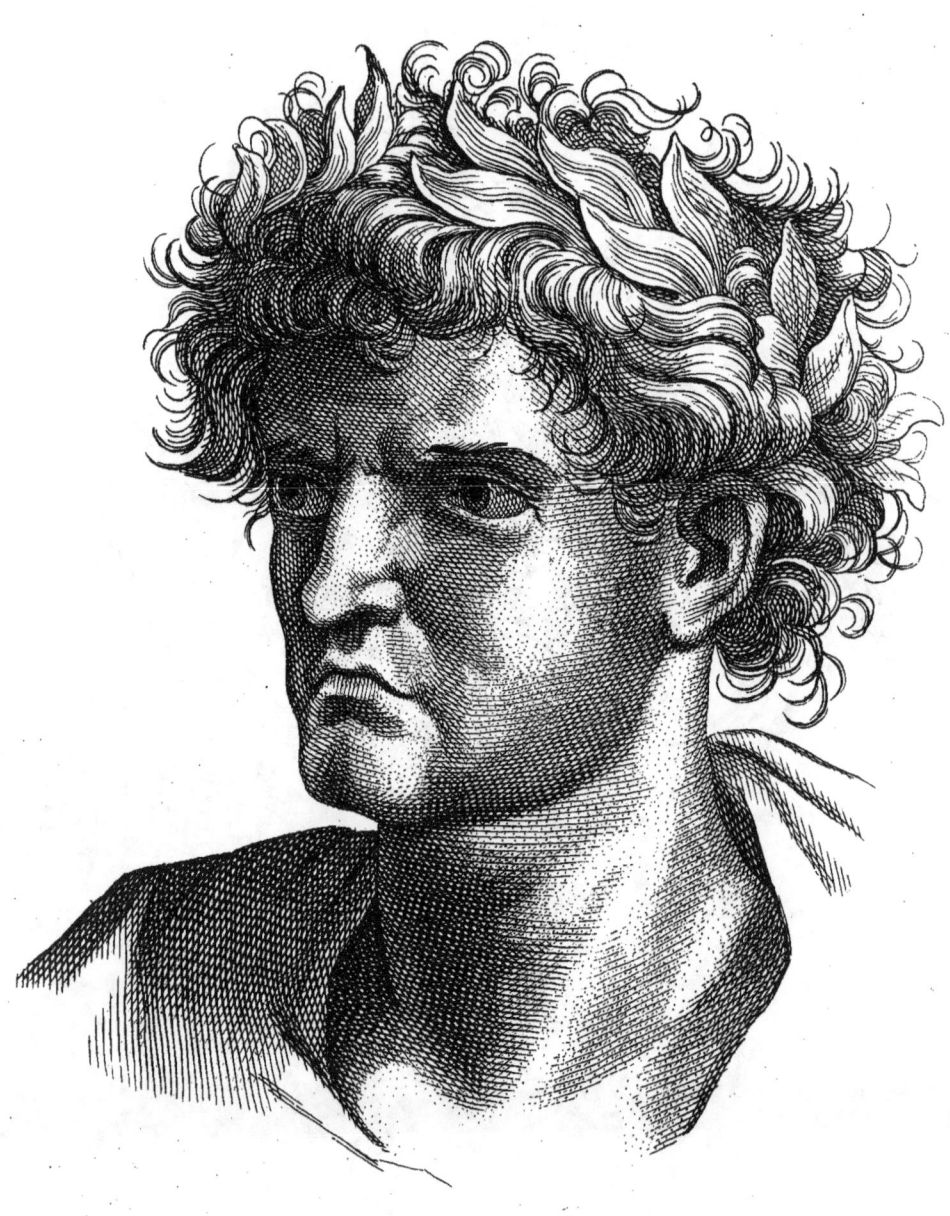

Raph . Urb.pin.

Plate 38.I. - from Elymas the Sorcerer

38

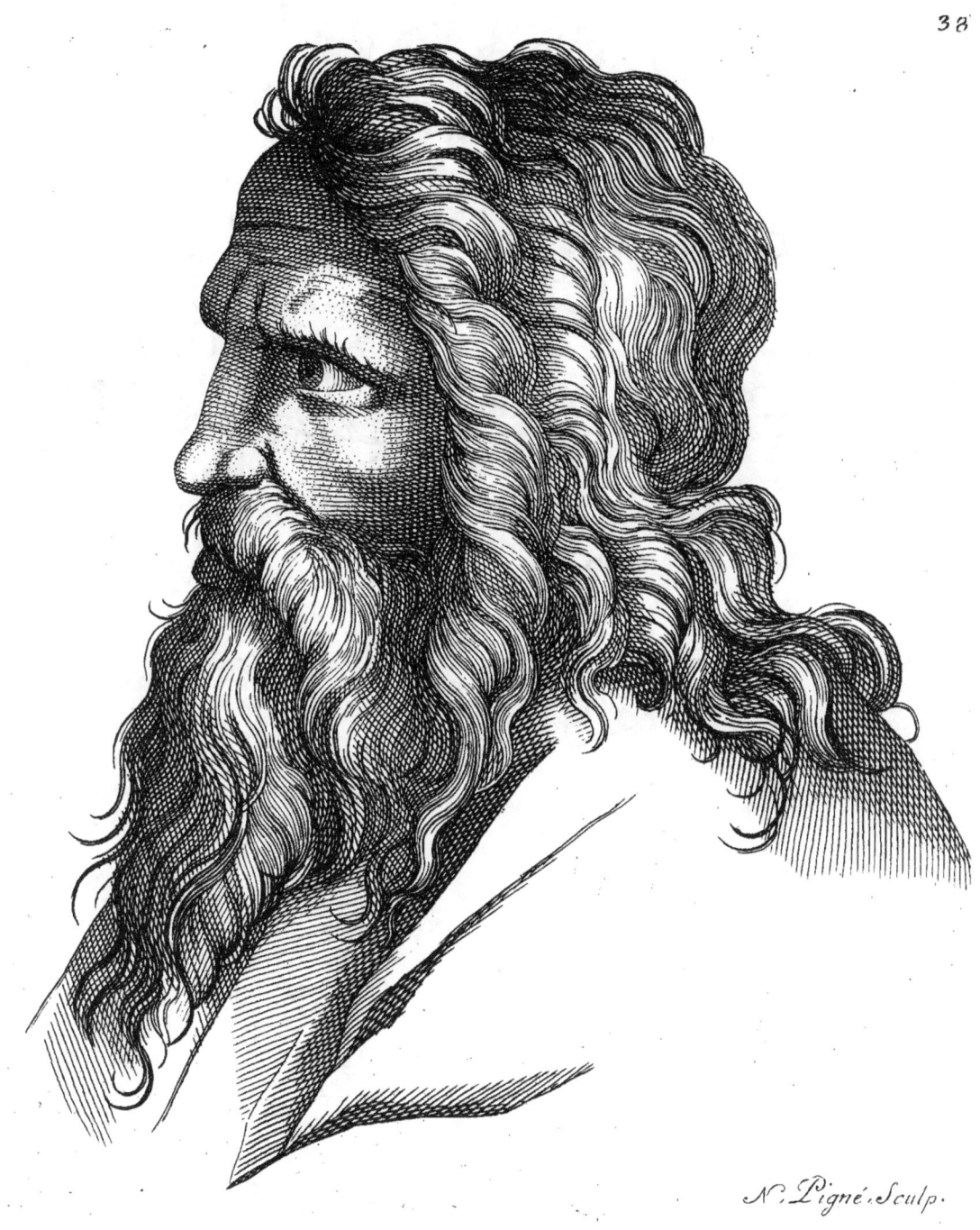

N. Pigné. Sculp.

Plate 38.II. - from Paul Preaching

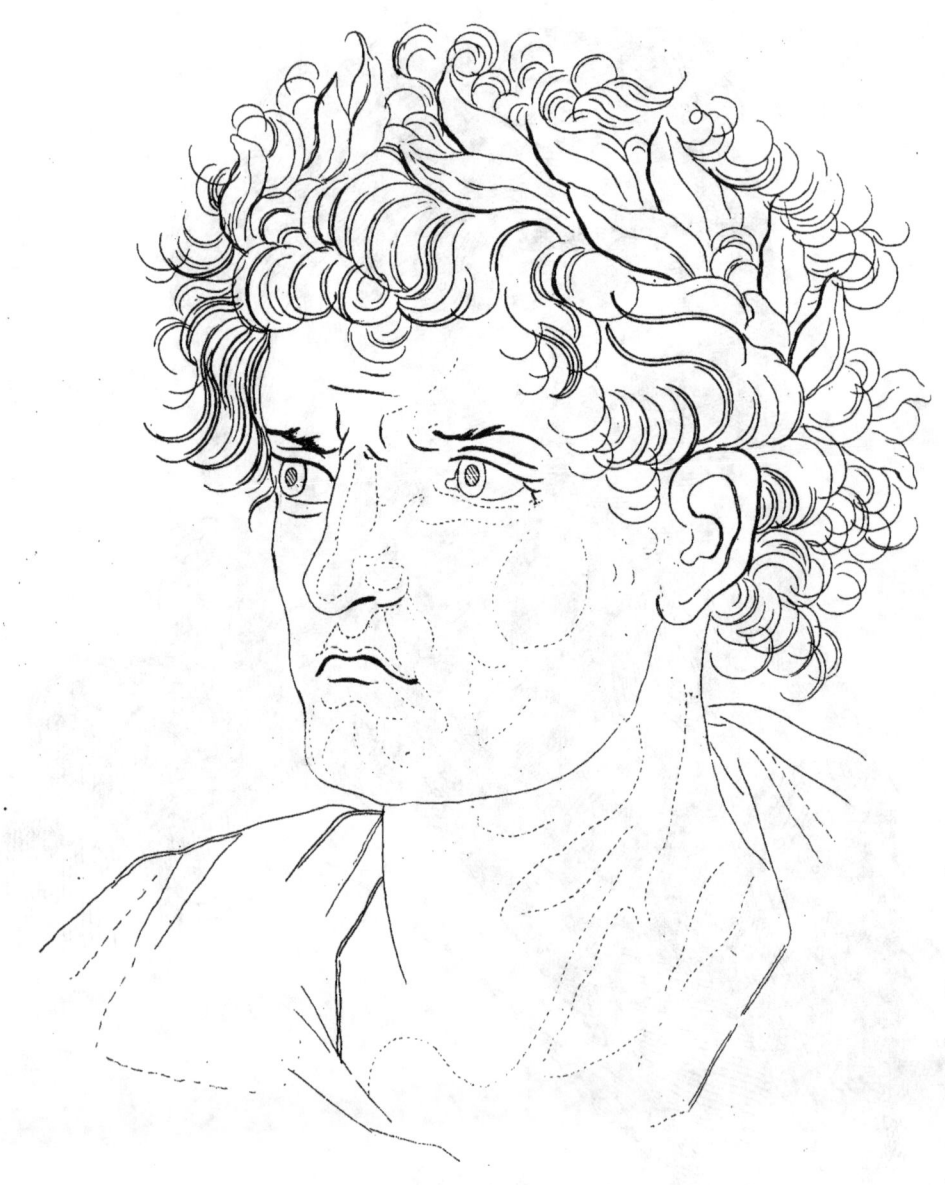

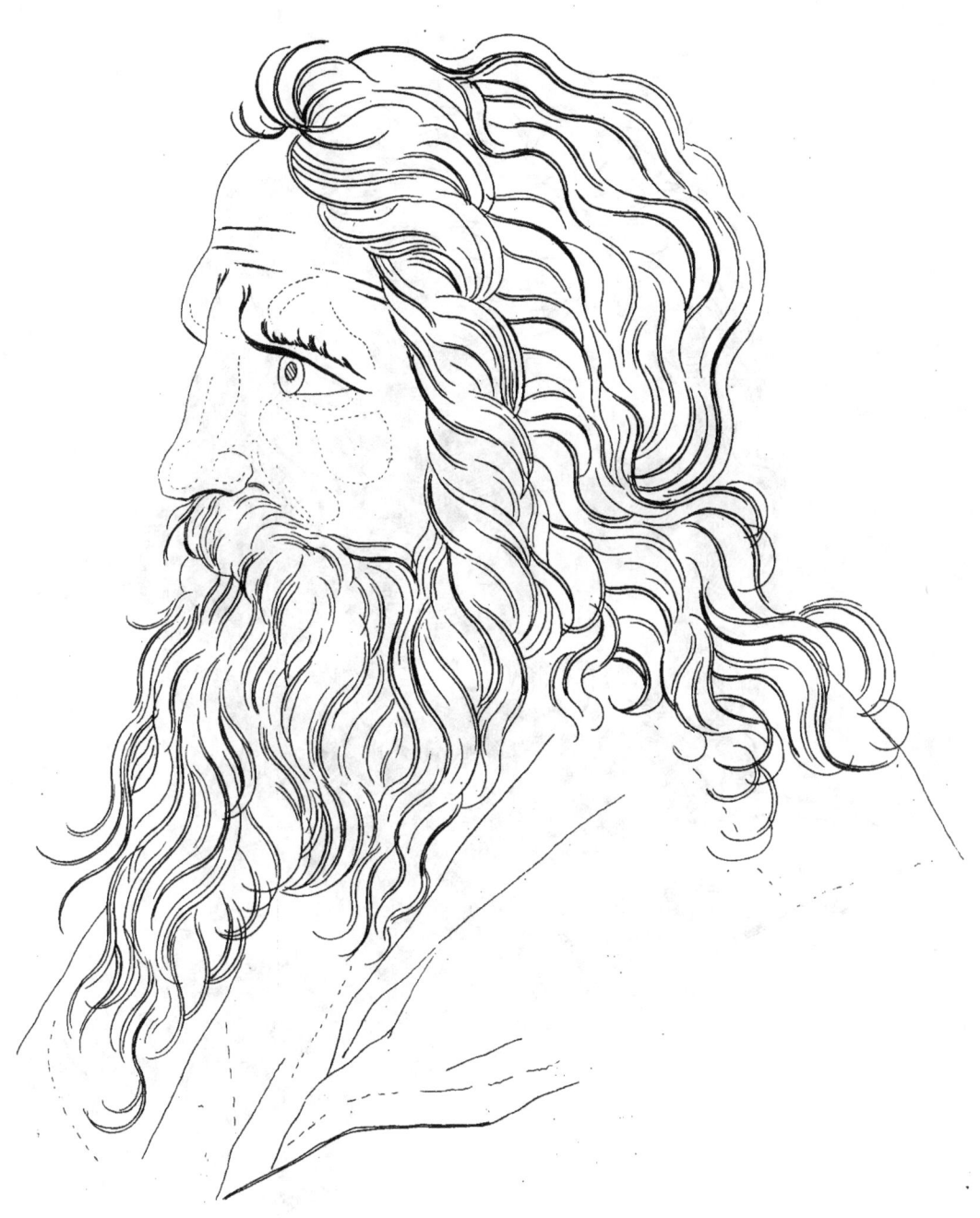

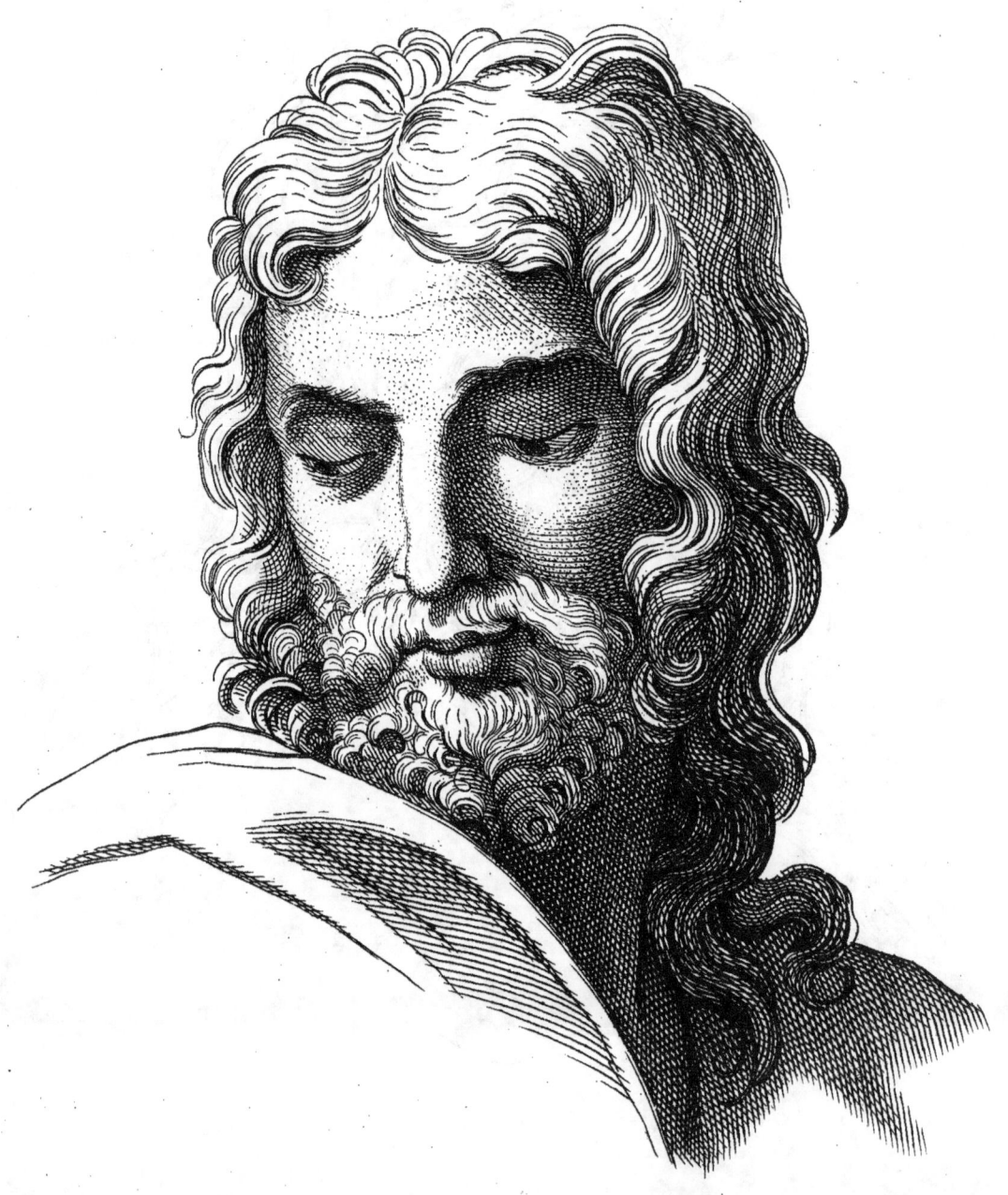

Raph.Vrb.pin.

Plate 39.I. - from The Death of Ananias

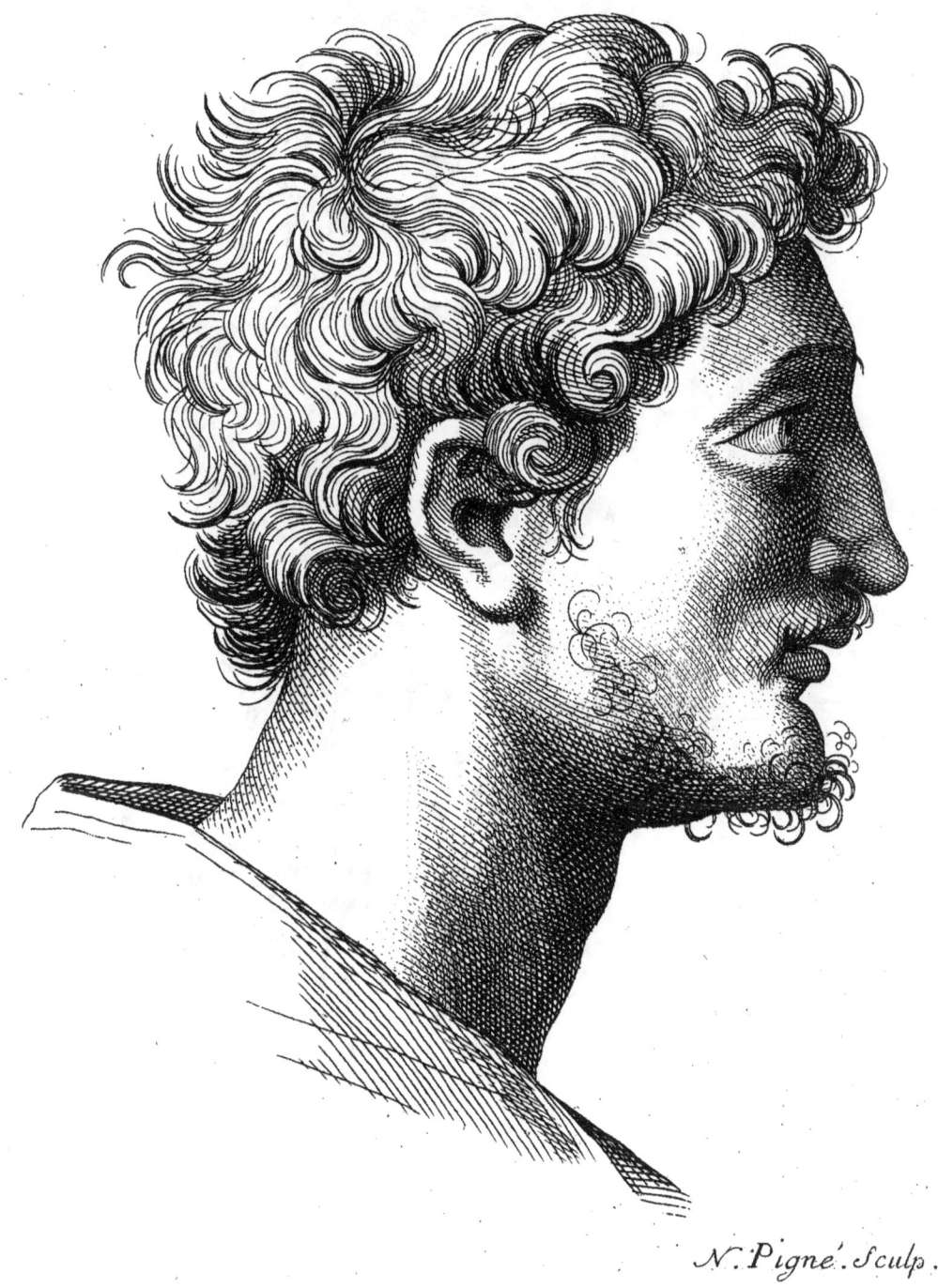

N. Pigné. Sculp.

Plate 39.II. - from Christ's Charge to Peter

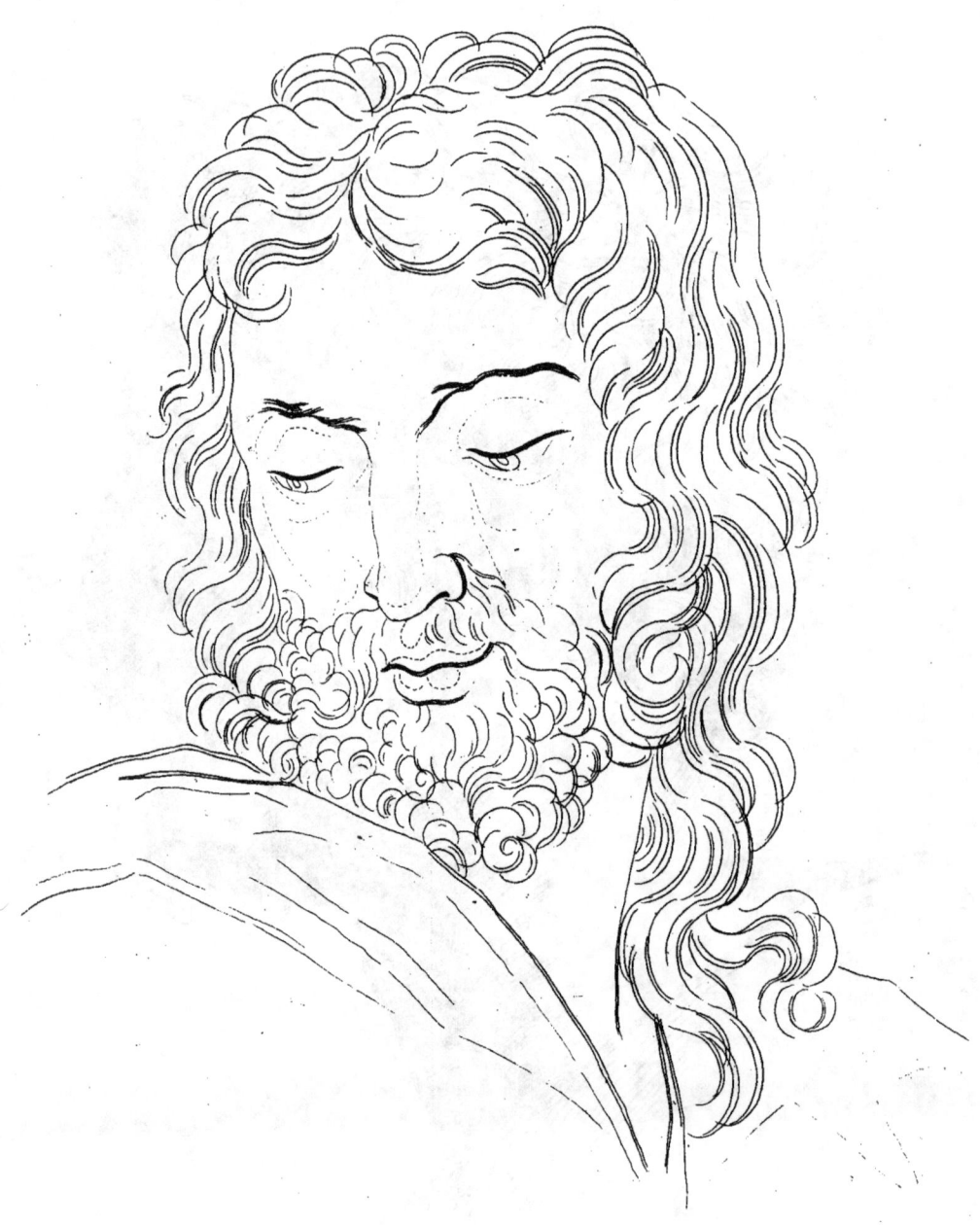

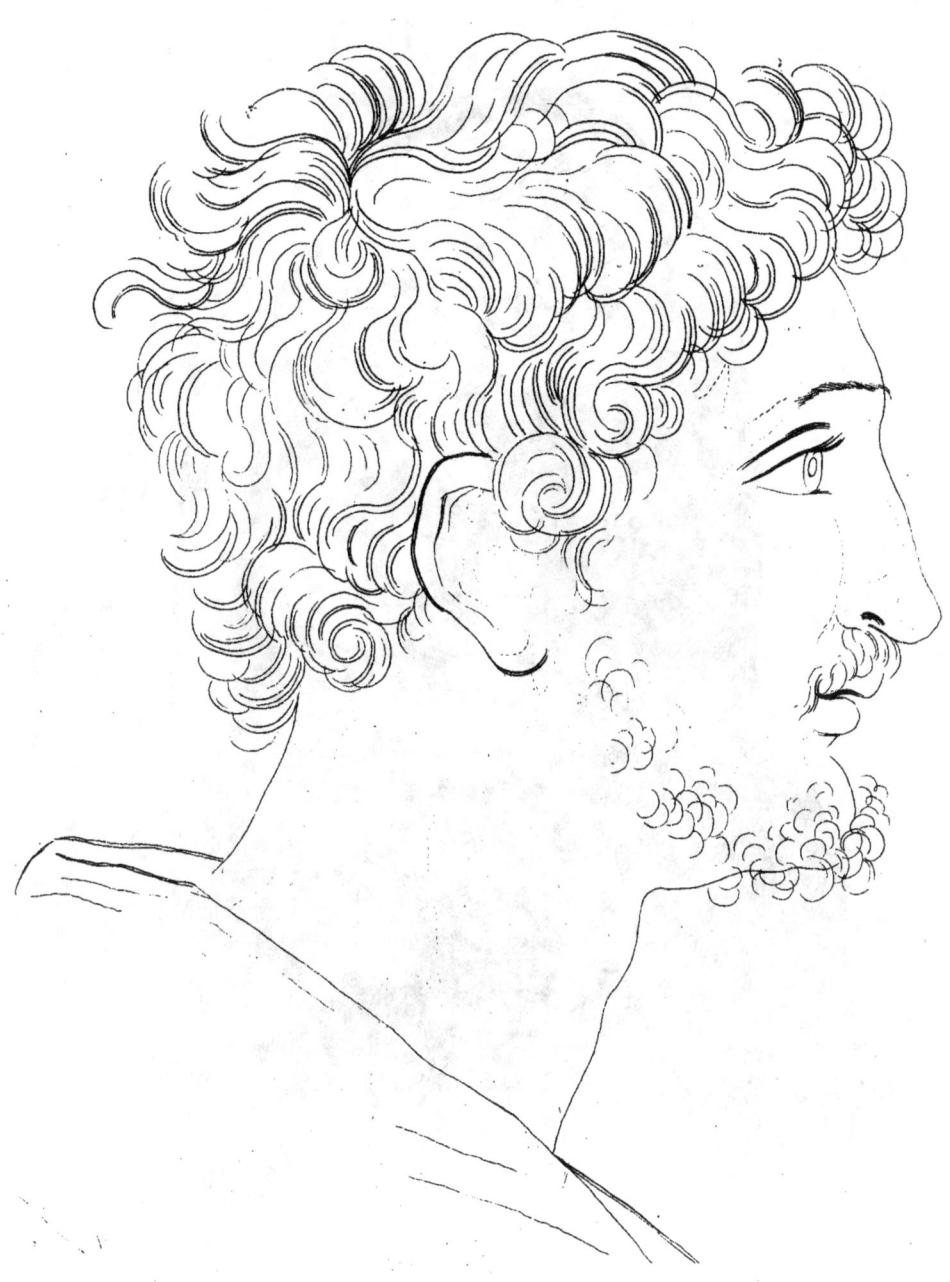

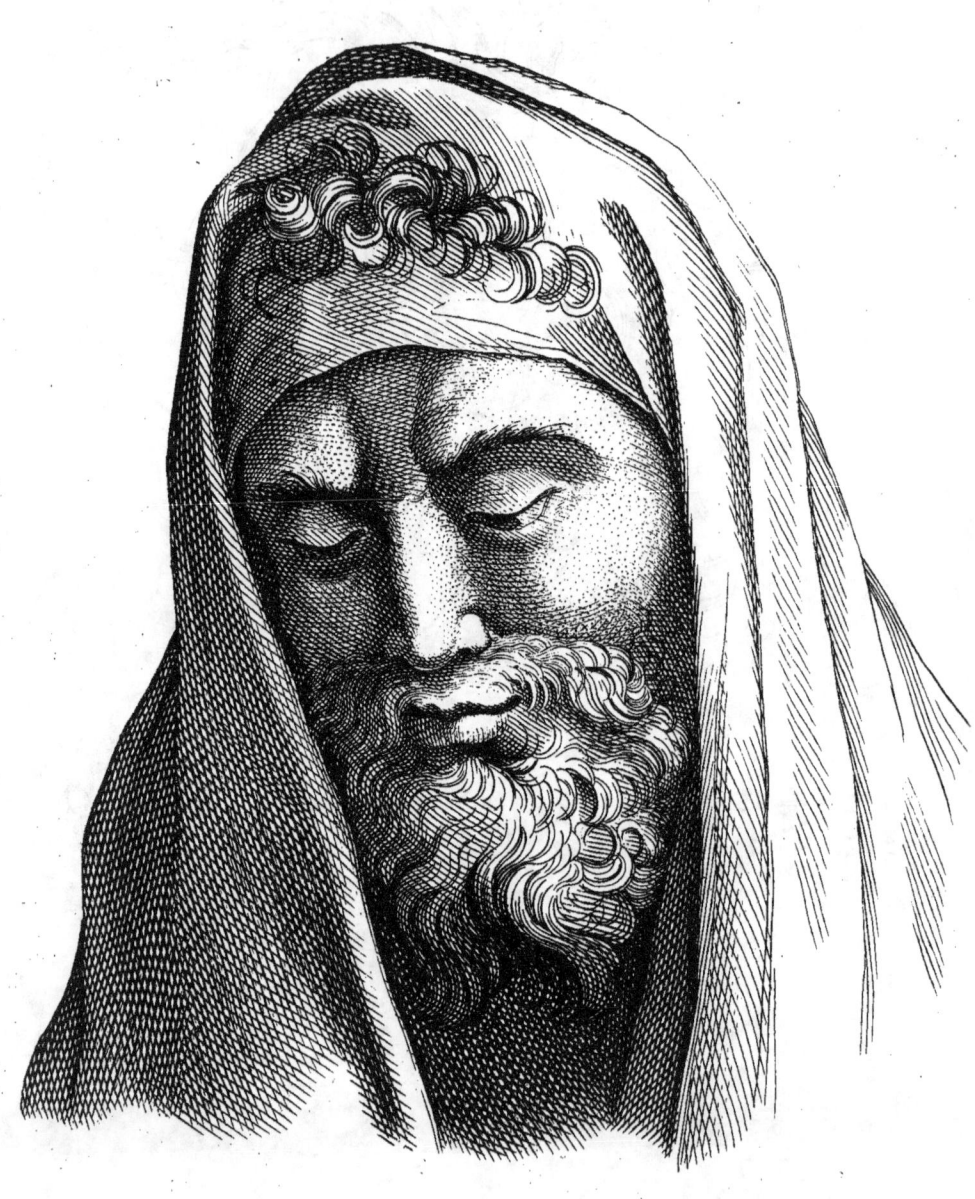

R aph.Vrb.pin .

Plate 40.I. - from Paul and Barnabas

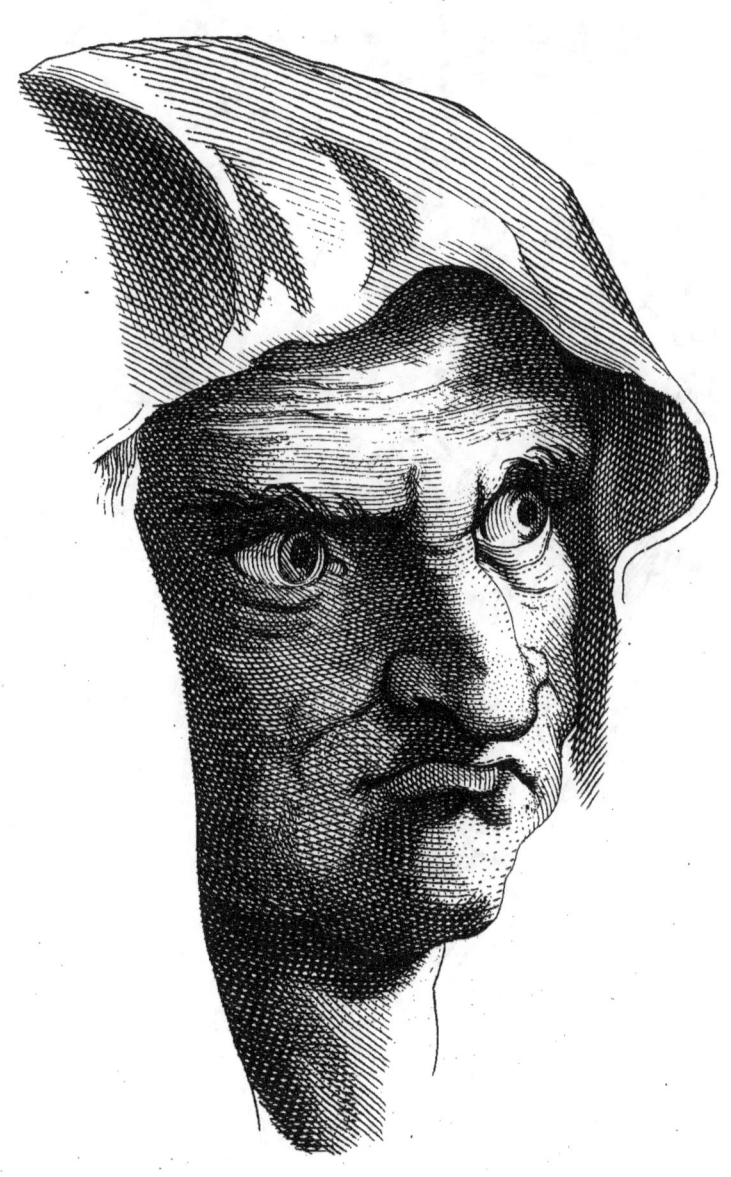

N. Pigné Sculp.

Plate 40.II. - from Paul and Barnabas

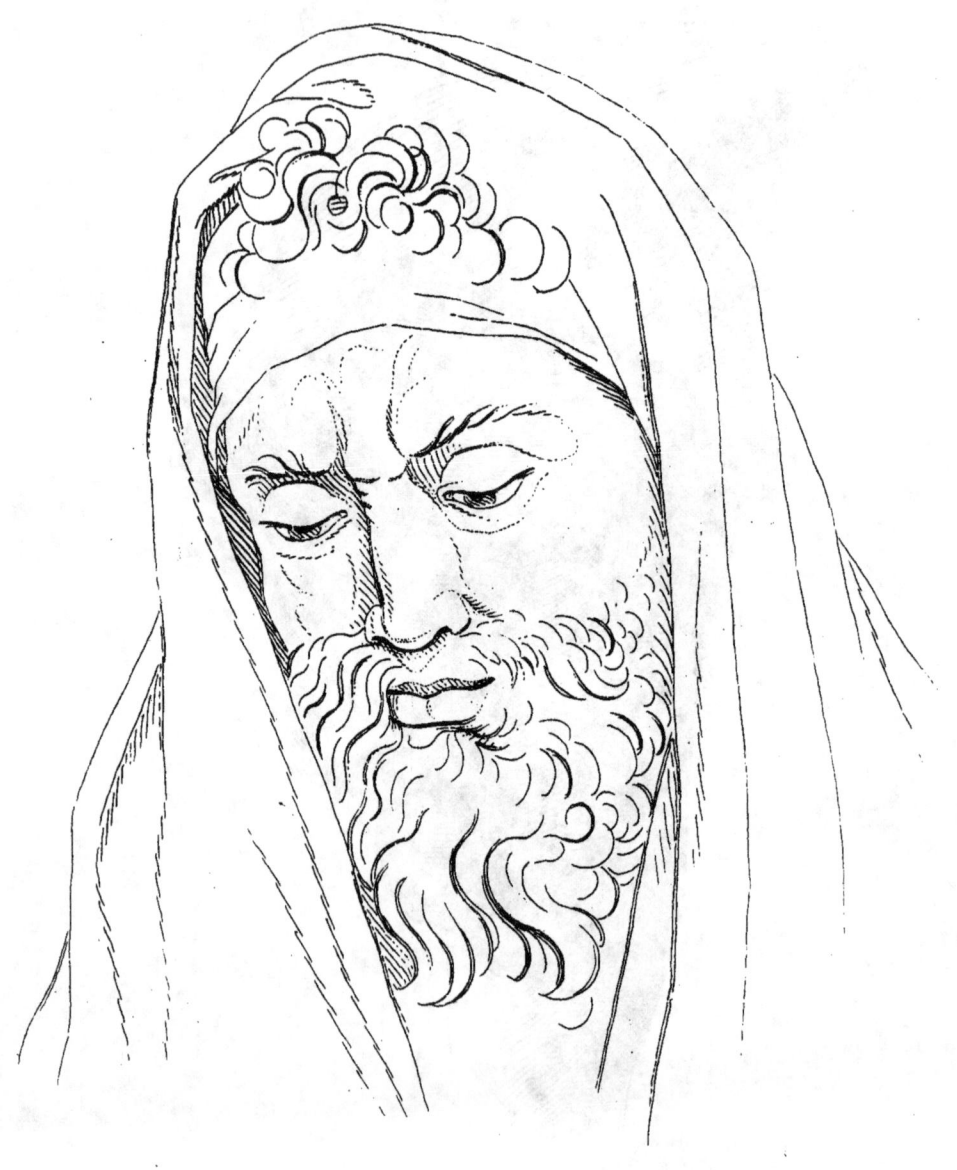

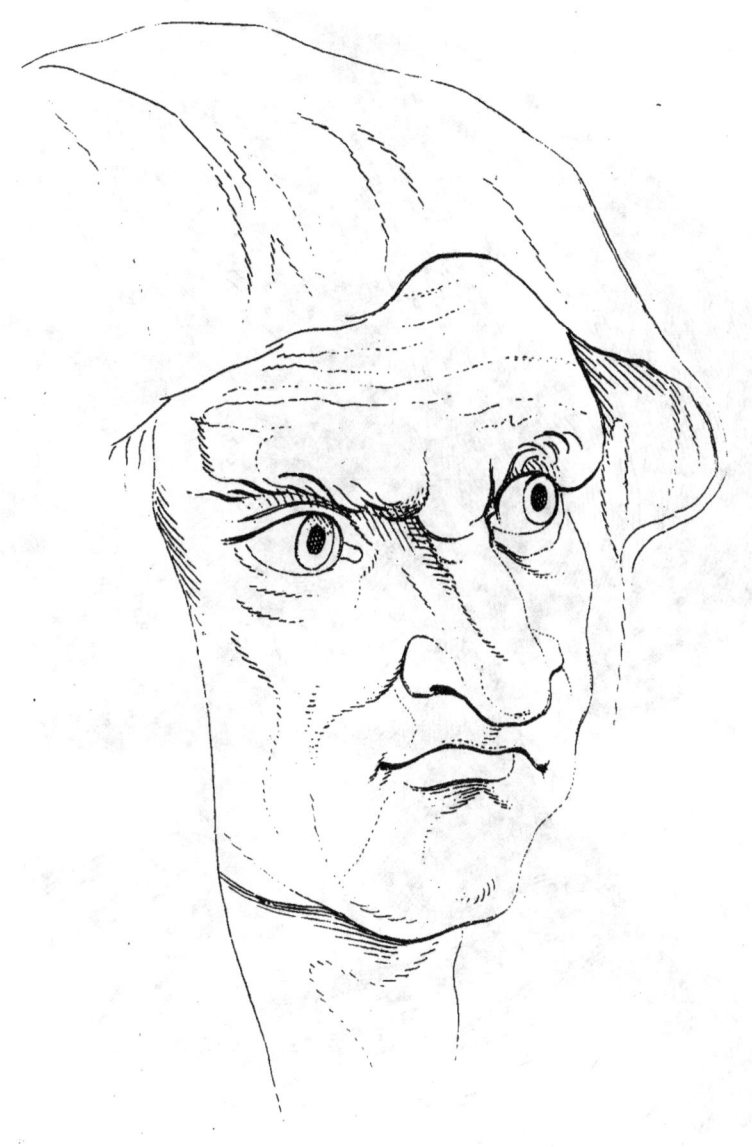

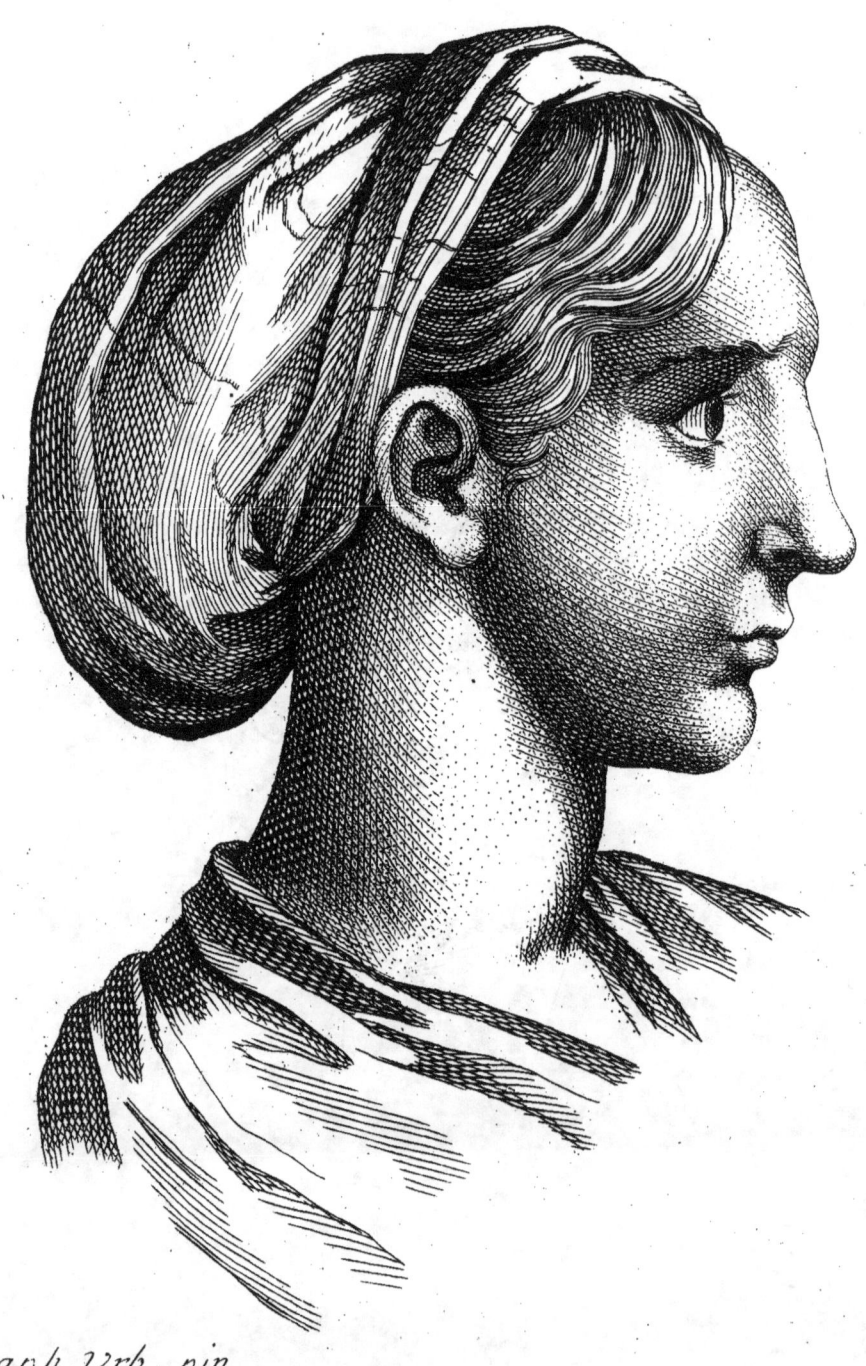

R.aph.Urb.pin.

Plate 41.I. - from Paul and Barnabas

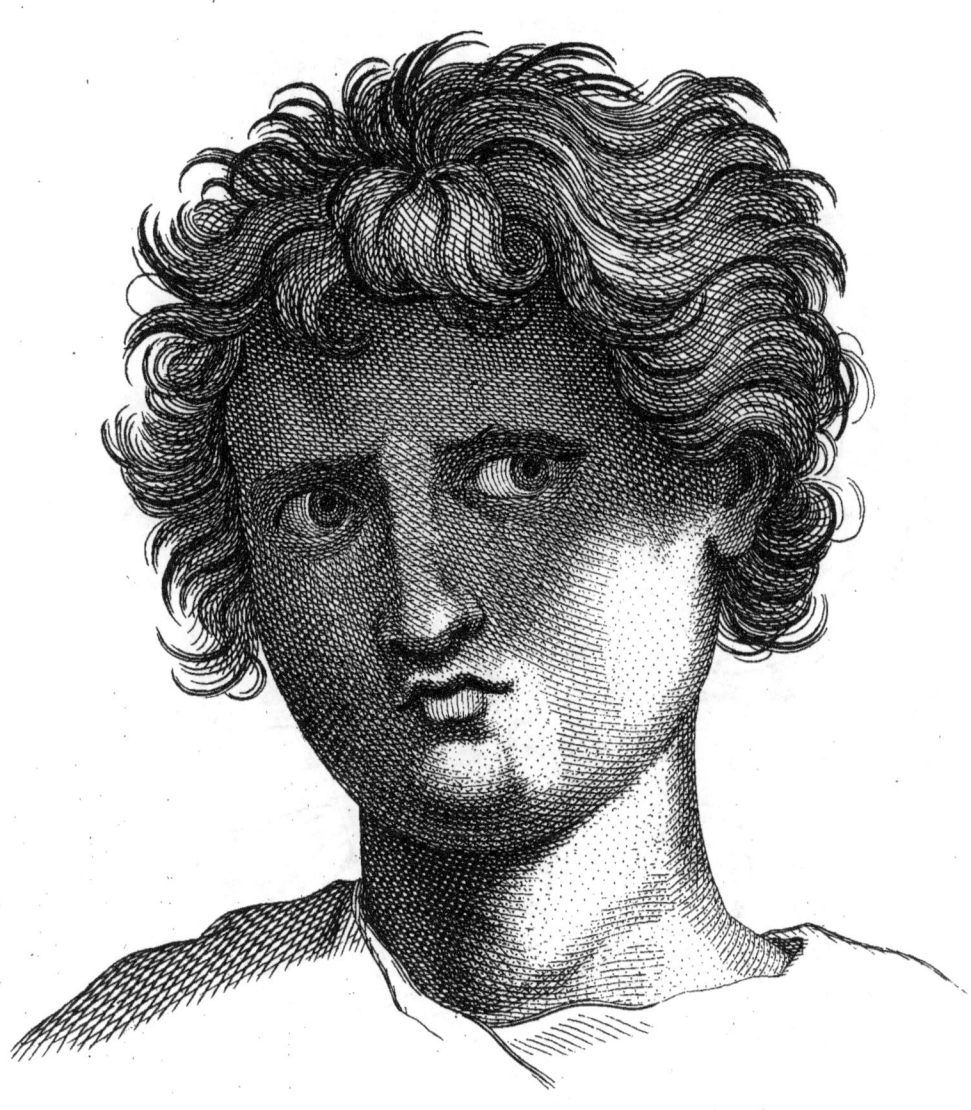

N. Pigné. Sculp.

Plate 41.II. - from Paul Preaching

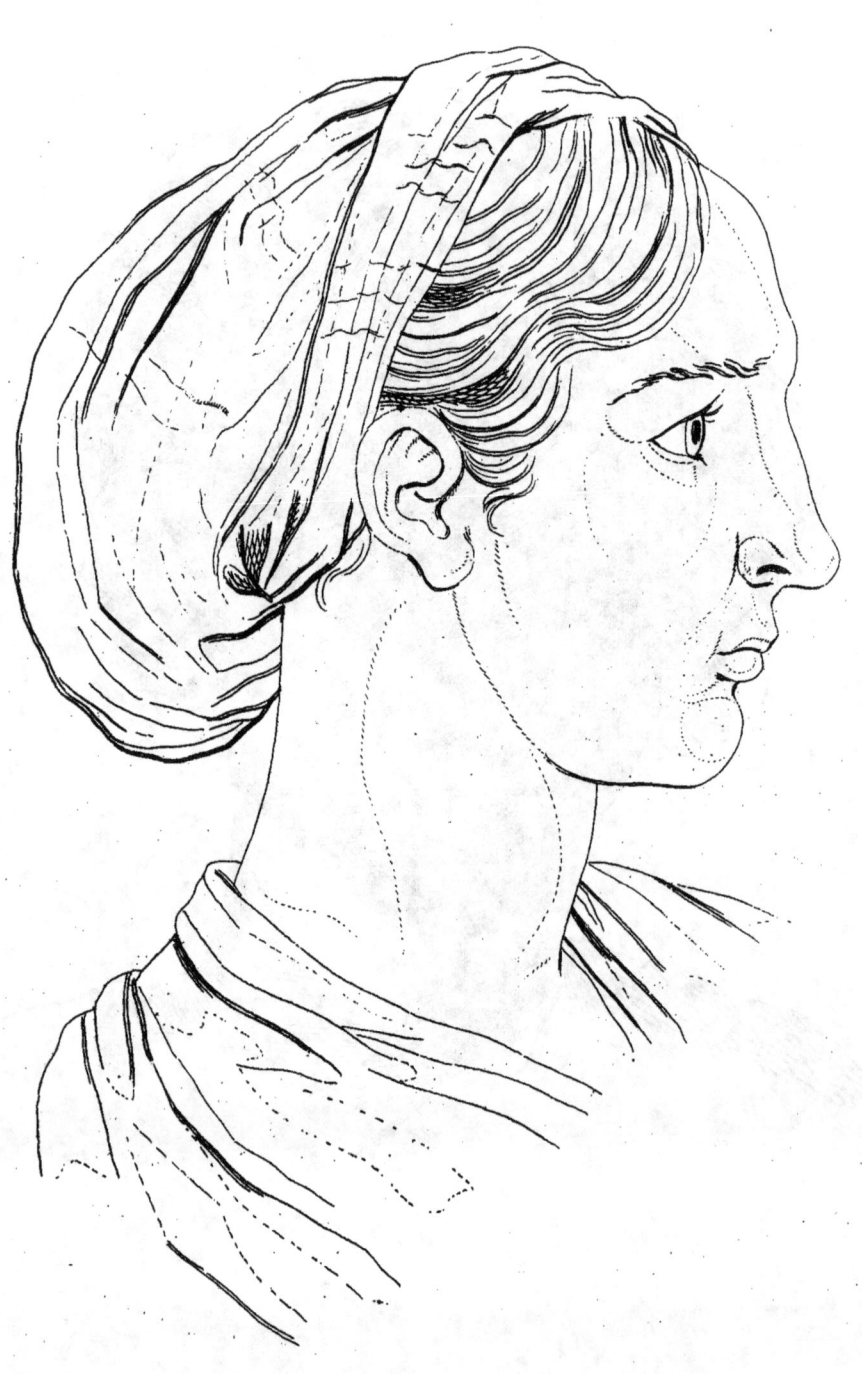

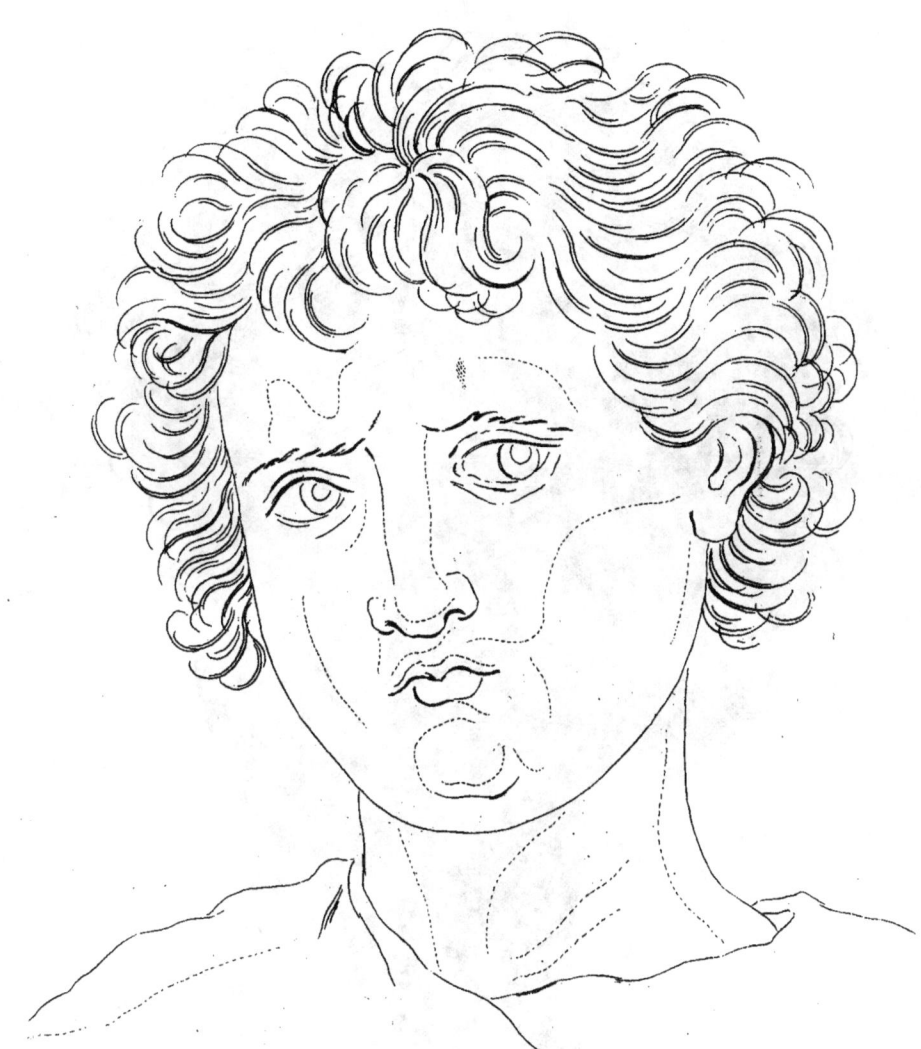

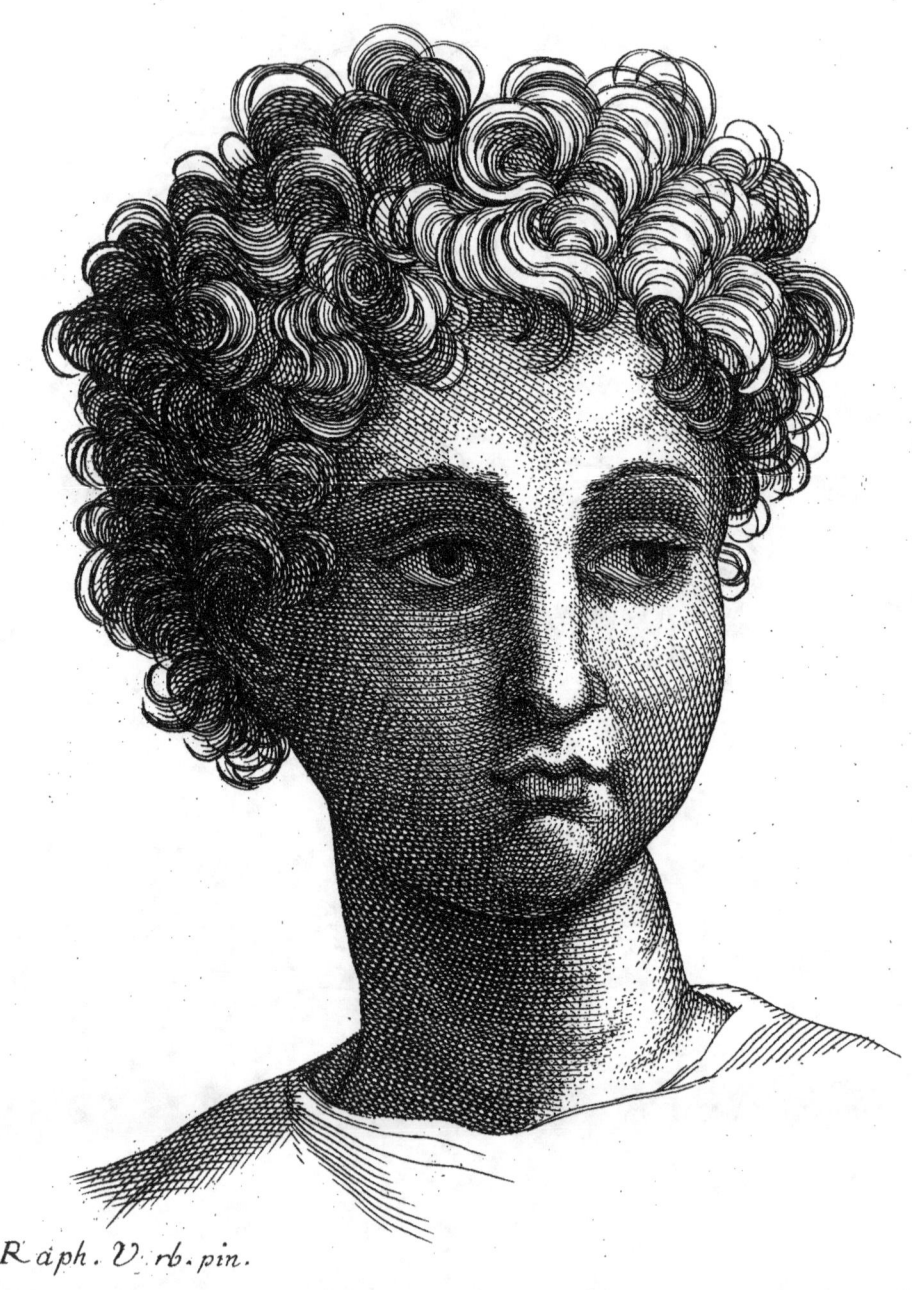

Raph. Urb. pin.

Plate 42.I. - from Paul Preaching

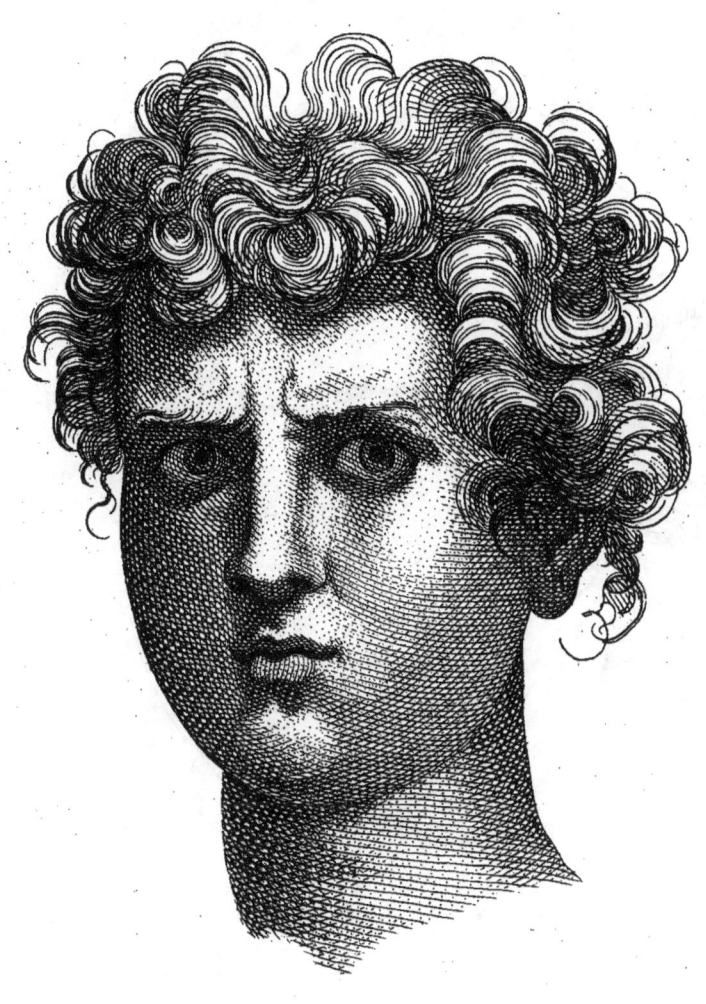

42

Nicolaus.Pigné.Sculp

Plate 42.II. - from Paul Preaching

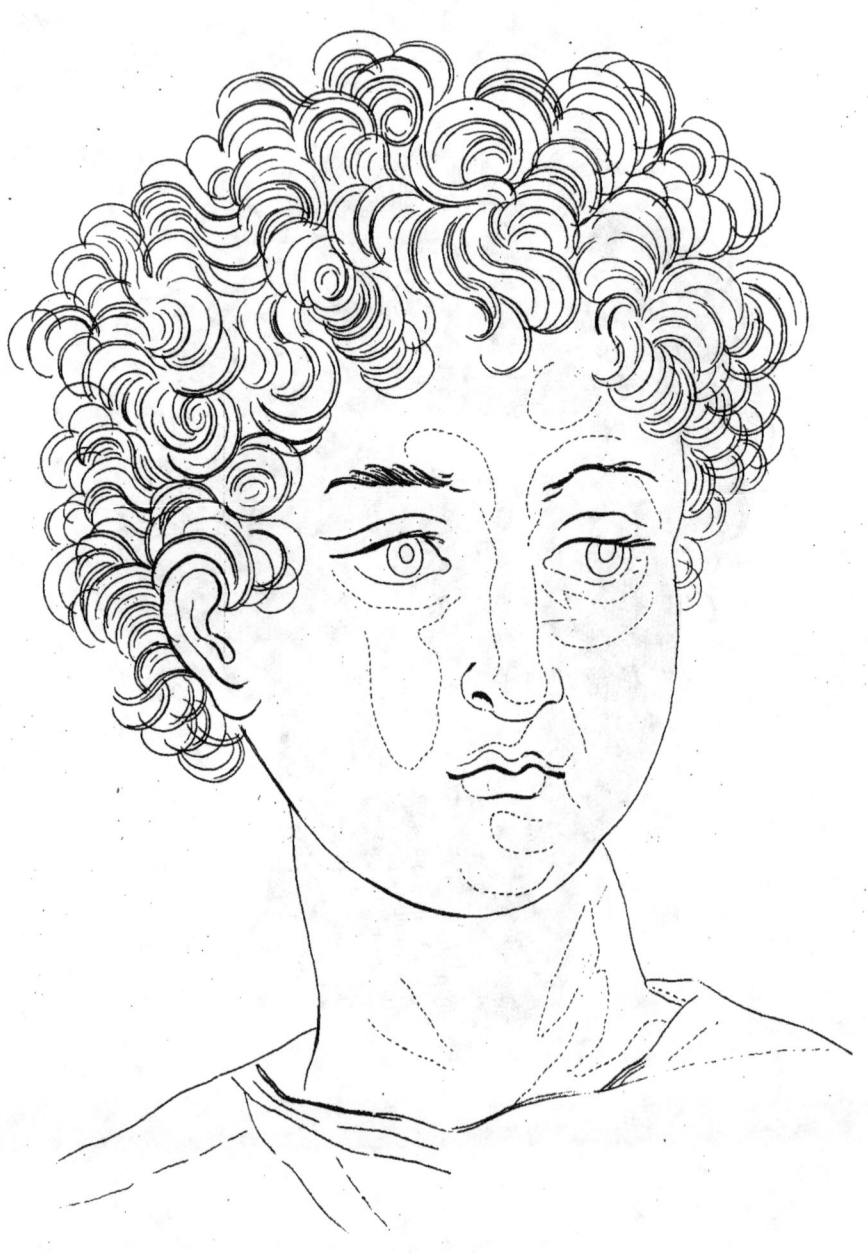

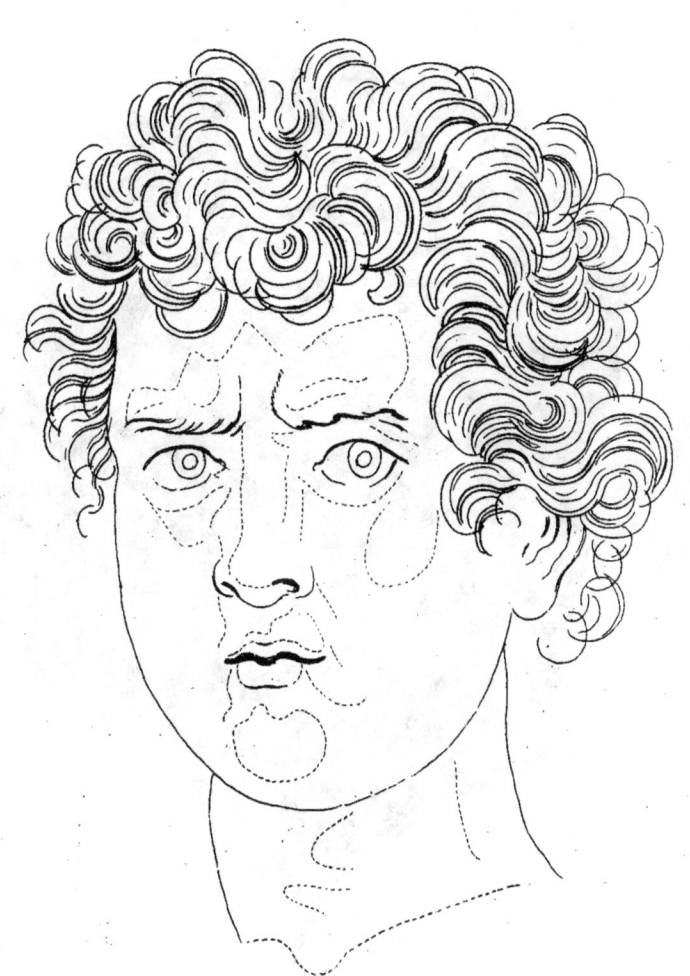

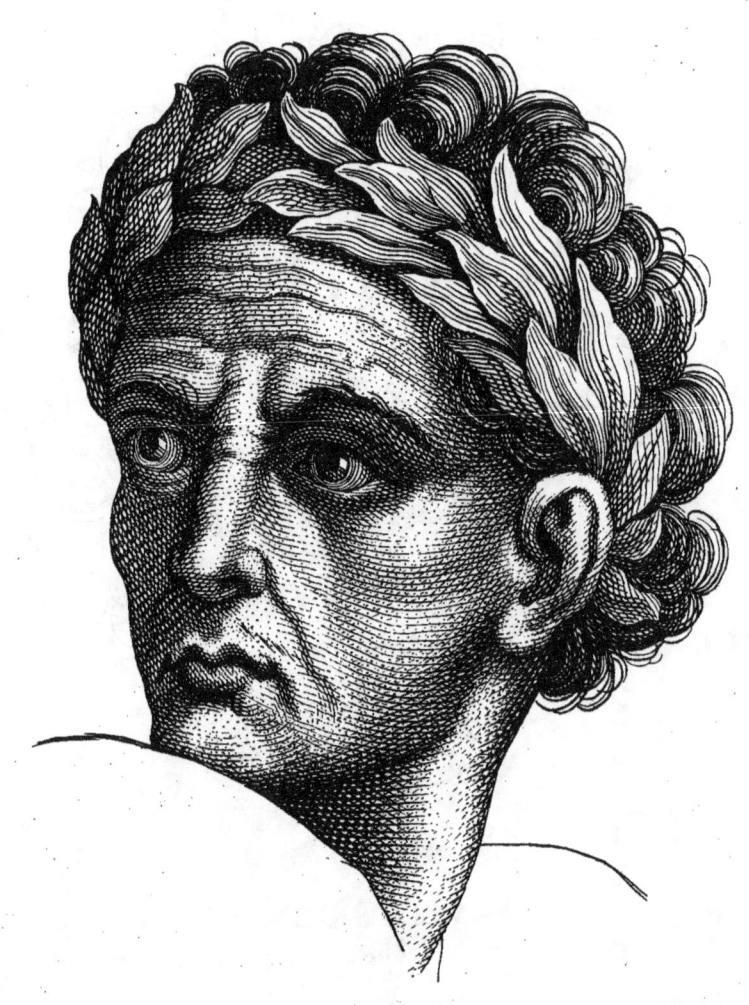

Raph . Urb . pin .

Plate 43.I. - from Paul and Barnabas

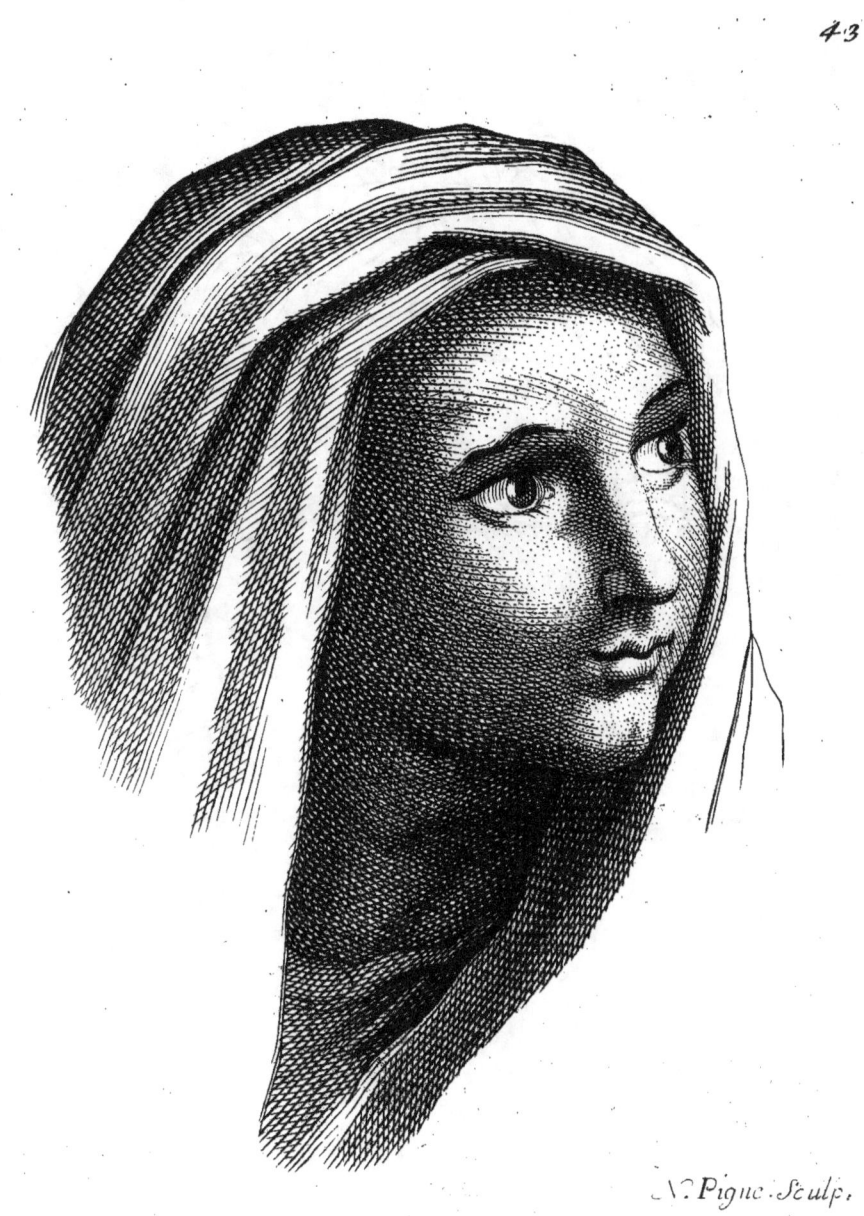

Plate 43.II. - from Paul and Barnabas

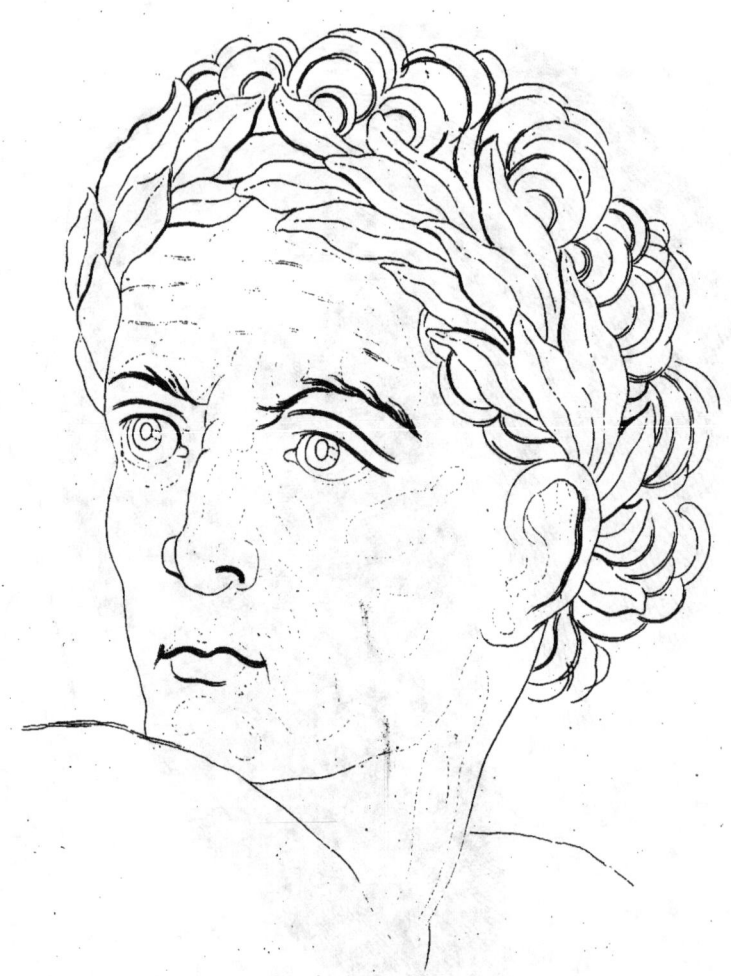

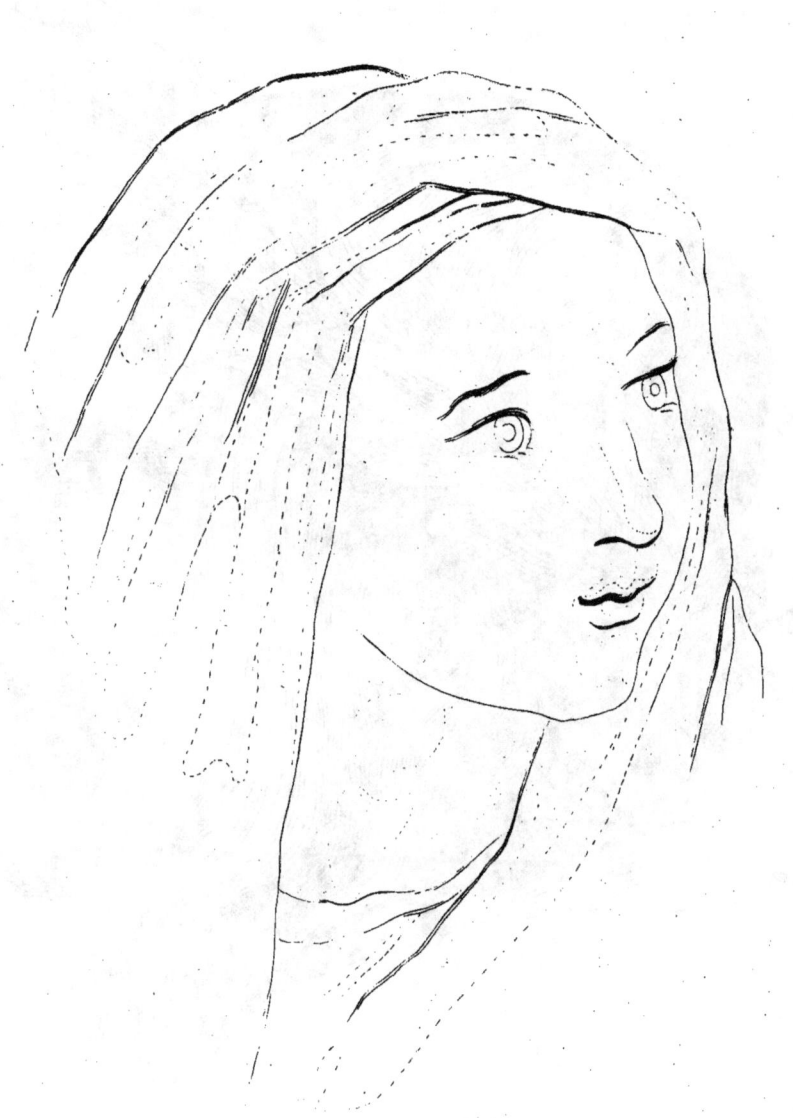

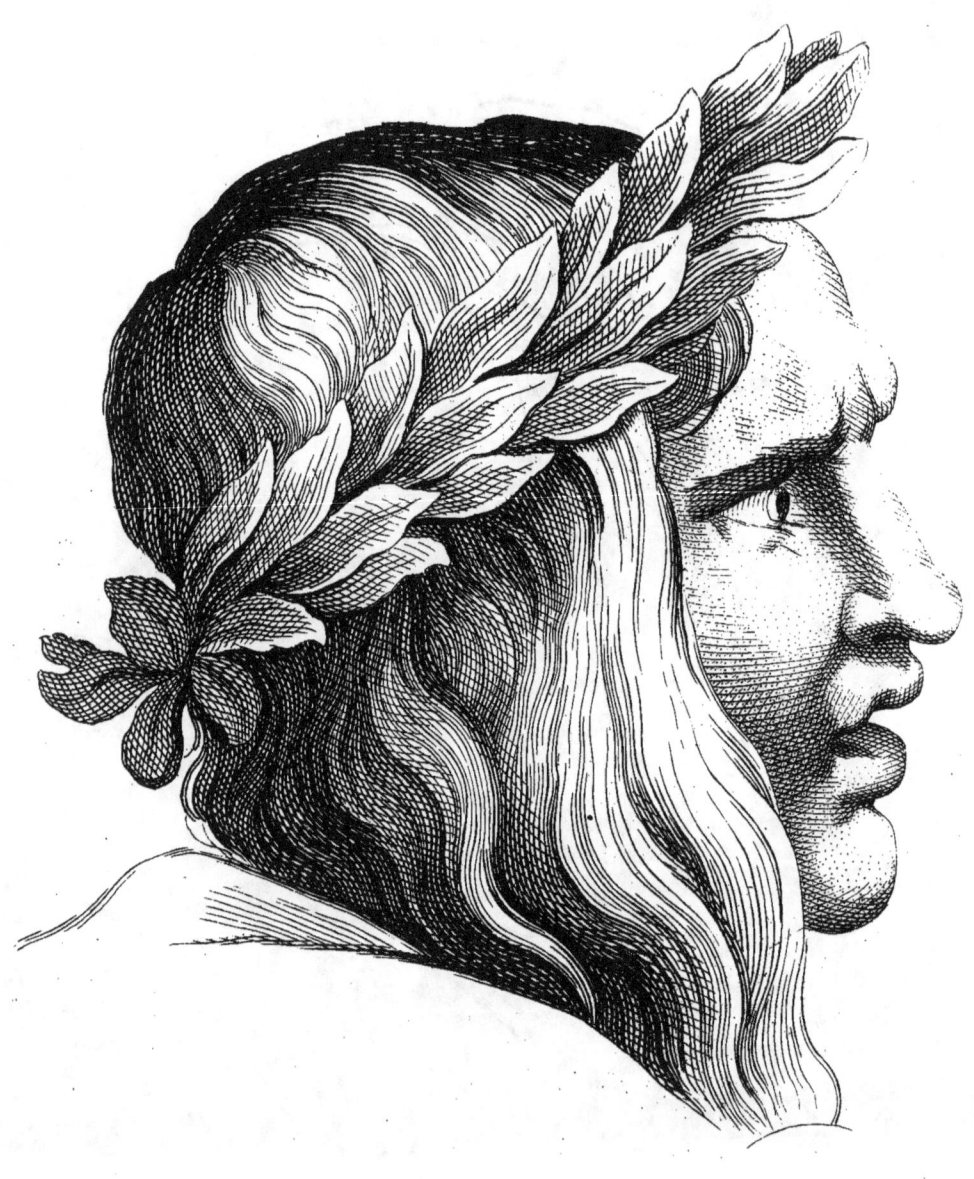

Raph . Vrb. pin.

Plate 44.I. - from Paul and Barnabas

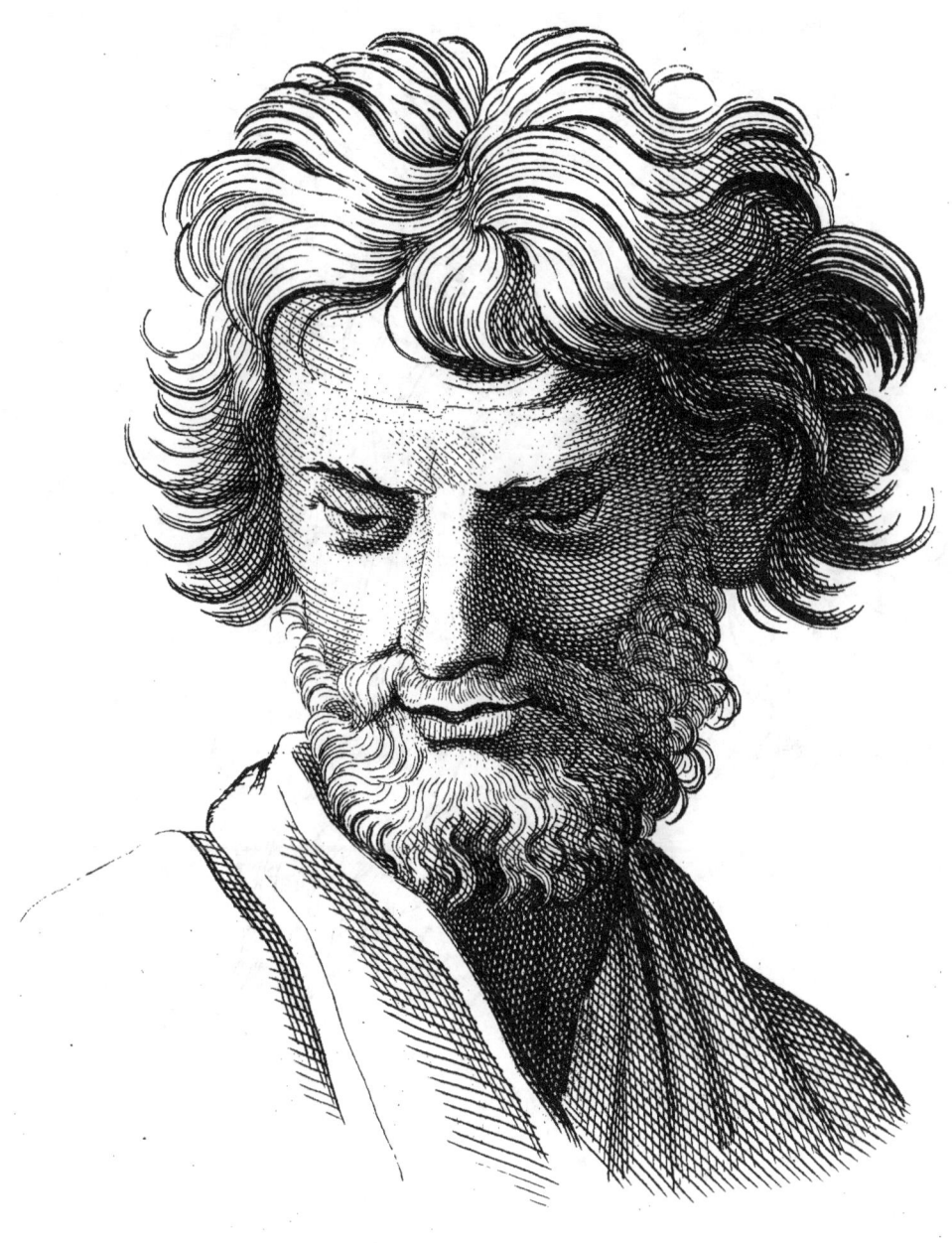

N. Pignc. Sculp

Plate 44.II. - from The Death of Ananias

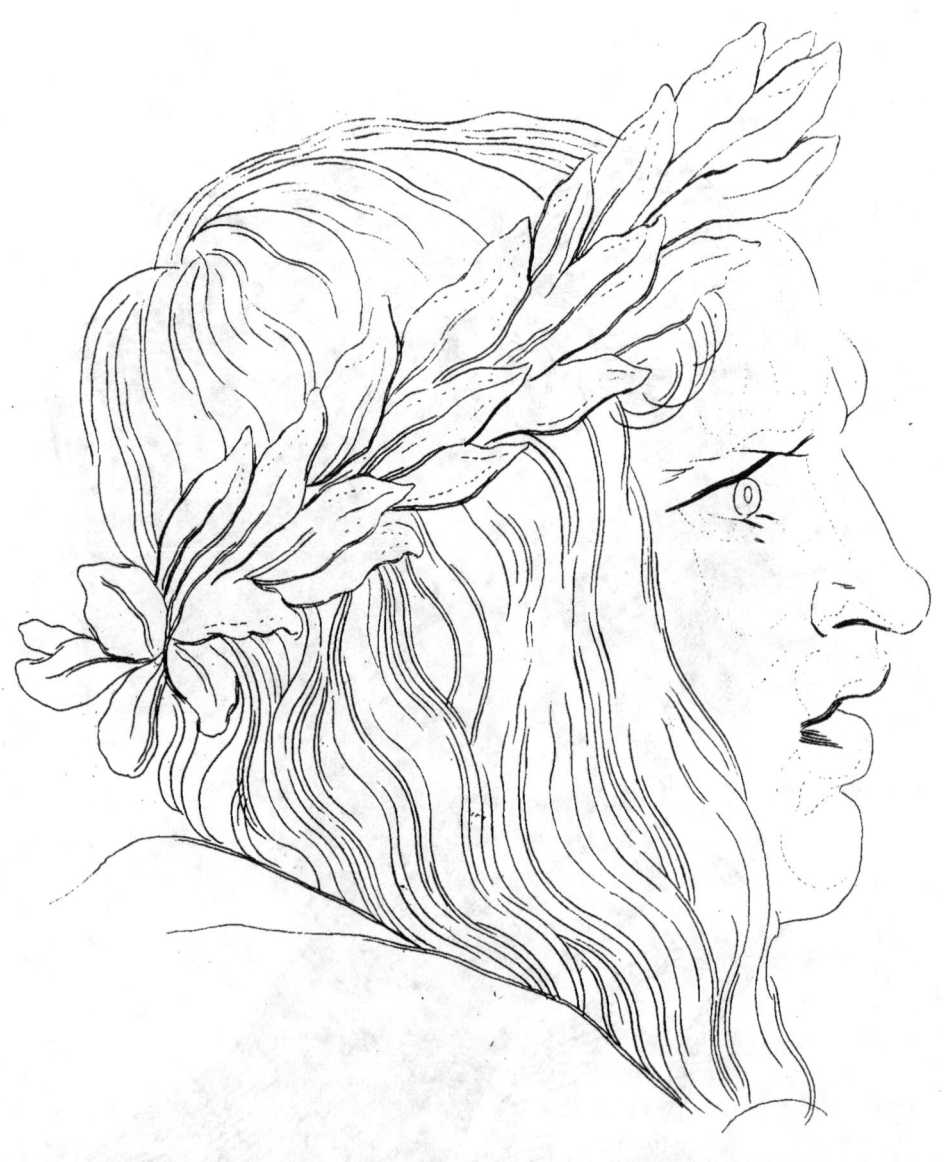

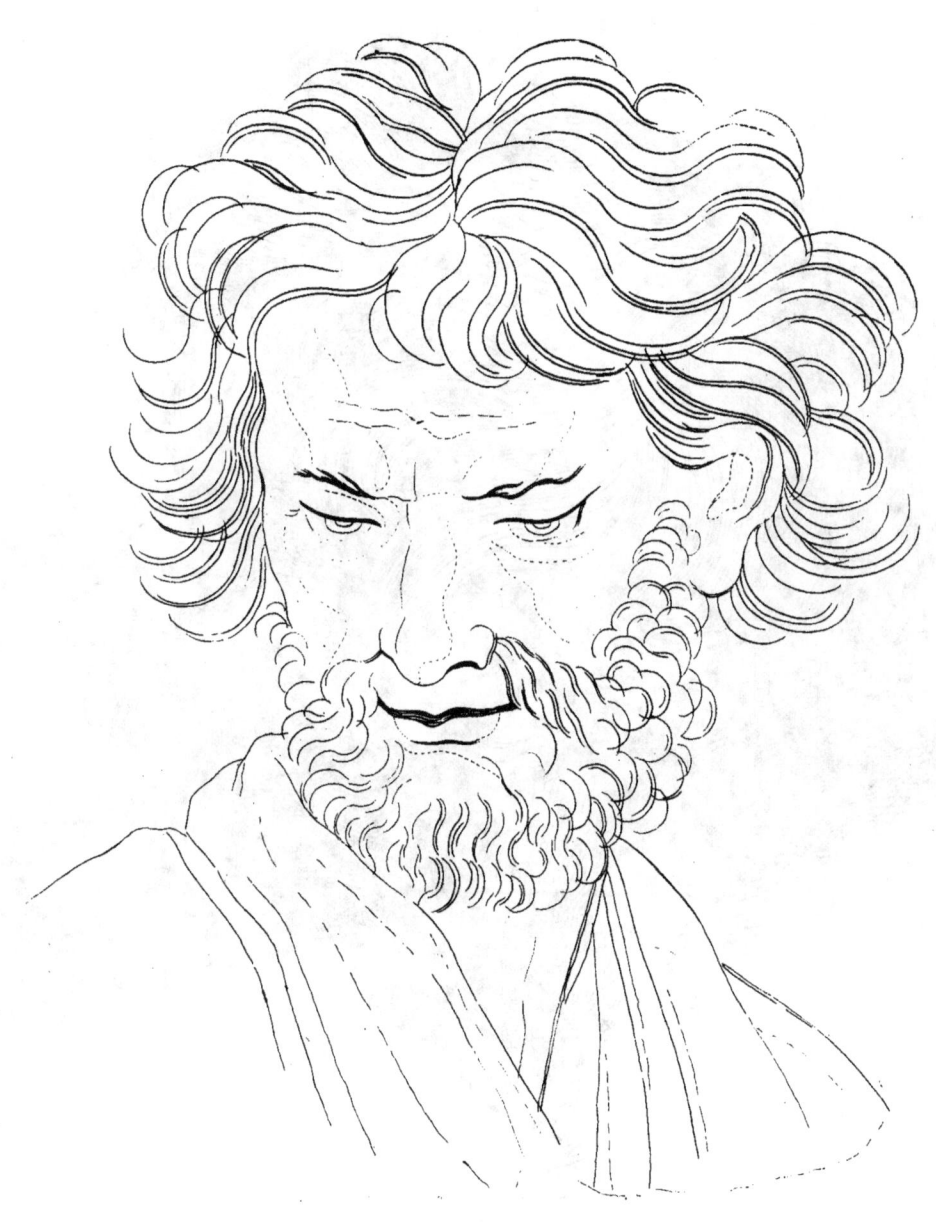

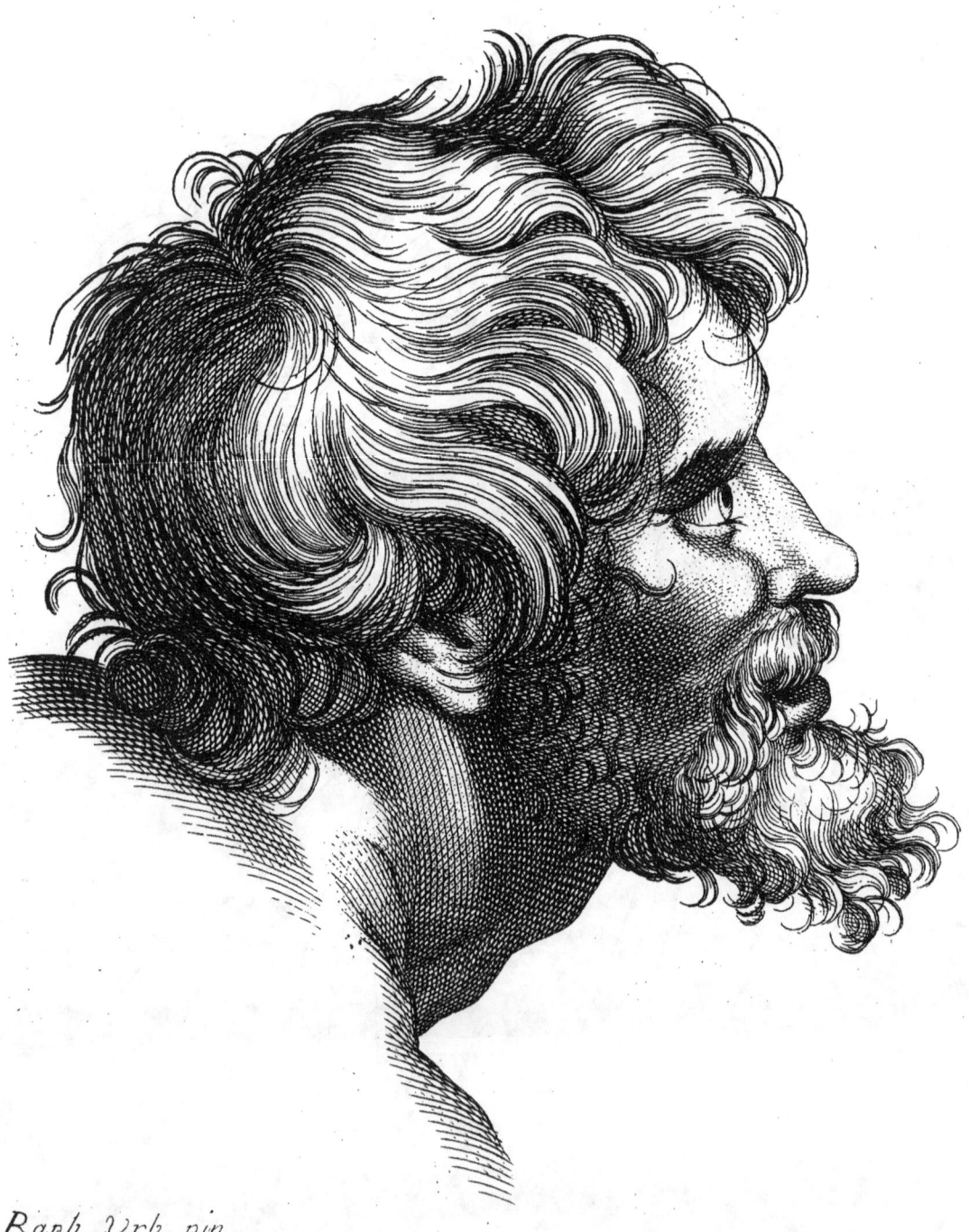

Raph. Urb. pin.

Plate 45.I. - from Paul and Barnabas

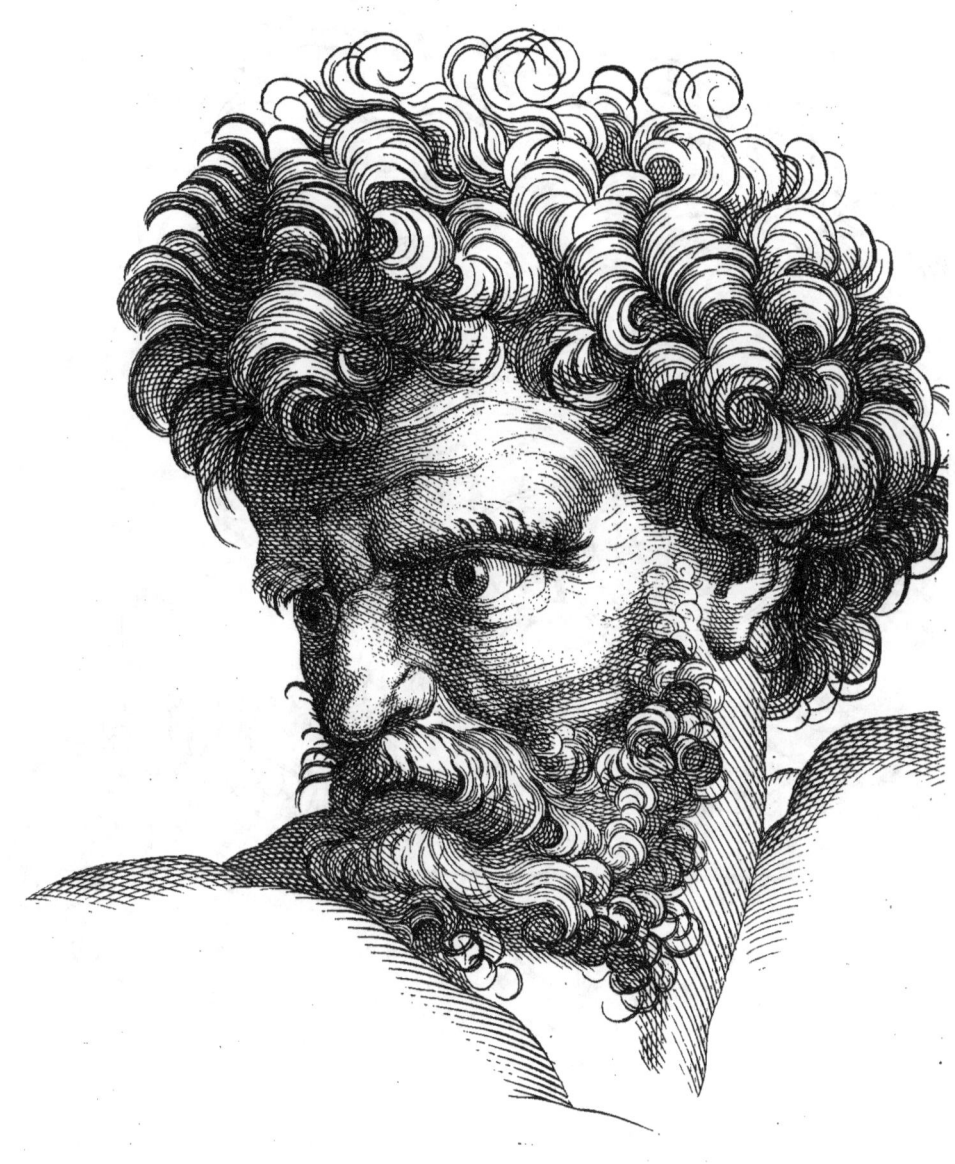

N? Pigné. Sculp.

Plate 45.II. - from Paul and Barnabas

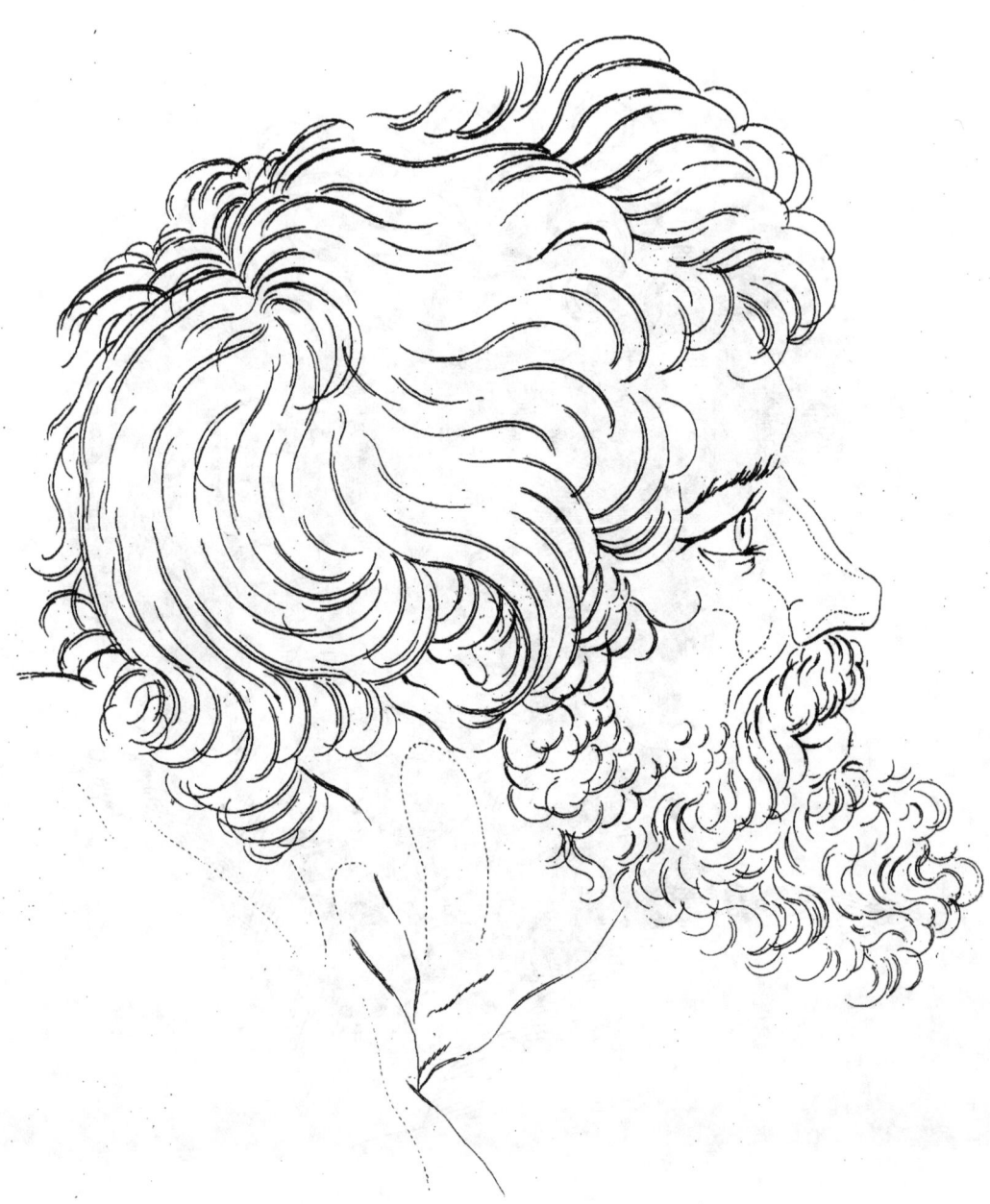

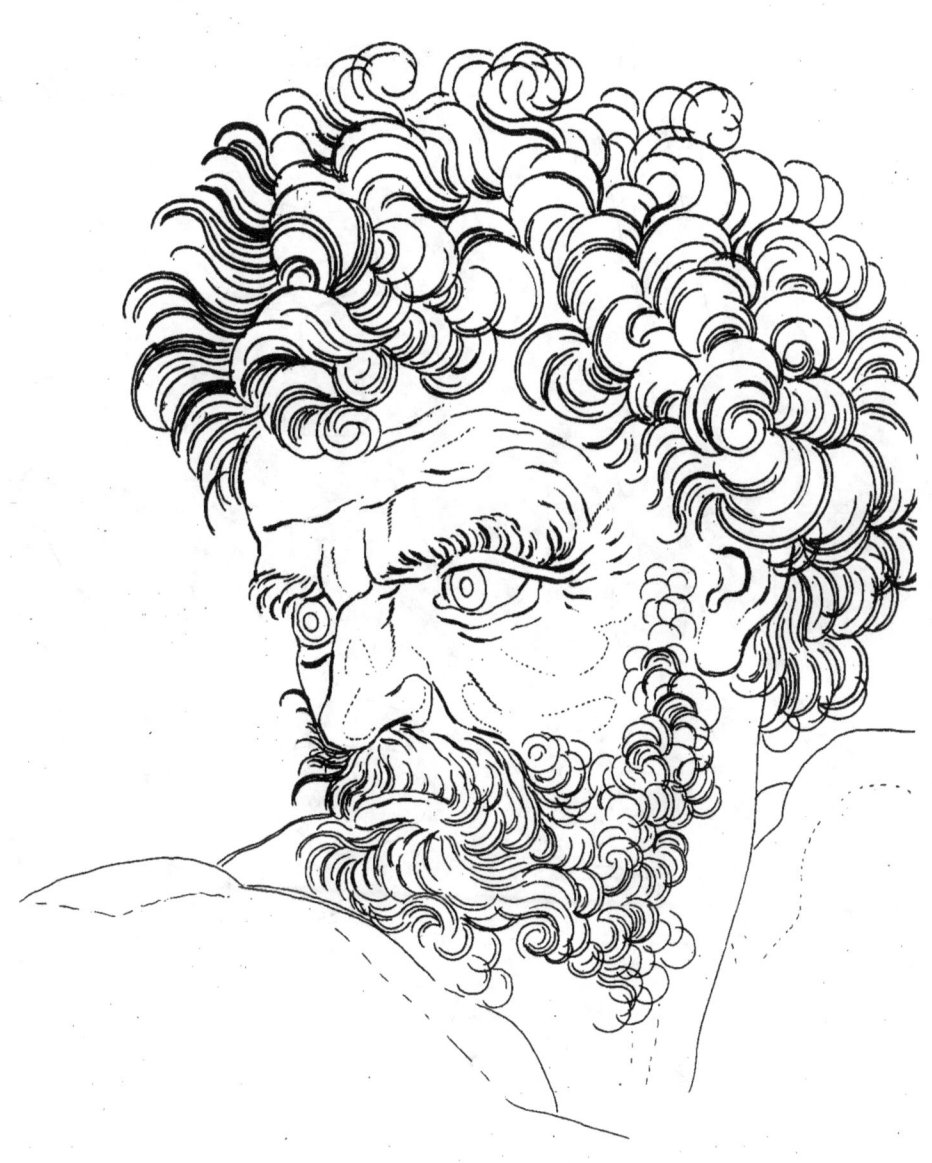

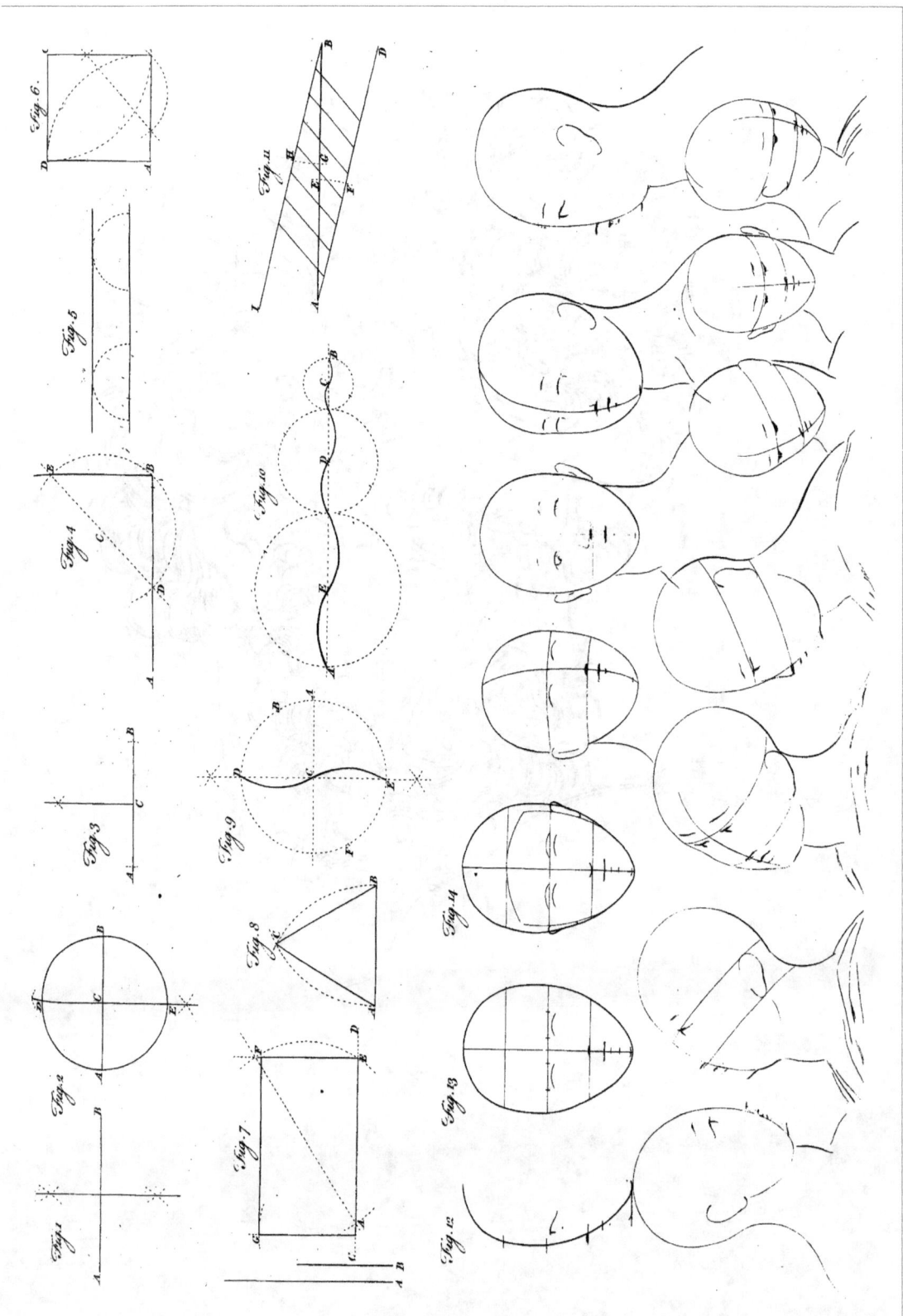

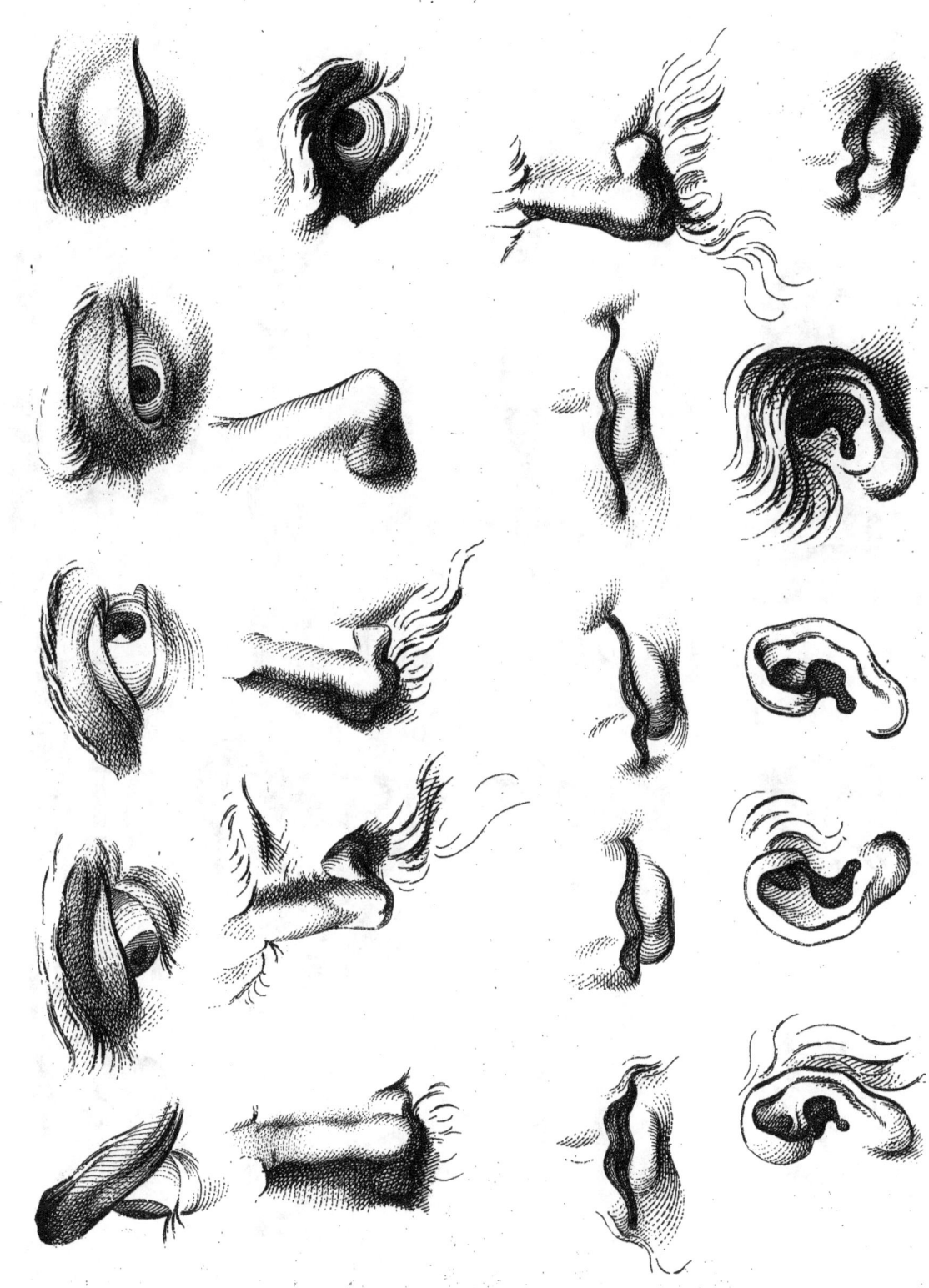

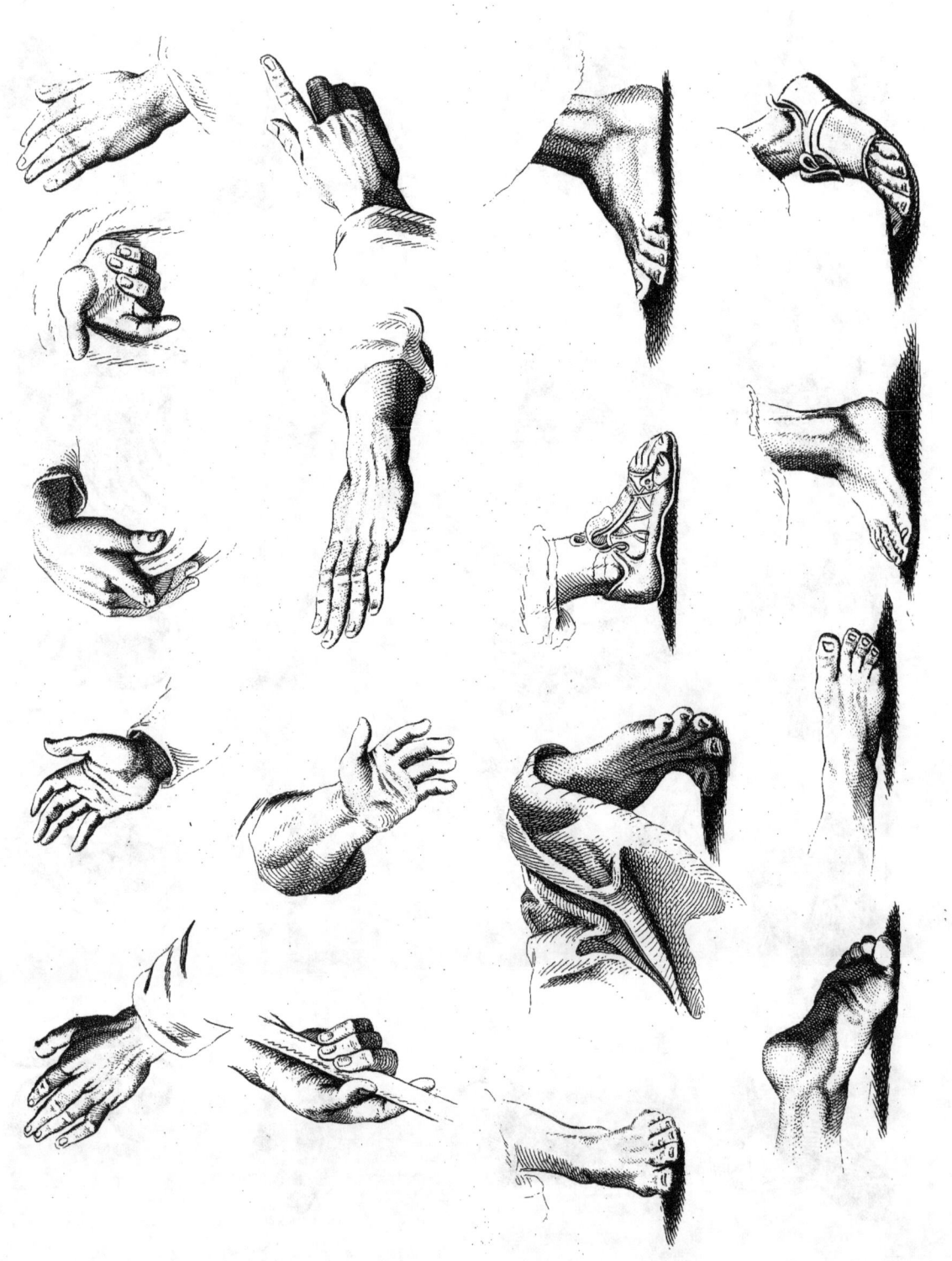

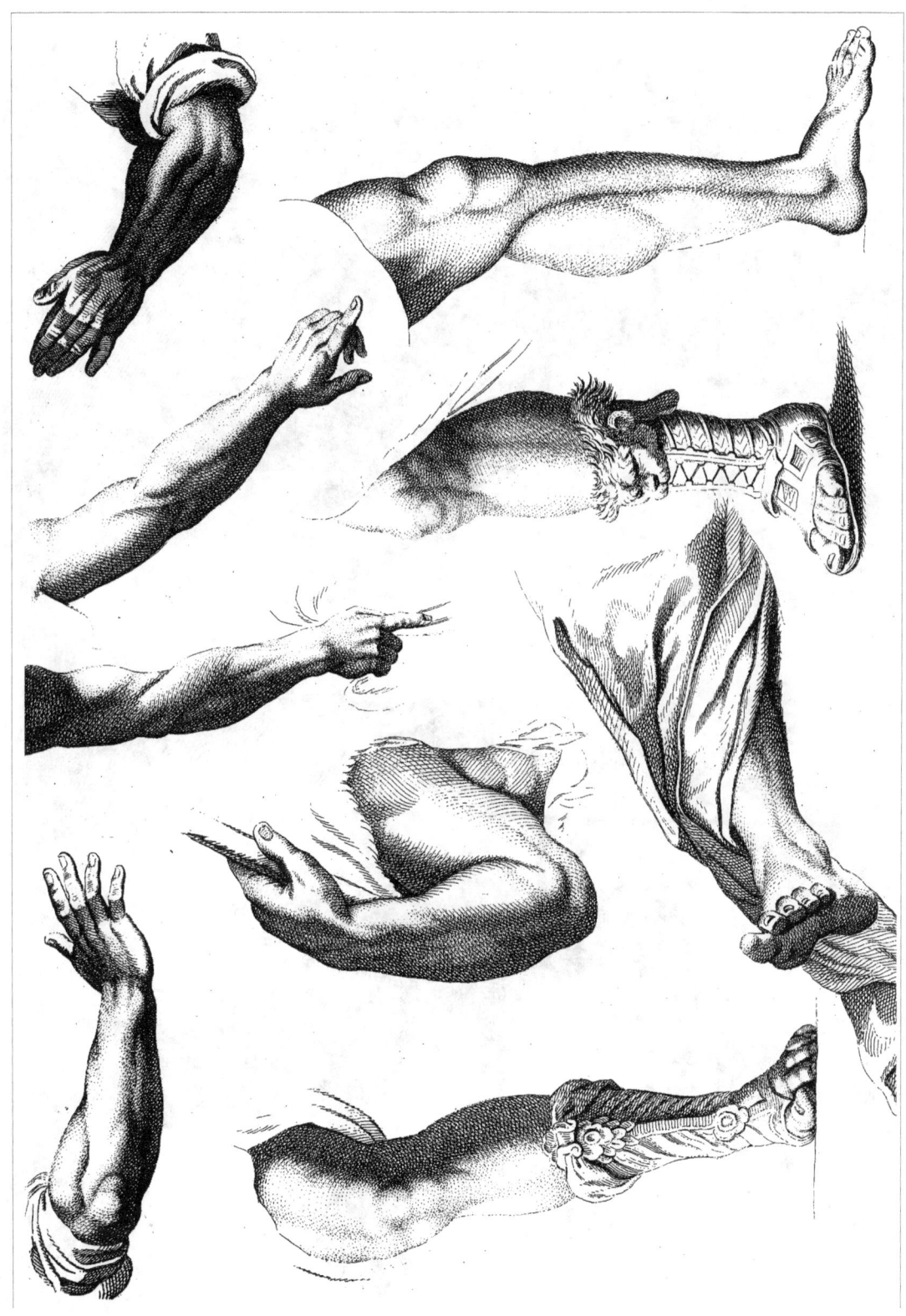

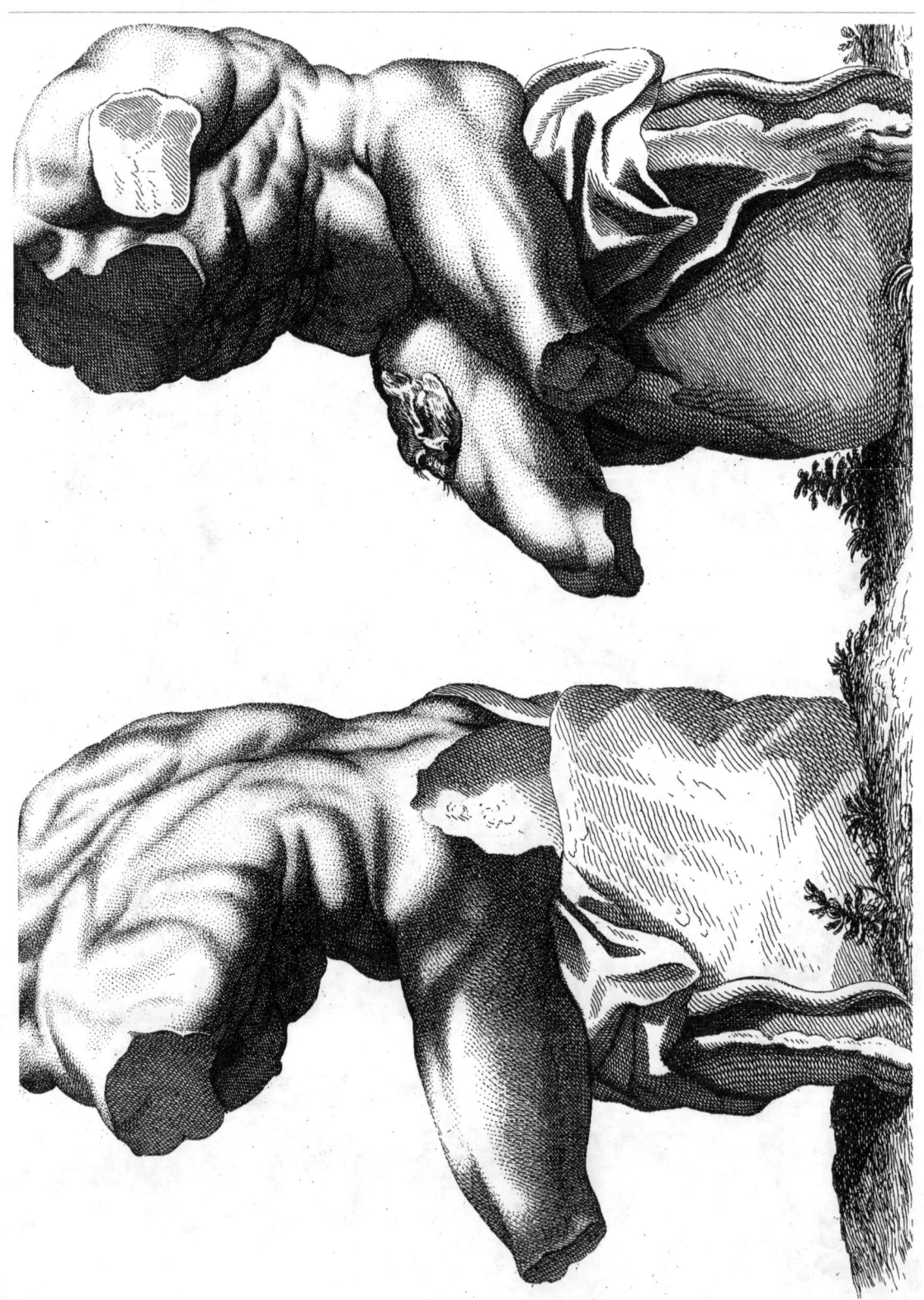

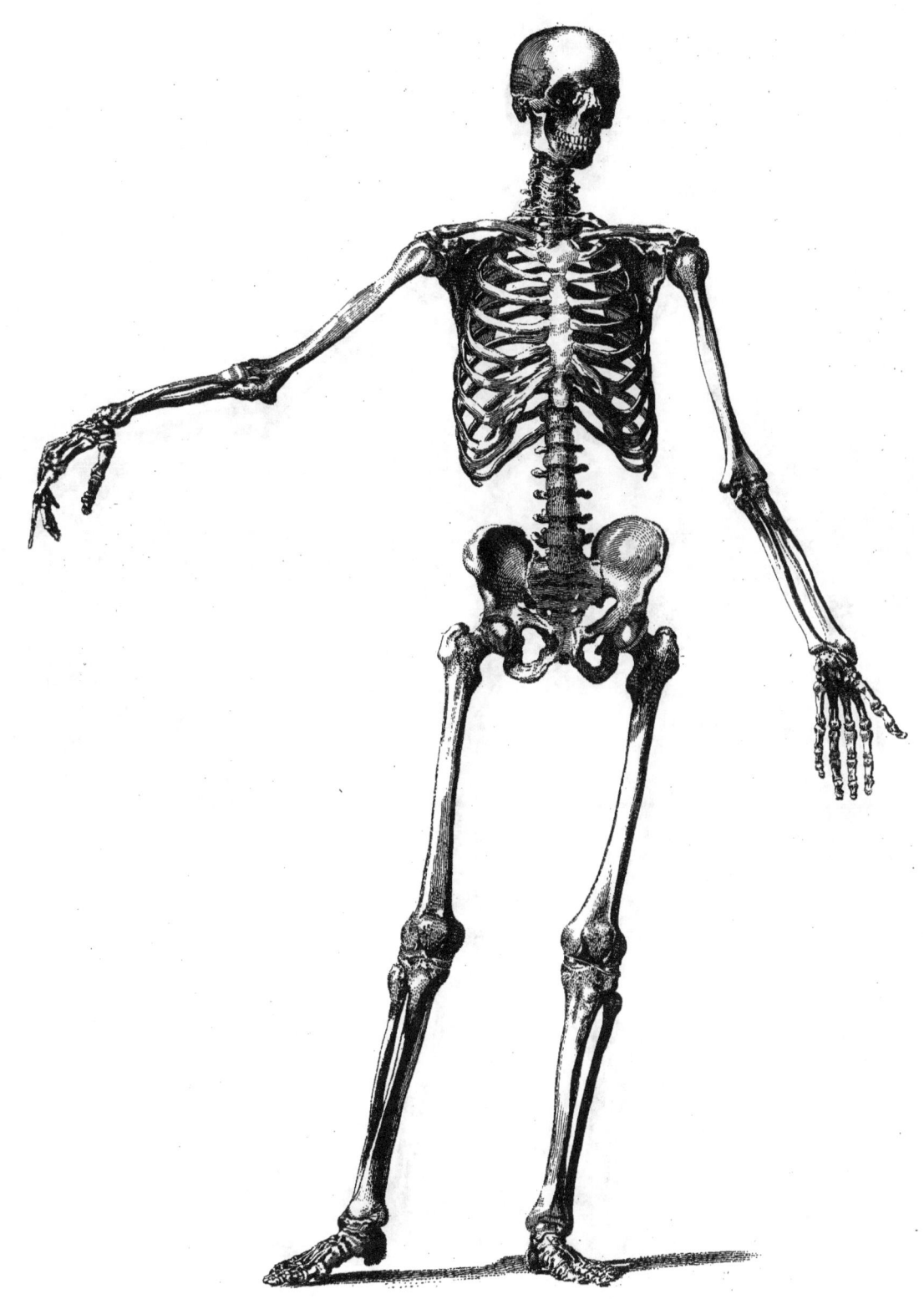

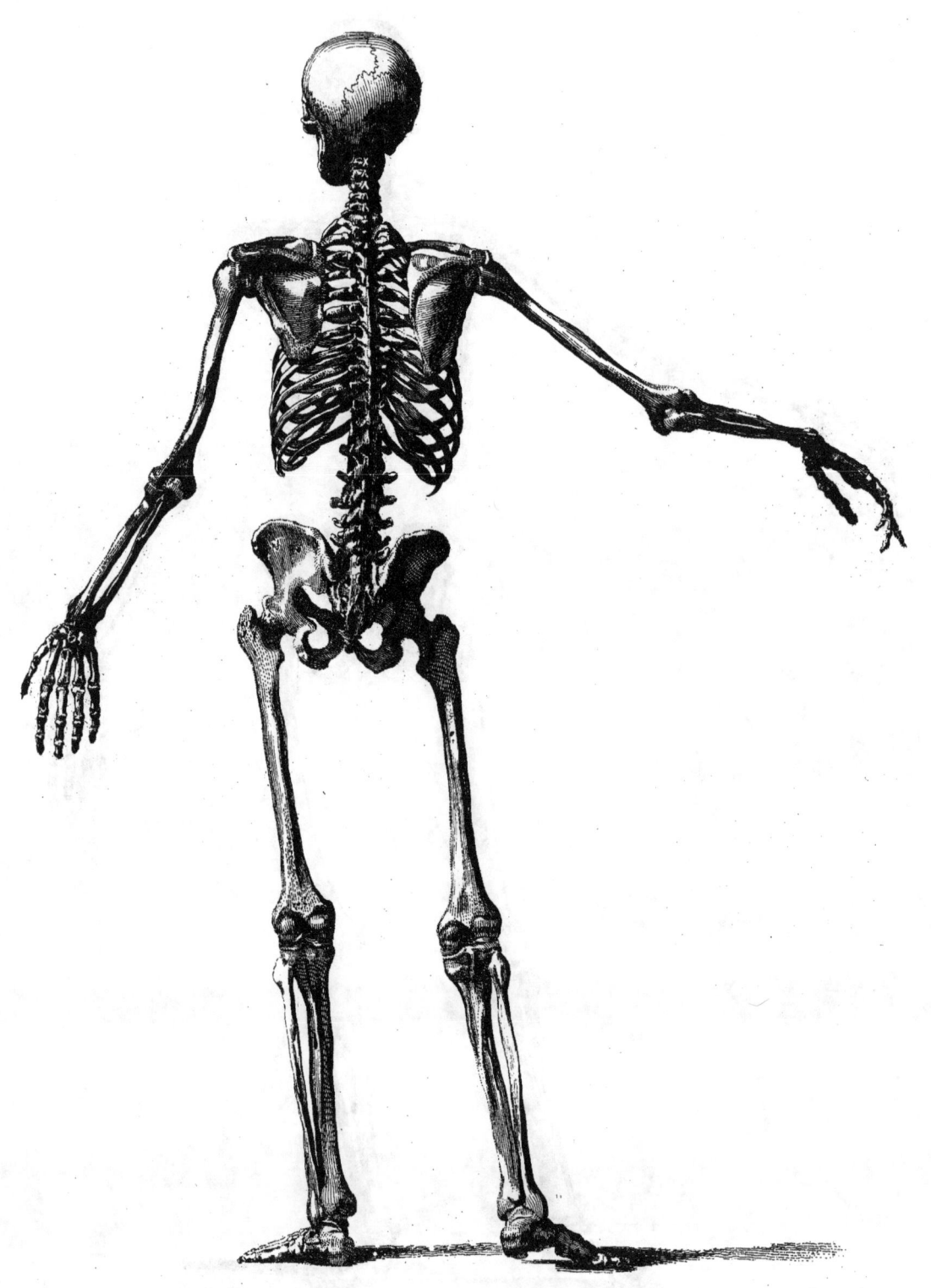

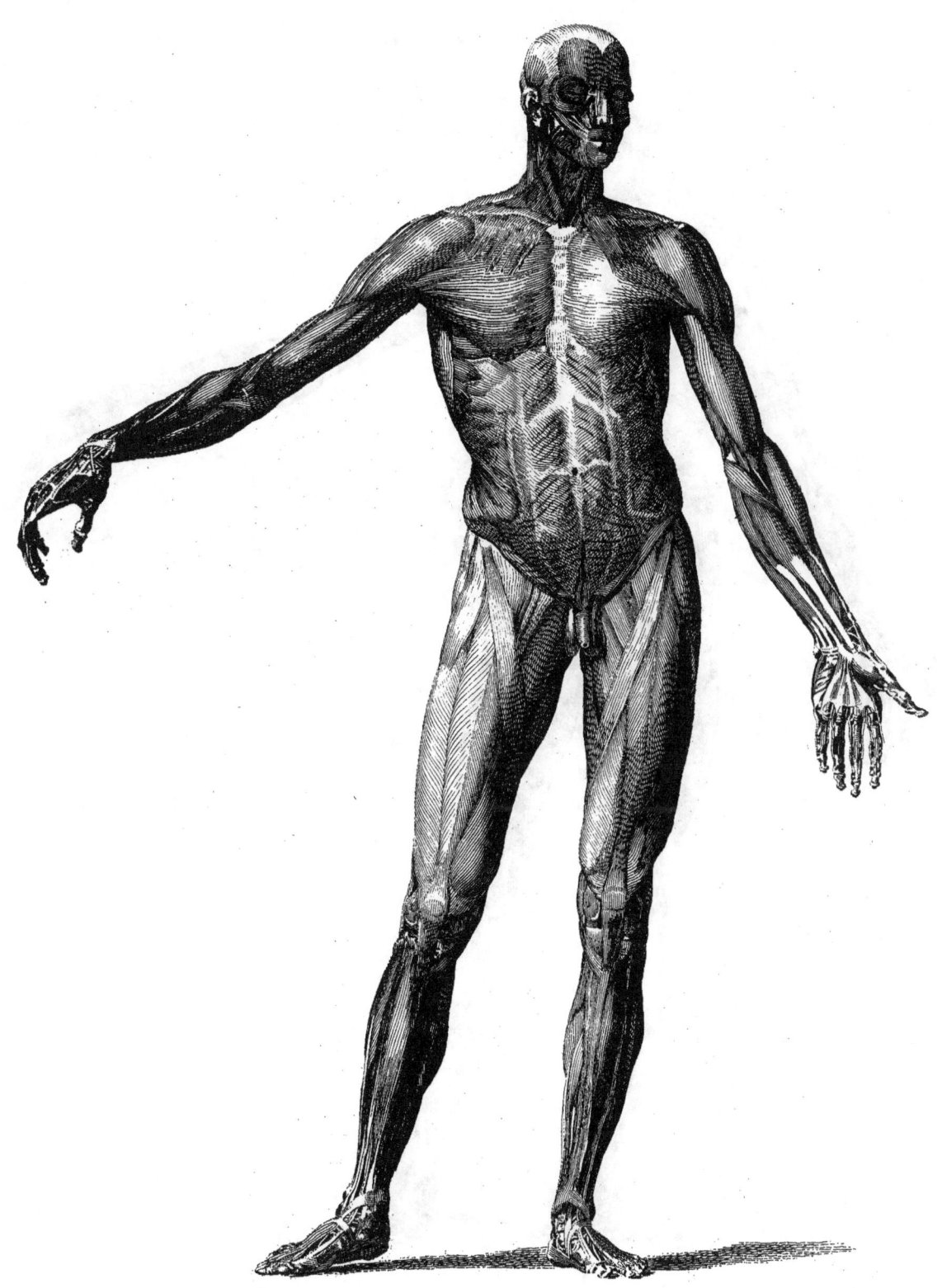

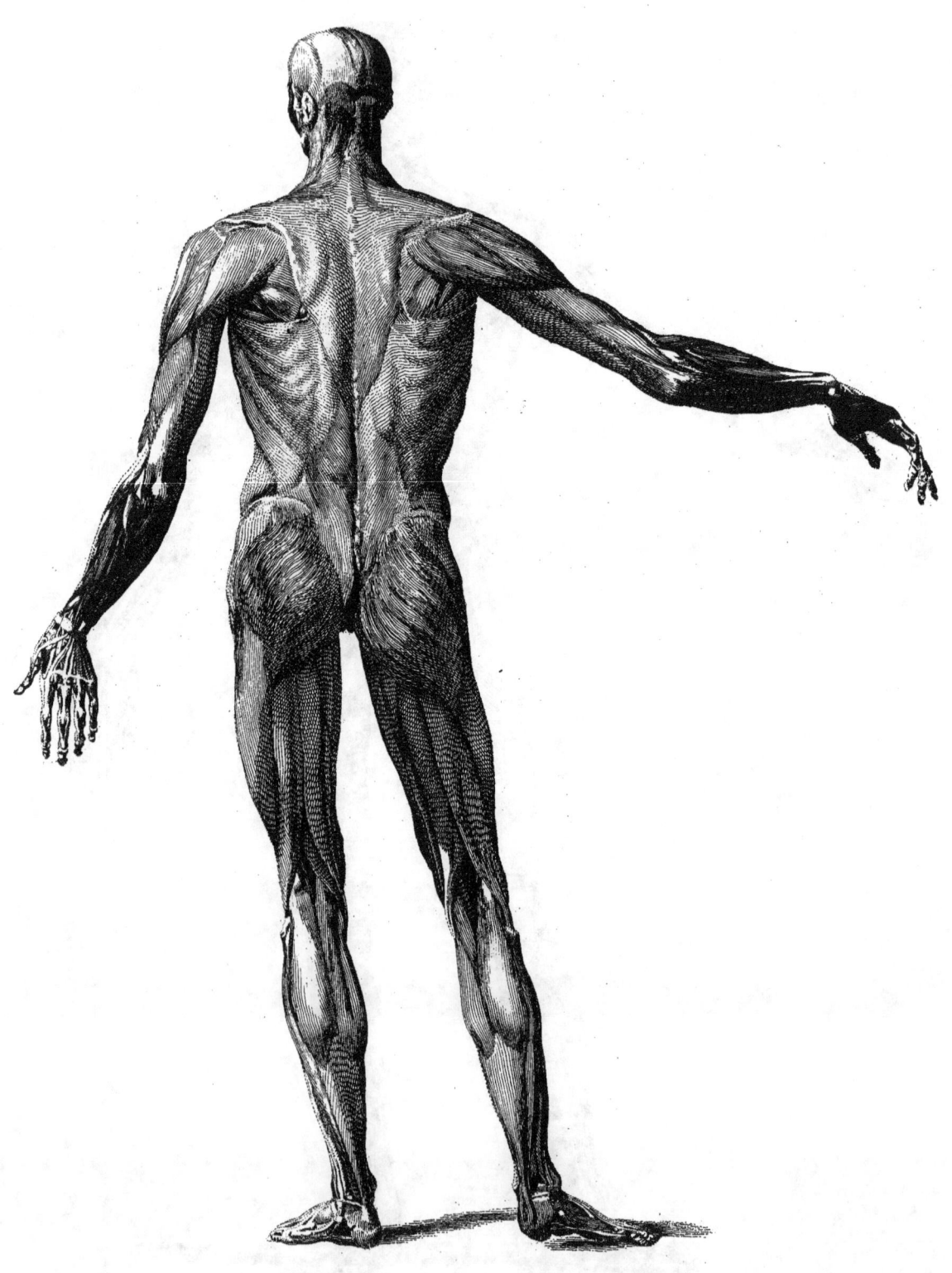

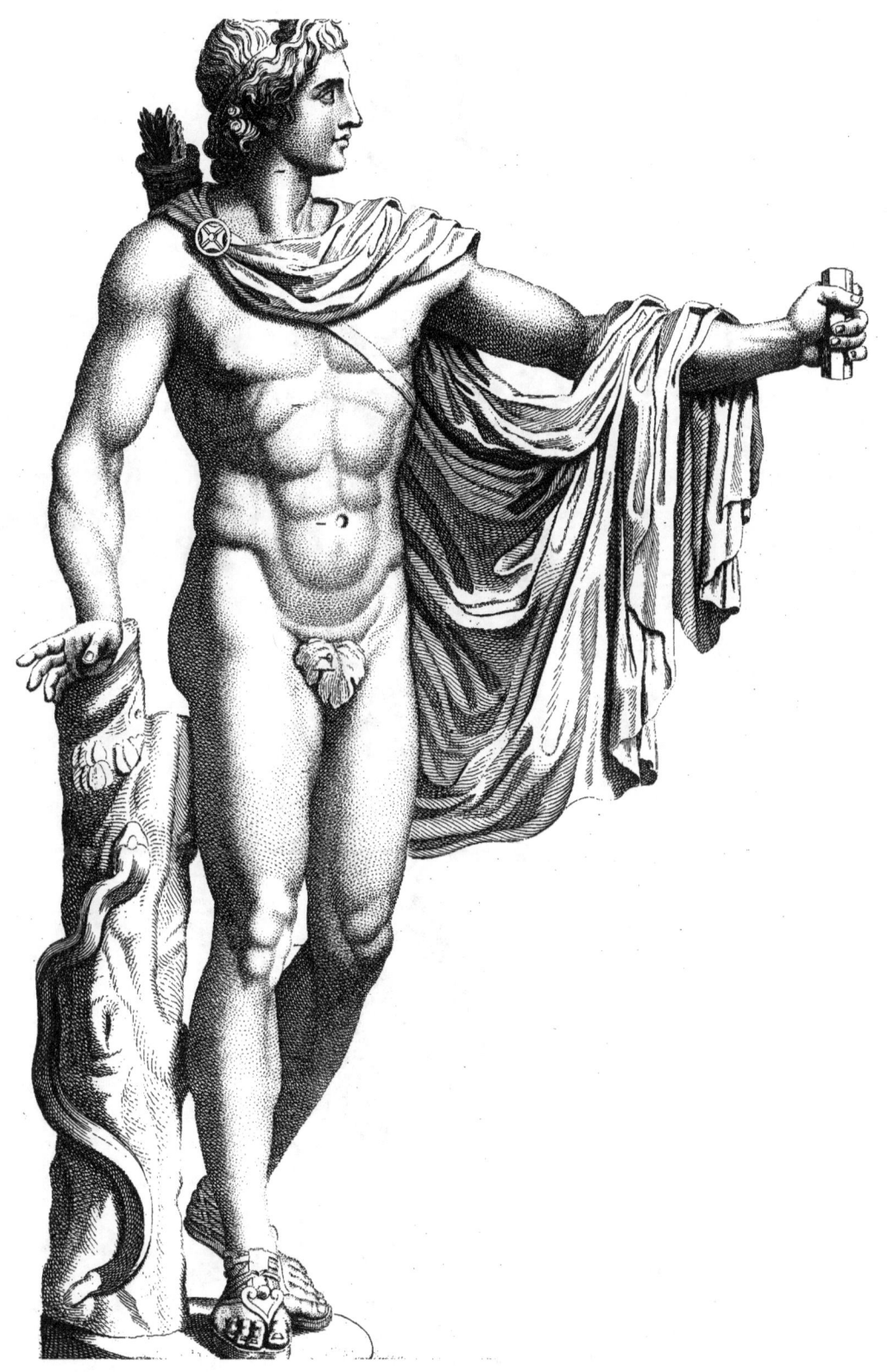

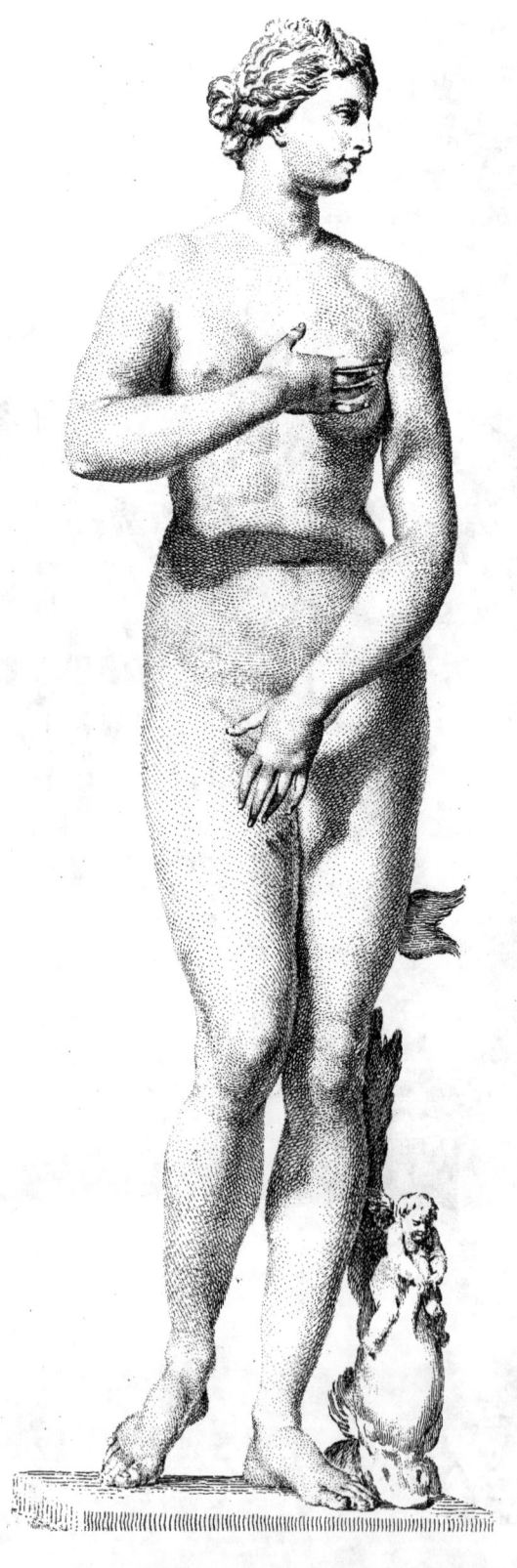

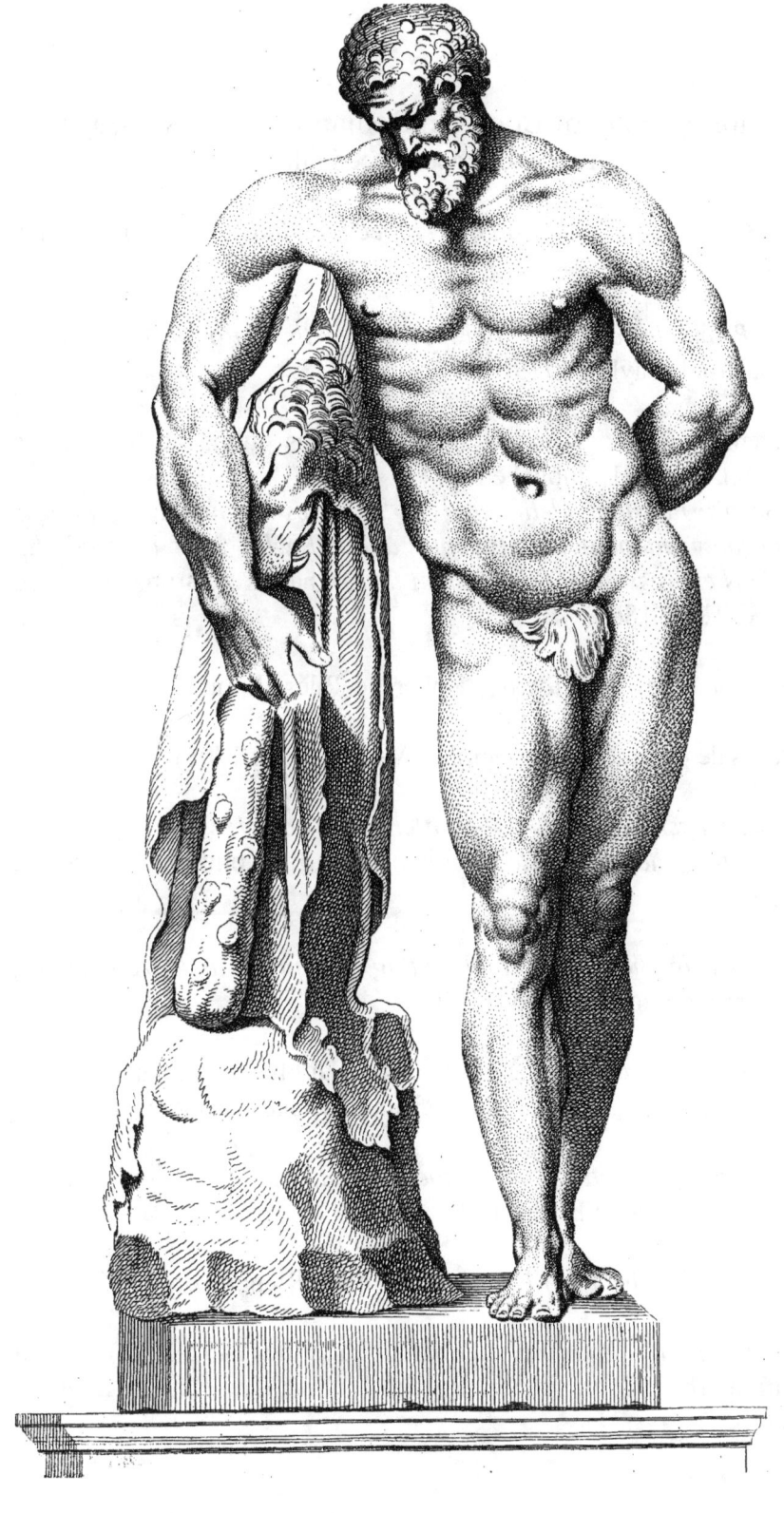

Bibliography of Books in Benjamin Ralph's Essays.
In order of appearance in the text.

Dr. Brook Taylor's Method of Perspective Made Easy, John Joshua Kirby, 1754.

New Principles of Linear Perspective: or the art of designing on a plan, Brook Taylor, 1719.

System of Physiognomy, a series of plates published by Charles LeBrun, ca. 1671. Published as:
LeBrun's Passions delineated in a series of nineteen studies: admirably adapted for students, and all who wish to read the various expressions of the human face, Charles LeBrun, Published for W. Tegg, 1863.

The Principles of Painting, Roger de Piles, London, J. Osborne, 1743.
(Cours de peinture par principles, Mr. De Piles, 1708)

The Analysis of Beauty: written with a view of fixing the fluctuating ideas of taste. William Hogarth, London, J. Reeeves, 1753.

The Idea of the Temple of Painting, Sculpture and Architecture, Giovanni Paolo Lomazzo, 1590.

The Art of Painting, Charles-Alphonse DuFresnoy, Charles Jarvis, Alexander Pope, John Dryden, Richard Graham, London, 1716.

The Art of Painting: after the Italian manner. with practical observations, John Elsum,1703.

Essay on the Theory of Painting, Jonathon Richardson, 1715.

A Treatise on Painting, Leonardo da Vinci(1452-1519), Milan edition, 1804; John Francis Rigaud English Translation, London, 1892.

Other Related Books:

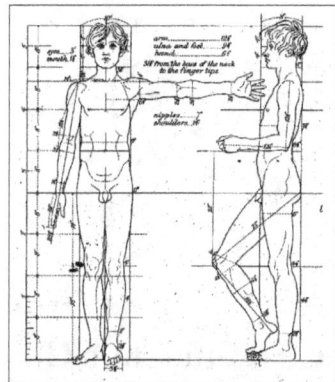

The Art Student's Guide
to the Proportions of the Human Form
By Dr. Johann Gottfried Schadow
edited by Tom Richardson
ISBN 978-0982167809

This is a republished edition of Dr. Schadow's famous work in which thirty plates demonstrate the proportions of the human form. It is based on the pioneering work of the Greek Sculptor Polycletus.

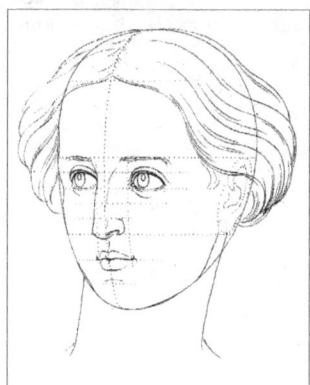

The Human Head
by Prof. Louis Bail
edited by Tom Richardson
ISBN 978-0982167830

How to draw the human head by the pre-eminent advocate for the teaching of drawing in schools in the mid nineteenth century, the inventor of the system of drawing used by many schools of the time.

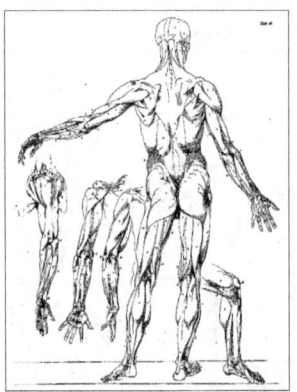

The Art Student's Guide
to the
Bones and Muscle of the Human Body:
and Lessons on Foreshortening
by Dr. Johann Gottfried Schadow
edited by Tom Richardson
ISBN 978-0982167823

This is a republished edition of Dr. Schadow's book which he designed for the benefit
of his students at the Berlin Art Academy. It combines studies of anatomy based on
his knowledge and the engravings of Bernhard Siegfried Albinus with three plates on
human proportions plus detailed studies of the head tilted in different directions to
demonstrate the effects of foreshortening.

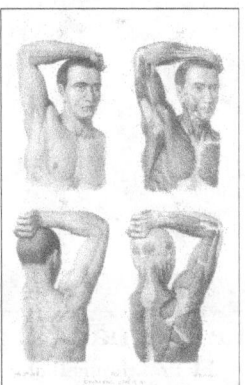

Anatomy for Art Students, Painters and Sculptors
by Dr. Julien Fau
edited by Tom Richardson
ISBN B002ACTVFG

This is a republished edition of Dr. Fau's book which was is wide circulation with as
many as ten editions in different languages and used by almost every art student in
Europe in the mid 19th century.

www.ingramcontent.com/pod-product-compliance
Lightning Source LLC
Chambersburg PA
CBHW080907170526
45158CB00008B/2028

* 9 7 8 0 9 8 2 1 6 7 8 4 7 *